AF361359

Plato's Politics of Passion

SUNY series in Ancient Greek Philosophy

____

Anthony Preus, editor

Plato's Politics of Passion

Erôs, Thumos, and Socratic Self-Knowledge in the
Charmides, *Republic*, and *Symposium*

ALAN PICHANICK

Cover image: *Cupid and Psyche*, by Antonio Canova (Italian, Possagno 1757–1822, Venice), 1794. Gift of Isidor Straus, 1905.

Published by State University of New York Press, Albany

© 2025 State University of New York

EU GPSR Authorised Representative:
Logos Europe, 9 rue Nicolas Poussin, 17000, La Rochelle, France
contact@logoseurope.eu

For information, contact State University of New York Press, Albany, NY
www.sunypress.edu

Library of Congress Cataloging-in-Publication Data

Name: Pichanick, Alan, 1975– author.
Title: Plato's politics of passion : erôs, thumos, and Socratic self-knowledge in the *Charmides, Republic*, and *Symposium* / Alan Pichanick.
Description: Albany : State University of New York Press, [2025] | Series: SUNY series in ancient Greek philosophy | Includes bibliographical references and index.
Identifiers: LCCN 2025003588 | ISBN 9798855803907 (hardcover : alk. paper) | ISBN 9798855803921 (ebook)
Subjects: LCSH: Plato. Charmides. | Plato. Republic. | Plato. Symposium. | Love. | Thymos (The Greek word) | Self-knowledge, Theory of.
Classification: LCC B366 .C64 2022 | DDC 184—dc23/eng/20250303
LC record available at https://lccn.loc.gov/2025003588

Contents

Part 3A: The Ending of the Dialogue and Socratic *Sôphrosunê*

Part 3B: *Thauma* and *Sôphrosunê* in the *Republic* and *Symposium*

Acknowledgments

I am lucky to have had the opportunity to learn from a number of people over the many years I have spent thinking about this project. It took its first shape at the University of Chicago, where I was fortunate to learn how to think with Plato from Jonathan Lear, Rachel Barney, Richard Kraut, Nathan Tarcov, and Leon Kass. In recent years, I have benefitted greatly from the insights and support of Angela DiBenedetto, Andy Bove, Walter Brogan, Peter Busch, Paul Camacho, Craig Carpenter, Marylu Hill, Greg Hoskins, Justin Humphreys, Brien Karas, Elizabeth-Jane McGuire, Brian Satterfield, Mark Schiffman, Tom Schmid, Bob Styer, Gina Talley, and Jim Wetzel. I thank Guy Aiken for being a translation and discussion partner for important sections of the *Symposium* and *Republic*, and Will Altman, Roslyn Weiss, Michael Weinman, and an anonymous reviewer for reading the manuscript and offering me invaluable advice and questions. I hope I was wise enough to put it to good use. I am deeply grateful to Mike Rinella and the editorial staff at SUNY Press for their assistance in the revising and production of the manuscript.

I owe much gratitude to the Augustine and Culture Seminar Program at Villanova, which in addition to providing me a community of interlocutors and freedom to explore and learn from texts, also awarded me (under the leadership of Marylu Hill and subsequently Greg Hoskins) two grants in the summers of 2021 and 2023 sponsored by the Patricia and Vincent J. Trosino '62 Fellowship to work on the chapters on the *Republic* and the *Symposium*. I am also grateful to Jess, Sophia, Katie, and Elie for unflagging belief in the value of this work.

Finally, three Socratic midwives helped me give birth to the idea, shape, and completion of this book: Dave Rudick, John-Paul Spiro, and Stewart Umphrey. I don't know how to express gratitude for their comments on the manuscript and for the numerous hours we have spent in conversation, pondering and wondering with courage and moderation. This work is dedicated to them.

Some of the work appears as modified forms of earlier publications. Part 1A, chapter 3 expands upon my "Sôphrosunê, Socratic Therapy, and Platonic Drama in Plato's *Charmides*" (*Epoché*, 21 [1], 2016). Part 2A, chapter 2, is a revised and expanded version of "Two Rival Conceptions of Sôphrosunê" (*Polis*, 22 [2], 2005).

Introduction

The guiding question of this investigation is: what is Socratic self-knowledge? But there is another question that concerns both scholars and students who read the Platonic dialogues, and it seems to become *more vital* as courses in the humanities at institutions of liberal learning continue to face more pressure to justify their existence, while our contemporary political discourse has become more and more polarized and beset by partisanship. The question can be put this way: *What good is it to seek Socratic self-knowledge? Why will it benefit me to undertake Socratic (or any) self-investigation?*

Plato's *Charmides* is <u>the</u> Platonic dialogue to work through this question, because it is there that the *use or uselessness of self-knowledge* becomes the predominant theme. In this dialogue, Socrates explores the possibility of the very culmination of his philosophical investigations—knowledge of ignorance. This happens through an investigation of the strange quality, *sôphrosunê*.

Sôphrosunê is the name of the virtue most commonly rendered as "moderation" or "temperance" but has also been translated as "sound-mindedness" and "discipline." Socrates discusses the virtue with Charmides, who was Plato's uncle, and with Critias, cousin to and guardian of Charmides. It is of the *utmost significance* that both are future members of the Thirty Tyrants responsible for overthrowing the democracy some years after this discussion has taken place. The definitions Critias and Charmides propose are examined and (at least apparently) refuted by Socrates, and the dialogue ends in aporia, a perplexity so profound that Socrates refers to himself as "a worthless inquirer" and a "babbler" (175e–176a), unable to reveal the essence of this elusive virtue.

It is here that perhaps the biggest problem with the dialogue emerges. For one definition that appears, "knowing what one knows and does not know," seems so Socratic. How could such a statement, which seems to be Socrates's description of his own activity in the *Apology*, fail to be shown to be possible or beneficial? Does the dialogue's ominous ending, in which Charmides and Critias threaten to force rather than persuade Socrates to continue conversations about this virtue with the young boy, imply that Socrates is either a teacher of tyrants or a failure at instilling moderation in his companions? I will argue that though Critias and Charmides fail to show *sôphrosunê*, Socrates actually demonstrates in word and deed the essential element of it—knowledge of ignorance coupled with wonder at the beautiful—and leaves hope for the reader that one may deal with the tyrannical ambition within oneself and perhaps the tyrannical ambitions of others. Therefore, it is in the character of Socrates and in Socratic philosophy, shown in sharp relief to the distorted tyrannical counterparts of Critias and Charmides, that one finds the possibility and benefit of Socratic self-knowledge.

I approach the perplexing exploration of *sôphrosunê* in the *Charmides* by placing much greater emphasis than previous scholarship on the neglected "erotic setting" in the dramatic introduction, and I argue that our reading of the rest of the dialogue should be done in light of this dramatic setting.[1] When the young, beautiful Charmides enters the room, he takes everyone's breath away. All are struck with *wonder* at his dazzling looks. His entrance to the dialogue dramatically displays this captivating, disruptive feature of *the beautiful* and provokes three intriguing reactions and orientations to it in the figures of Charmides himself, Critias his guardian, and the crowd who witnesses his entrance.

However, there is another aspect of *the beautiful* emphasized in this opening scene, shown especially by the ability of Socrates to gain control of himself upon seeing the beautiful Charmides. Socrates, as the fourth observer of this feature of experience of wonder, suggests that there is another orientation to the beautiful than what is shown by the crowd and the two future members of the Thirty Tyrants. I thus argue that these orientations toward the beautiful are connected to a distinction between philosophical wonder and tyrannical *erôs*, thereby drawing out the connection between one's orientation to the beautiful and the distinction Plato is highlighting between tyranny and philosophy themselves. The opening dramatic introduction has philosophical and political significance that sets the stage for the entire conversation about *sôphrosunê* and self-knowledge. In my commentary on the rest of the dialogue, I show that both inquiries to find a definition of *sôphrosunê* (with Charmides and Critias) fail because Charmides and Critias do not properly understand the nature of the beautiful, a failure that prevents their experience of genuine philosophical wonder, and this underlies their tyrannical impulses to seek to acquire beauty and knowledge. They understand them as possessions to be owned and exploited for their own self-interest.

I have organized the book into three main parts, dedicated principally to the three interlocutors Charmides, Critias, and Socrates. Corresponding to these three characters are three orientations to the nature of *sôphrosunê* itself, tied to different dimensions of *thumos* and *erôs*. The conversation with Charmides explores *sôphrosunê* in its behavior or moral aspect. This section culminates in the definition of *sôphrosunê* as "doing one's own things," the very definition of justice in the *Republic*. I thus turn in this part to the account of *thumos* in book 4 of the *Republic*, in which *thumos* is explicitly linked to "one's own things." I argue that the account of *thumos* sheds light on the character and behavior of Charmides as well as his definitions of *sôphrosunê*. This leads to a discussion of Aristophanes's speech about love in the *Symposium*, which I argue is a tragic portrayal of *erôs* fueled by *thumos* unencumbered by any restraining force, resulting in misery and unhappiness for the lovers. Such is the fate for Charmides under the guardianship of Critias.

The conversation with Critias explores a more intellectual dimension of *sôphrosunê* and culminates in his view of *sôphrosunê* as self-knowledge. This conversation takes up most of the dialogue, and this is the longest part of the present book. The actions and definitions of Critias are illuminated by the account in *Republic* VIII–IX of the tyrannical expansion of *thumos* into the lawless *pleonexia* and tragic self-dissolution that accompanies it. This psychogenetic account of tyranny demonstrates the connection between the "Critian" orientation to the beautiful and the tyrannical attitude toward unbounded, acquisitive desire for power. The account of tyranny in the *Republic* also prepares us for the ominous ending of the dialogue, in which Charmides and Critias threaten Socrates with force. Here is the final image of the *thumos* of Critias and Charmides as inquirers in the *Charmides*. The dominance of their *thumos* misleads them, and potentially all of us, as lovers of the beautiful.

In the third part, I begin with the closing section of the dialogue with these newfound insights about *thumotic erôs* and then return to Socrates's proposal for a benefit of *sôphrosunê* that his interlocutors and many readers neglect. Socrates's hypothesis speaks to his ability to inquire about that which he does not know, and is rendered more intelligible through an exploration of wonder at the beautiful itself in the *Symposium*. There is revealed a philosophical alternative to the tyrannical picture that has now emerged. I argue that Socrates in all three dialogues (*Charmides, Republic, Symposium*) sets the stage to be seen as a *theoros* who has come back to the city as witness. Socrates shares what he has *beheld*, rather than acquired, in order to help his fellow inquirers to behold the beautiful and experience wonder for themselves. I therefore turn to a discussion of Diotima's speech about love, which stands in contrast to Aristophanes's speech and the accompanying psychological and psychogenetic diagnosis in the *Republic*. Diotima gives a speech about an acquisitive *erôs* that by its end actually *transforms* into a contemplative wonder beholding the beautiful itself. Such wonder is a potential antidote to the tyrannical, acquisitive *erôs* that is made thematic in the *Republic*, and portrayed by Charmides's and Critias's speeches and deeds in the *Charmides*. Analysis of these two dialogues therefore sheds light on the impasse that is reached in the conversation between Critias and Socrates in the *Charmides*. The puzzle that remains at the end of the *Charmides*—how to define *sôphrosunê* and spell out its connection with Socratic philosophy—can best be answered, I argue, by paying attention to a proper understanding of the beautiful. It is *beauty* that leads to a definition of *sôphrosunê* and helps us to distinguish Socratic philosophy from its tyrannical image presented by the monstrous Critias. This definition, finally, would be a nonarchitectonic knowledge that originates in *thumos*, fueled by *erôs*, and culminates in wonder on beholding (the paradox of) one's kinship to and otherness of the beautiful itself, thereby giving birth to reverence and awe—ultimately preventing tyrannical impulses within.

The erotic setting of the *Charmides* combined with the discussion of philosophical wonder and the beautiful in the *Symposium* and tyrannical *erôs* in the *Republic* gives guidance about how to think about the potential connection between Socratic self-knowledge and knowledge of the good, but also shows why Charmides and Critias fail to come to such knowledge. Socratic conversations and Socratic self-knowledge appear, importantly, to do with the recognition of our *epistemic* limitations and require that we acknowledge ourselves as seekers of knowledge, rather than knowers. The *Symposium* thus gives us an account of an erotic pursuit that addresses and revises the *thumotic eros* described in the *Republic*. The ultimate goal of *sôphrosunê* and Socratic self-knowledge is generative and creative wonder at the beautiful itself, which is always coupled with an acknowledgement of our incompleteness. It is there, if anywhere, that self-knowledge and knowledge of the good must be put together. Charmides and Critias represent the failure of such wonder to bring about this result (or even to experience genuine wonder at all). Here we have the Platonic diagnosis of the tyrant, whose soul never wonders at anything beyond itself.

Part 1A

Socrates and Charmides on *Sôphrosunê*

Chapter One

Back from War (153a–153d)

The conversation about *sôphrosunê*[1] takes place between Critias, Charmides, and Socrates in the shadow of the Peloponnesian War. The first sentence of Plato's dialogue refers to this context succinctly: "We came (*hekomen*) yesterday evening from the army camp at Potidaea, and because I had arrived (*aphigmenos*) after some time away, I gladly sought my habitual conversations (*sunêtheis diatribas*)."[2] It is important to note three things about this opening to the dialogue. First, the whole discussion that follows is narrated by Socrates to an as yet anonymous addressee. Second, Socrates has been away from Athens and is reentering his customary way of life. Third, Socrates has returned from battle, indeed one of the battles that initiated the war between the Athenians and the Spartans.[3]

If we include dialogues whose authorship is controversial, these are the ones narrated in the first person: *Protagoras, Euthydemus, Charmides, Lysis, Republic, Lovers, Eryxias, Axiochus, Phaedo, Symposium,* and *Parmenides*. Plato begins only seven of this group with a recounting by Socrates to an anonymous addressee.[4] In the *Charmides*, Socrates never calls his listener by name, though he does address him as "friend" (*hetaire*)[5] and "noble gentleman" (*gennada*).[6] The gentleman Socrates seems to be telling his story to is described in no other way. Perhaps it is the case that the readers of the dialogue are the friends at whom Socrates's words are aimed and that the dialogue is for our benefit.[7] We are indeed Plato's intended listeners for this conversation. But this is surely true of any dialogue. More must be said to explain Plato's use of this *particular* form of address. In particular, few commentators have made much of his final address of "noble gentleman" (*gennada*). To use this particular appellation for any listener seems wrong.[8] Given the comments Socrates perhaps ironically makes about Critias's "noble line,"[9] he may be narrating this conversation to yet another "noble" listener who must learn from the failures of Charmides and Critias. That is, the "noble" listener is to become a spectator of Socrates's narration and should wonder about the "nobility" of the deeds done by Charmides and Critias, two members of the Thirty Tyrants. The dialogue, and its search for *sôphrosunê* and self-knowledge, is set in a thoroughly political context. Any Greek reader would be well familiar with the connotations of the presentation of the setting: the war, the political and erotic overtones of the Palaestra to which Socrates returns, and the deeds and fate of these future members of the Thirty Tyrants.[10]

Let us focus on the last first. Socrates points out that Charmides is the son of Glaucon, Plato's maternal grandfather. Charmides is the uncle of Plato, while Critias is the elder cousin of Plato's mother. Kahn remarks that this familial connection to Socrates's interlocutors here suggests that the *Charmides* is a dialogue in which "Plato takes an unusually personal interest."[11]

The family of Critias and Charmides shows their "aristocratic lineage," as Schmid says: "Charmides is a character-type of the Young Gentleman . . . [Critias] was a character-type of the Laconist or Oligarch . . . critical of Periclean democracy, closely associated with Spartan values, and excluded from the mainstream of Athenian political life. Moreover, he upheld conservative moral values, and particularly the ideal of *sôphrosunê*, in his writings."[12] Charmides exemplified the good Athenian youth. Critias wrote poetry praising the Spartan constitution and especially their *sôphrosunê*.[13] Yet after this, Charmides and Critias emerged as members of the thirty who ruled Athens after the Peloponnesian War. During this period, Xenophon called Critias "the most greedy and cruel of the thirty tyrants."[14] Critias along with Charmides were among the thirty who governed Athens from 404 to 403 BCE after the Athenians lost. He and the thirty came to power with force in an attempt to "purify the city of unjust men." They called themselves "the beautiful and the good," and Critias himself introduced Athens to a Spartan ideal of politics that he himself praised in writing.[15] Critias's government resulted in failure, as the oligarchy degenerated into the unjust and intemperate rule over the unwilling. They were both put to death later when the tyrants were overthrown by the democracy. Questions about Socrates's association with them, and Plato's as well, are thus urgently at issue as the dialogue unfolds. It is Critias in particular, with his history, who will become the target of Socrates's attack when the conversation with Charmides breaks down. And Critias makes it clear that he, like his young cousin and ward, also knows Socrates.[16] Therefore, Plato's personal interest in this conversation may be prompted by the question "How well does Critias know Socrates?"[17] Does Plato's ensuing depiction reveal that Socrates is indeed a corruptor of the youth who enabled Critias to lead Charmides down the road to tyranny? Or is Plato's depiction of the characters of Charmides and Critias meant to serve as a defense of Socrates? I will argue that just as Diogenes the Cynic may have rightly been called "Socrates gone mad," perhaps Critias is "Socrates gone tyrannical."[18] This tyrannical turn is exhibited throughout the *Charmides*, but is not properly and fully diagnosable from the perspective taken on *sôphrosunê* and self-knowledge therein. The discussion of *sôphrosunê* initiated in the *Charmides*, continued with an exploration of *thumos* in the *Republic*, and completed with an account of wonder (*thauma*) in the *Symposium* presents the full overcoming of Critias's oligarchic ideology.[19] At the end of this account, we can say why Critias ultimately lacked the *sôphrosunê* needed to save him from himself, and why this virtue becomes central for the leaders, citizens, and *city*.

It is illuminating therefore to compare Socrates's homecoming from war, as many scholars have pointed out, to Odysseus's return to Ithaca, and there are several allusions to the *Odyssey* throughout the text.[20] Christopher Moore and Chris Raymond have suggested that Socrates is returning home to reclaim his true love, *philosophia*, from unworthy suitors such as Critias.[21] Indeed Socrates cannot rest assured that the Athens he left has at all remained the same in his absence.

For Socrates has been away at war for three years. The dialogue takes place the day after Socrates returns from the battle at Potidaea.[22] Athens meanwhile has seen a plague that has destroyed a quarter of its population and even its great statesman, Pericles. But even worse than the scourge of human bodies, the plague created a sense of moral decay, depravity, and transvaluation of values:

> No one was held back in awe, either by fear of the gods or by the laws of men: not by the gods, because men concluded it was all the same whether they worshipped or not, seeing that they all perished alike; and not by the laws, because no one expected to live till he was tried and punished for his crimes. But they thought that a far greater sentence hung over their

heads now, and that before this fell they had a reason to get some pleasure in life.[23]

At the onset of the plague, Athenians came to resemble something other than citizens or full human beings. Having no assurance that they would see the fruit of any toil or even suffer the consequence for any action whatsoever, they lived only for momentary pleasures and were reduced to animalistic existences. Worse than any physical destruction the plague brought to the bodies of those inhabiting Athens, the plague wrought a devastation upon the quest for human goodness itself.[24] In the background of the discussion of the *Charmides* is a question about the benefit or even the utility of *sôphrosunê*—has it become a victim of the war, along with the citizens who have been wiped out? Has *sôphrosunê* lost its meaning in the face of the transvaluation of values that results when the plague forces citizens to confront their mortality? It is in this context that we see that Socrates's first action of note upon returning from the battle is to seek out his "habitual conversations" (*sunêtheis diatribes*), and go to the Palaestra—the wrestling school of Taureas.[25]

The Palaestra is a place for both physical and mental exercise: the improvement of the body by means of athletic training, and the improvement of the soul by means of conversation. And amid this war in this wrestling school Socrates is seated next to the future member of the Thirty Tyrants, Critias, the son of Callaeschrus.[26] It is Critias who introduces the other future member of the Thirty, Charmides, son of Glaucon.[27] The Palaestra is interestingly a place of "paiderastic pursuit," a place in which the younger beloved customarily arrives to receive cultural instruction from the wiser lover, in exchange for sexual favors.[28] We thus will find the answer to Socrates's opening question about the status of philosophy and the youths, by turning to an investigation of the nature, possibility, and benefit of wonder.[29]

Apparently all at the Palaestra are excited to see Socrates, for he can bring them news from the battle.[30] Given Socrates's three-year absence, it is understandable that many at the wrestling school rush in excitement to see *him*. Indeed, Chaerephon immediately asks him how he survived the battle—and thus provides the opening question of the dialogue.[31] For others, perhaps it is not Socrates himself that is their pressing concern but the news of what he went through. But none of this is the concern of Socrates, who responds quite simply, "Just as you see (*houtôsi hôs su horas*)."[32] At his appearance here, Chaerephon is described as manic[33] and thus not *sophron* in appearance at least, yet Socrates shows himself to be *always the same*, in battle or otherwise. His *sôphrosunê* shines through, no matter what the circumstances, and follows him wherever he goes.[34] Socrates, upon coming home from battle, returns to his customary conversations in the wrestling school and asks (once his peers "had enough" talk of war) about the state of the youths and philosophy in Athens: "When we had enough of these things, I in turn asked about things here: about philosophy, how it was doing now, about the youths, whether any had become distinguished in wisdom (*sophia*) or beauty (*kallei*) or both."[35] This is his opening question. While those at home in Athens are preoccupied, one might think rightly,[36] with the dangers posed by the violence of war abroad (made worse by the plague at home and its violent and abrupt transvaluation of values), Socrates asks about philosophy and the young. One may see him here as aloof and detached from his more rooted fellow citizens. But one should notice that Plato does not narrate to us Socrates talking about any heroic feats in battle or his achievement of any glory.[37] This, in fact, shows that Socrates's opening question is appropriately paired with Chaerephon's, for Socrates reveals his *sôphrosunê* while Chaerephon's question bespeaks his mania.[38] Indeed, their two questions are connected. While Chaerephon asks Socrates how he is alive, Socrates asks if Athens is *living well*. Socrates is asking about the genuine well-being of his community, if indeed part of its *good* consists in the thriving of philosophy and youths that are *truly* beautiful and wise. There is an important concern raised here, given the violence and disease in the background: what if the youths are not busying themselves with seeking wisdom (the proper meaning of *philosophia*) or not in any way seeking genuine wisdom and beauty but only pursuing shadows? The ensuing conversation about philosophy and the young therefore (1) takes place with the ideas of tyranny, violence, mortality, and freedom all in the background and is thus raised in a thoroughly political context,[39] and (2) compels us to wonder: what kind of political context is a necessary (and perhaps sufficient) condition for the search for self-knowledge to be possible and beneficial?[40] Finally, we should remind ourselves that Socrates's opening question is not at all about self-knowledge—but about wisdom and beauty, and only about these as they manifest in particular human beings: the young. Moreover, the search for *sôphrosunê* and self-knowledge is embedded in an examination of a particular beautiful individual: Charmides. Unfortunately, Charmides's own beauty, and his orientation to it, will turn out to lead directly to his lack of *sôphrosunê* and lack of self-knowledge. I will argue that Plato's point is nothing less than this: This disorientation to the beautiful is directly tied up with the downfall of Athens. For, to return to Chaerephon's question, the ultimate sign of Athens not living well is the death of Socrates. Can he survive the battle—the disease caused by the disorientation to the beautiful—that is happening at home?

Chapter Two

Beautiful Charmides (154a–155e)

In response to Socrates's opening question, Critias claims that Socrates will soon be satisfied with a response. For his attention has been caught by the noisy entrance of a crowd of lovers (*erastai*) of the young man he considers to be the most beautiful in Athens. It is noteworthy that Critias makes no mention at all of Charmides's wisdom; although Socrates had asked about it along with beauty, Critias is concerned only with the latter.[1] Socrates asks, "Who is he (*tis*) and of whom (*tou*)?"[2] The question should not be overlooked: it is about Charmides's identity and his lineage, his being and his genesis. And while it is tempting to read this as a question about Charmides's parentage (and thus translate *tou* as "Who is his father?" or "Whose son is he?"), the more literal meaning of Socrates's question connotes a more fundamental question that casts a shadow over the ensuing discussion, and (to mix a metaphor) fully comes to light by its end. The question could be put this way: who is Charmides and to whom does he belong? This is the true meaning of Socrates's second question in the dialogue. There is more at stake in answering it than in a mere ascertaining of Charmides's name and lineage. It becomes clear that Socrates throughout this dialogue is concerned whether the young man, beautiful as he is, is ready to take the step toward adulthood and stand on his own. If Critias is indeed presenting Charmides as a paragon of beauty among the young men, then perhaps this would show that he may indeed excel in wisdom as well. The answer to this second question thus will entail an answer to Socrates's first question about the youths in Athens. For what if, as the conversation continues, Charmides and

Critias reveal that the young man's beauty is only skin deep, his identity shallow, his wisdom superficial, and his motivations impure? Who then is Charmides and to whom does he belong? And if Charmides is the paragon of the youths, what should be made of philosophy and the youths at home?[3] Charmides's beauty may be remarkable for the effect it has on the beholder, but what is remarkable, as comes to light under Socrates's examination, is the disjunction between the presence of this beauty and Charmides's own ability to take beautiful actions, or his willingness to seek for anything beautiful himself.

Charmides's entrance as the stage for this investigation takes on particular significance because Socrates is describing it from his own personal first-person point of view.[4] When Critias tells Socrates that he is his cousin, Socrates confirms that he knows the young boy and that he was not at all bad looking before he left. In his narration of Charmides's entrance, Socrates reminds his anonymous listener that he is not the best expert on young male beauty:

> Now nothing is to be measured by me, friend (*hetaire*), for I am simply a white line when it comes to those who are beautiful (*kalous*). For almost all who have just reached maturity (*helikiai*) appear beautiful to me. But especially then he appeared wondrous (*thaumastos*) in stature (*megethos*) and beauty (*kallos*), and indeed, at least in my opinion, all the others were in love with (*eran*) him, so dazzled (*ekpeplêgmenoi*) and thrown into confusion (*tethorubêmenoi*) had they become as he came in. Indeed, many other lovers (*erastai*) followed behind him. Now this was not wondrous (*thaumaston*) on the part of us men, but turning my attention to the boys, I noticed that none of them, not even the smallest, looked anywhere else, but gazed (*etheonto*) at him as if he were a statue.[5]

The power of *erôs* is great, as Socrates's account of others' reactions makes clear. As stated above, Charmides's effect on those around him is remarkable. It seems that the power of his beauty to captivate those who gaze upon him is so all-encompassing that no one can look anywhere else. But if the reader looks away from Charmides and more closely at what Socrates describes in this first-person narrative of the reaction to Charmides's beauty, it is possible to distinguish four reactions to Charmides's looks, each representing four different orientations to beauty itself:[6]

1. **The Crowd (The Beautiful as the Tyrannical)**—Almost everyone who gazes upon Charmides sees only Charmides. Charmides's beauty causes a tumultuous noise amid a swarm of bystanders or followers. They are caught up in a confusion and uproar, and it is important to note that "*thorobeô*" is usually used of crowds.[7] Socrates even refers to the group that is overwhelmed by the beauty of Charmides as a crowd or mob (*ochlos*),[8] a word that has vicious political undertones, bringing to mind the transformation of the leader of the crowd into a tyrant.[9] The crowd looks at him as if he were a statue (*agalma*), a word in other contexts that is used of images of gods. The crowd, in its confusion, has become his devoted subject.[10] We should be careful to contrast this wonder, as we will below and later, with the kind of perplexity, confusion, and *wonder* associated with philosophical inquiry.

2. **Critias (The Beautiful as Possession)**—Socrates leaves Critias out of his narration. What is his reaction to Charmides's entrance? Either Critias has the same reaction as the crowd or he does not. It would be odd if Critias were included in Socrates's description of the tumultuous, noisy lovers of Charmides, since Critias is Charmides's older cousin and guardian. But there is a deeper point here too—intimated in Socrates's earlier question about Charmides ("Who is he and of whom?"). Critias possesses Charmides and is presenting him to Socrates—his relation to him is neither one of confusion nor of wonder. Charmides's beauty (just as Charmides is his younger cousin) is Critias's *own*. Critias's orientation to the beautiful Charmides and to beauty itself will not turn out to be properly erotic, in the sense that it can lead to wonder. It is only *thumoeidetic*, tied to an attachment to one's own things, which will also become clear later. In this light, Critias is the inversion of the crowd. As they are the ones tyrannized by the beautiful, Critias is the one who owns the beautiful and stands to rule over those so susceptible to its power.

3. **Charmides (The Beautiful and Self-Ignorance)**—What is beautiful Charmides's relation to his own beauty? Socrates

also leaves Charmides's reaction to those beholding him out of his own narration of the event. Both Critias's and Charmides's relationships to beauty are the phenomena *to be examined*. But Charmides's silence means something different than does the silence shown by his older cousin and guardian. For the experience of the beloved object of the gaze is not actually considered by the one who gazes. This is the case even if the one gazing, like Socrates, can present the other responses to Charmides by others gazing upon him. But this is precisely why Socrates will examine Charmides himself: to investigate his orientation to his own beauty and the beautiful itself. Is Charmides's orientation to his own beauty, like his identity ("Who is he and of whom?") defined by the view of others? It would only be fitting if he is the constant object of others' gaze. Indeed, can the one who is beautiful move past the ignorance of his own beauty, defined by the opinions of others, toward a genuine truth defined by real self-examination? What path lies open to Charmides, if this is possible? Will it be to be tyrannized by it as the crowd is or to rule over it as his own possession, as Critias appears to do? Perhaps another way lies open, as Socrates makes manifest.

4. **Socrates (The Beautiful as the Wondrous)**—Socrates certainly finds Charmides to be beautiful, but he also says that he is no good measure (he is like a "white line" on white stone). Socrates does not claim that he cannot make any measurements at all when it comes to beauty but that all who have reached maturity appear beautiful to him. And he makes a startling judgment, claiming that the boy appears wondrous (*thaumaston*). It is not clear what Socrates means by this at this point. I submit that it will make sense once we turn to Diotima's account of the ladder of love in the *Symposium*. For now, however, it is important to note that Socrates is not at all caught up like the crowd in their tumultuous uproar. He is able to observe them being so caught up, and thus to turn his gaze away from Charmides and observe others gazing at Charmides. He finds their response to be wondrous as well. Socrates's

relationship to beauty will turn out to be properly erotic, because philosophical *erôs* leads to wonder, where it is not plagued by one's own *need to possess it.*

I would thus classify these four orientations to the beautiful as four kinds of erotic relations. And they are presented to us in this dialogue about *sôphrosunê* because they bear essentially upon its theme. I will argue that only one of the four—the Socratic—is compatible with *sôphrosunê*, if *sôphrosunê* is to be understood in any way related to self-knowledge. Furthermore, if we are to understand how *sôphrosunê*—as Socratic knowledge of what one knows and does not know—is possible and beneficial, it will turn out to be necessary to connect it with the erotic orientation to beauty that culminates in the philosophical passion of wonder, as described by Diotima in Plato's *Symposium*.

At this point we should emphasize that Socrates is still in control. He is able to observe not only the beauty of Charmides but also able to evaluate the reactions of the other onlookers. He is in possession of himself and thus not blinded by the beauty of Charmides but able to see its effect on others. Charmides, therefore, does not have the effect on Socrates that a beautiful object can have—utterly distracting and confusing him, to the point of removing him from his circumstances.[11] But Chaerephon (with others seconding) now suggests that if Charmides were willing to strip, that Socrates would not even be able to see his face.[12] Still, Socrates here says that they are describing an "irresistible man" if he has a "small thing" in addition: a beautiful soul. While Critias had not guessed what this small ingredient was, he is no less quick to sing Charmides's praises, claiming that he is "exceptional in that respect" as well. Socrates remarks that this is fitting, since the boy comes from Critias's family. But at the same time he calls it into question, by getting permission from Critias to "gaze at" the boy's soul just as they had earlier been gazing at his bodily form. Critias is happy to agree to show off Charmides's soul to Socrates, but what should Socrates's examination really reveal? It should not go unnoticed by those watching the conversation, hearing Socrates's narration, and reading Plato's words, that were Charmides to demonstrate insufficiency of soul to Socrates and those present, the family of Critias would indeed be implicated in the failure to educate him, indeed, to corrupt him instead. For this reason, some have objected that Socrates is actually causing harm in carrying out his philosophical examination on young Charmides and is guilty of the corruption charges brought against him. But in fact, Socrates will be guilty only of exposing the miseducation of Charmides, for which Critias is most responsible.

Critias calls an attendant to bring in Charmides, but conspires with Socrates to use deception to invite the young boy:

> "Boy, call Charmides, tell him that I wish to introduce him to a doctor concerning the ailment (*asthenias*) from which he told me recently he was suffering." Then Critias said to me, "The other day he said he was heavy (*barunesthai*) in the head, upon rising at the dawn: now what prevents you from pretending to know a remedy (*pharmakon*) for his head?"
>
> "Nothing." I said. "Just let him come."[13]

The dialogue thus begins with a conspiracy.[14] For here it seems that Critias's motive for the deception is created when Socrates suggests that the two of them strip the boy's soul. Perhaps Critias realizes that he was too quick to assent to the stripping of Charmides's soul without getting his consent, so he concocts this scheme.[15] Critias's deception thus not only masks Socrates to allow Charmides to come forward but also diverts attention from the soul of the boy, back to his body (his head). Critias reveals thereby an attachment to the boy's appearance, his outer excellence, without any regard for a genuine soul stripping in search of wisdom. Those of us watching this will wonder: why has Socrates agreed to such a deception? Perhaps because it is not really a deception in Socrates's mind. It does not occur to Critias that Socrates agrees to this because, as Socrates goes on to discuss, there is a treatment (*therapeia*) for Charmides's head by investigating and treating his soul, to see if it is *really* beautiful and properly oriented toward what is *really* beautiful.

When Charmides is invited to come over, he takes a seat, sending some people head over heels as they attempt to make room for him. The scene provokes much laughter in the room.[16] Indeed, it is a funny scene, but the laughter here is not without its nervousness. Charmides's effect on others is dangerous. So blinding is his beauty that the men neglect each other, and perhaps even themselves, in pursuit of *him*. The laughter is rooted in the recognition that they have forgotten themselves. At this moment, Socrates is still in control of himself, but soon he experiences this same loss. On display is the disruptive tyranny of *erôs*, and given the ominous ending of the dialogue, we are compelled at this point to ask: can anyone, even one with *sôphrosunê*, escape it?[17]

Socrates becomes as confused as the others when Charmides takes a seat next to him.

> Then indeed, my friend (*phile*), I was at a loss (*êporoun*), and my former boldness (*thrasutês*), which I had as I was expecting to converse (*dialexomenos*) with him quite easily, had been knocked out of me. For when, as Critias was saying that I was the one who had knowledge (*epistamenos*) of the cure, he looked at me with his eyes in such an irresistible (*amêchanon*) way and was drawing himself up to ask a question, while everyone in the wrestling school flowed around us in a complete circle—then indeed, noble one (*gennada*), I saw inside his cloak, I was inflamed (*ephlegomen*), I was no longer in control of myself (*en emautou ên*) and I considered Cydias to be wisest in erotic things (*erotika*), who, speaking about a beautiful boy, advised someone that "a fawn coming opposite a lion should beware lest he be taken as a portion of meat."[18]

Socrates explains to his anonymous addressee that he was in aporia when Charmides looked at him in such an "irresistible way" and Socrates caught a glimpse of what was beneath his cloak. This aporia caused him to lose his boldness, a *thumotic* retreat, and to lose control of himself as well. The aporia he experiences here is one that seems to have an impact on his *thumos*, his courage and his *sôphrosunê*, understood at least in a traditional sense.

What then is the relation between *sôphrosunê* and *erôs*?[19] This is the question dramatically posed by Charmides's entrance. For the entire account of Zalmoxian medicine and discussion of *sôphrosunê* that follows is born in this erotic moment. As Benardete says: "We have then a split between the basis of the dialogue and the basis of the narrative. Charmides's experience of immoderation is the occasion for the form in which the question of *sôphrosunê* arises; but it is Socrates's immoderation that experientially grounds the Thracian teaching. What is theory for Charmides is fact for Socrates. The examination of Charmides's *sôphrosunê* serves Socrates's self-knowledge."[20] What is even more odd is that Socrates describes this experience by referring his addressee to the words of Cydias, the poet, who he claims in this moment to be wisest in erotic matters. Indeed, the image conjured up by the words of Cydias might be no comfort at all, when one considers that the relation between the fawn and the lion, if they are meant as stand-ins for the lover and the beloved, is antagonistic and brutal.[21] The lover is caught, fawnlike, before the more terrifying threat of the lion who will devour the beloved should the lover pursue him. In what sense then is the wisdom of Cydias helpful to Socrates? It is indeed a message of *sôphrosunê*, but not one that accords with our usual understanding of the virtue. The image is incommensurate with a notion of *sôphrosunê* as self-control, and we should not interpret it as an encouragement to restrain one's desires. The fawn (lover) *gazes upon* the lion (the beloved). But in such a circumstance, the lover may surrender (almost helplessly) to the vision of the beautiful that pursues him with irresistible force and will destroy him.[22] We should therefore not surrender to all that is beautiful, even though its pull over us may have an overwhelming effect. Not all experiences of wonder are the same. The wisdom of Cydias therefore reminds us to guard against the danger of surrender, if indeed the object of our gaze will devour us. If *sôphrosunê* emerges here, then, it is in a wisdom that allows us to take caution in the light of understanding one's enemies, however awe-inspiring and beautiful they may *appear* to be, when in fact they pose a real threat.

Charmides possesses an *ambiguous* beauty, one that at best threatens to bring its possessor and those who gaze upon it harm disguised as good. It raises a suspicion whether he is able to discuss, pursue, or possess a purely *unambiguous* beauty, one that may bring only good to its possessor. If such a beauty exists, then perhaps gazing upon it would bring about a kind of *sôphrosunê* that would not look like caution in the face of the ambiguous threat of the beautiful. Perhaps such *sôphrosunê* would look more like the quiet contemplation of the beautiful itself.[23] But to hear the wisdom of Cydias and take such caution in the light of this ambiguous beauty is to recognize oneself as vulnerable, while at the same time knowing oneself as lacking something beautiful *and* knowing that one's desires can be misled by what is not genuinely beautiful. Such caution therefore requires that Socrates be able to recognize his limits and admit his ignorance, while at the same time he is able to seek for what truly answers his opening question about wisdom and beauty. He sees himself as the fawn caught before a lion who may take him like meat, and in the dialogue from this point forward Socrates will attempt not to be swallowed.

Can the philosopher take caution to escape from the appetite of the tyrant? Socrates will need to do just that, for Charmides is now ready to hear his cure for what ails his head, and if Socrates is not cautious enough, he could end up as his meal. It is to counteract this that Socrates introduces a foreign teaching about medicine, in order to reorient Charmides's (and the listener's) relation to his own beauty and his own wisdom.

Chapter Three

Zalmoxian Medicine and Looking within Charmides (155e–159a)

When Socrates is perplexed upon seeing the beautiful Charmides up close, the boy asks him for a cure to his headache. Socrates has agreed with Critias to "pretend" to know this cure, and in his state of bewilderment, he barely manages an answer: "And I said that it was a certain leaf, but there was a charm (*epoidê*) in addition to the drug (*pharmakon*), and if one chanted (*epadoi*) it at the same as the treatment (*xroito*), then the drug would make him entirely healthy (*hugia*). But without the charm the leaf would be useless (*ouden ophelos*)."[1] Charmides immediately asks for the charm in writing, which prompts Socrates to ask if Charmides will even try to get his consent for this.

Socrates has thus asked four important questions about Charmides before the conversation about *sôphrosunê* and even begins:

1. Who is Charmides and of whom is he?[2]

2. Why don't we strip his soul and contemplate it before contemplating his looks?[3]

3. Whether you have a sufficient share of *sôphrosunê* or if you are in need.[4]

4. If you persuade me or even if you don't?[5]

In all four questions, the nature of *sôphrosunê* is not the primary emphasis, rather the stress of the questions is placed on the nature of Charmides and the nature of the society that has brought him up. I submit that (2), (3), and (4) are an attempt to answer (1). Can Charmides stand up and assert himself or is he a slave to his guardian Critias, who is possibly no more knowledgeable or free than the youth himself? It is this quest for identity that leads to the question of *sôphrosunê*, and Socrates is critiquing not only the young Charmides but Athens as well, and in so doing he raises wonder about the possibility of philosophy's success in this (or any?) city.[6]

The soul emerges for the first time in the dialogue as a result of question (2), and this makes it unambiguous that the conversation that follows is meant to shed light on Charmides's soul. The inquiry is not therefore primarily an impersonal search for a definition of a concept but rather starts with a very *psyche-analysis*: it is not only about *sôphrosunê* but also about Charmides himself.[7] Socrates tries to encourage Charmides to undertake this kind of self-examination when he urges the young boy to "say what he believes." It is his life that is being put on trial, and Socrates's question here demands that he put his very *self* on trial, and "courageously"[8] attempt the kind of questioning of his own beliefs in order to engage in true philosophical inquiry.[9] This is the basis for Socrates's questions (3) and (4), both of which require admitting his own ignorance and his submission to rational inquiry and dialogue. In addition, the final question ("If you persuade me or even if you don't?") suggests a violent undertone: the alternative to persuasion, especially for Charmides, the ward of Critias, would readily be force.[10] Plato has already alluded to this in depicting the tyrannical power of Charmides's own beauty over the crowd. Socrates is asking, in effect, whether Charmides will put away the force of his own beauty in favor of the collaborative discourse that philosophical dialogue requires. But Charmides's own beauty and others' reactions to it prevent him from taking such a stance. As we have seen in his entrance scene, *erôs* acts like a tyrant in his world.

In order to undertake an authentic quest for one's identity, and thus engage in genuine philosophy, there must be room for a dialogue that emerges from a kind of friendship between two seekers of wisdom. This demands a particular political context, one that is not plagued by a disease that sees *erôs* as exclusively predatory, violent, and forceful in all its manifestations. Such a diseased *erôs* breeds tyranny in the souls of the citizens and makes philosophic inquiry impossible. But there may yet be a nondiseased desire for what is beautiful: a desire that is nonpredatory, nonviolent, nonforceful, and it would legitimate philosophical investigation and the quest for self-knowledge and identity.

Recall at this point that the very question about Charmides's soul has been arrived at by means of a deception. Critias suggests that Socrates "pretend to be a doctor to treat Charmides's recent headache." Now we may see why Socrates assents to this ruse. As Hyland points out, the lie could be like the "grand lie" in book 3 of the *Republic*, and thus may serve a therapeutic end.[11] This implies that Socrates has already picked up from Critias that the boy himself may require something other than simple, honest persuasion to have his soul stripped. This is not unreasonable, given how beautiful the boy's body is. Socrates shrewdly sees already that the young, beautiful Charmides may have nothing underneath his good looks, and must be tricked to lay himself bare. For those watching (and reading) closely, the potential disjunction between Charmides's external beauty (and its captivating effect) and any *beauty of soul* is significant. The aporia Socrates will induce in Charmides will bring about a more important aporia for onlookers and readers. It compels them to question their own attachment and attraction to what is beautiful about Charmides, even to what is beautiful simply. Socrates's conversation with Charmides aims at a therapy of our desires.[12]

In response to Socrates's question (4), Charmides laughs. He then makes it clear that he thinks he knows who Socrates is. Readers should catch the joke that Socrates now says when he claims "he shall speak more freely" about the charm. Charmides has assented to Socrates's call for collaborative inquiry, rather than acting the tyrant, and thus Socrates is "more free." It is thus through conversation that Socrates comes to reorient himself before the tyrannical beauty of Charmides. In gazing at the beauty of Charmides's body, he risks being consumed by it. In attending to the soul and its good, he comes back to life.[13] But when Socrates finds out that young Charmides is familiar with him, should he not realize that his ruse with Critias has been unmasked? Instead, he now feels even more comfortable pressing forward with it. This is further evidence that what Socrates is about to communicate to Charmides is no mere deception, following the suggestion of Critias, but instead reveals something very true. Here then is Socrates's description of the nature of the charm.

> For it is such that it cannot make the head alone healthy, but just as you too perhaps have heard from good doctors (*agathôn iatrôn*), whenever someone comes to them with his eyes in pain—they may say that it is not possible (*ouch hoion te*) to try to cure (*iasthai*) alone, but it is necessary at the same time

> to treat the head as well, if one intends the condition of the eyes to be well; so also they say it is quite mindless (*anoian*) to suppose that one could ever treat the head itself without the whole body (*holou tou sômatos*). Because of this argument (*logou*) they turn to the whole body with their regimens and attempt to treat and heal (*therapeuein te kai iasthai*) the part along with the whole (*meta tou holou to meros*).[14]

Socrates here reports a principle that the health of the body must be attained holistically. The example is easy enough to follow. If a pain in one's eyes is in fact caused by a cerebral injury, then treating the eyes by themselves would not cure the sickness that *caused* their disease. Now this may not be the case always, and Socrates does not say that parts cannot malfunction by themselves, but the suggestion he is following is that we must first look at the whole body to understand the health of its parts. If one does not do this, then one takes a great risk of not treating the real cause of disease. Charmides agrees to this principle, and Socrates now takes the principle one step further:

> Such, then, is how it is with this charm (*epoidê*), Charmides. I learned it there in the army from one of the Thracian doctors of Zalmoxis, who they say even makes one immortal (*apathanatizein*). This Thracian said that the Greeks say beautifully (*kalôs legoien*) what I was now saying. But Zalmoxis, our king, who is a god, says that just as one must not attempt to heal (*iasthai*) eyes without head or head without body, so also not body without soul (*psuchês*); and that the cause (*aition*) of many diseases eluding the doctors among the Greeks is that they neglect the whole (*tou holou ameleoien*), to which care (*epimeleian*) must be given, because if it is not in beautiful condition (*kalôs echontos*), the part is not able to be well (*eu echein*).[15]

What does this account mean? What kind of medicine is this charm, and how does it work? The first thing to notice is that Socrates seems to be suggesting that the charm addresses itself to the whole human being. It is not meant for merely physiological correction or restoration. The doctor who gives a merely "physiological" treatment takes the risk of missing the whole, for having an only partial view he mistakes the body for all there is, and neglects the soul.

Socrates claims that a good doctor should not treat the eyes without the head, nor the head without the body, and accordingly not the body without the soul either. But this implies that the body belongs to the soul in the same way that eyes belong to the head, and this is not easy to grasp. This is made even more complicated when Socrates implies that the *entire human being* is a part of the soul.[16] What then does the relation of part to whole mean here? Socrates's Thracian God-King explains it by calling the soul the normative source: "For he said that everything springs from the soul, both bad things and good things (*ta kaka kai ta agatha*) for the body and the entire human being (*anthropoi*), and they flow from there just as from the head to the eyes. And so one must treat (*therapeuein*) first and foremost [the soul] if one wishes the head and the rest of the body to do well (*eu echein*)."[17] The body then is a part of the soul in the sense that the soul is the ultimate *source* of what is good and bad for the rest of the human being. Many commentators take this to mean that Socrates is talking about "the whole human being" here.[18] To take an analogy, we could consider the case of a person's legs. The knee is not just a part of the leg because the leg "contains" the knee but because the knee's "good" or "function"—bending—is part of the leg's "good" or "function"—walking. The end knees serve is subordinate then to the end of the leg. The end of the leg is going to be subordinate to the end of the body, and ultimately the soul. For walking may be the function of the leg, but why should the *whole person* be walking? Is he escaping quietly from his enemy? Is he on his way to teach a class? Or perhaps wandering aimlessly trying to figure out the purpose of his legs? Each part of the body has its own proper "good," but this good is only partial. On this reading, the whole good cannot be perceived unless ones pays attention not only to the body but also to the good embedded in the *best kind of life* appropriate to a human being. Now it is in trying to live a particular kind of life, say student, parent, or athlete, that we follow goals and norms that guide us to achieving the good in that life. But the kind of life that Socrates is asking about is the life of *human being qua human being*. Socrates asks: is there such a thing as the *human* good, life appropriate to the human? What kind of goals and norms come along with defining it?

If we had knowledge of the *best kind of human life*, then surely the well-being of the soul would be a cause of the well-being of the body. For if one's soul is truly oriented to the *human* good understood in this way, then one will also practice such actions that will actually contribute to the health of the body as well. Socrates is not asserting that all disease is psychosomatic, or that no disease belongs just to the body, or that bodily medicine is unnecessary. As Coolidge asserts, Socrates's Thracian doctor is only saying that if there is disease in the body, there was a disease in the soul at some prior time that was the original cause of it.[19] This would indeed be the case if one takes "disease in the soul" to denote a kind of life.[20]

Therefore, our understanding of ourselves cannot stop with the body, unless we wish to say that something like the soul does not exist. But if Socrates is saying that our soul is the source of what is good and bad, then it is this capacity to judge our lives as good or bad, well or badly lived, that seems essential to being human.[21] And it is just this capacity that Socrates associates with the soul in the *Charmides* and nothing more. Other than this, Socrates gives no more information to us about *what the soul is.*[22] But we may doubt that it is possible to answer the question, What *is the soul*? Or what *is the human being*? How do we examine these, and how does examination of them then yield knowledge of the good?[23] The *Charmides* shows that the young boy and his guardian are unable to answer this question, and Socrates discovers that their souls themselves are ill suited to even attempt to answer the question. Deep down they cannot accept the truth of the Thracian teaching, and so discussion with them can never reach this level. They are clearly in need of the charms Socrates is talking about, but it is not clear that they would do any good.[24] Other interlocutors may be necessary to have the deeper conversation with Socrates about the human soul.

Socrates presents this teaching in sharp contrast to the way that medicine is conducted "here in Athens." The principle behind the practice of Greek medicine is only partially correct: Greek doctors treat the whole body, and not just its part, but they stop short of the true whole. It is noteworthy that Socrates claims that he learned of this error from outsiders: the source is Zalmoxis, the God-King of Thrace. The implication is that the notion of good according to Athenian conventions may be too narrow. One must transcend this culture in order to set it on the right track. Here then we see that he is already expressing concern about the potential answer to his opening question.[25] It is also not only a foreign teaching but a teaching that comes from a being who is both god and king. This would be an individual, if he exists, who possesses the highest authority from both a political and theological standpoint, and it is this individual who sends Socrates as a messenger to Athens. Socrates would then potentially be comparable to a *theoros*, a spectator who has obtained some theoretical wisdom via philosophical inquiry about it, and, having attained this wisdom, has returned to his polis in order to share it with his fellow citizens, and thus complete his journey.[26] But the wisdom Socrates brings upon completing this journey is connected to an attention to *the whole* that will be inextricably to linked to *sôphrosunê* and self-knowledge as Socrates conceives it—knowing what one does and does not know. Consequently, and because of the role that *wonder* plays in Socratic philosophical investigation, it is not without reason that Socrates says these Thracian doctors can make human beings immortal. For in Socrates's view, it is in bringing humans to contemplate and wonder about the limits of their wisdom that they are brought the closest they can come to divinity. On this reading, Socrates is not suggesting here a transcendence into the eternal realm but instead highlighting that what we could call "human divinity" rests in a recognition of one's finitude that is (somewhat paradoxically) simultaneous with the glimpse of what lies beyond one's mortal grasp. It is, as we have begun to see with the striking entrance of Charmides, the beautiful itself that gives paradigm experiences of this, such as the trancelike states of those who gaze upon beautiful Charmides.

Indeed, Socrates asserts that the charms that treat the soul are "beautiful speeches" (*kaloi logoi*) and even says earlier that the Thracian speech was "beautifully spoken" and led to a "beautiful condition of the soul."[27] It is these beautiful speeches that engender *sôphrosunê* in the soul, and once *sôphrosunê* is present, one can provide health for the head and the rest of the body. Tuckey claims that it is Socrates's *elenchus*, his method of demonstrating inconsistencies in an interlocutor's set of beliefs, that serves as the model of these beautiful speeches that induce *sôphrosunê*.[28] Schmid claims that this ability shows Socrates to be this kind of Thracian physician, for in using his elenctic method to demonstrate inconsistency, he brings his interlocutors to realize what they do not know. On Schmid's view Socrates seems to know what is good is for the soul and how to bring about this good both for himself and others.[29]

I believe Schmid (who is following Vlastos here) is right that Socrates's elenctic method could be a tool that the physician uses to engender *sôphrosunê* in the soul. For the interlocutor is brought via the *elenchus* to see that his beliefs are inconsistent with one another, and he must reject some of them, which usually entails the abandonment of his original thesis.[30] Because this method is "highly personal"—that is, it requires the interlocutor to say in public what he believes and to examine deeply held beliefs and values about which he is quite confident—Socrates acts as a "therapist" to his particular interlocutor, and not simply an investigator of the truth of the matter at hand.[31] The goal then of the *elenchus* is the freedom from dogmatic authority for the interlocutor.[32]

What then will be the aim of Socrates's *beautiful speeches* for beautiful Charmides? Socrates's own beautiful speech should render Charmides able to examine his relation to his own beauty, primarily the power his own beauty has over him to impede his inquiry into what might be genuinely beautiful. On this reading, we can think of Socrates's beautiful speeches as therapeutically designed to bring Charmides to recognize himself not as the beautiful object of others' gaze but as himself lacking genuine beauty and therefore in need of searching for it—so that he eventually comes to wonder at the beautiful itself.

Socrates now asks whether Charmides can submit his soul to Socrates, and avoid the error of human beings: " 'Now in teaching me both the drug (*pharmakon*) and the charm (*epoidas*),' he said, 'Let no one persuade you to treat (*therapeuthênai*) his head with the drug unless he first submits (*paraschê*) his soul to be treated by you with the charm. For as it is now,' he said, 'this is the error (*hamartêma*) common among human beings (*peri tous anthropous*), that some attempt to be doctors of *sôphrosunê* and health separately.' "[33] Notice that Socrates makes it clear how much control he has over his *erôs* here. It is no coincidence that Socrates reminds Charmides that *persuasion* is critical here. The force of Charmides's beauty, according to the God-King Zalmoxis, can have no influence over his decision to pass on the drug, without charming his soul into *sôphrosunê* first. The presence of *sôphrosunê*, attained through beautiful speeches, must precede treatment of the body. We cannot understand the goodness of the body fully until we have understood the good of the soul—philosophical dialogue is the precondition of the search for *sôphrosunê* and health. Nor can these be separated, and the common error of human beings results from their mistake in this regard. In supposing that health resides only in the body, they lose sight of the soul and what is truly good and live their lives in the partial realm of appearances, rather than inhabiting the reality of the whole. But what does it actually mean to be oriented to the whole? According to the myth, it involves an understanding of the soul that is nowhere given in the dialogue except to say that it is the source of all that is good and bad. Understanding of soul is thus inextricably bound up, as self-knowledge, with knowledge of good and evil.

At this point we should recall the setting of the dialogue in war, and consider how Socrates's account here, as I have presented it, is tied to the political context of the dialogue. Recall that Socrates's opening questions concerned the state of the youth and philosophy "here in Athens." Now that we have discussed the physician of the soul, it can be seen that this healer, if he were successful, would also be an indispensable physician of the city.

For Socrates has claimed that those who practice Greek medicine are ignorant of the whole, and as such they are sadly deceived about what is truly good for the citizens. Charmides, as the representative youth, will show at the end of the dialogue whether his city has failed him or not by demonstrating whether he can or cannot break the hold of his elders' opinions in order to examine them for himself.[34] These two, Charmides and Critias, will later be followed by the Athenians as they overthrow the Athenian democracy. In this dialogue, then, we are seeing an exploration of characters responsible for the bloody downfall of their community. Recall too that Socrates claimed he learned the teaching about the whole from the foreigner Zalmoxis, who was not only a god, but a *king*. Understanding good and evil is something that is required for a political leader to guide his city to flourish. Spelling this out, of course, is a task that is undertaken in the *Republic*.[35]

The *sôphrosunê* engendered by the physician of the soul lifts one out of the potentially enslaving opinions of one's culture, doctrines that one has ingested before having the ability to rationally examine their truth or goodness. The city built upon these opinions is one that risks keeping its citizens from seeing what is good, and even if they try to break free, it wields a tyrant's power over their souls.

As Schmid says, there are certainly two sickness Socrates is trying to cure. He is: "the logotherapist of the two chief illnesses of the Athenian mind—the psychic diseases of moral heteronomy, on the one hand, and of Sophistry and self-conceit, on the other."[36] Socrates is certainly worried about these, but Socrates has not only promoted here the idea of critical reason and rationality as a cure to these diseases. I believe his use of myth shows us that he is discovering and examining the nature of the irrational element of human beings, and what philosophical and political methods might be necessary to combat the irrational forces with any hope of efficacy. The discovery of the irrational is thus crucial to one who seeks to have "knowledge of the whole," and this grounds the multifaceted approach that is Socrates's therapeutic examination. With its mixture of myth and *elenchus*, hypothesis and analysis, its aim throughout is to produce *sôphrosunê* in the soul: to bring authentic self-understanding to both participants in this dialectic. Socrates examines our orientation (or disorientation) to beauty in order to work on the prephilosophical conditions of the pursuit of self-knowledge. Having the right orientation prevents us from tyrannizing others or subjecting ourselves to tyranny, and moreover, enables us to pursue what is genuinely good for us.

This motivation, then, underlies Socrates's question to Charmides after he has given his account of Thracian medicine. Socrates asks, finally, if Charmides can say whether he needs Socrates to charm him with *sôphrosunê*: can he affirm that he has the virtue, or can he admit that he is deficient?[37] Socrates has asked Charmides—can you admit ignorance and ask for treatment?

Charmides responds with a blush,[38] then puts forth a dilemma. He cannot admit possession or nonpossession of *sôphrosunê*. Charmides is in a kind of aporia. Socrates was earlier placed in a kind of aporia by witnessing Charmides's beauty. Now Socrates turns the tables and produces aporia in Charmides with his own beautiful speech. Charmides says that to claim that he is not *sophron* would be "strange"[39] to say against himself, as it would give the lie to Critias and others who say he is *sophron*. On the other hand, Charmides continues, he cannot say he is *sophron* for that might appear "obnoxious" (*epachthês*) to those present. Notice that Charmides does not say it is logically impossible to assert either of these claims: he only says that both make him uncomfortable in the view of those around him. The paradox Charmides faces here is not a logical one but a political one. Behind his answer—or lack thereof—is a fear for his reputation and nothing more. Any inconsistency in his opinions is rooted in his allegiance to others' views of him. So far, Charmides has answered definitively Socrates's questions ("Who is he? And of whom?"). He is Critias's slave and a slave to his beauty. His blush is indicative of not modesty but embarrassment.

However, when Charmides blushes, Socrates communicates to his anonymous addressee a beauty even greater than the bodily one that was able to tyrannically captivate those who beheld it: "Blushing, Charmides first appeared even more beautiful—for a sense of shame (*aischuntêlon*) suited his age."[40] It is not the physical appearance that is powerfully moving to Socrates, here but what is revealed about the soul beneath it.[41] For a moment Socrates is able to get a glimpse into the *moral beauty* of Charmides.

He claims, first of all, that it was Charmides's look in his eyes and his asking a question that first moved him to lose control. Furthermore, he says that the praise from Charmides emboldens him to go on and even rekindles him to life. If this is coupled with Charmides's willingness to ask Socrates a question, then we might say that what Socrates finds particularly attractive about the boy is not his beautiful looks but the boy's own erotic nature. This is why Socrates finds all mature boys to be beautiful—they are the ones who are beginning to seek wisdom.[42] For Socrates himself, it seems quite important that *thumos* (seen in Socrates's own self-regard and his response to Charmides's praise) and *erôs* (seen in his attraction to Charmides) are both at play. But Socrates's *thumos* is capable of profound transformation into something more and more erotic as the conversation proceeds until finally Socratic *erôs* looks indistinguishable from wonder itself. It is at this point that philosophy must begin. Socrates's concern is to provoke such wonder in Charmides. Whether he can depends on whether Charmides can be freed from his dependence on Critias, whose own *thumos* never becomes erotic, let alone capable of wonder.

We know Socrates has come back to himself fully when Charmides blushes, for now Socrates does not become enflamed again and instead reflects upon the fittingness of the blush. Socrates sees the place of the beautiful blush in the whole of things, thus revealing already a different orientation to the beautiful itself, one that now becomes central in his discussion of Thracian medicine. Socrates is able to move Charmides beyond this dilemma by suggesting that they shall investigate together whether the boy possesses *sôphrosunê* or not. This is satisfactory to Charmides, and the conversation continues. Charmides is not swift enough to anticipate Socrates's next move, which subtly puts the same question back to Charmides, only now compelling him to answer, rather than allowing him the possibility of silence: "Now it is clear that, if *sôphrosunê* is present (*paresti*) in you, you have some opinion (*doxazein*) about it. For it is necessary (*ananchê*) that being in (*enousan*) you, if it is in you, it produces some perception (*aisthêsin*) from which you have some opinion (*doxa*) about what it is and what sort of thing it is. Do you not think so?"[43] If it is truly in him, Charmides must have an opinion and thus answer the "What is" question.[44] A refusal to answer now shows him to lack *sôphrosunê*, for he has just admitted that if he has it, he must have some perception from which to form an opinion. Charmides obviously cannot admit that he does not have *sôphrosunê* in front of Critias. But Socrates's request for an opinion is designed not to elicit an answer that would appear "onerous." Charmides thus has no choice but to answer, and his response reveals what we have already suspected about the not-yet-mature ward of Critias. Charmides is unable to do anything but report the traditional, cultural views he has been given, not only because he is young (which is of course understandable) but because shame and concern for others prevent him from thinking for himself. Underneath Charmides's beautiful exterior there lies only the ugliness of heteronomy.

Chapter Four

Charmides's First Definition—
A Sort of Quietness (159b–160d)

The search for *sôphrosunê* itself has thus begun in an unusual way. For the first step in the conversation is not, as would be expected, a question of the ilk: "What is *sôphrosunê*?" The conversation arrives at this question only secondarily, after encountering a minor setback when the primary question of the dialogue is put forth. The inquiry thus begins not with a question about the nature of this virtue but with a direct interrogation of Charmides's possession of it. From the outset the emphasis is placed on the psychological rather than the metaphysical, the personal rather than the universal. It is only after a blushing Charmides is unable to answer Socrates's question that the dialogue seems to take a more conventional turn. Socrates releases Charmides from the position of having to answer the question "Do you have *sôphrosunê*?" and suggests that the two of them search for the quality together. It should be kept in mind, however, that Socrates remains concerned with the prior question. For though he has softened the blow of his interrogation by joining Charmides in this quest, his goal still remains to determine whether or not Charmides has *sôphrosunê*. When the beautiful Charmides enters the room, and all other observers are captured by the boy's stunning appearance, it is the beauty of the soul that Socrates seeks to determine. Such beauty of soul may very well be the essence of *sôphrosunê*, which Charmides may or may not have, but which Critias claims the boy indeed has. An additional byproduct then of the investigation would be to reveal whether or not Critias knows of what he speaks.

When Charmides is finally willing to answer, his first attempt comes out as follows: "He said that, in his opinion (*dokoi*), *sôphrosunê* was doing everything orderly (*kosmiôs*) and quietly (*hesuchê*), in walking in the streets, and talking, and doing all other things similarly. 'So it seems to me (*moi dokei*),' he said, 'that what you ask about is a sort of quietness (*hesuchiotês tis*).'"[1] Now this answer is actually a perfect resolution to the political paradox Charmides faces. For, as Santas suggests, the definition itself allows him to "avoid praising himself without at the same time denying that he possesses this desirable quality."[2] The reason for this is that Charmides has reported a quality of *sôphrosunê* that he has been taught by his culture. Consider Schmid's description: "The first definition presents the most obvious element in the traditional understanding: whatever the social station, the *sophron* person is expected to exhibit behavior that is bounded, restrained, temperate. The opposite of such behavior—behavior that is extreme, impulsive, and violent—is prohibited, if the traditional virtue is practiced."[3] Charmides is thus able to escape his political paradox not by standing on his own and ignoring the expectations of those around him but by regurgitating the imbibed but undigested views of his culture.

Indeed, Socrates is immediately aware that Charmides's definition is indeed what "they say."[4] But this reveals that the examination of Charmides's soul has gotten off to a bad start. His first definition reveals that his soul is *filled* with his culture, perhaps to the exclusion of *Charmides's own thoughts*. Given his youth, Charmides should not be blamed for what is merely his immaturity. It is after all just his youth that has displayed itself so far. But then Socrates is more concerned with what the youth displays about the teaching of the culture—how are the young being educated and what is the state of their souls? This is close to Socrates's opening question of the dialogue.[5] Charmides has revealed that he is approaching the question—"What is *sôphrosunê*?"—with an already formed outlook, an outlook that was formed before Charmides had the ability to examine it critically, and consequently Socrates may here be discovering how difficult it is to alter. Even at this stage, it may already be too late for Charmides.[6] Given how beautiful Charmides is, and how much he is praised for his physical beauty by those powerful men in Athens who are responsible for his education, Charmides could stand to lose more than he would gain by questioning the value of his looks, his gifts, and the authority of his guardian Critias. He is thus highly motivated and trained to speak with his culture.

The notion itself—"quietness"—may seem strange at first, because we are tempted to associate the quality of being *sophron* with the control of desires, and this first definition omits this image, as does the rest of the entire dialogue. The picture of an individual who is master of his desires, even master of himself, is not taken up here, though it is discussed elsewhere by Socrates.[7] What can account for this puzzling fact?

First of all, it should be noted that the coupling of *sôphrosunê* with *hesuchia is* seen elsewhere in Plato's dialogues.[8] But far from coming out of thin air, as some have supposed, this definition has roots in the traditional understanding of *sôphrosunê*.[9] For what has been offered is "the reply that might be expected from a noble young Athenian, for it describes the conduct required of him by the conventions of Athenian society."[10] If we see this quality as an external, observable element in the behavior of the *sophron* individual, it becomes less surprising and more understandable that this is Charmides's first utterance. He is reporting the conventions, he is a voice of his culture.[11]

Most importantly, what could be more apt than *beautiful Charmides* offering as his definition of *sôphrosunê* a likely description of his own behavior (behavior for which he has received praise from others)? For if we imagine again the scene that has preceded the encounter between Socrates and Charmides, we can recall the manic crowd whipped into a frenzy as they were dumbstruck by Charmides, the object of the beloved gaze of everyone. But what was Charmides doing as they all stared at him in wonder? Walking orderly and quietly into the room.[12] By offering this definition, Charmides suggests that he understands his *sôphrosunê* to be that which makes him beloved by others. He also places the virtue solidly in the realm of power relations between himself and those others, and we have already seen that Charmides's own "quietness" is not mere submissiveness—it acts tyrannically over those who witness it.

When Charmides offers it as a definition, however, he seems very concerned to echo others' praise. Socrates indicates precisely this in his first response, when he tells the youth he has indeed uttered what "they say."[13] Socrates thus says to Charmides: *they* do say this about your beauty and your virtue, but have *you* examined it for yourself to see if there is more there than only appearances? And it is here that Socrates asks Charmides about his notion of what is beautiful itself, asking him "Is not *sôphrosunê* one of the beautiful things (*tôn kalon*)?"[14] Socrates gets Charmides to agree to this two more times,[15] and mentions it as an assumption two additional times.[16] It is the key to his argument, and is thus mentioned no less than five times.

Socrates's argument is then divided into two parts, regarding the body (159c–d) and the soul (159e–160b). He concludes with a recapitulation that appears to be more than mere summary. His strategy first involves getting Charmides to admit that in the activities of the body (writing, reading, playing the lyre, wrestling, boxing, running, jumping) and in the activities of the soul (learning, teaching, remembering, understanding, deliberating) it is not acting "with quietness but as quickly as possible [which] is the most *kalos*."[17] Since they agreed that *sôphrosunê* was *kalos*, Socrates then concludes that *sôphrosunê* cannot be quietness, nor can the *sophron* life be the life of quietness.[18]

It might already be apparent from this presentation that Socrates's argument cannot do the job, as it stands. The biggest problem with the argument so far is an egregious non sequitur. Socrates persuades Charmides that his activities are all more worthy of praise when they are done quickly rather than with quietness,[19] and then concludes that *sôphrosunê* cannot be quietness. But in order to show that Charmides's beliefs are inconsistent, he has to bring Charmides to say that quietness is not *kalos*. For if *sôphrosunê* is *kalos*, and quietness is not, then the two can clearly not be identical. Charmides thinks Socrates has succeeded when they agree that quickness is more admirable than quietness, but this claim is entirely compatible with the assertion that quietness itself is still *kalos*. The only way of making Socrates's argument work here would be to concede that since quickness is more *kalos* than quietness, then quietness is not *kalos*, and so on. But such a concession would be worthy of ridicule.

Charmides is not astute enough to be aware of this, but it should not surprise the reader of the dialogue that the interchange continues in a way that reflects the prior suspect logic. For though Socrates begins by concluding that *sôphrosunê* cannot be quietness, he qualifies this claim as he develops his thought:

> *Sôphrosunê* would not be a sort of quietness, nor the *sophron* life quiet, *at least from this argument* (*logou*), since being *sophron* needs to be *kalon*. For there are two possibilities for us, either *in no cases are the quiet actions in life more honorable* (*kallious*) *than the quick and strong ones, or in very few*. If then, my friend, even quite a few quiet actions should turn out to be more admirable than the violent and quick ones,

> *not even on this assumption would* sôphrosunê *be doing things with quietness any more than (mallon) doing things violently and quickly,* neither in walking nor in speech nor in anything else; *nor would the quiet life have more (sôphrosunê) than the unquiet.*[20]

This apparent summary puts a slightly different spin on the argument than the one Socrates has been making thus far. For the missing step that Socrates seemed to overlook heretofore involved some kind of claim that quietness is, in fact, *not kalon*. And this could not be established from the claim that quickness appears to be more worthy of praise than quietness. But here the assertion is not that quietness is not *kalon* but that quietness is only a part of *sôphrosunê no less than is its opposite, quickness.* This is a case of Socrates's interlocutor casting his net too wide in his attempt at definition. To be more explicit, it seems that the argument Socrates has given is not adequate to refute the conception at hand because. as Santas points out, it relies on a missing premise: "[The argument] remains faulty because Socrates has not produced a single case of quietness of behavior which, so characterized and no further, is either not praiseworthy or disgraceful. Without such an instance, he would need in place of [the premise that *sôphrosunê* is an honorable or praiseworthy thing] either a premise that [*sôphrosunê*] is the *most* praiseworthy thing or a premise that *sôphrosunê* is the *only* praiseworthy thing."[21] I will argue that Santas's call for an additional premise, that is, that *sôphrosunê* is indeed the most beautiful thing, can be supplied by Socrates's own view the nature of *sôphrosunê*, as is made clear not only in his discussion with Charmides and Critias but with Glaucon and Adeimantus in the *Republic*, and Diotima in the *Symposium* as well. Had Socrates been conversing with someone other than Charmides, perhaps a better attempt could have been made to qualify this definition suitably and place quietness in the proper context such that it seems most praiseworthy and beautiful. In fact, from the outset it appears that Socrates has interpreted Charmides's suggestion in an unfair way. For Charmides begins by talking not just about quietness but quietness and order (*kosmos*). It is doing things calmly and orderly which seems to him *sophron*, and which he calls a kind of quietness.[22] But Socrates makes no mention of actions that are disorderly, or unharmonious. He instead focuses on the contrast between quickness and quietness. Surely Socrates would not argue that the actions done with less order are more worthy of praise.[23]

In addition, in concluding his qualified statement Socrates once again brings up the examples of walking and speaking.[24] This may be no coincidence. For these are exactly the two examples that Charmides first introduces when talking about quietness and order. Then, in Socrates's refutations, these two examples are simply omitted. Is quickness in speaking and walking more praiseworthy, simply, than slowness in walking and speaking?[25] Socrates himself would surely point to counterexamples. It seems that Plato is subtly arousing wonder in us about the discussion that has preceded, and if there might be some truth in the definition after all. What might that truth be?

Here is Kosman's attempt to qualify the definition, which he puts in the mouth of Charmides:

> You have not understood the quietness I am speaking of, our Charmides replies. I mean the quiet *mastery* that may characterize any action, fast or slow, energetic or leisurely, loud or soft; I mean the quiet, smooth *rightness* of the master artisan or statesman or warrior, which alone makes possible their acting swiftly and vigorously. You think I mean not moving fast, I mean *not speeding*. I mean the calm quietness that is *knowing who you are, what you want, how to do it;* that is always admirable. And that is why the quietness of which I speak, rightly understood by my aristocratic friends and teachers to be associated with *modest reverence* and the *self-knowing of which the god speaks*, is the *sôphrosunê* after which you ask.[26]

Obviously, there are elements in this definition (i.e., mastery, modesty, and self-knowledge) that have not yet made an appearance in the conversation between Socrates and Charmides. But their absence here points to the real problem, finally, with the definition that Charmides has offered. His understanding of *sôphrosunê* is limited purely to the external appearances and lacks any normative dimension at all.[27] What Charmides overlooks is the possibility of doing activities more quickly but doing them *badly*. Writing, for example, done slowly, if it is done better, would indeed be more admirable. Charmides does not see this essential missing element in Socrates's formulation.[28] *The handwriting that is produced with quietness may yet be more beautiful.* It is to the point that we would not be sure what we mean in making a claim about the beautiful handwriting—what features to draw attention to in either the activity or the finished product that we could say were necessary to make it genuinely beautiful—but our deficiency about this knowledge shows us to be at a different stage of the inquiry than Charmides. He does not see that there is a question needing investigation here.

If one were to defend Charmides, perhaps one could say that he assumes the example takes it as given that the same level of correctness is achieved by both the quiet writer and the quick writer. But not a word of this is spoken in the dialogue, and it seems more likely that Socrates narrates this to his unnamed interlocutor (or Plato presents this interchange for the reader) to notice what is missing: the oversight suggests that Charmides "too quickly" follows Socrates in looking at human activity from a narrow point of view that neglects a sufficient account of the beautiful. Charmides's view of human activity seems almost behaviorist. This is only confirmed by the further examples.

It is fitting that Socrates's second example is reading, and Charmides too quickly concurs that reading quickly is more admirable than reading with quietness. There is no mention of reading well or badly, let alone reading that is beautifully done. Surely Plato is counting on *his reader* to wonder about the example here. Should we also be quick readers and just go along with Socrates and Charmides? Or would a quiet, beautiful reading of Plato's text be such a kind that wonders about the perplexities that Charmides in his quickness passes over? To put it in language from the earlier part of the dialogue, Charmides so far seems to mistake the part for the whole. While the further examples seem to hammer home this point further, none do so more ironically than the final case of thinking. For at this point one wonders: what if Charmides had been more quiet than quick in his thinking? Perhaps his answers would have shown more understanding than less. For his answers suggest that he thinks about both the body and the soul only in bodily terms, and he therefore appears not to understand the story Socrates has told about the doctors of Zalmoxis. Charmides moves too "quickly" to notice this, for he is distracted by his concern for others watching him. He thus has shown, rather than said, that just as his beauty is only skin-deep, so is his quietness: he does not have a nonsuperficial, genuine quietness that might actually be a quality of *sôphrosunê*. He is too quick, because he is too dependent on others. This is an amazing reversal, for it is those "others," gazing at his beauty, who have bestowed upon him in their love the idea that quietness is what *sôphrosunê* is.

Socrates initially asked Charmides about his internal perception and whether that led to some opinion about his *sôphrosunê*. The preliminary results of this investigation are not good. Charmides's internal perception and his judgment are clouded by his view of others' perceptions of him. He has been praised for his quiet and ordered behavior, and so he reports this to Socrates as his definition of *sôphrosunê*. Because the boy's exceeding bodily beauty prompts such praise for physical behavior and form, he comes to see them as his virtue—what he is truly worth, who he is.

Socrates's first response therefore appears to be two things. In addition to being a typical *elenchus* that shows that Charmides's answer captures only the effect, rather than the essence of *sôphrosunê*, it is also a kind of test. For his questions elicit answers that reveal that Charmides has not yet properly appreciated Socrates's Thracian story, and that he consequently has a deeply flawed understanding of the human soul and the world it confronts. Socrates refutes Charmides by appealing to *to kalon*, a notion that is deeply embedded in Charmides and his culture. Charmides's conception of what is beautiful, because he is the beloved object of the gaze, cannot help but conceive of the beautiful in physical or behaviorist terms. In exposing his flawed conception of the beautiful, Socrates has shown that there is a deep problem in Charmides's way of thinking about being human. Socrates thus learns that he must clear away this ground, if this youth is to truly learn. Socrates sees that Charmides must free himself from his dependence on others and reorient him to the beautiful itself. Such a reorientation will bring him to look within himself if he is to approach wisdom. This is the result of his test.[29]

There are results for the more quiet readers as well. For in displaying Charmides's inability to notice Socrates's specious logic, Plato has forced us to ponder a set of questions that now press for answers and will continue to do so in the remainder of the dialogue. We suspect that Charmides has a flawed understanding of the soul, and more generally of "the whole" as well. We thus must ask: how do we properly understand the soul, not in terms that reduce it to the body but in its own terms? This would perhaps lead to an understanding of the body and soul as "a whole," but what does it take to understand something as a whole? And what would it be to have knowledge that glimpsed or even grasped *the* whole, whatever that might be?

It is no coincidence that in his refutation Socrates appeals to the beautiful (*to kalon*). For, as effective as it is in showing an inconsistency in Charmides's set of beliefs, it should also be introduced into our thinking not as an answer but as another question. As we have seen, Charmides's conception of what is *kalos* finally seems to imply nothing more than that something is "worthy of praise," which again reveals his dependence on others and his value of reputation.[30] He therefore understands what is *kalos*, and consequently what is *sophron* and everything else, in terms of the body, for he has learned in his youth is that it is only *his body* that is worthy of praise. Recall that Charmides's physical beauty is so overwhelming that he turns all heads and causes a noisy commotion when he enters the room, and his beauty is even equated with his virtue.[31] This very noisy tumultuous commotion is the consequence of the crowd's erotic response to Charmides's physical beauty. It is, indeed, the opposite of the first definition he gives to Socrates. But the beloved is the calm, quiet one at the center of the storm. Charmides then offers this definition from his point of view as the object of *erôs*.

But Socrates, we saw, initiated this inquiry doubting that this bodily beauty entailed beauty of soul. This, combined with Charmides's flawed understanding put on display, reveals a possible disjunction between what is *kalos* and what is *sôphrosunê*. That is, it might be the case that Charmides, contrary to the claim of Critias, has the former without having the latter: Charmides may be an object of *erôs* for the crowd because of his physical beauty, but Socrates is interested in whether the boy is capable of philosophy. If Charmides were to demonstrate this, he would reveal a more complete understanding of *to kalon*—for he would show that he is not only experienced as a beloved object of *erôs* by the crowd for his physical beauty but is erotic himself, desiring wisdom. Perhaps this motivation to seek wisdom could apply to all others in the dialogue as well, for on seeing Charmides they are overwhelmed.[32]

Socrates, though, is somehow able to transcend this stance, and in bringing up the relation of *sôphrosunê* to *to kalon* and then refuting Charmides, he incites the reader to uncover a relation that is more complex than the one Charmides and his teachers espouse and represent, a relation that gets past the appearance of *to kalon* and *sôphrosunê*, toward their real essence.[33] So at the end of Socrates's refutation we are merely left wondering about the true relation between these notions. I will show that an inability to get past the crowd's reaction to Charmides, or Charmides's own reaction to the crowd, is inextricably linked to a particular understanding of *erôs*—that it is finally an acquisitive desire that can be gratified only by possessing what is outside and taking it in to oneself. Such a desire is ultimately dangerous because its utmost manifestation is not the quietness, in any sense, of *sôphrosunê* but the tumultuous commotion of tyranny. It is the quietness of wonder that is the alternative to such a picture of desire. But at this point, Socrates has raised a crucial question about Charmides's self. What really is *kalos* in the young boy?

Chapter Five

Charmides's Second Definition— A Sense of Shame (160d–161a)

For all of the problems in the first interchange between Charmides and Socrates, there is an immediate positive result in the dialogue. At the end of the first refutation, Socrates successfully encourages Charmides to stand on his own and look within himself for *sôphrosunê*:

> Then again Charmides, I said, attend more closely (*mallon prosechon ton noun*) and look into yourself; consider (*ennoesas*) the sort of thing (*hopoion tina*) that *sôphrosunê* makes in you and what sort of being it must be to accomplish this. Put all these things together and say well and courageously (*andreiôs*) what it appears to you to be.
>
> He paused and, examining himself very courageously (*andrikôs*), he said, it seems to me that *sôphrosunê* makes men ashamed (*aischunesthai*) and bashful (*aischuntelon*), and *sôphrosunê* is the same thing as shame (*aidôs*).[1]

Before considering the content of Charmides's answer, it should be noted what Charmides has (and has not) accomplished. Socrates tells Charmides more than once to have the courage[2] to look inside himself, and then narrates to his unnamed interlocutor that Charmides did so courageously. This is the most praise awarded by Socrates in the entire dialogue. The prior refutation then has at least partially succeeded in its goal. The emphasis on quickness has transformed the quiet Charmides who refused to answer.

The answer Charmides has offered has also accordingly moved in the right direction. The difficulty with Charmides's first response ("a sort of quietness") was its narrow view of the soul in terms of the body, his reduction of all to the physical so that he could not appreciate any normative dimension to *sôphrosunê*. By looking into himself, and coming up with "shame," he has not only tried to show what *he* thinks as opposed to what others have told him, but he has also moved from the purely external to the internal, from the outer to the inner. He has gone past the appearances, closer to the real essence of *sôphrosunê*, and subsequently self-knowledge now becomes even more visible in the discussion.[3]

Yet why does Charmides offer "shame" as his definition of *sôphrosunê*? I argued earlier that it is likely that Charmides took his first definition from the praise he received from his own quiet and orderly behavior. Now Socrates has asked him to look within, away from what others say about him and his virtue, in order to examine himself and say whether he has *sôphrosunê*. It's not clear what we readers would find if similarly called to look within and answer this question, and we should pause to ask whether we would come up with the same answer that Charmides offers. Charmides is right to say that he sees shame within: he has blushed, experienced a political paradox in which he did not know whom to please, and has seen that he did not himself understand why praise of his own behavior was praiseworthy. But it is interesting that he does not look within, see this situation, and see something akin to his ignorance, or desire for wisdom. For shame, let us not forget, depends essentially on the view of others. It is impossible to experience shame without being embedded in one's relation with others. So Charmides's look within, even as it has been courageous, has still been underpinned by a looking without. Charmides's admission of shame is indeed a self-knowing insight. Charmides is made of shame. Unfortunately, his shame prevents him from knowing about his shame and questioning its sources.

Therefore, the answer Charmides gives is not praised as much as his effort prior to formulating it. Socrates is able to dispatch of it quite quickly. Once again, Socrates turns to Charmides's conception of the *beautiful*. Socrates's response opens with, "Didn't you just now agree that *sôphrosunê* is *kalon*?"[4] The questions about the *beautiful* raised by the previous inquiry are thus still with us in this interchange as well, but now they are more complicated. For we saw that in the prior exchange Charmides understood *to kalon* externally, in terms of the body alone. Now he has offered a quality that is located more inside than out, and is willing to say that it is *kalos*. It is unclear how his prior understanding of *to kalon* can fit in with this new definition he has offered. However, we might suspect that Socrates's own understanding may be able to make room for it. But then Socrates turns the discussion in a new direction, seemingly leaving behind what is *kalos* behind for what is *good*.

> Well now, I said, didn't you just now agree that *sôphrosunê* is *kalos*?

> Certainly, he said.

> And accordingly, men [possessing *sôphrosunê*] are good?

> Yes.

> And could that be good, which does not bring about *(apergazetai)* good men?

> No, indeed.

> Then *sôphrosunê* is not only *kalos*, but is also good.[5]

Socrates gets Charmides to jump from the *kalos* to the good without any hesitation. This is not too surprising when we consider the first appearance of these notions in the dialogue: Critias claims that Charmides himself is both *kalos* and good.[6] Charmides then is supposed to be an embodiment of all three qualities, *sôphrosunê*, *to kalon*, and the good. Consequently, he has no reason to see any a problem with coextension of the beautiful and the good. But for the reader the question is again raised regarding the relation between these two notions.[7] Are the two truly coextensive? Might they ever conflict?[8]

Surely, if one were like Charmides and understood what is *kalos* in terms of the body, then there will be cases when what is *kalos* and what is good do not coincide. What is *kalos* would purely reside in the aesthetic domain, while the good would potentially elicit questions that are ethical and political. There should be room for these two realms to overlap in some way, but it is not clear where and how, especially if one reduces beauty to physical appearances as Charmides does. Perhaps the proper understanding of *kalos* will resolve this difficulty, but in this part of the conversation, as soon as it appears, it drops out of sight. We are left with questions once again, as Socrates moves on to refuting *sôphrosunê*-as-*aidôs* by appealing to Charmides's conception of the good.

The argument Socrates makes appeals to Charmides's trust in the authority of Homer, explicitly asking him "Do you not trust Homer?" He then claims Charmides cannot assert this trio:[9]

1. *Sôphrosunê* is a sense of shame (*aidôs*).

2. *Sôphrosunê* is good (without qualification).

3. It is right to trust Homer that *aidôs* is not good for a man in need.

Charmides cannot reject (3), and so he hastily abandons (1) (even though [3] does not necessarily entail the rejection of [2][10]). Homer turns out to be an additional authority who has his grip on Charmides. Although he is able momentarily to take a look within himself, he is not able to continue to do so and courageously stand against the cultural icon. Just as Charmides was too quick in his thinking to examine carefully the argument Socrates launched against his first definition of *sôphrosunê* as quietness, now he betrays himself as too ashamed to question the authority of Homer and examine the argument Socrates launches against his own definition of *sôphrosunê* as shame. Were he less ashamed before the cultural icon, he could perhaps defend his position against Socrates and still attempt to qualify his definition rather than abandon it entirely. *Aidôs*, like quietness, could be part of a more complete picture of *sôphrosunê*, but Charmides too quickly and shamefully moves on.

This exchange not only reveals more about Charmides's character to Socrates but also raises questions about Socrates for us, especially if we reflect further on the quote from Homer. The speaker of this quote is Telemachus, and it is addressed to the disguised Odysseus,[11] a character often linked to Socrates in the Platonic dialogues.[12] We readers are aware that Socrates strongly questions the authority of Homer in the *Republic*.[13] But consider also what Moore and Raymond suggest about the passage that Socrates quotes from the *Odyssey*:

> The swineherd Eumaeus advises Odysseus, newly returned to Ithaca and disguised as a beggar, not to let his sense of shame prevent him from begging at his suitors' tables. Filling

his stomach is more important. But it is also a message from Telemachus to his father, with a different understanding of what Odysseus needs: not to let his shame at being abused by the suitors prevent him from carrying out the plot to regain his kingdom and restore his honor. But Socrates advises Charmides not to let shame prevent him from satisfying his, and indeed everyone's, most essential human need: to care for his soul, by examining himself and others about the "greatest matters."[14]

If Moore and Raymond are right, the appeal to the quote from Homer can be seen as a test on Socrates's part. He has encouraged Charmides to look within and is challenging him to undertake genuine Socratic self-examination, rooted in the fear of only one thing—self-ignorance.[15] Charmides fails the test when Socrates learns that Charmides cannot question Homer's authority, placing his shame before others above his desire for wisdom. Charmides knows he has shame, but this is not the same as undertaking self-examination. He cannot explain to us whether he *should* feel shame, and if he were pressed to explain why he feels shame, he would be compelled to resort to the praise of others. There are no internal justifications for his sense of shame.

It is thus no accident that Socrates appeals to Homer's authority in discussing Charmides's shame. The Homeric view subordinates the good to the *kalos*. Schmid puts the point well: "The Homeric warrior and the Spartan citizen—the man who lives morally within a shame-culture—simply does not consider whether he must violate the noble or beautiful [*to kalon*], in order to preserve his own good, much less his moral self-respect."[16] The problem with this is clear from the question raised from the beginning of this inquiry: how should we properly understand the good and *to kalon*, and the relationship between them? It is the task of the philosopher to face this question, if he is to live an examined life. As Schmid says, Socrates really is trying to get Charmides to confront this inquiry: "Is the *kalon*, as my society defines it, really what I ought to do?"[17] Charmides and others bound to the traditional conception do not ask, perhaps cannot ask, this question. But it is in asking this question that one begins to engage in philosophy, and Charmides accordingly shows his nonphilosophical nature once more.

The presence of *kalos* and *agathos* in this passage thus do give us a clue as to Socrates's own view of the discussion. For we keep seeing reasons to doubt that Charmides is as good as he is *kalos* (at least if this is taken to mean "physically beautiful"). This is not surprising: the relation between the two notions is not a clear one. But Charmides seems to want to subordinate the good to the *kalos*, even though this is inconsistent with claiming that *aidôs* is *sôphrosunê*. As before, Charmides has failed to appreciate Socrates's lesson regarding the part and the whole. For in the notion of *to kalon* he sees the all-encompassing whole that includes, but really engulfs, the good as one of its parts. We now wonder whether in this way, too, he is like the doctor who attempts to cure the eyes without looking at the head. In the prior discussion he showed that he understood the soul only in terms of the body, but now he seems to understand the good only in terms of *to kalon*. And his nature prevents him from seeing that, perhaps in Socrates's view, he has mistaken the part for the whole both times.[18] But rather than give up on his view of *to kalon*, and admit his ignorance, he now gives up on *aidôs*, in speech and in deed, and attacks. This is the moment most revealing of Charmides's character, and thus Socrates's goal has been well achieved. For this moment allows him to conclusively determine whether Charmides has a philosophical nature, and confirm that Charmides does not, after all, possess *sôphrosunê*. To this moment I will now turn.

Chapter Six

Charmides's Final Definition— Doing One's Own Things (161b–162c)

Having been refuted a second time, Charmides does not once again look within himself as Socrates previously encouraged him to do. Instead, he now openly resorts to what he has heard another say. Though his first two responses had origins outside of himself, he at least presented them as his own opinion. Here he does not present his own opinion at all: "But how does this view (*skepsai*) of *sôphrosunê* seem to be to you? For I remembered just now what I heard someone say, that *sôphrosunê* could be doing one's own things (*to ta heautou prattein*). Inquire (*skopei*) then if the speaker seems to you to speak correctly."[1] Charmides thus withdraws himself from Socrates's examination. This brings about the end of Socrates's dialogue with him. For Socrates's method, the *elenchus*, requires that the interlocutor put forth his own opinions, for otherwise his soul remains untouched by Socrates's arguments. Any aporia ultimately reached will be a false one, and there will be no motivation to escape this aporia. In short, true philosophy cannot begin. But the problem is even further compounded in the present circumstances. For Socrates and Charmides agreed that they would jointly inquire whether Charmides has *sôphrosunê*. Charmides then agreed that if he had it, he had some opinion about it. Charmides has abandoned the search for his *sôphrosunê*—such an abandonment demonstrates his very need of it.

The question could not have been put more strongly: if Charmides truly is *sophron*, he must have some opinion about what makes him so. If he is unable to explain it, then he cannot possess the quality after all. Self-knowledge is inextricably linked to the nature of *sôphrosunê* for

Socrates: the very act of looking for *sôphrosunê* and finding it requires self-knowledge and produces perhaps more.[2] But Charmides's answer upon completing this self-examination reveals that his "look within" is superficial and inauthentic. Charmides cannot abandon tradition, and is still controlled by his dependence on Critias's and others' views of him. This dependence is what is within him.

For though Charmides reports his emotions and not just his behavior, he is refuted again by Socrates's appeal to the *kalon* and the authority of Homer. Charmides is not willing to abandon either his culture's attachment to its view of the *kalon* or Homer's authority in order to truly look within himself. Were he able to question his culture, he could question Socrates's refutation here. Indeed, Socrates's refutation is effective because it is aimed at the conventional, incoherent understanding of the soul, an understanding that Charmides has imbibed.[3] The Homeric view, oriented around shame, is at odds with the Socratic view, oriented around philosophical wonder. The latter inevitably leads its initiates to question the norms and conventions that are the source of one's shame. It is for this reason that Socrates comes to be seen as a corruptor.

But in this episode, we can perhaps see that Charmides is the one who is corrupt—and not because of Socrates's influence. Rather than report his own opinion, Charmides now flees from Socrates's examination of his soul. For he had agreed that they would investigate together whether Charmides had *sôphrosunê*, and this required Charmides to give *his* opinions about it. Charmides is fed up with the embarrassing refutations and decides that it is Critias's turn. For Socrates immediately grasps that the source of this opinion is Critias, calling Charmides a "wretch" (*miare*).[4] Socrates claims Charmides has heard this definition from Critias or "some other of the wise men."[5] Critias first denies that he is the origin of the boy's opinion but later makes it clear that this denial is false when Socrates chops apart the definition.[6]

Socrates agrees with Charmides that it makes no difference who the source of the opinion is, which may seem surprising for the one who has urged Charmides to lay bare *his soul*. But this begins to make sense when we consider that Socrates has already learned from Charmides's first two definitions that he is controlled by Critias and others, and it is these others whom Socrates must examine now. Charmides's turn on Critias here is not, therefore, the attempt to stand on his own that Socrates is looking for: it is a thinly disguised retreat to his guardian himself.[7]

Socrates begins his argument by first calling the definition a "riddle" (*ainigma*).[8] This is the first (and only) definition in the dialogue to elicit such a comment. When Charmides puts forth his first two definitions, Socrates immediately goes to work refuting them, without any pause to consider how one should understand the words "*hesuchia*" and "*aidôs*." As Bruell says, Socrates implies that in this particular case "their failure to find for [the definition "doing one's own things"] a reasonable or acceptable meaning will not necessarily be taken to bear on its ultimate validity. It might even be that such an answer as is given in the dialogue to the question, what is [*sôphrosunê*], can be understood as a modification or development of the answer now given."[9] Given that we know that Socrates discusses "doing one's own things" in great detail elsewhere, we need to be careful to understand the phrase in this context. For Socrates emphasizes that it takes a great deal of thought to come to understand it, as we shall see. Ultimately, the failure to understand it will be disastrous.

Socrates shows that Charmides clearly has no understanding of the notion, even if he is still engaged as a serious interlocutor, which is doubtful. Socrates's argument works on two levels. He presents counterexamples in terms of the individual and the city. The former are part of a theoretical objection, and the latter a practical objection. Regarding the individual, Charmides agrees that the scribe (*grammatistês*) writes and reads not only his own name and his friends' names but the names of his enemies as well. His students, including Charmides, are taught this practice as well, and Charmides does not consider it to be *asophron*. The claim is generalized to other activities, such as medicine, building, weaving, and production in general, and so it seems that doing one's own things is not *sôphrosunê* from the point of view of the individual.[10]

Charmides then agrees that the same follows from the point of view of the city. Socrates asks if a city would be well managed if a law commanded that everyone should make their own clothes, tools, and everything else in order not to violate the principle of doing one's own things. Charmides claims such a city would be poorly managed, and therefore not governed with *sôphrosunê*, since a city governed with *sôphrosunê* would indeed be managed well, not poorly.[11] The conclusion then is that doing one's own things *seems* not to be *sôphrosunê*. For now Socrates ends not by saying that *sôphrosunê* is not doing one's own things but by again calling the phrase a riddle[12] and pleading with Charmides to explain to him what indeed the phrase really means. Charmides responds that he doesn't know and suggests that the person who uttered it to him does not know either, with an illuminating laugh and glance at Critias. Charmides has exposed not only Critias but also the incoherence at the heart at the Athenian elite ethos. The quiet shameful one who couldn't question the norms found another way to cope with his embarrassment. He turns the questions upon his own guardian. It is at this point that Critias can no longer restrain himself and bursts with anger into the conversation.[13]

Charmides's admission of ignorance is thus no advance. His admission of ignorance, like his look within himself, is only on the surface. For he does not care that he does not understand a claim that he has put forward, which is the requirement for undergoing a Socratic self-examination. He only cares that Critias has now been put to the test, a move motivated by his perception of others' view of him. Charmides—the object of everyone's erotic gaze—is ignorant of his ignorance, and has no desire to pass beyond this state. Once and for all, he has shown that he cannot submit his soul for treatment, though it is clear by now that he needs it. This is why Socrates turns to Critias (and Athenian culture), for if he can refute them, perhaps Charmides can still be rescued, should he himself see *their* ignorance. But we should not be optimistic. Socrates's initial question to Charmides asked him if he already had an "adequate share" of *sôphrosunê* or if he needed it. The goal of this question is to determine if the boy has a need—a desire—for a kind of knowledge in order to become genuinely beautiful and good. It is finally a question about whether Charmides is *philosophical* or, better, *erotic*. This final movement in the conversation does not bode well for any philosophical future for Charmides.

Charmides remains the quiet spectator while Critias takes over the argument with Socrates. He does not speak again until the closing scene, when he once again admits ignorance, and again only in a superficial way. Charmides continues looking to others and remains under Critias's control. By the end of the dialogue, he has answered Socrates's opening question about the youth of Athens: they are corrupted, perhaps beyond help.[14] It is for this reason that Socrates responds by calling Charmides *miare*, a word that often gets translated as "wretch" but has deeper significance than this word connotes. A more literal translation of *miaros* would be "defiled with blood" or "bloodstained."[15] The word refers to a polluted state that accompanies a murderer.[16] Socrates uses it again in the *Charmides*, directed at Critias.[17] Why do these two receive such harsh language from Socrates? The image of Charmides and Critias polluted and stained with blood should not escape the attention of the reader, given the violent future of these later members of the Thirty Tyrants.[18] The moments that Socrates chooses to give Critias and Charmides this appellation are thus significant: they are the moments in which we can see their future.[19]

Charmides's response confirms that he has abandoned dialogue with Socrates and is again retreating from their search for his possession of *sôphrosunê*. It has become clear to Socrates that Charmides does not possess the proper philosophical nature to engage in this search. He thus goes along with Charmides in order to attack the strong influence on Charmides that Socrates suspects is primarily responsible for corrupting his soul: his guardian Critias. The next interchange is aimed directly at Critias, rather than Charmides, and it is successful. For at its end an embarrassed and rageful Critias can no longer remain silent, and the dialogue shifts to him.

Critias here responds that Charmides's ignorance of the meaning of the phrase does not imply that the one who spoke it is ignorant also.[20] This is a fair response from Critias, for it seems that the phrase has been mangled quite badly in Charmides's care. For regarding the individual, Charmides quickly agrees that the learning of one's enemies' names would be an act of not doing one's own things. But surely Charmides could respond, if he were either more astute or more inclined to defend this definition, that "one's own" can be understood widely enough to include one's enemies in certain spheres. The same goes for the practical objection as well: "one's own" may be defined in another way such that the city is not ultimately managed poorly but well.[21]

For regarding the case of an individual learning the names of his enemies, there may be a number of possible descriptions for this activity that are consistent with calling them "doing one's own things." Here are two such descriptions: First, the student learns the names of his enemies, because they are still his own, in that they are also human beings. Second, the student learns the names of his enemies because they are still his own, in that he must, after all, wage war upon them. These two descriptions emphasize different elements. In fact, they seem to be activities with two different goals. But both descriptions have this in common: they attempt to account for human conduct by appealing to a broader context that makes more sense of that conduct. They are descriptions that attempt to move beyond the part to the whole.

Charmides has been unable to do this time and time again, and he fails again to do it here. For perhaps Charmides has no problem in counting his body, beauty, reputation, family, and friends as his own, for this has earned him praise and admiration. But he is unable to see a larger sphere than this. Charmides's sense of "one's own things" does therefore not transcend the immediate. He is myopic in the presence of his desires and the desires of others for his beauty. This ultimately leads to a more significant failure: Charmides has again not succeeded in asking the question that coincides with the starting point of philosophy. Previously he failed to consider whether *he ought to follow to kalon*: he did not ask, Is the *kalos* really good, and in what way? Now he does not sufficiently reflect on whether and how he ought to follow one's own: he does not ask, Are one's own things beautiful or good, and in what way? Once again, there may be a way of understanding "one's own things" so that its relation to the beautiful or the good becomes clear, but Charmides does not possess this understanding. Ironically, Charmides's attempt to put forward "doing one's own things" as a definition of *sôphrosunê* shows that Charmides himself does not reveal his own beliefs to be his own things, for he is unable to give an account of their meaning or give reasons for believing them. In giving in to his view of others, he himself does not know his own things but is himself the object of others. But now Socrates has succeeded in initiating a new inquiry. He has brought Critias into the conversation, and will now attempt to dismantle his influence on Charmides.[22]

At this point we ignorant readers, hopefully aware of our ignorance, are left with a riddle (*ainigma*). The meaning of "one's own things" remains unclear and problematic. Self-knowledge has come to the foreground even more strongly than before, for it is in wondering about what is *truly ours* that we begin to think about who we truly are. Charmides's understanding of "his own" surely reveals something about who he is: a lover of vanity and therefore a slave to others. He has also revealed that in being ignorant of his own things, he must not possess *sôphrosunê* after all. For he cannot truly be so and not fully understand what in his life is properly his. His *sôphrosunê* and, consequently, his genuine well-being remain at the level of appearances, mere shadows. But his failure to understand leaves our questions open. For the definitions that have appeared have not been refuted entirely but have just been improperly understood by Charmides. It remains to be seen whether given the right understanding they can be incorporated into a genuine definition of *sôphrosunê*. Such a right understanding will somehow have to face the problems that have emerged regarding the relation of *to kalon* to the good, and the relation of the good to one's own. And we are further beginning to see that these three notions themselves will have to cohere with a picture of authentic self-knowledge, which soon becomes the central issue of the dialogue. Perhaps achieving the proper understanding of these notions would involve transcending one's partial view, in an attempt to grasp the whole, and thus becoming erotic in a different sense, one that Charmides may not understand. But it remains mysterious here how this will ultimately look. We are ignorant, and we should note that it is here that Charmides truly disappoints: *he* is unable to admit his own deep ignorance. This too will play an important role in the remainder of the dialogue, and it will be essential to our understanding of the problems intrinsic to thinking about *sôphrosunê*. In part 1B we will delve into two discussions (in the *Republic* and *Symposium*) that link "one's own things" explicitly to *erôs* and *thumos*.

Part 1B

Thumos in the *Republic* and the *Symposium*

Chapter One

The Psychology of *Thumos*
(*Republic* 4.437a–441c)

We have seen that Charmides fails to engage with Socrates in genuine philosophical inquiry. He is unable to define *sôphrosunê* and is prevented from doing so by his *thumos*, which is manifested in both his speeches and deeds. We see Charmides's *thumos* early in the conversation (when he blushes before Socrates) and offers definitions (quietness and shame) that stay focused on the external beauty he has come to identify with himself, based on the gaze of others. Charmides is through and through dependent on the views of others, especially his guardian and authority Critias. This desire for external validation persists even in his eventual attempt to turn the tables on Critias, culminating in his offer of "doing one's own things" as the definition of *sôphrosunê*. In the *Republic*, of course, justice itself is defined in terms of one's own things.[1] But it is important that "doing one's own things" in that context involves a taming of *thumos* by reason. The *thumotic* attachment to one own's things, unchecked by reason, is the subject of our discussion here. Indeed, the definition of justice in the *Republic* is a direct response to this uneducated, uncontrolled, and dangerous attachment to one's own things. But Charmides resists an encounter with a philosophical inquiry that seeks to transcend such tribalism and partisanship. His rebellion against Critias (as we will see by the end of the dialogue) is only temporary. A real rebellion would involve a more profound taming of his *thumotic* attachment to the views of others. In the *Republic*, we find a deeper psychological investigation into the nature of *thumos*, and I will argue that the account there helps us provide an analysis of the failures of Charmides (and, subsequently, Critias). We must begin with an account of the nature of *thumos* itself.

A puzzle confronts all readers of the *Republic* who wish to understand the nature of *thumos*. It is clear that *thumos* is in some way deeply connected to anger: indeed, if we are to believe the discussion in the *Cratylus*, its very etymology reveals this (*thuô* = seethe or rage).[2] But beyond this, it seems to have several different aspects, as Hobbs notes:[3] "anger, aggression and courage; self-disgust and shame; a sense of justice, indignation and the desire for revenge; obedience to the political authorities though not necessarily to one's father; a longing for honour, glory and worldly success; some interest in the arts but a fear of intellectualism; a preference for war over peace and increasing meanness over money." This multiplicity has provoked a skepticism among some readers about its usefulness as a psychological concept, for it seems difficult, if not impossible, to unify these various aspects under one central trait.[4] Many commentators suggest that these various aspects of *thumos* can be united under the notion of "self-assertion," while connecting the notion of self-assertion primarily to a desire for recognition.[5] I will argue that self-assertion—what Hobbs describes as one's need to "count for something"—is crucial to understanding *thumos*. Indeed, if we reflect for a moment on the nature of anger, we see so clearly how intertwined it is with our sense of self. That which angers me or offends me, in many cases, is that which is a threat to my own sense of self-worth. I will be arguing, however, that the desire for recognition is a secondary rather than primary manifestation of this part of the soul. By this I mean to say that in Plato's account *thumos*, when it is uneducated, uncontrolled, and in all ways unacculturated by reason, does not manifest most vividly in the desire for recognition from others. Although this desire for recognition is indeed *thumotic* (and we have seen it on display in the character of Charmides), the primary—because unchecked—element of *thumos* is a self-assertion rooted less in the aspiration for superiority over others and more in the defiance of vulnerability, rendered most vivid in the disintegration that death threatens to the self. In response to the danger that death presents, *thumos* acts as an engine for the desire of what we can call the *boundless propagation and expansion of the self*.[6] It is this primary motivation that sheds indispensable light on the failures of Critias and Charmides to turn away from tyranny and toward genuine philosophical inquiry. In order to see this, let us turn to the discussion of *thumos* in the *Republic*.

Thumos makes its first major appearance in book 2 of the *Republic* when Socrates introduces it in order to talk about the courage needed for the guardian of the city in speech.[7] Courage is the quality most necessary for such guardians, and Socrates is quick to remark that there is no courage where there is no *thumos*. Indeed, any dog or horse or other animal, if indeed it is to be brave, must be possessed of *thumos*: "Haven't you noticed how irresistible (*amachon*) and unbeatable (*anikêton*) spiritedness (*to thumoeidês*) is, so that its presence makes every soul (*psuchê*) fearless (*aphobos*) and invincible (*aêttêtos*) in the face of everything?"[8] *Thumos* is thus described in this first instance as that which allows one to endure, remain steadfast, and achieve victory in the face of a fearful threat. The language of *thumos* is the language of war.[9] *Thumos*, in truth, *is* the part of the soul most needed for the warrior in battle. Indeed, the original city of pigs (as Glaucon called it) had no need of *thumos* because there was no reason for the citizens of this city to be engaged in war. It is only in the feverish city, which is beset by an "unlimited acquisition of money,"[10] that it becomes essential to have warriors who are guided by *thumos*. *Thumos* then comes on the scene with *pleonexia*. Though usually translated as "greed" (literally "having more"), it is important to recognize that the excessiveness of appetite does not capture the full meaning of *pleonexia*, nor does this grasp its rootedness in the nature of *thumos*. Tom Smith argues that Plato sees *pleonexia* as a "clinging possessiveness that arises in the spirited part of the soul that issues in projects of power and self-protection."[11] Indeed, *thumos* is inextricable from *pleonexia*, as Glaucon indicates in his challenge to Socrates in book 2 regarding the Ring of Gyges:

> We can see that those who practice justice do so unwillingly, from an incapacity (*adunamiai*) to do injustice, if we think about something like this: let's give a just man and an unjust man the license to do whatever he wants, and then let's follow and watch where their desires lead them; we'll catch the just man red-handed following the same way as the unjust man out of *pleonexia*. This is what any nature naturally pursues as good, but the law forcefully (*biai*) diverts it into honoring equality.[12]

As Arruzza suggests in commenting on this passage, "Glaucon establishes a causal link between [*pleonexia*] and injustice"[13] and he also suggests that without the limits placed by law, the nature of the human being would not respect equality but feel entitled to satisfy any desire. Human nature without law is described as lacking power to fight its own boundless appetites. It is only the strong force (*bia*) of *nomos* that can restrain these boundless appetites. Moreover, the root of *pleonexia* is *thumotic*. *Thumos*, unlike appetite, is not at all based on need. It is the threat of vulnerability that gives rise to the particular kind of possessiveness that seeks to have more than one's share. It is *thumos* that makes humans possessive, self-protective, and self-assertive in the face of imposed limits, which it seeks to throw off in the name of expanding the self. As Adeimantus says in his challenge to Socrates, unless someone has a divine nature, they are not willingly just but only reject injustice "because of a lack of courage, or old age, or some other weakness . . . lacking the power to do it."[14] The nature of human beings, according to Glaucon and Adeimantus, reveal that our *pleonectic* urges can only be dealt with by attending to and controlling *thumos*.

And it is here that a problem arises: given their potential *pleonectic* urges, how will spirited natures not be savage to one another and the rest of the citizens? From its first appearance, *thumos* is thus not only tied to *pleonexia* but also strongly associated with savagery.[15] Violence and aggression seem part of its basic, primitive, uneducated nature. *Thumos* is therefore as dangerous as it is powerful. As we have already noted in discussing the different aspects of *thumos*, there appears to be a tension built into its nature, a tension so profound it makes Socrates doubt the possibility it can be resolved.[16] Tarnopolsky and others[17] suggest that there is a bidirectionality to *thumos*: it points "simultaneously in two directions . . . both inwards to one's own advantage and outwards towards those whom one loves and cares about" and moreover is caught between "the desire either to remake the world complete in own's own image or . . . remake oneself in the image of the others from whom one desires recognition."[18] It is important that both these sides of *thumos* be considered when discussing it. And it is important to note that these two features, because they aim at two different objects, should not be considered inconsistent. In fact, we may see them as complementary when we consider that the bidirectionality of *thumos* lines up with what I will come to call below the *oikeion* principle—our attachment to what we identify as our own things paired with our repulsion from what is *other*. Socrates refers to this in arguing that a harmony between these two longings must be achieved, so that the spirited guardian is harmful only to enemies while being gentle to friends. He suggests that we can see this in the example of "well-bred dogs"[19] who are indeed gentle to their familiars and the opposite with those they don't know. Socrates says twice that this is *worthy of wonder*,[20] and he goes so far as to call them philosophical because they are acting on knowledge. As Wilburn points out, it is noteworthy that Socrates uses the word "*aspazesthai*" to describe a dog's treatment of those it recognizes.[21] The word, meaning primarily "to welcome or greet warmly with kindness," is used by Aristophanes in the *Symposium* to describe the love between young men and their older lovers. As we will see in the next chapter, Aristophanes's speech about *erôs* builds upon and deepens the account of *thumos* presented here. But here, something strange happens. Socrates asks Glaucon if they should "be bold" (*tharrountes*)[22] and assert that a human being, if he is to be kind to friends and harmful to enemies, must also be a lover of learning,[23] and that the guardian who is both *thumotic* and philosophic will be good and *kalos*.[24] We should note the irony that it is courage (and therefore *thumos*) that moves them to make these assertions, in spite of the possibility that the comparison to dogs is a problematic analogy.[25]

Let us emphasize here that Socrates has introduced a most fundamental aspect of spiritedness that we can call the *oikeion* principle.[26] *Thumos* is essentially connected with an emotional attachment to what one sees as one's own things, and thus also an antipathy to what is perceived as alien, *other*. The significant feature of these "well-bred" dogs is their *loyalty* to those they identify as *theirs*.[27] This lies at the root of everything that is potentially protective and destructive about *thumos*. Both the communal bond with those one identifies as one's "tribe," and the hostility toward those outside the tribe, spring forth from this psychic part that in a very basic, primitive way divides the world into friend and foe. For this reason, as I will discuss below, several commentators emphasize the social rootedness of *thumos*—and analyze it primarily as the part of the soul that longs for recognition. As I will make clear, I believe that Socrates's discussion of it in the *Republic* suggests that this is a misleading picture of the true nature of *thumos*. In my view, the story of Leontius reveals that the *oikeion* principle points to a darker motivation, lying "beneath" human sociality, and perhaps impossible to disentangle from savagery and violence. At the root of *thumos* and thus at the root of the human soul, Socrates suggests, is an aggressive part that detests most of all its own vulnerability to dissolution. The question raised by this insight will be, How can we deal with this aggression so that it does not destroy us?

How might we diagnose and hopefully respond to the threat that Charmides and Critias will pose to Socrates at the end of their conversation?[28]

To see this come to light in Socrates's account of *thumos*, let us turn to the text of the Leontius[29] story in book 4 of the *Republic*. Socrates tells the story of Leontius's glimpse of corpses in an attempt to distinguish spiritedness (*thumos*) from appetite as a real and separate part of the soul. Differentiating the rational part (*logistikon*) from the appetitive (*epithumotikon*) is relatively easy (439c–d). Once one grants the principle of noncontradiction and that it applies to psychological experience, then it is clear that reason is not the same thing as appetite.[30] Socrates then asks Glaucon if *thumos* (and that with which we become *thumotic*) is a third part or is the same as one of the two already distinguished: reason and appetite. It is Glaucon who first attempts to associate *thumos* with appetite,[31] and thus Socrates responds with the story of Leontius:

> So then, I said, I have distinguished these two kinds (*eide*)[32] as being in the soul; now is the one of spirit (*thumou*) and with which we are spirited (*thumoumetha*) a third thing, or would it be of the same nature (*homophues*) with either of the other ones?
>
> Perhaps, he said, with one of them, the appetitive.
>
> But, I said, I once heard something that I believe, namely that Leontius, the son of Aglaion was going up from the Piraeus along the outside of the North wall when he noticed corpses lying by the executioner. He had an appetite (*epithumoi*) to look at them but at the same time he was disgusted (*duscherainoi*) and turned himself away; and for a time he struggled with himself and covered his face. But finally overpowered by the appetite, he opened his eyes wide, ran toward the corpses and said "Look for yourselves, you evil wretches (*kakodaimones*), take your fill of the beautiful sight (*kalou theamatos*)."[33]

Socrates goes on to say that the story demonstrates that "anger (*orgê*) sometimes makes war against the appetites as one thing against another thing."[34]

It is an odd story to communicate such a message. Indeed, Socrates might have argued instead that surely Glaucon himself has had an experience in which his anger has been roused against himself—in the act, perhaps, of seeking to satisfy an appetite for sweet desserts which he knows he should avoid. In such a case, the satisfaction comes with a sense of guilt that suggests there are indeed two warring parts, and if we grant Socrates's claims about the application of the principle of noncontradiction to psychological experience, then appetite and *thumos* would not be the same thing. In fact, Socrates makes such a case at 440b. How then does the story of Leontius contribute to this argument? For instead of arguing from Glaucon's personal experience of psychological conflict, Socrates chooses to tell a story of a man who catches sight of corpses and reproaches himself—to be precise, his own eyes—for taking in the sight. How exactly are *thumos* and appetite at war with one another in this story? And why does Socrates tell such a strange story to differentiate them?

I suggest that the answers to these questions highlight two essential and important features of *thumos*, as human beings experience it. First, the arousal of *thumos* comes, often, from a sudden awareness of our ultimate vulnerability to death. Second, when *thumos* is aroused it manifests in the assertion of self, subsequent to its desire for self-sufficiency. To put it another way, *thumos* is ultimately aroused by the threat of self-dissolution, and it is this feature that distinguishes it from the other two parts of the soul. Were we to exist as rational appetitive but non-*thumotic* beings, we would not have a part of us with which we express our desire for agency—and thus *thumos* is the part of the self that is most invested in the expression, protection, and propagation of the self. Indeed, we will come to see that it is this very reflexivity of *thumos*—its pointing to no end beyond itself—that comes to define the most dangerous and powerful feature of this part of the soul. It is this *thumotic* boundless self-propagation that is constitutive of the tyrannical soul and is enacted in the speeches and deeds of Charmides and Critias.

In order to see this, we must first interrogate the desire of Leontius as he gazes upon the illicit sight of the decaying corpses: What is the object of Leontius's desire to look at the corpses? Why does such a desire elicit a reaction of disgust? Some have suggested that the appetite to see the corpses is sexual.[35] But indeed, the textual evidence for this is not strong. Contrary to this, some commentators, such as Allan Bloom, suggest that the *thumos* of Leontius is actually fighting the curiosity of reason, and Socrates here is giving an inadequate account of *thumos*.[36] But on this view, Socrates is intentionally misleading Glaucon, and we would be forced to say that Socrates actually means the precise opposite of what he says, when he claims that the story shows that anger takes up arms against appetite. In addition, both these interpretations downplay the punitive context of the sight—the corpses are, after all, lying by the public executioner. The setting of the story thus brings to the reader's attention the justice system of democratic Athens. Leontius is not seeing just any old corpses on the side of the road. They are corpses belonging to convicted criminals. So the discussion of justice and punishment in Athens is in the background of the story that Socrates recalls to Glaucon. And indeed, the discussion of justice and punishment is in the background of this entire conversation about the nature of the soul. For this reason, Danielle Allen connects Leontius's appetite to see the corpses with pity for the dead. Disgust at oneself, according to Allen, would be atypical of an Athenian response to such a sight, and thus Leontius shows the possibility for his *thumos* to turn against "the politics of punishment as it was practiced in Athens."[37]

Though I find this interpretation interesting, I would still suggest that the importance of the image should be more squarely placed on the threat that the corpses present. Leontius is disgusted with himself and sarcastically refers to the corpses as a beautiful sight. So however we understand the motivation behind the appetite to look at the corpses, the story still implies that there is a fundamental conflict between a *rational* antipathy to look at corpses and the appetite to look. To be clear: it is only *after* reason suffers a *defeat* and appetite takes over, that Leontius becomes angry at himself. In my view, the arousal of *thumos* comes from a threat that exposes his vulnerability on two fronts. First, the very image of the corpse is not merely frightening but disgusting.[38] It is of course a memento mori—a visual reminder of our mortality that forces us to confront our finitude. And because of this, it is reasonable that seeing them might provoke a fearful response. But more than that, the sight of corpses is associated with what the Greeks called *miasma*: contact with the pollution of the corpses is a threat to the person in contact with them, because they are both dangerous (fearful) and impure (disgusting).[39] I will come back to this below.

Second, Leontius struggles but finally loses. He does not walk away from the sight but looks and screams at his eyes in anger. The anger reveals a true self that longs to be in control of his appetite, which he does not identify as truly himself. If this is right, then the *thumos* of Leontius, which reproaches his own wretched eyes, is an assertion of self in response to this threat of vulnerability to the pollution of death and to his perceived loss of autonomy. Several commentators[40] emphasize the presence of other potential witnesses of the action of Leontius and argue that Leontius is acting out of a spirited shame that is motivated by respect for the view of others. But it stretches the text too far to say that Leontius covers his eyes out of shame rather than out of his desire to prevent them getting what they want. And at no point in the story does Leontius say anything that indicates that his concern is with others who might be watching. Neither he nor Socrates as narrator draw our attention to the emotional effect of any onlookers. Although *thumos* is often talked about as being fundamentally social and connected to one's desire to receive approval from others, the emphasis is different in this story, and I would say more fundamental. Leontius may indeed feel ashamed of himself, but not shame before others. The disgust he feels in this story, like so many experiences of disgusts that are misplaced, can actually be traced to a yearning for agency, control—even a fantasy of omnipotence. Think of a person who blames herself for her very own victimhood, in an attempt to control and bring order to a situation in which her own power has been threatened and for which no other psychic solution seems available. I would suggest that such a person is indeed being directed by an aggressive but untrained *thumos*. It is *thumos* that hates the vulnerability exposed by the acknowledgment of one's own finitude, loss of power and agency, and potential dissolution, and thus resists identification with the appetite that threatens such dissolution. Finally, then, *thumos* is connected to a desire for control. A *thumotic* soul will indeed be one that is occupied with thoughts about what is shameful and admirable, but Leontius's desire to look at the corpses suggests that there is a deeper psychological root or motivation that underlies such thoughts—that deeper motivation is connected to the propagation of self that becomes manifest in confronting one's own vulnerability to death, and, as I will argue below, the loss of order, agency, and meaning that such vulnerability threatens.

In this light, we should then ask: Why does Leontius not identify with his own appetite? Why does he feel that his appetite to look at the corpses is in some way an alien, hostile part of himself? Tarnopolsky has suggested that it is a "debased *thumos*" that treats death "as strange and hence foreign, arbitrary, illegal and not part of human existence."[41] I would only disagree with her claim that it is a debased *thumos* that does this. I would suggest instead that this is the natural disposition of *thumos*, which must be educated and trained rightly if we are to expect of it a different attitude toward death. Recall the *oikeion* principle—*thumos* is especially concerned with the preservation, protection, and propagation of what is seen as "one's own things." Death is so threatening because it is finally the most threatening *other*.

To return to Leontius's appetite to look at the corpses, then, we should ask: why is this appetite *deserving* of such disgust and self-reproach? In my view, it is neither a pity for the dead nor an appetite for sex that calls forth the reproach of the disciplinarian within him. The desire to look upon the corpse is that of an untrained appetite that pursues a gaze upon that which *reason* sees as bringing a threat, that is, dissolution. This is why it is only reason's defeat that arouses the *thumotic* reproach, for *thumos* naturally allies itself with reason, as Socrates suggests at 440e. It is reason that communicates the threat to *thumos*. For it is reason that sees that death, presented in the image of a decaying corpse, is a pollution (*miasma*) that will bring harm in the form of dissolution to the self. Why should we attribute the aversion to *miasma* to the rational part of the soul? The pollution of *miasma* is, as I have earlier suggested, connected with our notions not only of danger but of impurity as well. To speak of corpses as a *miasma* is to utter a word with religious and ritualistic overtones about the stain and filth that now hovers around the corpse like bad air. But what is stained and filthy is different from what is merely frightening. The stained and the filthy is repellent and disgusting to us because it is a violation of our conceptual categories or way of ordering the world. Following the work of Noel Carroll and Mary Douglas, we could thus say that the disgust provoked by the impurity of the corpse is a reaction upon being confronted with "interstitiality [and] categorical contradictoriness."[42] The polluted object in its impurity presents us with a disordering: it either violates the separations of things which, according to our conceptual schemes, ought to be kept separated or it violates by breaking apart that which we take to be wholes. In the case of the unburied, decaying corpse, we have on display a human being that is not only bereft of life and incapable of performing any *human* activities but thoroughly reduced to nothing but matter, eventual earth. We are face to face with human as *dirt*. The sight of the decaying corpse is a sight of not only the dissolution of the self but the dissolution of our fundamental categories related to living. This impure object is rejected by the rational part of the self, which eschews the impure as the alien harbinger of the irrational.[43]

But without *thumos*, it is not clear that the self as a whole would follow this rational norm. Reason is not talking to our appetites in a language that the appetites can understand. The appetites care not a bit about the dissolution of the self but only for the immediate pleasure that gratifies their need. It is the *thumos* of Leontius that understands this message from reason, and because it is allied with reason, it thus rebels at the untrained appetite that moves him toward that which is corrupt, ugly, threatening, and rationally forbidden. As we have seen, the disgust Leontius experiences has its ultimate source in a rational recognition of the *miasma* that the corpse displays. It is therefore a rational rejection of that which threatens disorder. *Miasma* is always connected to an "impairment of form," and is thus evocative of what I have now been referring to as "dissolution" of the self. When confronted with *miasma*, it is *thumos* that becomes protective of the self and strives to hold on to self-integration. The Leontius story thus reveals *thumos* primarily as a desire for victory,[44] self-sufficiency, and self-control in the attempt to side with reason and not be defeated by one's unrestrained appetite to descend into the muck of pollution. The definition of courage in the individual that soon follows depends upon *thumos* understood in this manner—a courageous individual is one whose spirited part (*to thumoeides*) will "preserve, through pains and pleasures what has been proclaimed by reasonable speeches (*ton logon*) about what is fearful (*deinon*) and what is not."[45] A person with a *thumos* that acts as an auxiliary to reason in this way identifies his core self as something other than his appetite. The *thumotic* individual transcends the lowly body,[46] which the image of the corpse presents to the conflicted Leontius.

Leontius's anger, even if it shows a man in conflict and not fully successful against his own appetites, still reveals that the *thumos* of Leontius itself can't be identified with an appetite. Moreover, it is in an alliance with a rational rejection of what reason sees as a threat to the body and soul, in the guise of the *miasma* of death. This alliance with reason speaks to its obedient, rather than deliberative, nature.[47] *Thumos* is much more concerned with defending what reason demands rather than thinking about it. This is connected to Socrates's proposed definition of what he calls "political courage,"[48] which is entirely parasitic on the norms set by reason. Perhaps at this point, then, it could be objected that *thumos* is not then a third thing in the soul. Is it a kind of rationality or a part of the rational part of the soul?

Socrates argues that this can't be the case either.[49] Three examples are discussed to distinguish *thumos* from reason: children, animals, and Odysseus—whom Socrates quotes without identifying. Glaucon gives the example of children who are "full of spirit straight from birth," well before they have the capacity to reason well. Socrates says that the same is true of animals. But the brunt of the argument is borne by the example of Odysseus. As commentators have noticed, this quote comes from book 20 of the *Odyssey*, when Odysseus, having returned home, stands over the sleeping suitors and debates with himself whether he should slaughter them all right there and then.[50] The *thumos* of Odysseus growls (literally) for revenge, while his rational part engages in strategy about the most effective and safest way to get revenge. His *thumos* is exclusively concerned in this moment with vengeance upon those who have harmed him, but reason must come in with its awareness of circumstances that *thumos*, in its narrow purview, does not consider. It is interesting that reason eventually persuades *thumos* using language that it understands. Odysseus reminds himself how strong he is and that he *can endure* this yet further. While *thumos* and reason begin in opposition to one another, his rational part wins by appealing to what *thumos* itself wants. This is how reason takes *thumos* on to its own side in pursuit of its cause. *Thumos* is itself irrational, and needs the guidance of reason from which it receives norms that it longs to preserve, protect, and propagate, in its attempt to assert the self.[51] The reason of Odysseus is able to persuade his *thumos* how to bring that about most effectively.

In the stories of Leontius and Odysseus, we see that *thumos* is neither appetite nor reason but appears more naturally allied with reason, especially in a soul that is not corrupted by bad education.[52] What, then, is it finally? I would suggest that it is most visible in its hatred, in its aversion to vulnerability, ultimately in the guise of the *miasma* of death, and in its subsequent assertion of the self at all costs against that which threatens the self with dissolution. At the same time, it is, like the dog to its owner, obedient to norms not set by itself but set by reason. *Thumos* is therefore bidirectional: it is at times the enforcer of the rational part of us and is able to keep appetites in check, and at other times it becomes the accomplice of the appetites in overcoming reason's control over the self. In fact, I would suggest that this bidirectionality is actually a feature of a healthy soul. In an untrained or even corrupted soul, *thumos* can fail to be *thumotic* enough: in such a case, it is so obedient to the norms provided by reason that it does not courageously defend itself against threat, nor assert itself in a situation that calls for it. Imagine Odysseus saying, "I guess I should just leave. It's too dangerous to take my home back. Penelope would be better off without me." However, *thumos* can also fail by being *too thumotic*, when it becomes excessively savage and it asserts its demand for control and victory without boundary. In such a case, it rushes headlong, not out of courage but out of rashness, into its own eventual destruction. This would be true in the case of Odysseus seeking revenge upon the suitors right there and then, and then suffering the consequences.

But what about an uncorrupted or properly trained soul? In this case, both the desires of *thumos*—for obedience and control—are satisfied. It obeys reason and controls appetite. It is thus most at peace when it is able to perform these two functions that answer to its bidirectional longing. And it is in this balance that *thumos* can assert and protect itself and thus be rightly attached to its own things. But if nurtured in the wrong way, if subject to corruption, this attachment to one's own things can bring about violence upon oneself and others, as Leontius's own self-reproach implies.

In conclusion, we should agree with those readers who suggest that *thumos* is not merely divisive. It is importantly self-protective and integrative. This is why it is associated with courage, one's sense of justice, and loyalty to one's family and friends. It is in this context that it makes sense to talk of *thumos* as "self-assertion." It is in fact best described as our adamant attachment to our own things—where one's own things includes not just to one's property but extends to one's family, friends, institutions, and cherished *beliefs*. This, finally, is how I would describe the nature of *thumos*—it is the part of the soul that attaches to our own things *as ours*, to what we feel properly belongs to us.[53] Without *thumos*, no appetite would be satisfied because the soul would not see any object as *deserved*. Nor would any reason count as being a good one to follow, for no justification would count as good, right, or owed *to me*. *Thumos* therefore turns out to be the engine for desire, and not the other way around. The problem, however, is that *thumos* is expansive and has no natural end beyond itself. No amount of self-protection is enough, and so *thumos* comes to express itself in what Socrates calls *pleonexia*—the boundless desire to acquire more and more and more. The *thumotic* need to self-replicate and self-propagate will stop only when self encompasses all there is. But a tragedy awaits us as the natural end of this *thumotic* self-expansion. That tragedy is expressed in Aristophanes's myth about the origin of *erôs* in the *Symposium*.

Chapter Two

The Psychogenesis of *Erôs*

Aristophanes's Critique of Love of One's Own Things (*Symposium* 189c–193d)

Aristophanes's speech[1] offers what I call a "psychogenesis," in that it gives a mythic account of how *erôs* came to be in the psychic structure of human beings. I will argue that it is a tragic portrayal of *erôs*. Most importantly, *erôs* is fueled by *thumos* unencumbered by any restraining force, resulting in misery for the lovers. It thus responds directly to our misguided *thumotic* "attachment to our own things." The speech reveals the tragic consequences of the dark side of *thumos*, manifested in the human longing to remake the world in one's own image.

In the *Symposium*, Plato ironically puts a speech in the mouth of Aristophanes, the comic playwright, that should not make us laugh. His account of love is not only pessimistic but also really a tragedy, portraying humans as having an "irrational urge, incapable of satisfaction."[2] It tells us also that a human being is doomed to live with a "permanent separation from his truest nature, along with an unremitting longing to correct this separation."[3] In my view, this is because it is finally a mythological account of *thumos* disguised as *erôs* that can never truly find its fulfillment in the human sphere. The problem with Aristophanes's account of *erôs* is therefore not merely that it is irrational. It is that is not about love properly understood—it is finally about *thumos* and its *pleonectic* desire for self-expansion.[4]

Aristophanes's account of human nature begins by pointing out that humans did not always exist in the form they currently have. Originally there were three sexes, not two, and they were spherical people with four arms, four legs, two faces, and two sets of genitals. They rolled around cartwheel-like from place to place whenever they wanted to move quickly.[5] In addition, human beings used to be powerful because of their double-bodies. "In strength and power, they were terrible, and they had great ambitions (*phronêmata megala*)."[6] It is pride that defines the soul of these original protohumans. They are protohumans not only in their physical form[7] but also in their souls—*erôs* is not yet part of their psychic structure. But it is clear that even at this early point of their history, they do have *thumos*. So while they are not yet properly erotic, they are indeed *thumotic*, as seen in their *phronêmata megala*. These ambitions grow to the point of inciting rebellion[8] against the gods. Because the spherical protohumans are so powerful, Zeus and the other gods deliberate about what to do, but find themselves in an aporia[9] about how to defeat them. The gods themselves are thus also motivated by *thumos*: they fear losing the honors and sacrifices that humans give them.[10] But Zeus knows that something has to be done about the humans "running riot" (*aselgainein*). At this point Zeus conceives of an innovative *mêchanê* that will crush the pride of these spherical protohumans while at the same time doubling their worship!

> I think I have a contrivance (*mêchanên*) . . . that would allow human beings to exist, while having become weaker (*asthenesteroi*), stopping their indiscipline (*akolasia*). I shall now cut each of them in two. And they will be weaker (*asthenesteroi*) and also become more profitable (*chrêsimôteroi*) to us, owing to the increase in their numbers. They shall walk upright on two legs. But if they seem (*dokôsin*) to still run riot (*aselgainein*) and are not willing keep quiet (*hesuchian*) . . . I will cut them in two again, and they'll have to make their way on one leg, hopping.[11]

Zeus thus splits human beings down the middle, through a contrivance (*mêchanên*), an artificial device,[12] that changes human nature from what it once was. This contrivance will give birth to *erôs*, which "calls the halves of our original nature together; it tries to make one out of two and heal the wound of human nature."[13] According to Aristophanes's speech *erôs* is not natural to human beings but is the result of a divine intervention to interfere with the original protohuman nature.[14] What we call *erôs* has emerged from a wound in human nature that resulted from a corrective by the gods. The original, spherical protohumans lacked *erôs* but were not at all lacking in *thumos*. In Aristophanes's account, then, we can say that *thumos* is more basic and primitive to the original human nature. It is only after *thumos* is seen as a threat to the gods that *erôs* is brought to human beings. The *thumos* of these protohumans led to a state of licentiousness or indiscipline (*akolasia*), rioting (*aselgainen*), and ambition (*phronêmata megala*) that caused them to make an assault on the gods. Zeus wounds these original beings in order to weaken them, and so *erôs* itself is a *mêchanê* that distracts these protohumans from their original strength and power. Indeed, Zeus threatens to cut human beings in two if they do not keep quiet (*hesuchia*)—the very first definition of *sôphrosunê* offered by Charmides. In Aristophanes's story both *erôs* and *sôphrosunê* are not original to human beings. It does not occur to Zeus that these ambitious human beings could be educated or trained to moderate their *thumotic* desire for power. Perhaps such training is possible only in the new form that humans will take. It is only after the divine punishment that *erôs* and *sôphrosunê* come to be as balms for humans to cope with the unconscious wound in human nature—the wound that traces its origin to a *thumotic* sickness.

But *erôs*, and any accompanying quietness, will turn out to be an unsatisfying salve to the wound that human beings now have. The *erôs* that emerges for human beings is not essentially different from the kind of *thumos* that preceded it. Indeed, *erôs* in Aristophanes's speech is a kind of *thumotic* attachment to one's own things. Finding one's beloved—one's other half, from whom one has been disconnected—is the ultimate paradigm of attaching to what is *one's own* insofar as one's beloved was formerly not at all separate from oneself.[15] It is only through an artificial contrivance brought about by hostile gods that human beings now live separated from their former selves. Now one has a memory—a very bodily one[16]—of one's own former self, deeply buried beneath conscious awareness. But this memory drives us to what we once were: erotic longing is a desire *to reclaim what used to belong to us. Erôs* turns out to be a desire for wholeness, whose goal is self-completion,[17] but only *thumos*—by definition—could set this in motion. Although the account of *erôs* here makes no direct mention of *thumos* by name, we can see its essence in the actions of the original protohumans and the description of love that comes as a result of Zeus's manipulation of their nature. Human beings are indeed distracted from their original ambitions, for they now long for their original selves instead. The story of love is a story of finding oneself in the guise of the other.

But it is here that Aristophanes's tragedy comes to light. Any sense of power once associated with the original wholeness is gone. Now when two people love each other, they never wish to be apart, thinking of nothing but their embrace of one another.[18] At the beginning of human existence as halves, the situation is so bad that human beings are unable to distract themselves long enough from their embrace of one another to even feed themselves. They quickly begin to die off. Only when Zeus introduces orgasm are they then able to separate, after temporary satisfaction, for the sake of survival.[19] But even this seems to be done to benefit the gods, according to Aristophanes's story. Sexual gratification serves, at best, as a continual temporary distraction from our deeper alienated state—our permanent forgetfulness of our own being, our incapability to gratify our *thumos*. The present state of things is thus a great step down from the grand strength of the original spherical protohumans. Our halfness has irrevocably removed us from the potential to overthrow the gods, and our memory has been transformed: what remains of our former self is an unconscious, faint image of our other half, which we cannot even articulate.[20] Humans carry the scar of long ago in their navels as a reminder not of the power they are seeking but of the punishment they suffered. To rebel against the gods again would bring about another split, which would result in death or worse. Instead, Aristophanes suggests that "we find the young men that are meant for us and win their love, as very few men do nowadays."[21] Aristophanes's speech, ostensibly about love, is a direct call for moderation (*sôphrosunê*) in the face of the hubris that our natural, original *thumos* breeds.

Consider now what Aristophanes presents in his speech as Hephaestus's offer to two lovers: "Is it this you desire (*epithumeite*)—to become parts of the same thing (*en toi autoi*), as much as possible, and never to separate, day or night? Because if you desire (*epithumeite*) this, I'd like to weld you together and fuse you into one mass, so that the two of you become one."[22] There is something importantly correct about the offer Hephaestus makes to the two human beings. Human beings cannot say exactly what it is about their beloveds that they find so compelling and attractive, but they know that they long for something that transcends the temporary connection that they have with their beloved. In this way, we could say that Hephaestus's offer reminds readers of the dialogue of the unspoken *mortality* of the lover and the beloved. Hephaestus's offer, if it points at anything attractive at all, does so because it provokes us to wonder about the connection between love and transcendence of our bodies, bodies that are vulnerable to decay, death, and dissolution. In its attractiveness, then, it speaks to our *thumotic* longing to overcome such vulnerability.

Yet there is also something particularly unattractive about Hephaestus's offer. Indeed, I submit that Plato intends readers to be disgusted with this element of Aristophanes's speech. Agathon himself in his next speech about love refers to Hephaestus, in an action motivated by his *thumos*, entrapping his own adulterous wife Aphrodite and her lover Ares in such an embrace in order to humiliate them before all the gods.[23] So there is something missing from this account of loving communion, and I suggest that Plato intends the reader to feel that. *Erôs*, when it is a disguise for *thumos*, can't be satisfied by the romantic love of another individual, even if this may very well be the truest fulfillment of one's desire.[24] The difficulty revealed here is not that this kind of union is untrue to love but that love's object (as described by Aristophanes) is ultimately and permanently unsatisfying and one's *thumos* won't let one forget that. The unity that Hephaestus offers will not ultimately be the true wholeness and self-completion that is the truest desire of human beings, according to Aristophanes's myth. The erotic embrace of another, even if welded together, will finally leave human beings dissatisfied because the union does not satisfy their deeper yearnings to reclaim their lost selves. Though Hephaestus talks about joining the two lovers into a near indissoluble unity, his language is silent about making them truly whole. Love as longing for wholeness can be satisfied only by becoming one's full original self. Aristophanes thus brilliantly portrays how weakly the erotic longing for another responds to the *thumotic* attachment to ourselves. Behind *Aristophanic erôs* is a *thumos* that hates alterity and strives for self-propagation. This is why Aristophanes desperately makes a plea for moderation. He is calling for a restraining force that will combat the potentially boundless yearning for self-propagation for which human beings naturally yearn. Aristophanes sees human beings as essentially incomplete. Indeed, their incompleteness is finally the most important feature of their erotic longings. On this, as will become clear, Socrates and Aristophanes agree. But in Aristophanes's view, *erôs* for other human beings may indeed not be strong enough to fight our *thumotic* yearning for our original godlike and powerful selves. Indeed, *thumos* finally aims at a goal that will bring about its own destruction. For a boundless self-propagation ultimately leads to a need for self-transcendence that can only be seen as self-destructive by the *thumotic* soul. In part 3, I will show that Socrates agrees with this Aristophanic worry, but he will suggest, instead, that *thumos* can be satisfied only by being properly transformed, trained, and educated by the beauty of wisdom attained by philosophical inquiry that acknowledges one's own incompleteness—if done rightly, the *thumotic* attachment to one's own things can receive a kind of therapy from the only non-*thumotic erôs* there is—*wonder*.

But here in Aristophanes's speech we have what I call a psychogenesis of an *erôs that* on closer inspection turns out to be *thumotic* through and through. Indeed, we can call it *thumos* in disguise. As such, this *erôs will* be permanently unsatisfied until it is finally destructive of others and itself. The unity promised to it by Hephaestus is a poor substitute for the lost self-completion and wholeness that was a part of its original state. While human beings used to be on par with the gods, and thus cosmically connected to them, their assault has brought about a separation that is now permanent. Because of the permanent separation from the gods, their *thumotic* longing can only meet with frustration and eventual disappointment when it attempts to take hold of the realm that lies beyond the reach of their desires.

Chapter Three

The *Thumotic Erôs* of Charmides

Using the story of Leontius and the speech of Aristophanes, we can better assess the failure of Charmides. We have seen the *thumotic* desire for recognition of Charmides in his actions. Charmides blushes upon Socrates's examination and is at first caught in a political aporia about his own reputation and that of Critias; Charmides's definitions of *sôphrosunê* are deeply tied to his views of others' expectations of him; and Charmides turns upon his own guardian in an attempt to free himself from embarrassment and embarrass Critias instead. All this clearly points to his concern for praise—to look good in the eyes of others. But if I am right, there is a deeply troubling root of this desire for recognition: a fear of vulnerability.

In the case of Charmides, we can say that his concern for praise from others is better understood using the language of vulnerability and control. Of the three definitions he gives of *sôphrosunê*, the first two ("quietness" and "shame") reveal a naïve neglect of a good that transcends the authority of Critias and Socrates, while his third ("doing one's own things") manifests his desire to escape being refuted again, a desire that conflicts with a genuine curiosity and philosophical wonder that perhaps would inspire a different interlocutor to investigate further, through more conversation, into the nature of *sôphrosunê*. Charmides never escapes his *thumos*. He is at first obedient to authority, then seeks to overthrow it, but in no way is he free from the dialectic of ruling and being ruled.

Charmides's *thumos* underlies his identification of himself with his erotic power (his sexual allure). The very conversation with Socrates ensues only after Socrates himself shows himself not to be threatened to be consumed by the beauty of Charmides's body. Socrates's question to

Charmides about his possession of *sôphrosunê* is actually threatening to Charmides. It is a call to him to be willing to give up power, admit his ignorance, and render his soul up for examination and treatment. But such a task would require Charmides to turn away from his own things—from the authority of Critias and from the identification of himself as beautiful in the eyes of others. When Charmides turns the tables on Critias, it is thus a false rebellion. It is instead a rejection of Socrates. In Charmides, the *oikeion* principle is strong. His *thumos* has become so assertive that he is ignorant of his ignorance of what lies beyond. It seeks completeness in an other that blinds him, and it will rise up against the questions from Socrates that threaten to expose him as still deficient. He will fight against the painful acknowledgment that he is incomplete and ignorant and take solace in what others have defined for him. If unchecked and corrupted by the wrong guardian, the fate of Charmides is thus the very dissolution of self. But Charmides has no more interest in investigating, if it means being refuted again. Socrates thus has only one hope for Charmides, and perhaps for the other youths of Athens who admire him. He must show him and those watching that his guardian is ignorant, and that this ignorance is dangerous if he and his guardian refuse to search for wisdom. We will now turn to Socrates's attempt to examine Critias.

Part 2A

Socrates and Critias on *Sôphrosunê*

Chapter One

Ugly Critias

Sôphrosunê as Doing One's Own Things
(Part 2: 162c–163c)

Socrates's dialogue with Charmides ends and his discussion with Critias begins when the young boy's guardian is no longer able to restrain himself but bursts in a fury into the conversation.[1] His entrance into the investigation into *sôphrosunê* is fueled completely by his *thumos*, to the extent that he *loses his self-control*. Socrates's discussion with him thus begins with a tension between word and deed. Critias is enraged at hearing his own doctrine mishandled and mangled, and Socrates himself narrates to his unnamed listener that Critias had long been eager to contend to "win honor" (*philotimôs echôn*) in the eyes of Charmides and the others watching.[2] His reputation for wisdom has been damaged, and so he comes to rescue it, even if it means publicly shaming young Charmides. Socrates adds that his earlier suspicion has now been confirmed: Charmides has heard this definition of *sôphrosunê* from Critias, and Charmides has grown weary of going under the knife of Socrates's examination. He thus incites Critias to take over Charmides's role, for Critias (as Socrates recounts it) has become angry at Charmides the way a poet is with an actor who recites his poems badly.[3] Faced with an image of himself that looks bad, Critias is more upset about his own reputation than the soul of young Charmides, it turns out. The two future tyrants thus battle each other with shame.[4] Critias, however, has more power than Charmides, and when the young boy steps outside of his role as Critias's beautiful possession, Critias puts him back in his place. Critias cares for Charmides "in an instrumental manner only."[5] But it was Critias who said the boy was a gifted poet. How well then does Critias "know his own things?" In fact, Critias manifests here the dangerous *thumos* we saw emerge in the speech of Aristophanes. He shows a love of honor that despises the shame and vulnerability of being refuted. His knowledge of his "own things" (his ward, Charmides) has been exposed as ignorance. Critias will attempt to defend *his own* definition of *sôphrosunê* in order to show that he himself does have knowledge of his own things. We will see that he will turn out to doubly fail. His definition will be deficient because it is tied to the *thumotic* character of his soul. His own *thumos* extends past the boundaries of Charmides's, which is predominantly motivated by the approval of others. This is natural for the young boy because he sees himself finally as the possession of Critias. It is when he turns against his guardian that it reaches its peak. Critias, who has no guardian over him, sees his own power threatened most vividly in the rebellion of the youth. His response is thus more menacing than Charmides's not merely because he is older and more powerful but also because his own *thumos* is potentially boundless. As the discussion of one's own things continues, Critias's boundless *thumos* will come more and more to the surface, culminating in his vision of the nature and benefit of *sôphrosunê*.

Socrates's strategy now plays directly into the anger and love of honor that he sees in Critias. Having seen immediately that Charmides is now willing to offer up Critias's words for examination, he baits Critias into his trap, and in so doing he attempts to magnify for Charmides the import of the forthcoming refutation of his elder cousin: "But Critias, good friend (*beltiste*), I said, it is not wondrous (*thaumaston*) that he is ignorant (*agnoein*) at his age; but you, on account of your age and attention (*epimeleias*), likely know (*eidenai*)."[6] Socrates emphasizes to those listening that Charmides is only a youth after all, and that his ignorance should really provoke *no wonder*, despite Critias's and others' great respect for the boy's maturity. Socrates has thus begun to show that what Critias and the others thought they knew about the boy turned out to be mere shadow. But still, what would really provoke wonder would be the revelation of ignorance of the boy's elder and experienced guardian. This can only cause even more anger in Critias, and a strengthening desire to defend himself in front of the watching crowd. But Charmides is Socrates's primary listener, and if Charmides is paying attention,[7] Socrates will attempt to bring him to the beginning point of philosophy: the boy will experience wonder if he can see that even his guardian does not know what he thinks he knows.[8] For Critias presumes that he does indeed know what *sôphrosunê* is—a remarkable, if not humorous, state of affairs, since only moments ago he could not remember the very quality Socrates had been asking about.

Critias thus unknowingly plays into Socrates's plan and accepts the definition as it stands. Not only is he blind to the role he will play in Socrates's scheme, but he also does not see that the revelation of Charmides's ignorance has already refuted him, for it was Critias who claimed that the boy had *sôphrosunê*. Despite his ardent willingness to hold on to "doing one's own things" as a definition of *sôphrosunê*, Critias seems not even know his own things, if he really believes his earlier praise of Charmides. And, more importantly, his ignorance of *this* ignorance will be further illuminated by Socrates. The drama of the dialogue thus brings the reader to ask *if* and *how* "one's own things" are good, just as Critias is ready to assert that they are.

Socrates begins by asking Critias about the same craftsmen who proved to be too troublesome for Charmides: "Do they seem to you to make (*poiein*) their own things or those of others also?"[9] Critias accepts that they make the things of others and insists that they still possess *sôphrosunê*. One expects Critias here to account for this apparent contradiction by getting clear about what "one's own" means, and how it can include things that are, in the usual sense, the things of "others." This would answer directly the questions raised by Socrates's discussion with Charmides. If one did know "one's own things," one would have to have a kind of self-knowledge, and we would be compelled to ask, What is self-knowledge? This moment in the dialogue is as opportune as any for the conversation to turn in this direction. Instead, it follows a different path.

Critias responds to Socrates with a distinction not between what is "one's own" and what is not but between *doing* and *making*. Critias quotes from Hesiod: "Work is no disgrace (*ergon d'ouden einai oneidos*)"[10] and interprets it in the following way: Hesiod did not mean that cobbling, selling salt fish, or prostitution are activities without disgrace. Rather they are "makings," and not works. No *work* is a disgrace, for a work, just by definition, is connected to the beautiful and the useful or beneficial (*to kalon kai to ôphelêma*). But "makings" may or may not be so connected: if not, they are harmful and disgraceful, and are therefore "others' things." But if they are so connected, they are "one's own things."[11] To put it simply: "doing one's own things" = making + beauty + benefit.

So, though we and Socrates might expect Critias to begin with a distinction between what is one's own and what is not (and thus move toward an account of the nature of self-knowledge), he instead furnishes a distinction between making and doing, a verbal maneuver that rests on two further distinctions—between what is and is not beautiful and between what is and is not beneficial. The reoccurrence of "the beautiful" (*to kalon*) is not surprising. Recall that it played such a crucial role in Charmides's first two definitions: "quietness" and "shame." Charmides's understanding of beauty, framed by others' approval of his own physical prowess, proved to be his guiding ideal, supplanting all others. Therefore, it is no coincidence that it should appear again in the speech of his guardian, Critias. But just as Charmides had an understanding of *to kalon* that led him astray in the inquiry into *sôphrosunê*, so too will Critias reveal himself to understand *to kalon* in a way that is inextricably linked to a contradictory notion of *sôphrosunê* that only a tyrant would refuse to revise.

For Critias adds to the notion of *to kalon* the notion of the useful or beneficial (*to ôphelêma*), which here makes an appearance for the first time. On hearing Critias's words, one wonders: What exactly is beneficial or useful? How does Critias conceive of "benefit" and how should we?[12] Again, we seem to have arrived at a moment that strongly points toward a discussion of self-knowledge. For does it not require self-knowledge to understand what is truly beneficial or harmful to us?[13]

Critias does not immediately see this path in the discussion. And before moving forward, we should pause a little longer over the details of his current proposal, in order to shed light on his seeming oversight. First, consider the citation from Hesiod. What is immediately striking is that it makes no mention of doings and makings but only of works. Consequently, one wonders why Critias would be introducing such a distinction here at all. Surely there would be another more appropriate quote on which to rest this distinction. But as has been pointed out, the citation makes another illuminating appearance in Xenophon's *Memorabilia*.[14] There it is put forward by Socrates's accusers as an example of his corrupt teachings of tyrants. The meaning of the phrase in context is that Socrates claims "one should refrain from nothing, no matter how wicked."[15] Plato appears to have put this enigmatic citation here, in the mouth of Critias, to say something about Critias's use of the phrase to defend his own vision of *sôphrosunê*, not that of Socrates. It is thus Critias who should be guilty of the charge made by these accusers, if anyone is.

Consider briefly the examples that Critias supplies in explaining the Hesiod quote: shoemaking, salt-fish selling, prostitution. It is strange that these three should be lumped together in one category. It is quite clear that Critias's tone when discussing these "makings" is quite derisive. Shoemaking and selling salt fish are as "disgraceful" to him as prostitution. Whereas Socrates seems to introduce examples such as these without judging them, Critias clearly sees them as inferior human activities. This is quite a perversion of the passage in Hesiod.[16] Secondly, perhaps it is because he blends all these lowly activities together that Critias does not see two key differences between prostitution and the others. Prostitution would not exist without *erôs* and is an art with no separable product. The former detail not only points us back to the beginning of the dialogue, during Charmides's entrance, where *erôs* played a crucial role. It also puts us in mind of Critias's own erotic stance toward Charmides's beauty. Unlike everyone else who beholds Charmides's beauty, Critias himself has no reaction to it, for he treats it as his possession. Charmides is the one whom Critias has been prostituting all along. The latter detail—that prostitution appears to be like an art with no separable product—points the reader forward, to the challenges that Socrates will make to Critias's reformulated definition. Both details are connected to Critias's failure to give an account of *sôphrosunê*, for he will not meet Socrates's challenges later, nor will his account include any reference to *erôs*.

We should thus make clear what Critias is actually endorsing in affirming that what is beautiful and beneficial is "one's own." For it is in fact an extraordinary claim, that amounts ultimately to a doctrine of self-benefit.[17] For Critias, all harmful things are the affairs of others (*ta blabera panta allotria*),[18] while the beneficial things are one's own. It might be tempting to hear Critias as saying that the "good" is his guiding principle, and that what is one's own is defined in reference to this ideal.[19] But precisely the reverse is true: it is one's own benefit, even though this is not defined, that is the standard for good and bad. Hyland writes, comparing Critias's position to that of Thrasymachus, "One is *sophron* who does only that which is useful to oneself; anything that is harmful is someone else's business, and so *sôphrosunê* as doing one's own business is to be understood as doing only what is useful to oneself."[20] This will be confirmed when Socrates clarifies Critias's position.[21] Critias and Socrates cannot understand "one's own things" in the same way. They take very different views of the relation of one's own to the good, in no small part because their views of the good are radically opposed.[22]

Socrates begins by saying that he immediately understood what Critias was saying when he had hardly begun. He summarizes Critias's speech as "You call what belongs to oneself (*ta oikeia*) and one's own things (*ta hautou*) good, and the makings of the good things doings."[23] Socrates's emphasis is illuminating and renders unambiguous Critias's meaning. For Critias, it is one's own things—and notice the addition of "*ta oikeia*"—that is the standard for the good, and not vice versa. Critias's definition of "good," it should be kept in mind, is the beautiful and beneficial (*to kalon kai to ôphelêma*). Socrates thus summarizes Critias's current doctrine in a sentence: the beautiful is now subordinate to what is one's own. This is why Critias is not *struck* by the beauty of Charmides. Because it does not present itself as something *other*, from which one's distance creates a reverence and a longing. Rather it is seen, through the eyes of Critias, as an extension of himself—as what belongs to him. Ultimately, to define the good as subordinate to what belongs to one ("one's own things") is the mark of one ruled by *thumos*, as we saw in the speech of Aristophanes.

Socrates comments on Critias's distinction, "For indeed I have heard from Prodicus countless distinctions between names (*onomatôn*)."[24] This quick remark may be lost on Critias, but Socrates has subtly called attention to the superficial quality of Critias's response. For he implies that Critias has culled a distinction between names but not necessarily between things. The precision required to distinguish names may not be enough to distinguish being, and perhaps Critias's thinking so far is not quite deep enough to touch the real being of *sôphrosunê*, still stuck like his younger cousin at the level of appearances—for he, too, is concerned primarily with how he appears to others. Secondly, consider the mention of the person from whom he has heard this superficial activity before. Prodicus is a sophist, and is also mentioned in the *Laches* as a source of the sophistic definition of courage that is discussed there.[25] In that context Socrates clearly is trying to distance himself, in front of Nicias, from the doctrine that the general hints he has heard from Socrates.[26] The mention of Prodicus here thus may have the effect of showing that Socrates wants to distance himself from Critias's doctrine as well and from his distorted vision of the good and the beautiful.[27]

Socrates confirms this is as he goes on. He is content to allow Critias any distinctions between names he wants, but he must say clearly the referent of each name. With that in mind, Socrates initiates a new beginning: "Therefore begin again from the beginning (*archês*) and define (*horisai*) more plainly."[28] This is the first of two new beginnings that Socrates suggests to Critias.[29] Finally, Socrates emphasizes at the beginning of his response that he understood Critias's own speech "from the beginning." If one keeps in mind Charmides's own attempts to begin again and again in the quest to define *sôphrosunê*, a question emerges. What is the proper *archê* for finding *sôphrosunê*? What is the beginning point in examining this virtue, or any virtue for that matter? This question will loom in the background for the remainder of the dialogue, and then come into the spotlight by its conclusion. It is perhaps *the* question of the dialogue and both its argument and action detail competing ways of coming to grips with it. It is akin to thinking about the beginning point of philosophy, which is wonder, and may also be the beginning point for thinking about *sôphrosunê*.

Chapter Two

Sôphrosunê as Self-Knowledge (163d–165b)

Socrates begins his rebuttal by saying, "I wonder (*thaumazô*) if you believe men possessing *sôphrosunê* are ignorant (*agnoiein*) of their *sôphrosunê*."[1] Recall that "*thaumazô*" was used by Socrates earlier, when he said it would be no wonder if Charmides turned out to be ignorant.[2] Rather, he implied, it would be wondrous if Critias, in his years and experience, turned out to be ignorant as well. Socrates's comment about what is and is not wondrous is coupled with his question to Critias about self-knowledge. There is indeed a deep connection between wonder and self-knowledge properly understood that will come to light in sharp contrast to the lack of wonder and false self-knowledge exhibited by Critias. Socrates actually refers to knowledge only indirectly, by calling attention to the *ignorance* of the *sophron* individual. This small difference is not seen by Critias, and he will fail to appreciate its implications as the discussion continues. One who fails to appreciate one's self-ignorance is incapable of wonder.

It might seem surprising that Socrates chooses to proceed in this manner. Why does he not, rather, press Critias to explain the nature of the good? As Schmid points out, Socrates could very well employ arguments about the good that he uses elsewhere in the *Republic* and the *Gorgias*: "Socrates does not argue here, as he does in the first book of the *Republic* (341b–342e), that the artist qua artist is essentially oriented to the good of the other, only accidentally to his own good, nor, as he insists in his dialogue with Callicles in the *Gorgias* (511c–513c), that the artist must distinguish the immediate service his craft may convey from the larger question of benefit and harm."[3] Socrates clearly has the means to pick apart Critias's notion of the good and move the discussion accordingly. But he chooses to ask about self-knowledge instead. Socrates appears to be willing to go along with Critias's conception of the good and to explore whether such a conception is compatible with self-knowledge properly understood. The focus of the discussion in the remainder of this dialogue thus concerns the relation between knowledge of the good and self-knowledge, and in what way, if at all, *sôphrosunê* bridges these two.

The suspicion that there might be such a relation—between knowledge of the good and self-knowledge—is justified. The notions that have been dancing about in the background and the foreground of the dialogue—the useful and the harmful, the beautiful and the ugly, the good and the bad—all seem to require a kind of self-knowledge for their proper understanding. Even in Critias's self-interested sense, can one really know if something is good for oneself without any kind of self-awareness? That is, if Critias is aiming to achieve a good that is good for Critias, qua human being, must he not have some understanding of human nature, and of its needs and limitations?[4]

Perhaps none of this is on Critias's mind when he answers Socrates's question about the *sophron* individual's ignorance.[5] Critias claims that an individual possessing *sôphrosunê* cannot be ignorant of it,[6] and thus unknowingly refutes his own praise of Charmides. Charmides showed himself to be ignorant of his own *sôphrosunê*, if indeed he had it, and by Critias's own words this amounts to proof that he does not have it after all. Critias thus was wrong to boast about the *sôphrosunê* of young Charmides, but he does not give any indication that he recognizes this. He is too concerned with defending himself now to notice the implications of his words on his previous statements about his ward.

So now Socrates again brings up the example of the doctor, recalling the image of the Greek and Thracian doctors at the beginning of the dialogue. Critias consistently claims that a doctor, in making someone healthy, makes a benefit both for himself and for the person whom he heals. Socrates then asks if this is done dutifully, according to what is "needful" (*ta deonta*).[7] Critias agrees and claims that someone who does the needful is *sophron*. Critias's view is continually augmented. It now seems that what is done beautifully, beneficially, *and* needfully is *sophron*.

Socrates, however, gets Critias to agree that a doctor's knowledge is incomplete: the doctor will sometimes act beneficially without knowing that he does so. He therefore, according to Critias's account, has *sôphrosunê* but is ignorant of it. The structure of this argument is as follows. After introducing the notion of "the needful," Socrates asks two questions.

First, must the doctor know when he heals beneficially and when not? Second, must each craftsman know when he will profit (*onêsesthai*) from his work? The second question is easier to answer, for the term "profit" is unambiguous. The craftsmen do not know when their activities will bring them profit and when they will not. But it is less clear in the case of the doctors: are they ignorant of their own benefit, the patient's, or both?[8] Socrates leaves this ambiguous. But surely the Thracian doctors of "the whole" are not ignorant of themselves, either their own benefit or that of their patients, for they treat the body only by attending to the good of the soul. Profit and benefit also appear to be lumped together by Critias when perhaps they should be distinguished: this is further vindication that his own view of what is good amounts to a doctrine of self-interest. It is this doctrine that is being damaged by Socrates, and perhaps if one truly understood what real benefit were—as perhaps a *sophron* individual might—then one would not be led, like Critias, to the conclusion that one could be ignorant of it in this way. At this point, then, it should be clear how intertwined this question is with the mysterious nature of self-knowledge, to which Critias finally turns, struggling desperately to save his doctrine and to save face.

Critias has run into a self-contradiction. He cannot assert that the craftsman with *sôphrosunê* can be ignorant of the benefit of his actions. The consequences of this inconsistency are quite dire for the older and more experienced gentleman. Not only does it now look that he himself may not know what *sôphrosunê* is, but Socrates's response is a damaging blow to his doctrine of self-interest. It raises the possibility that Critias himself may not understand what really is "his own benefit," much less what is good simply. Critias himself is ignorant of himself.

The way has been paved for his longest speech in the dialogue, standing at its center, which now unambiguously asserts the primacy of self-knowledge. Critias has finally gotten a glimpse, perhaps not a true one, of what his account needs: he sees that Socrates is pointing to self-knowledge and is thus prompted to suggest it as a definition.[9] He now dispatches with Hesiod and calls up the Oracle at Delphi as his authoritative witness:

> For I would almost assert this to be *sôphrosunê*: knowing or recognizing oneself (*to gignoskein heauton*); and I go along with the one who put up a prescription of this sort in Delphi. For it seems to me that this inscription was put up as if it were a

> greeting (*prosrêsis*) from the god to those coming in instead of "rejoice" (*chaire*), as if "rejoice" were not correct, and they must not exhort (*parakeleuesthai*) one other to say this, but to say "be *sophron*." Thus the god addresses (*prosagoreuei*) the ones coming into the temple differently than do human beings. Such was the thinking of the one who put up the inscription, it seems to me, and he asserts that the god always says to those coming in nothing but "be *sophron*." But he says it in a quite riddling way (*ainigmatôdesteron*), like a prophet (*mantis*). For "know yourself" (*gnôthi sauton*) and "be *sophron*" are the same, as the inscription and I assert. But perhaps someone might consider (*oiêtheiê*) them to be different, which happened, it seems to me, to the ones laying down the later prescriptions, "Nothing too much" (*mêden agan*) and "A pledge, and ruin is near" (*to enguê para d' atê*). For they supposed "know yourself" to be advice or counsel (*sumboulên*), not a greeting from the god to those coming in. And so, in order that they might put up (*anatheien*) counsels no less useful (*chrêsimous*), they wrote these and put them up.[10]

Critias points out that there are a number of interpreters of the oracle who have not understood the real meaning of *gnôthi sauton*. How lucky, then, for Socrates: he is discussing *sôphrosunê* with someone who seems to think he understands the intention of the Delphic Oracle, and what self-knowledge really is! Clearly, we have already seen hints that we should be suspicious of Critias's view of self-knowledge, and ultimately, he will not be able to coherently defend it. This should not be too surprising, for the words he is claiming to understand are indeed mysterious, as Critias himself admits—calling them a riddle, as Socrates called his teaching when it was in the mouth of Charmides. But Critias seems to be riddling again, for his own words are rather mysterious as well, and even he himself may not understand their full implication.[11]

First of all, we should again note the traditional link between *gnôthi sauton* and *sôphrosunê*, which serves as the background for this move by Critias. Briefly, the traditional view emphasized the *restraining* value of *sôphrosunê*: living a *sophron* life entailed shunning one's hubris, containing ones' ambition, and having the self-knowledge to bring this about, that is, *knowing one's own human limitations*.[12] But Critias's own version will twist this conventional view of *sôphrosunê* and self-knowledge. Rather than an exhortation to human beings to recognize their human limits, and not attempt to transcend them, Critias's view carries with it his doctrine of self-benefit that will be shown to be more and more radical as the dialogue progresses. What emerges from this first speech are further suggestions that will be vindicated during Socrates's challenges that the self-knowledge Critias values is incompatible with *sôphrosunê*, conventionally understood, while also in tension with a Socratic notion of *sôphrosunê*. The conception Critias is here putting forward is essentially connected to the definitions and account he has already presented, and he is attempting to defend his self-interested view in calling upon and *departing from* the Delphic oracle.[13]

Critias begins by agreeing with the authoritative Oracle and begins to describe the intention of the person who put up the inscription. One expects to hear an explanation of the words that are written in Delphi, but this is not forthcoming from Critias. Rather, his first comment about the Delphic inscription is that "be *sophron*" is a greeting (*prosrêsis*), and a more correct greeting than "Rejoice!" (*Chaire!*). The god thus greets humans coming into the temple in a different way than human beings greet each other, and Critias asserts that the god is really exhorting (*parakeleuesthai*) human beings to greet each other similarly.

But what does it mean to say that "be *sophron*" is a kind of *greeting*? Second, why is Critias talking about this "greeting" from the Delphic Oracle? For, even though there is the traditional link, the Delphic oracle does not mention *sôphrosunê* but only self-knowledge. As Critias continues, his speech takes up the latter question first, and later the first question becomes his theme.

First, Critias claims the inscription makes the connection between *sôphrosunê* and self-knowledge in a riddling (*ainigmatôdesteron*) manner, because it is done, after all, by a prophet (*mantis*). This is his answer to the latter question: the inscription does not say "be *sophron*" but "*gnôthi sauton*," because they are the same and because it is written by a riddler.[14] As Critias continues explaining the "riddling" manner of the oracle, the traditional link between self-knowledge and *sôphrosunê* comes more into focus. For he mentions the two other inscriptions that were put up in Delphi: "Nothing too much" (*mêden agan*) and "A pledge, and ruin is near" (*to enguê para d' atê*).[15] The appearance of these inscriptions alongside "know yourself" emphasize the traditional meaning that the Oracular inscription had. For the latter two remind human beings to recognize their limits: their inability to understand, predict, or rule all that is around them. Both emphasize the importance of knowing one's place and not transcending it.

Now previous conversation with Critias has already suggested that his own deepest views are not identical to the traditional ones, but at best they might be self-interested twistings and perversions of the views, in the service of his own ends. This is only further suggested by Critias's explanation of these inscriptions that stand alongside "know yourself" in Delphi. For he claims that the ones who put up these inscriptions made an error, the very error Critias is denying, namely, that "be *sophron*" and "know yourself" are *different*.[16] Those who put up these inscriptions did not understand the real meaning of "know yourself," and consequently put up these later, misleading additions. Critias is ready and willing to kick away the ground on which the traditional link between *sôphrosunê* and self-knowledge appeared to be standing and assert his own *correct* understanding of the true Delphic inscription. Critias thus presents himself as one with knowledge and authority to give a correct interpretation of the riddling Oracle. But we have no reason to believe that Critias has insight into these divine matters. Without any reason, Critias asserts authority to interpret as if he were equal to the gods. Such a claim is hubristic, at best.

Critias asserts that the latter dedicators misinterpreted "know yourself" as advice or counsel (*sumboulên*) rather than as a greeting. They consequently decided, erroneously, to put up advice that was no less "useful" (*chrêsimous*).[17] Critias here appears to unknowingly refute his earlier definition (as he unknowingly refutes his own claim that Charmides possesses *sôphrosunê*). His notion "doing one's own things" depended on "the useful," a concept that he now disparages. But the "useful" necessarily points to a standard beyond itself: nothing is useful simply; we must always ask "useful for what"? It is thus unlike Critias's conception of self-knowledge, which has no standard outside of itself. Consider Levine's description: "Advice is above all prescriptive, value laden. As such it proposes, in the case of deficiency, a change in another's doing or thinking, in one's way of life."[18] Seen in this light, a greeting is unlike advice in all these ways. It is not value-laden or prescriptive; its goal is not change in the other. Advice such as "nothing too much" holds one to a higher standard, but with regard to a greeting this is just not so. A greeting such as "Rejoice!" (*Chaire!*) seems to be value-free and imposes no view of what is good and bad on the other.[19] Thus *sôphrosunê* as self-knowledge now turns out to be only tenuously connected to knowledge of the good. It is here that we further see Critias's radical view come to light. For his words ultimately bring the god down to a human level: he is vitiating the notion that the "superior" god may be giving "mere humans" advice, and is asserting that the gods are really participating in a value-free practice that humans engage in with one another.[20] At the same time, however, Critias is asserting that few human beings have actually understood this correctly, and that he himself is one of those who sees into the mysteries, who is really at the level of the "god."

True self-knowledge and *sôphrosunê* are thus only in the domain of the elite: it seems only the superior can be truly *sophron*. So at the same time that Critias has brought the god down from the divine, he has elevated himself and others like him to the superhuman. In sum, Critias's description of the greeting "know yourself" reveals his belief that *sôphrosunê* is somehow "value-free," his belief that *sôphrosunê* or self-knowledge belongs only to the superior, "godlike" human beings, and his belief that these superior, "godlike" human beings have replaced the gods. The picture yielded by these beliefs coincides with the doctrine of self-benefit that earlier appeared. As Schmid sums it up, Critias's views are the "amoral human praise of self-certainty, not the divine moral counsel of self-restraint."[21]

It is thus surprising that this passage has not aroused more suspicion. As I mentioned above, commentators have identified, or come close to identifying, the speech Critias makes here with Plato's own opinion.[22] But consider once again how Critias was drawn into making this speech. His first definition, "doing one's own things," failed insofar as it was unclear what one's own things were. Critias then amended his definition to define the beneficial and useful things as one's own, so that *sôphrosunê* became "the doing of good things." In making this move, Critias implied that the good was defined by one's own things and not vice versa. But this definition, "the doing of good things," failed too insofar as it seemed that the *sophron* individual could do good things without self-knowledge, that is, without knowing his own things. Socrates thus implied that Critias himself, believer as he is in his doctrine of self-benefit, may not in fact know what is really good for him. But what is revealed here is deeply connected to his *thumotic* entrance to the conversation. Critias sees the good as what belongs to him and defines the bad as what is other. When *his own* ward Charmides betrays him by mangling *his own* words, he lashes out in fury. Self-knowledge, according to Critias, is similarly *thumotic* through and through. It defines its standards (what is good and bad) according to what it sees as its own and what belongs to another, a distinction not imposed from without but constructed from within. Critias's Delphic speech places Critias himself at the center of all.

Tuozzo argues that readers who suppose Critias here has completely lost sight of the good are mistaken,[23] and that Critias rather sees self-knowledge as the *highest good*.[24] In a sense, this is correct. Self-knowledge is supremely *important* for Critias because, as Socrates has shown, without it Critias's doctrine of self-benefit and thus his life may be based on shadows and illusions. But Critias never really has sight of the good, let alone the "highest good." His self-knowledge is purely constrained only by his view of what belongs to him, which determines his view of the good. So, while the goal of Critias's speech *should* be to bring together the epistemological and moral inquiries of the dialogue,[25] in fact it highlights the failure of Critias's outlook to do just this. For it will ultimately be fatal for Critias's position that he cannot overcome his *thumos:* he does not see past the distinction between what belongs to him and what is another, nor is he able to let the good itself ground this distinction. This leads him into incoherence, for it will turn out that his view of self-knowledge and his notion of the good are unbridgeable. I believe this is what is at issue at the center of the dialogue, and what Socrates will now explore, raising the question for us of another way of understanding *sôphrosunê*.

But Critias cannot really revise his words and thereby admit ignorance. Immediately following his claim that *sôphrosunê* is self-knowledge in his Delphic speech, Critias makes the following statement: "Why I am saying all this, Socrates, is this. Everything earlier I am taking back for you. For perhaps in some way you were speaking more correctly about them, perhaps I was, but nothing of what we were saying was quite plain."[26] Let us be clear about Critias's words here. Critias does not (because he cannot) simply say he was wrong and accept the consequences of admitting his ignorance. Rather, he asserts that perhaps Socrates was correct, but perhaps *he himself was* and that *neither of them* was speaking clearly. Rather than take responsibility for his own deficiency and accept the invitation of Socrates for transformative conversation, Critias shares out the blame with Socrates and denies ignorance. He exposes his desire not to be refuted in front of those watching and his consequent inability to understand his own real ignorance. Underlying both of these dispositions is the sickness in his soul that tyrannizes him, that is connected to his ruling *thumos*. It prevents him from abandoning his belief that he is a "knower," and thus he cannot in this moment experience genuine philosophical wonder. The tyranny of this belief, on the inside, creates the tyrant himself, when it is turned outward. It is thus significant that Socrates's own response to Critias is not agreement or endorsement but a confession of ignorance.[27]

Chapter Three

The Intentionality of Critian Self-Knowledge (165b–166c)

Socrates's opening question in response to Critias's speech is remarkably brief, but has been one of the biggest centers of controversy among readers of the dialogue. He says, "If acknowledgement (*gignoskein*)[1] is what *sôphrosunê* is, then clearly it is some knowledge (*epistêmê*), and a knowledge of something (*tinos*). Or not?"[2] Critias agrees. Since he has asserted that "*gnôthi sauton*" is the same as "be *sophron*," then *sôphrosunê* is clearly a *gnosis* (an acknowledgement or recognition), and is therefore also an *epistêmê*.

The terms *epistêmê* and *technê* are often interchangeable in the Platonic dialogues.[3] However, it is not clear that these notions are so similar that one should readily go along with Socrates and say that the former implies the latter. Some commentators suppose that the move from one to the other is confused, if not illicit. Consider the remarks by Tuckey:

> In this argument, therefore, there is a confusion between two senses of the word 'knowledge,' the first being instanced in the precept [*gnôthi sauton*], the second in the words [*iatrikê hugieinou epistêmê ousa* (medicine is the *epistêmê* of health)]. But it was in this second sense that the Socratic *arête = epistêmê* was used. Thus, coupled with the confusion between the senses of the word 'knowledge' there is a linking together of the two Socratic sayings 'know thyself' and 'virtue is knowledge.'[4]

On Tuckey's reading, this move is consequently the key moment in the dialogue, because he sees the equation of the two notions here as illegitimate. In his view, not only is Critias wrong to agree that a *gnôsis* is an *epistêmê* but he is also incorrect in claiming that self-knowledge itself is an *epistêmê*.[5]

But we must be careful in moving to this conclusion too quickly from the verbal transition here. For it is not immediately clear what Critias believes he is affirming when he affirmatively answers Socrates's question about the status of *sôphrosunê* as a "knowledge." Nor is it obvious what Socrates intends in asking the question in the first place. The most we can assert at this point is this: it is fair to ask both Critias *and* Socrates whether or why they would agree that all forms of knowing (including self-knowledge) are encapsulated in the word "*epistêmê*."[6]

What is at issue here is not the relation between *gnôsis* and *epistêmê* and self-knowledge, abstracted from the present dramatic situation, but between Critias's own views, which may be suspect because they spring from an ill-formed conception of the best life. For we will see that Critias's answer to this question is only fully revealed when he finally spells out in detail his answer to Socrates's next question ("of what" is *sôphrosunê* the knowledge?).

Having agreed that *sôphrosunê* is an *epistêmê* and is "of something," he says that the object of this *epistêmê* is "oneself" (*heautou*).[7] This is the first direct reference to *reflexivity* in the argument of the dialogue, but it remains opaque what Critias means by his claim. In order to proceed, Socrates does not investigate the faculty or activity of knowing that takes "oneself" as one's object but instead asks Critias about the object of the knowing.[8] Socrates introduces the examples of medicine (again)[9] and house building, referring to each as an *epistêmê*, and shows that in these cases we can point to an object or product distinct from the *epistêmê* itself: medicine has health as its product (*ergon*) that Socrates links with its benefit,[10] and even calls it beautiful (*kalos*), recalling his earlier appeal to *to kalon* in order to refute Charmides's first definitions. In what way, we might ask, is *this* knowledge oriented toward something beautiful or good beyond it?

We can see how one might answer this question in the examples that Socrates uses. For he goes on to say that the product (*ergon*) of house building is the finished house, and one could say something similar for all the other *technai*.[11] Socrates then encourages Critias to point to the distinct object of the *epistêmê* that is *sôphrosunê*, to say what "beautiful work (*kalon ergon*)" it produces. At this point Critias claims that Socrates is inquiring incorrectly. But perhaps Critias does not understand the significance of Socrates's question.[12]

We should consider why Socrates is so insistent on getting at the "of what (*tinos*)?" regarding this *epistêmê*. His question implies that we define "knowledges" (*epistêmai*) not by investigating the subjective cognitive faculty we call knowing but by considering the specific object known, which delimits the knowledge under investigation.[13] Socrates is implying that knowledge is essentially *intentional*, for it is defined by an object other than itself.[14] But recall that Critias has already suggested that the knowledge he is talking about should be seen as a kind of "greeting" rather than advice. This is how "the god" intends us to understand the phrase "know yourself." In removing the phrase from the realm of advice, and thus stripping it of its normative quality, Critias has also taken away the intentional attribute of self-knowledge. Since the action "know yourself," according to him, does not aim to bring about change at all, for there is no standard outside of self-knowledge that delimits it and defines it, Critias will have difficulty relating his conception of self-knowledge to the notion of knowledge that Socrates seeks, one that is *intentional*, defined by the object outside it. Critias might be able to offer a suitable candidate in response to Socrates's question by claiming that the object of this self-knowledge, distinct from the knowing activity, is the *soul*. In fact, this *seems* to be what he is suggesting when he first mentions "oneself."[15] If he were to say this, the conversation would take a quite different turn from the one it actually does. For Socrates and Critias could at this point begin discussing more explicitly the nature of the soul, and could end up with a conversation similar to the one that occurs in *Alcibiades I*.[16]

But Critias chooses to respond to Socrates's request for a "beautiful work" by claiming that *sôphrosunê* is not like the other *epistêmai*. In his view, *sôphrosunê* does not have a separable product like house building and medicine. He claims that Socrates is wrong to compare it to these *epistêmai* or *technai*, and then asserts that even arithmetic and geometry are unlike house building and medicine in this way. His response thus ends with a challenge: "What is such a work of the art of arithmetic or of geometry, in the way a house is of house building or a cloak is of weaving? . . . Can you show me any works like these? But you will not be able to."[17] According to Critias, *sôphrosunê* is more like geometry or arithmetic than house building or weaving.[18] Critias is right that while house building and weaving focus on a tangible material product, there is properly no parallel tangible material product for geometry and arithmetic. It is therefore Critias, not Socrates, who categorically rejects productive *technai* as appropriate models for understanding *sôphrosunê*.[19]

Socrates agrees with Critias (*alêthê legeis*) that these knowledges do not issue in a separable product in the same way.[20] But he now claims that they have similarly distinct objects, if we consider what they are *about*. In this sense, they are still *intentional*, because they are "of something":

> But I can show you of what (*tinos*) each of these knowledges (*epistêmai*) is, which happens to be different from the knowledge itself. Thus arithmetic is of the even and the odd, how many they are in themselves and with respect to other numbers. . . . Now aren't the odd and the even different from arithmetic itself? . . . And again, weighing is of the heavier and lighter weight. But the heavy and the light are different from weighing. . . . Then tell me, what is *sôphrosunê* the knowledge of, which happens to be different from *sôphrosunê*?[21]

Socrates thus continues to press Critias for the "of what." For although Critias has made clear that he rejects productive *technai* as a model of self-knowledge, he still needs his conception of self-knowledge to be "beneficial" if he is to avoid being shown that he doesn't know what is even to his own good. But he is not willing to say that this benefit comes from it having an object that is different from itself.

Critias thus claims that Socrates is still attempting to seek sameness where there is only heterogeneity. *Sôphrosunê* is unlike the other *epistêmai* in just this way, "for while all other *epistêmai* are of something else, but not of themselves, this one alone is an *epistêmê* of all the others and of itself."[22] This statement has been the center of an enormous and confused controversy, even more so than the previous move from *gnôsis* to *epistêmê*. What has caused such debate is the move from "knowledge of *oneself*" to the present formulation "knowledge of *itself*."[23] Socrates does not make anything of this move: for him it is not the strange and confusing transition that many readers have taken it to be. I believe the best way of seeing why this is so has been explained by Schmid: "Critias would appear to assume that self-knowledge takes the form of knowing that one knows [an *epistêmê*], that is, self-knowledge is of oneself qua knower, qua cognitive self. . . . Thus Socrates may well agree with the transition, even if he understands self-knowledge differently than Critias."[24] Schmid's proposal makes sense of the movement of the text, which is a smooth transition, though one wouldn't think so based on the controversy it has generated. But what has been eclipsed by this controversy is the larger question of the meaning of this statement that Critias makes. For along with the claims made that this transition is nonsensical comes the implication that Critias's statement here has no serious basis.[25] But if we consider carefully what is implied in this definition, then we will see that it rests on Critias's doctrine of self-benefit that has previously appeared.

To possess a knowledge which has all others and itself as its object, is to have a knowledge that is both all-inclusive and reflexive. It has generality *and* self-reference. Critias offers it in an attempt to explain how his conception of self-knowledge can indeed benefit the one who possess it, even if it is not defined by an object that is distinct from it.[26] Therefore, he puts forward "knowledge of the other knowledges and of itself" in order to describe a knowledge that is "architectonic," in its subordination of the other knowledges. So, for example, the knowledge of bridle making appears subordinate to the knowledge of horse riding, for it is the person who rides the horse who puts the bridle to test, and thus supplies the standard to the bridle maker. Such a conception is not unique in Plato's dialogues.[27] If this knowledge is possible, Critias seems to be claiming that the person who possessed this would seem to know the purpose of all such subordinated knowledges. The one with *sôphrosunê* would not be a lowly prostitute or fish-salt seller but the one with the knowledge that somehow stands above all these others, and because of its reflexivity, needs nothing beyond itself. It is the *ruling science*, that subordinates all others to serve its proper ends.

Although we do not have reason to reject the notion outright, we should regard this notion with suspicion. *Sôphrosunê*, as defined by Critias, seems to be a divine wisdom.[28] It should not be surprising that Critias promotes such a conception. In his Delphic speech he showed himself willing to bring the god down and elevate himself. He has also listened to Socrates's account of the Thracian doctors, whose goal it is to treat "the whole," and thus gives an image of *sôphrosunê* that attempts to encompass "the whole" within it. Far from coming out of nowhere, this is the logical outcome—the ultimate culmination—of the views that Critias has expressed so far.[29] Self-knowledge, according to Critias, does have an aim. Its goal is all-encompassing, totalizing knowledge. But Critias has not shown that such a conception, like his own account of the Delphic injunction as a greeting, is oriented to any standard outside of itself. Indeed, at this point we should wonder if this is the self-knowledge a tyrant would promote—totalizing in its purview, it seeks no object beyond itself and what it rules. Critias's account of self-knowledge here is through and through *thumotic,* just as it fails to be properly *erotic.*[30] In not being oriented to anything beyond itself, it aims to spread itself throughout the whole and loses sight of the individual human soul that is the proper object of the person seeking self-knowledge. Critias's account therefore abstracts from the situation that he himself is in with Socrates—a conversation in which the participants are seeking knowledge they lack about themselves.[31] Therefore, even if we assume the possibility of this attempt, it is not clear that this vision of self-knowledge reveals knowledge of the *self* at all. In sum, Critias's reply to Socrates's question ("of what?") concerning the object of this self-knowledge: it is "of" everything. Socrates will show that this answer is equivalent to saying that is actually "of" nothing.

But perhaps it will be objected that these suspicions are not well-grounded, or that they do not take seriously enough the proposal Critias is putting forward. So, if we are to take seriously the proposal of Critias, it is necessary not to dismiss it outright (as Socrates does not), but to consider carefully (as Socrates does) what it implies and whether such self-knowledge is indeed possible for and beneficial to its possessor. This is precisely what Socrates begins to do in his forthcoming questions. But before turning to these questions, it is important to consider Socrates's small but significant addition to the notion Critias has proposed.

Chapter Four

Socrates's Addition—Knowledge of What One Knows and Does Not Know (166c–166e)

Critias's formulation is coupled with an attack on Socrates's method in the conversation so far. In addition to claiming that Socrates is not inquiring correctly, Critias asserts that Socrates knows very well the truth of the phrase he has just uttered, and is only seeking to refute Critias, regardless of what he says. Socrates once again takes this opportunity to profess his ignorance, but now sees that Critias is in danger of not continuing the conversation.[1] He is able to calm Critias down and reengage with him by telling him not to worry whether it is Critias or Socrates who is refuted but to focus solely on the argument itself.[2] Socrates then makes a small comment to Critias, in which his own *sôphrosunê* comes to light. " 'But Critias,' I said, 'you come at (*prospherê*) me as though I claim (*phaskontos*) to know what I am asking about, and would agree with you, if only I were willing (*boulômai*). But that is not how it is, for I am inquiring (*zêtô*) along with you about whatever is proposed because I don't know (*eidenai*). Therefore, after I investigate (*skepsamenos*) I am willing to say whether I agree or not. But wait until I investigate.' "[3] Critias thinks that Socrates already agrees with his claim that *sôphrosunê* is self-knowledge, and thus he implies that from where he sits, Socrates already knows what *sôphrosunê* is.[4] But Socrates's response reveals that Critias does not grasp Socrates's view at all. For Socrates claims that he does not know and cannot yet say whether he agrees or disagrees with Critias. He must investigate *what Critias means by these words* in order to discover whether they are true. While Critias supposes he has the answers and is ready to argue for them, Socrates claims he does not know and is ready to inquire.

His ignorance motivates his search for knowledge, while Critias's claim to know conceals his own ignorance.[5] As Schmid says, "Socrates has before his mind an epistemological distinction that Critias seems not to appreciate—knowledge vs. opinion. Critias has before his mind a political distinction that Socrates seems to disregard—that of authority vs. disgrace."[6] The former distinction is essential to the philosopher's outlook—that is, it becomes relevant if one has a genuine desire (*erôs*) for wisdom. But for Critias this distinction is outweighed by the latter, political distinction. His *thumos* trumps such *erôs*, if there is any. Whereas Socrates sees the need for investigation, and thus recognizes the limits of Critias's definition of *sôphrosunê*, Critias in no way seeks to investigate. After Socrates claims it is necessary to do so, Critias responds, "Investigate then." The command is in the second person, rather than the hortatory ("let us") that would be heard from one who actually wished to discover the truth with Socrates. Critias is unable to do what Socrates himself shows. Socrates's inquiry, and any *inquiry* deserving of the name, is an act of a philosophical soul motivated by recognition of ignorance and a genuine desire to transcend this ignorance.

Critias does not see that his agreement to put aside considerations about whether he or Socrates is being refuted actually undercuts his own view of *sôphrosunê* itself. For in saying this, he agrees to detach his own view from the inquiry they are conducting. But his own conception of *sôphrosunê* placed the *sophron* individual at the center as the supreme ruling *knower*, surrounded by *epistêmai* that work toward his benefit. Such an image is in sharp tension with a philosophic detachment from one's interests in favor of finding the truth, especially given the addition that Socrates will now make.[7]

Socrates asks a small question of no small import: "Therefore . . . [is *sôphrosunê*] also a knowledge (*epistêmê*) of ignorance (*anepistêmosunês*), if indeed it is of knowledge (*epistêmês*)."[8] Socrates's question here sounds almost exactly like his description of his own famous claim to knowledge of ignorance in the *Apology*.[9] After provoking wonder about the refutation of "Critias" and "Socrates," Socrates now explicitly brings to the conversation a notion that seems to be the very depiction of his own vision of self-knowledge. By doing it in this manner, he prepares us for a discussion of two conceptions of *sôphrosunê*: the Critian and the Socratic.[10] The advice Socrates earlier gave now invites us to suspect that though Critias's understanding of *sôphrosunê* will be shown to be untenable, perhaps the Socratic view will escape refutation, even if it needs further elaboration.[11]

That there are really two images here, Critias's and Socrates's, is also suggested by the way Socrates induced Critias to bring self-knowledge into the discussion. Socrates asked about the *ignorance*, rather than knowledge, of the individual who does good things.[12] Critias leaves ignorance far behind, and it is not until this moment that it is rekindled in the discussion. Critias's omission of ignorance is not merely accidental: For Critias, it appears there are no limits to this wisdom he calls *sôphrosunê*, a fact he does not realize will cause trouble when he agrees to Socrates's small addition.

Socrates's addition implies that the *sophron* individual is open to what is beyond his limits, in that there is a recognition of what is beyond his knowledge. This calls for a very different orientation to the good, for the knowledge of limits removes the individual from the center of his world. Rather than being elevated to the godlike, as in Critias's description of the Delphic Oracle, human beings now properly stand in that in-between realm, the realm between beast and god.[13] Consequently, the Socratic account of the good is not gobbled up by "one's own things." For it is the neglect of the knowledge of ignorance, the elevation of ourselves to the gods, that seems to carry with it a confusion between one's own and the good.[14]

When Critias agrees to Socrates's small addition, Socrates elaborates on an important activity that is essential to and unique to the individual who possesses *sôphrosunê* so described. This individual, and only this individual, has self-knowledge and knowledge of *others*:

> Then only the one who is *sophron* will himself both acknowledge (*gnosetai*) himself and be able to examine both what he happens to know (*eidos*) and what not, and in like manner will have the power to inspect others, what they know and think they know, if indeed they know, and also what they think they know but do not know. But nobody else will be able to do this. And this is what "being *sophron*" and "*sôphrosunê*" and acknowledging oneself are: knowing what one knows and one does not know. Is that what you are saying?[15]

Critias agrees. But what has he agreed to? Does he himself know what he thinks he knows in agreeing with Socrates here? Or has he instead assumed that his all-encompassing architectonic knowledge, because it is all-encompassing, will also rule over Socrates's small addition and be able to accomplish the task Socrates assigns to it? There are reasons to suppose that it is the latter case. For Socrates's elaboration here adds elements to the Critian vision of *sôphrosunê* that have no proper place for them. It thus turns out that Socrates is presenting an alternative vision of *sôphrosunê* that is *incompatible* with the description put forth by Critias. Critias describes an all-encompassing architectonic knowledge of knowledges that is closed to what is beyond its limits because it dictates that there is nothing beyond its scope. Socrates's account claims the opposite of *sôphrosunê*: it is an "open self-knowledge not limited to one's own knowing situation."[16] Moreover, Socrates has insisted that only the person with such knowledge of limits will be able to examine himself and *others*. The examination that is essential to the *sophron* individual is remarkably parallel to Socrates's description of his response to the Delphic Oracle in the *Apology*, which will further reveal how different the Socratic understanding is from that of Critias.

In the *Apology*, Socrates begins his speech about the Delphic Oracle by suggesting that someone in the audience might rightly ask, "But Socrates, what is your occupation or task (*pragma*)?"[17] Socrates raises this question after he has begun to debunk the slanders against him that ultimately have brought him to trial. It is against this background that he calls upon the Oracle at Delphi as *his authoritative witness.*[18] For he uses the words of the oracle to explain the cause of his slandered reputation: "What has caused my reputation (*onoma*) is nothing other than a certain kind of wisdom (*sophian*). What kind of wisdom is this? Perhaps it is human wisdom (*anthropinê sophia*). For perhaps I may be wise in this wisdom, while those whom I mentioned just now are wise in something greater than human wisdom, or I do not know what to say, for I do not understand it (*epistamai*)."[19] From the outset Socrates emphasizes that the difference between his own "wisdom" and that claimed by those he examines is the difference between the human and what is beyond the human. While his wisdom is confined to the limits of human beings, theirs, if it is true "wisdom," somehow transcends these limits. But as Socrates interprets the Delphic Oracle, the highest "wisdom" human beings are capable of achieving is defined by these limits and does not reach beyond them.

Socrates explains that Chaerephon, the well-liked companion of Socrates who also happens to be present for the discussion in the *Charmides*, was the individual who found out from the Delphic Oracle that no one is wiser than Socrates.[20] Socrates's response is one of utter incredulity. Echoing the passages in the *Charmides*, he says that the god is riddling (*ainittetai*), for he knows (*xunoida*) that he is wise with respect to nothing either great or small.[21] Socrates assumes the god told a riddle, for the only alternative is that he is lying. This he says is impossible for him: whereas Critias seemed to suggest that the god bestowed upon humans a "value free exhortation," Socrates here makes us wonder if this too might be absurd behavior for the god.

Socrates was perplexed, in aporia, for a long time and then began an investigation that became his way of life, his well-known *pragma*. Going to people who had a reputation for wisdom, he attempted to show that there must be at least one human being wiser than he himself was. He thus submits even the words of the god to examination: his desire for wisdom prompts a philosophical inquiry that subordinates all claims to wisdom, even including one from a divine authority that makes a claim about Socrates's wisdom. It thus could appear that Socrates himself is pursuing an activity that is impious, in his questioning (indirectly, at the very least)—he is submitting the divine authority itself to the test of reason. But each time he does so he discovers that what the god says is true. For though each person "appeared wise to many people and especially himself, he was not."[22] Socrates's restless search to refute the god ends up as vindication. And the fundamental difference between Socrates and his interlocutors is essentially connected to his recognition of limits:

> So I withdrew and thought to myself, "I am wiser than this man, for it is likely that neither of us knows anything beautiful and good (*kalon kagathon*), but this man thinks he knows something when he does not, but I, when I do not know, do not think I do either. I seem then to be wiser than this man in just this little thing: that what I do not know (*oida*) I do not think I know either.[23]

Socrates's proclamations of ignorance thus contain what he thinks to be a significant insight into the human soul. The proper understanding of human wisdom and its difference from the wisdom of the gods leads one to the highest wisdom that mere human beings can reach. This is the recognition of limits that seems to come out of Socrates's small addition in the *Charmides*, "knowledge of ignorance." The description in the *Apology* also illustrates that Socrates's pursuit of self-knowledge shows it to be inextricably connected with knowledge of *another*. The pursuit of self-knowledge, the accomplishment of *sôphrosunê*, comes about through exploratory conversation, and conversation begins only with its partners admitting their deficiencies and being genuinely open to the good of the other that is potentially transformative for each of them.[24] For such self-knowledge frees one from standards imposed without reason by others and brings about an ability to think independently about one's beliefs and commitments, especially ones we come to see are only founded on the desires and expectations of others.[25] In acknowledging what lies beyond the scope of our wisdom, and standing apart from beliefs that find their origin in authorities that we have not examined, we then can come to see and claim what properly belongs to us—a true notion of "our own things" is inseparable from an acknowledgment of our ignorance. It may seem paradoxical, but Socrates's account of *sôphrosunê* suggest to us that this acknowledgement of our own ignorance brings us closer to a genuine self-knowledge.

Critias seeks however to make *sôphrosunê* and human wisdom "something greater than it is."[26] He attempts to replace the human wisdom that recognizes its very human limits with the wisdom of the gods. Critian *sôphrosunê* claims that nothing is beyond its scope and is instead aggressively *thumotic*. It dictates that the good be defined according to its own standards, and it subjects itself to no standards beyond itself. It is anything but open. Rather, it is the doctrine rooted in a will that makes itself and what it defines as beneficial to it to be the measure of all things.[27] Critian *sôphrosunê* is best described as the "dialectical deformity"[28] of Socratic *sôphrosunê*. For both notions are rooted in a desire (*erôs*) for wisdom of the whole. But Socrates's desire leads him to a genuine openness to what is beyond the reach of this desire, and an acknowledgement of his own limits as they come to light in knowing others' limits. No such openness will be possible for Critias's conception.[29] Critias is ignorant of his ignorance. He has not understood the nature and benefit of *sôphrosunê*. It will be shown that his own self-knowledge is an illusion, a fantasy for humans who have Critian self-knowledge only in their dreams.[30] The waking reality of the tyrant's view of self-knowledge and the good is fundamentally incoherent, for it is rooted in a totalizing desire that refuses to acknowledge that the most divine wisdom is beyond human reach. It will therefore turn out to be Critias's doctrine, not Socrates's examination, that is impious and hubristic. Critias fails to acknowledge the essentially limited nature of human beings, and this failure will lead his account of *sôphrosunê* to be neither possible nor beneficial for the *sophron* individual. But while his vision dwindles into absurd fantasy, the Socratic conception of *sôphrosunê* may be able to wake us from this *thumotic* nightmare, and on awaking, achieve authentic self-knowledge in wonder about the beautiful and the good.

Chapter Five

Is Knowledge of Knowledge Possible?
(167a–169c)

A. Argument One (167a–168b)

Socrates begins his response to Critias's latest formulation with a "third offering to Zeus the Savior" and initiates another new beginning.[1] After he is led to the implication that Critias's *sophron* individual (and Critias himself) may not know his own good, Critias brought self-knowledge into the discussion, which he finally defined with Socrates as an *epistêmê* of itself and all the others and the lack of *epistêmê*.[2]

The two new beginnings are initiated only after Critias has revealed something about his unconventional view of the issues at hand. The first moment follows Critias's assertion that the good is swallowed up by "one's own things," and the second moment follows Critias's *un-Socratic* picture of self-knowledge as hierarchical, unbounded, godlike, and "ignorant of ignorance."[3] But Socrates now indicates that this second new beginning is the final one, for the libation to Zeus is the third and final one made after the one to the heroes.[4] Socrates does not say why this most recent definition of *sôphrosunê* should be the last one they offer up in the conversation. But the conception of self-knowledge that is now on the table must somehow address the problems that have appeared already, problems that made the new beginnings necessary. Perhaps then the finality at issue here is connected to the *fatality* or *survival* of Critias's deepest beliefs about the good.[5] That is, Socrates seems to suggest that it is only through defending this conception that Critias can vindicate his doctrine of self-benefit that is in peril. At the same time, Socrates also hints that this finality suggests something ultimately true in the definition, which gets close to the real nature of *sôphrosunê*, which I take to be its awareness of ignorance.[6]

Therefore, the third libation to the savior ushers in a new inquiry, concerning the possibility and benefit of this latest definition of *sôphrosunê*: "So from the beginning let us examine (*episkepsômetha*) first whether this is possible to be or not—the knowing (*eidenai*) of *what* one knows and *what* one does not know (*ha oide kai ha mê*), *that* one knows and *that* one does not know (*oiden hoti oide kai hoti ouk oiden*). Then if it is quite possible, what benefit (*ôphelia*) there would be for us by knowing it (*eidosin*)."[7] Socrates raises two questions: about *possibility* and *benefit*, but of what? The phrase is ambiguous. There seem to be two pictures, the former narrower than the latter:

A. Socrates and Critias are talking only about the possibility of and benefit for the individual who knows that he knows (whatever he knows), and knows that he doesn't know (whatever he doesn't know).

B. Socrates and Critias are talking about the further possibility of and benefit for the individual who knows (A) *and also knows what he knows and doesn't know.*

It is not clear from the text here which meaning is intended. But as the discussion continues, it will become clear that the "that" cannot be separated from the "what," and Socrates's words will show that the latter possibility is what is at issue. This renders the more restrictive first interpretation possibly misleading.[8]

Without resolving this ambiguity, Socrates turns to examine the possibility and benefit of this mysterious knowledge. He turns to "possibility" first. Socrates begins his refutation by telling Critias to inquire (*skepsai*) whether he can show himself to be more resourceful (*euporôteros*), for he himself is at a loss (*aporô*).[9] Socrates thus continues the inquiry with a claim of ignorance: he does not know the way they should proceed from here. But the two words—*euporôteros* and *aporô*—are opposite in meaning: Socrates thinks himself to be ignorant, so Critias had better be the resourceful one if they are to get anywhere.

Socrates suggests that Critias will see that this new definition, again recapitulated as the *epistêmê* of itself and all others and of the lack of *epistêmê*, is strange (*atopon*), and that "it will seem to you, so I believe, to be impossible (*adunaton*)."[10] By the end of this first challenge, he will have only suggested that *some* cases analogous to "knowledge of knowledge" are impossible, while others are merely "not to be seriously trusted (*apisteitai sphodra mê*)."[11] The difference here is telling. Socrates begins by suggesting that it is Critias who will think, inevitably, that Socrates's argument will demonstrate impossibility, rather than mere strangeness. For the Critian understanding of the good and self-knowledge will be unable to meet Socrates's objections. But this leaves open the possibility of a kind of non-Critian conception of the good and self-knowledge that will not be victim to Socrates's challenges here.

What, then, is the content of Socrates's aporia? The investigation of possibility of this *epistêmê* (of itself, all others, and the lack of *epistêmê*) involves an examination of mental faculties and quantitative relations. His first step is to show that the picture Critias gives of self-knowledge is unlike any *dunamis* of the soul. His second step is to show that it is unlike any quantitative relation, which then sheds further light on their preceding talk of mental faculties.

Socrates begins with mental faculties, the very first example being seeing: "For reflect (*ennoei*) if there seems to be to you some seeing (*opsis*), which is not a seeing of the same things that other seeings are of, but is a seeing of itself and the other seeings, and of the lack of seeing likewise. And although it is seeing, it does not see color, but just itself and the other visions. Does there seem to be to you some seeing like this?"[12] Socrates is asking about a seeing that would be structurally similar to the *epistêmê* whose possibility they are seeking to establish. The question is meant to ask Critias if he has ever run across a seeing that does not see what other seeings see[13] but instead sees only itself, other seeings, and the lack of seeing. By mentioning the "lack of seeing," Socrates has therefore included an analogue to knowledge of ignorance in his question.[14] Critias emphatically denies the existence of such a seeing (*Ma Di' ouk emoige*), showing almost immediately that Socrates's suspicion was well-placed: he will see impossibility where Socrates is showing strangeness. The example does show the strangeness of a self-relating faculty that does not see what other faculties like it, that are non-self-relating faculties, see. For, as Socrates suggests, what would a vision *be* that saw no color but only itself and other visions and nonvisions? Socrates brings up seven more examples to expound this strangeness: hearing, perception (*aesthesis*), desire (*epithumia*), wish (*boulêsis*), love (*erôs*), fear (*phobos*), opinion (*doxa*), and then returns to *epistêmê*. In each case Socrates asks if the faculty can be directed at itself and not at the usual object of the faculty, but the questioning proceeds in an odd way.[15]

First of all, we should note the three groups that the faculties constitute:[16]

1. The "perception" group: sight, hearing, all *aisthesis*

2. The "desire" group: *epithumia, boulêsis, erôs*

3. The "emotion and cognition" group: fear, opinion, *epistêmê*

Though this seems to carve up the examples quite nicely, further examination complicates the picture somewhat. For instance, the first two cases, vision and hearing, are spelled out with a structure precisely parallel to the case at hand, the case of *epistêmê*: Socrates explicitly inquires about the seeing and hearing that are not of color or sound but of (1) themselves, (2) others, and the (3) nonvisions and nonhearings. But as he continues, he drops reference to (3) and asks only about (1) and (2). That is, when he turns to *aisthesis*, he spells out only "the other perceptions and itself" and leaves out "the non-perceptions."[17] The same follows for *epithumia, boulêsis, erôs, phobos,* and *doxa*, until finally the "strange" conception Socrates is talking about is not the knowledge of ignorance but the *epistêmê* of itself and the others. If one were to read only the passage at 168b, one would have no reason to suppose that Socrates calls into question Socratic knowledge of ignorance in the *Charmides*. One must wonder about this repeated dropping of the "lack" in these seven cases, which seems to emphasize that the view of self-knowledge that Socrates is calling into question is the Critian one, not the Socratic.[18]

Critias does not see this, nor perhaps does he see that mere strangeness rather than complete impossibility is the result of his admissions, as he emphatically rejects the cases Socrates puts forth. His rejections are so emphatic that he does not pause over the significance of the examples or even their relevance. For starters, Critias himself earlier charged Socrates repeatedly with inquiring incorrectly, even dishonestly, claiming that the uniqueness of *sôphrosunê* would not allow it to be compared to the other *technai*. Why does he not make the same claim here? Might this *epistêmê* also not be comparable to the other faculties of the soul that Socrates is mentioning? Critias does not raise this question, but it is raised for us.

Critias also does not seem to make much of a *kind* of self-relation that could be observed in the cases Socrates is mentioning. For though the example of *aisthesis* seems to require a distinct object, yet there is still a higher awareness that we perceive.[19] The point becomes more debatable with the later examples: clearly one can have desires of desires, beliefs of beliefs, opinions of opinions, fears of fears.[20] Critias does not pursue this question, but obviously the astute listener will wonder about it, and in this wondering show that we are indeed psychologically capable, just as we observe ourselves listening to this conversation, of some kind of opinion of opinions, at least. But it would be odd to have an opinion that is only of itself, and not of things that other opinions take as their objects.[21] Therefore, the strangeness Socrates points to seems to amount to a suspicion that the faculties, by nature, are all—even if they are self-relating—also necessarily directed at an object distinct from themselves. Indeed, it is only because the faculty might become like the distinct object of the faculty that it appears possible for the faculty to be self-relating. Put another way, in order for faculties to be self-relating, they themselves must have the quality of the distinct, intentional object. For example, a fear is by nature "of" a terrible thing (*to deinon* is the distinct, intentional object of fear), but perhaps certain fears may turn out to be dreadful things as well. In this case there would be good reason for a fear of fear to come about. Such a case may be the fear of one's fear of the enemy, a terrible thing itself.[22] This makes it all the more necessary for us to determine what the proper object of knowledge is, such that the faculty of knowing could take on this attribute and thus be capable of self-relation.[23]

An appropriate response to this section of the dialogue would thus be connected to the perplexities aroused by the previous discussion. Both Charmides's and Critias's answers raised puzzles for us about the relation between one's own things, the beautiful, the good, and the soul. Socrates now seems to spell out different capacities of the soul, all pointed at different objects, among them the good and the beautiful. We should wonder again here not only how are these objects related to each other but also how are the parts of the soul that "move toward" them related to one another?[24] And is not this "moving toward" or "intentionality" what binds these faculties together in some way? Wish, desire, and love all seem to be a kind of need. I will argue in part 3B that a deeper examination of this "need" is essential to bring us closer to self-knowledge and understand the possibilities (and accompanying failures) of the self-relations discussed here. It is no coincidence that Critias does not see the role of "need" as something necessary to explore for his own "seeing" of self-knowledge is blind to need.

Socrates therefore sums up the discussion by saying that this *epistêmê* would be strange (*atopon*), and explicitly says that he and Critias should not yet claim that it is impossible but investigate further whether it does or doesn't exist. When Critias sees that Socrates is implicating himself and Critias jointly in this claim of ignorance, he agrees. But Critias will be no help in a real investigation into the nature of self-relation and the soul.

B. Argument Two (168b–168e)

Socrates now turns to a second set of examples and proceeds to make an argument that is different from his first.[25] The first argument proceeds by examining analogues of knowledge of itself, others, and ignorance and showing how odd (*atopon*) it would be for them to only be directed at these three elements while not also having the characteristic attribute of the distinct, intentional object of the particular faculty. As we have seen, this implies (*if* the strangeness is not mere strangeness but impossibility) that all faculties (self-relating or otherwise) might *necessarily* be related to a distinct, intentional object. It is precisely this principle with which Socrates now begins his second argument. Socrates now establishes that this *epistêmê* has "a power (*dunamis*) such as to be of something."[26] Having just put forth every *dunamis*, Socrates now explicitly asks about the *dunamis* that *sôphrosunê* has to be. But in continuing, he asks Critias to compare this *dunamis* not to the mental faculties that we have just seen but to the faculties in quantitative relations. Socrates points out that with regard to magnitude and multitude, self-relation is not just strange but clearly impossible:

> For do we say the greater (*to meizon*) has a certain faculty (*dunamin*) of this sort, so that it is greater than something?
>> Yes, it has.
>> Indeed of something smaller (*elattonos*), if it will be greater?
>> Necessarily (*Anankê*).
>> Therefore, if we could find something greater which is greater than the greater things and itself, but not greater than the *things* beside which the others are greater, surely what would

happen (*huparchoi*) to it is that, if indeed it were greater than itself, it would also be less than itself, would it not?

Most necessarily, Socrates, he said.[27]

These quantitative relations run into logical contradictions when one tries to apply self-relation to them. Something greater than itself would be less than itself. Something double itself would be half itself. What is more than itself will be less than itself, and what is heavier will be lighter.[28] In contrast to the first argument, which proceeded on the assumption that the self-relating faculty did not have the quality of their distinct, intentional object and yet "strangely" were still of themselves, this second argument proceeds on the opposite assumption. These quantitative relatives (greater/smaller; more/lesser; double/half) *do* have the quality of their relata while at the same time being related to themselves. In such a case, such self-relating seems to be not only strange but manifestly impossible.

Critias is therefore right to say that these quantitative relations "necessarily" can't relate to themselves. But the story should not end here. For he could interject, as he did so forcefully earlier in the dialogue, that the *epistêmê* that is of itself and the others is different.[29] It is unlike these quantitative relations. Could he not suggest that quantitative relations are a bad model for this self-relating *epistêmê*, *sôphrosunê*?[30] Such an interjection does not occur to Critias. Either he is not thinking seriously about the examples Socrates is putting forward or he is persuaded by the force of Socrates's analogy.

The problem, again, is that these quantitative relations imply that "whatever has its own faculty (*dunamin*) applied to itself (*pros heautou*) will also have that being (*ousian*), to which the faculty was directed (*pros hên hê dunamis autou*)."[31] Having now made this principle explicit, Socrates calls Critias's attention again to mental faculties, and thus introduces his final set of examples: hearing and sight. Socrates's *reexamination* of the mental faculties actually suggests that it is not sufficient to model self-knowledge on quantitative relations.[32] But just as the quantitative relations exemplify, Socrates suggests that these two capacities, hearing and seeing, must have the "being"—what I earlier called the attribute of the distinct intentional object—at which their faculties are directed, namely, sound and color. Unlike his first argument, in which he asked Critias to imagine a hearing that hears no sound and a seeing that sees no color, Socrates now points out that a hearing, in order to be heard, must make a sound. For a seeing to be seen, it too must have color.[33]

In returning to the mental faculties, we thus are working with a different image of self-relation. When previously Socrates turned to the faculties to demonstrate to Critias what a strange notion they were entertaining, Socrates specified that the perplexity arose from the existence of a vision that was not of any color but just of itself and the other visions and nonvisions. Likewise for hearing, Critias had earlier agreed that this self-relating hearing would hear no sound.[34] But the exact opposite is affirmed here. If a hearing is to hear itself, it must also hear "by having a sound."[35] Socrates's new argument therefore causes us to wonder again what the distinct, intentional object of knowing is, such that knowledge could know itself, by having the attribute of that object.

It is here that Socrates asks Critias if he "sees" how some of the cases they have discussed are impossible, while others are "not to be trusted" (*apistetai*).[36] This talk of seeing is no mere joke. Socrates's use of the word "see" here, and all along, shows how connected *seeing* appears to be *knowing*.[37] We ourselves can "see" here that Socrates is asking Critias if he has not actually *learned* something about this knowledge they are seeking, and thus demonstrating the possibility of knowledge of knowledge, through showing the possibility of learning. Socrates also suggests that there is possibility here, rather than simply impossibility, by claiming that *only some* cases seem to be impossible, while others seem to provoke only "distrust" to some but not to others.[38] Finally he mentions examples—"heat burning" and "motion moving itself"—that seem utterly unlike the quantitative relations and thus not impossible.

But Critias may not be able to hold this stance of "distrust" toward these relations, for his view of knowledge is based on his conviction that the hierarchical, architectonic *epistêmai* are the true models of wisdom. This view may not be the right kind to allow for such a middle ground as "distrust." But Socrates may know what he knows and does not know, for he here claims that they have reached the limits of their knowledge, and he will call for some "great man" to solve the problems that face him and Critias. In doing so, he is demonstrating in deed the possibility he hopes to establish in speech, and he is explicitly stating that he makes room for possibility, saying what problems need solutions in order to continue their investigation into *sôphrosunê*. Here is a moment, therefore, for Critias to show whether he is capable of genuine wonder about this perplexity and admit his ignorance, and then possibly show courage and attempt to turn his soul toward what might be its real good.

C. Some Great Man Is Needed

Whereas Critias sees only the impossibility of knowledge of knowledge, Socrates suggests that these problems can be solved by one with the right understanding. He calls for "some great man" (*megalou tinos andros*) to aid them in their inquiry: "So, my friend, we need some great man to make an adequate division (*diairêsetai*) among all things, (1) whether none of the beings (*tôn ontôn*) can by nature apply its own faculty (*dunamin*) to itself but only toward something else, or whether some can, but others cannot. (2) And if there are some things that have [their power] toward themselves, whether the *epistêmê* which we say is *sôphrosunê* is among them."[39] Socrates suggests that the inquiry into self-relation *simpliciter* must precede the inquiry into *sôphrosunê* and self-knowledge. Given the examples of the quantitative relation, there are really only two possibilities: either nothing is capable of self-relation, or only some things are. We need to know which is the case, and if the latter, whether Critias's *epistêmê* is in the self-relating category. Socrates "distrusts" himself to sufficiently determine these questions and concludes once again that he cannot say whether it is possible that there should be an *epistêmê* of *epistêmê*.[40] Again he thereby indicates that he does not think impossibility has been shown and that the proper attitude to take *until one has investigated* is "distrust." Socrates thus puts the question to Critias. Can he be the knowing great man who can solve these problems? As Charmides watches on, Critias must admit his ignorance in the face of a question too difficult for him. But he does not do so nobly.[41]

Socrates puts the problem to the "son of Callaeschrus":[42] he must establish the possibility of this *epistêmê*, for he is the one, after all, who says that *sôphrosunê* is this very *epistêmê* of *epistêmê*, and of the lack of *epistêmê*. Reintroducing the "lack" here puts before our mind the real problem that Critias really has. He cannot combine his own conception of self-knowledge with the Socratic one. It is no coincidence that Socrates refers to him here as the son of Callaeschrus, for this recalls Critias's connection to his family and his earlier claim that *sôphrosunê* is connected to doing "ones' own things." But earlier it remained opaque how to give meaningful content to the phrase "one's own things," and Critias's actions toward his ward Charmides betrayed that he himself did not sufficiently understand "his own things." Critias himself is capable of self-relation, it seems, insomuch as his behavior and account of *sôphrosunê* both point to a commitment to praise *his own* wisdom and authority. But such self-relation does not seem to reveal *self-knowledge*.[43] Critias demonstrates that he does not understand his own claims to wisdom and also can't see or acknowledge his own limitations.[44] He lacks both knowledge of knowledge and knowledge of ignorance. Accordingly, Critias cannot show the possibility of self-knowledge, but unfortunately his perplexity does not run deep:

> Now when Critias heard this and saw my perplexity (*aporounta*), then—just like people who start yawning when they see other people doing it—he seemed to be compelled (*anankasthênai*) by my perplexity (*aporountos*) and to be seized by perplexity himself. But since he always valued his reputation (*eudokimôn hekastote*), he was ashamed (*êskuneto*) in front of those present and he was not willing to admit to me that he was unable (*adunatos*) to determine the questions which I asked him, and said nothing clear, covering up (*epikaluptôn*) his perplexity (*aporian*).[45]

Critias saw no problem earlier but now has caught the apparently contagious perplexity that grips Socrates. Socrates's account of this "yawn-catching" perplexity reveals that it is only a superficial admission of ignorance that Critias makes. Critias is *compelled* into such perplexity only by the behavior of Socrates. But because he so highly regards the views of others, because his *thumos* dominates him, he is unable to expose himself, even to himself, *as unable*. Critias's experience of perplexity does not go deep enough for him to forsake his love of his reputation, in favor of admitting ignorance and getting at the truth of the matters they are discussing. So nothing important that Socrates has said has had any effect on his soul. Though Critias's "yawn perplexity" may reveal that he cares what Socrates thinks and how he looks to others, it does not reveal that he is truly aware of his ignorance, nor that he desires to learn the truth. He hides himself not only from those who are observing but also from himself. But his attempt to conceal himself fails to hide who he is from those listening. For his very attempt to hide reveals to those watching who he truly is: one whose *thumos* prevents him from engaging in philosophy.[46]

Socrates has now presented to Critias the opportunity to demonstrate practically the theory he has been putting forward, to act in a way that would imply the possibility of knowledge of knowledge. Socrates is essentially asking Critias and those watching if the perplexity that confronts them instills *wonder* that would inspire and motivate one to seek wisdom by pursuing the fundamental questions about knowledge and the soul.[47] But Critias does not experience such wonder, and it is related that he cannot explain self-relation. His desire for the approval of others actually chains him to a condition of the soul from which wonder could potentially liberate him. The dialogue thus shows dramatically what Critias failed to establish in the discussion itself. His lack of understanding and the way he lives his life are intertwined, and Charmides himself must break free of both Critias's perverted understanding of the beautiful and the good as well as the practices that have shaped this, in order to attain an authentic and liberating self-knowledge. For Critias is incapable of the wonder that would lead to critical self-examination that might make this possible.[48]

It is thus no surprise that Socrates ultimately takes responsibility for the failure of the conversation to show what *sôphrosunê* is and what it is good for. In doing so, he suggests that Critias never really had any substantial contribution to this inquiry, and thus Critias has once again enacted what his speech has implied: his vision of *sôphrosunê* really is of no benefit whatsoever.[49] This could very well be the result Socrates sought to show to Charmides and those present: the end of this strange interchange shows that Critias is ignorant of his ignorance and that Charmides and those present—including the reader—should seek a better teacher than him, if they care about what is *good for them.*

Who then is the better teacher? Who could be such a great man? The reader of the dialogue may well wonder at the similarity here to a passage in Plato's *Parmenides*, where a young Socrates cannot meet Parmenides's objections to his view of the Forms. Parmenides calls upon a "very gifted (*panu euphuês*) man" to resolve the problems they have encountered.[50] It may turn out to be no coincidence that two such gifted men are called upon to resolve the problem of self-relation *and* the problems attendant upon the nature of the Forms. For the nature of the Forms has been alluded to in some way throughout Socrates's first challenge. In the *Parmenides*, for instance, the one is said to be paradoxically both greater and less than itself. Self-relation also seems to show up in talk of the soul. For one of Socrates's final images is that of a motion moving itself: such self-motion is given the name of soul in the *Phaedrus* and the *Laws*.[51] The result seems to be that the nature of the soul and the Forms seems strongly connected to the nature of self-relation. But who can explain it?[52]

It is beyond Critias's reach. For such engagement with "the beings" would require a great transcendence of his love of reputation, narrow view of knowledge and the good, and unwillingness to admit ignorance. In a word, the great man that Socrates calls for must be more *erotic* than *thumotic*, moved by a desire that pulls him beyond his own myopic attachment to what he holds to be his own things toward the greater whole in which he might see himself embedded, or better yet, which eludes his ability to grasp it in its entirety. Critias's view of knowledge, as Socrates has shown, is problematic in its self-related aspect, while it attempts to be comprehensive, all inclusive, and ignore what lies beyond its scope. But the Socratic conception, knowledge of *ignorance*, has not been under the same attack in this conversation. Critias has shown, and will continue to show, that he cannot make room for knowledge of ignorance, and through his "yawn perplexity" he shows that he is deeply ignorant of his own ignorance. Yet if Critias did know what he did not know, he would then *see* how his convictions mislead him to an illusory good. Such knowledge of ignorance might be the ultimate *self-relation* and presents a different ideal from the reflexive knowledge Critias has suggested: Critias's reflexivity, too, is mere "yawn reflexivity."

Further, Critias's failure to be the great man that can determine the questions necessary for a proper investigation into *sôphrosunê* stems from a failure to rightly grasp the nature of the soul.[53] Because he sees nothing beyond what his own *thumos* reveals, Critias attempts to erase the boundaries of the human world, *his world*, and his view of the good and self-knowledge are constructed out of nothing beyond this sensible, political realm in which he retains authority. But others who are not consumed by such destructive *thumos* may experience wonder at the realms that transcend their merely partial worlds.

Chapter Six

Is Knowledge of Knowledge Beneficial? (169d–173a)

A. Socrates's Initial Question (169d–170a)

In order to move the discussion forward, Socrates releases Critias from this shameful situation and suggests that they grant (*sunchôrêsômen*) the possibility of an *epistêmê epistêmês*.[1] The argument is now conditional: Socrates and Critias will assume the possibility of knowledge of knowledge, and then draw out the implications of this assumption, returning only later to examine the provisional assumption itself.[2] Instead, Socrates now asks how this conception of self-knowledge as "knowledge of knowledge" is linked to the Socratic notion of "knowledge of ignorance": "Come then, if this [*epistêmên epistêmês*] is perfectly possible, how is someone better able to know what he knows and does not know (*eidenai ha . . . ode kai ha mê*)? For this, I think, we said to be self-knowledge (*to gignoskein hauton*) and *sôphrosunê*. Or not?"[3] In this introductory statement, Socrates has put forth the two conceptions—*epistêmê epistêmês* and knowing what one does and does not know—and suggested that the two may not in fact be identical. Again, the former view is the one Critias expounded in his discussion of the Delphic Oracle. The latter view came along with Socrates's small addition at 166e. Socrates's question here implies that even if one grants the possibility of the former, one is not thereby given the possibility of the latter.[4] Critias, in fact, will not be able to get to the Socratic view from his own standpoint. The result of this will be that it is not Socrates's conception of *sôphrosunê* that is refuted in this section of the dialogue but only that of Critias.[5]

This is further confirmed by the answer Critias now makes to Socrates. "By all means (*Pane ge*)," he responds to Socrates, and then explains himself: "And it follows (*sumbainei*), Socrates, for if a man has an *epistêmê* of this sort, he would be the same sort of man as that which he has. Just as whenever someone has quickness, he is quick, and whenever he has beauty, he is beautiful (*kalos*), and whenever he has knowledge (*gnosin*), he knows. And whenever he has a knowledge that is of itself, then he will be, I think, a man who knows (*gignoskôn*) himself."[6] Critias's answer is puzzling. It does not in fact seem to address the very question that Socrates has put to Charmides. Socrates assumed the possibility of *epistêmê epistêmês*, and then asked how it leads to knowledge of ignorance, which they had taken to be the meaning of self-knowledge and *sôphrosunê*. Critias now responds by saying that of course this follows, because whoever has a knowledge of itself, will thereby have a knowledge of himself. Critias has completely overlooked or ignored the brunt of Socrates question. Whereas Socrates was concerned with establishing the link between *epistêmê epistêmês* and knowledge of ignorance, Critias's response only addresses the issue of the link between *epistêmê epistêmês* and knowing oneself. Knowledge of ignorance is still not at the forefront of Critias's mind.[7]

But Critias is not concerned with knowledge of ignorance because he sees knowledge as a possession—akin to his "own things." Critias has said that both beauty and self-knowledge are things one has, and this compels readers to wonder how properly acquisitive our relation to beauty and self-knowledge really are. His answer here harks back to the earlier discussion between Socrates and Charmides. For the two examples Critias suggests in explaining how *epistêmê epistêmês* leads to self-knowledge are quickness and beauty. Both were terms used to refute Charmides's first superficial definition, *sôphrosunê* as quietness. It was the superior "beauty" of "quickness" in action that brought Charmides to admit that quietness by itself was no more *sophron* than not. It is impossible to hear Critias talk about beauty without recalling that it is the captivating trait that Critias and everyone else had attributed to Charmides. But all this takes place before Critias watched his young ward manhandle his own doctrines. Critias's answer therefore betrays more of his anger at the youth over whom he has lost control. He is here attempting to demonstrate that this knowledge does indeed belong to him, and so therefore should Charmides.

But Socrates makes clear that Critias has not, in fact, grasped the meaning of his question, and further indicates that there is still a gap between "knowledge of knowledge" and "knowledge of ignorance": "This,

I said, I do not dispute (*amphisbêtô*), that when someone has that which knows itself (*to hauto gignôskon*), he will know himself, but having this how is it necessary to know what he knows and does not know?"[8] This is the main issue that concerns Socrates, for it will highlight the problematic nature of Critias's view of *sôphrosunê*.[9] Critias responds that these two things are the same: his own knowledge of knowledge, *epistêmê epistêmês*, and Socratic knowledge of ignorance are identical. This is a remarkable claim to make, for if it is true, then the former always leads to the latter. But Critias himself, if he has the former, surely has shown himself not to have the latter.[10] Regardless, Socrates responds again by averring his ignorance: "Perhaps, I said, but I worry I am the same (*homoios*). For I still do not understand (*manthanô*) how this is the same thing as knowing what one does and does not know."[11] Again Socrates seems to show *sôphrosunê*: he knows what he doesn't know, for he has just said that he does not know what the bridge is between *epistêmê epistêmês* and knowledge of ignorance, and for the third time Socrates asks Critias to establish this link, and finally Critias listens. His answer, on finally hearing Socrates's question, is telling: "How do you mean? (*Pôs legeis*)"[12] Critias sees no problem here, and so Socrates will begin his first of two arguments in response to Critias's claim to derive the Socratic description of self-knowledge from the Critian. His first argument is meant to show that Critias's account of an *epistêmê epistêmês* will not be able to explain what a person knows and does not know. His second argument is more general than the first[13] and will establish that the possession of *epistêmê epistêmês* will not enable its possessor to know anything about *any other knowledge* except itself. *Sôphrosunê*, if it is an *epistêmê epistêmês* as conceived by Critias, turns out to be useless.

B. Argument One (170a–170e)

Socrates asks Critias, "Will an *epistêmê epistêmês*, if such exists, be anything more than the ability to determine (*diairein*) whether one of these things is *epistêmê*, and the other is not *epistêmê*?" Critias says that it is nothing but this.[14] Socrates then introduces the examples of the *epistêmai*—and lack of *epistêmai*—of health and justice, asking Critias whether these are the same as each other. When Critias responds that they are not, they then agree that the former is medicine (*iatrikê*) and the latter politics (*politikê*).[15] Socrates's point in bringing up these examples is to remind Critias that the other *epistêmai* have objects that are distinct from the *epistêmê* itself, while *epistêmê epistêmês* is unique in its self-relation. Medicine aims at health; politics aims at justice;[16] but this *epistêmê* that Critias has suggested aims only at—*epistêmê*.

The problem for Critias's view here emerges with Socrates next comments:

> Therefore if someone has no added knowledge (*prosepistêtai*) of health and justice, but recognizes (*gignoskê*) only justice because he only (*monon*) has *epistêmên* of this, he will likely recognize (*gignôskoi*) about himself and others that he knows (*epistatai*) something and that he has some *epistêmên*, won't he?
> Yes.
> But how will he know (*eisetai*) what he recognizes (*gignoskei*), by means of this *epistêmê*? For he recognizes (*gignoskei*) health by healing but not by *sôphrosunê*, and harmony by music but not by *sôphrosunê*, and housebuilding by that art but not by *sôphrosunê*, and so it will be in every case, or not?[17]

The problem for Critias is that *sôphrosunê*, as an *epistêmê* of *epistêmê*, is empty of content. This appears to be so when Critias admits that any object that could conceivably be the object is known by another *epistêmê* or *technê*, but not by *sôphrosunê*. Therefore, if an individual possessed this *sôphrosunê* and did not in addition know (*prosepistêtai*) health or justice, he would know only that the politicians knew something but not whether it was justice or medicine or anything else for that matter. Now divorced from all subject matter, *epistêmê epistêmês* appears to be empty, narrow, and restrictive. This picture is quite surprising, though. Critias had aimed at a comprehensive, all-encompassing view of *sôphrosunê* that included itself and all the other *epistêmai*. But this first examination has revealed that Critias's view cannot bring him the good he hopes to attain, for his view of the *sophron* individual turns out to posit an individual whose "knowledge" is ignorant of all content. The Critian *sophron* will only know *that* he knows something, but in no way will his *sôphrosunê* give him knowledge about what he knows. This is the limit of Critias's "knowledge of knowledge." It shows that Socratic self-knowledge and Critian self-knowledge cannot be the same.[18] In fact, the *sophron* for

Critias seems closest to Critias himself. He seems to claim to know that he knows, but Socrates has shown that the gentleman is ignorant of what he knows and what he does not know.[19]

Now Socrates makes a *second* point:[20] if we suppose that *sôphrosunê* is an *epistêmê epistêmôn* (and not just an *epistêmê epistêmês*), that is, a knowledge of the *other* knowledges and not only a knowledge of itself, then the problem *still* is not solved. As has already been established, the "whatness" of each *epistêmê* is confined to each *epistêmê* that is in turn defined by its distinct, intentional object. Health is known by medicine, but not a by a knowledge of knowledge. If Critias were to possess this knowledge of knowledge, he would not actually be able to tell if Socrates is or is not a physician, only that he has knowledge of something.[21]

At the end of this argument Socrates conspicuously omits the third element of the definition so proposed: the *epistêmê* of the lack of *epistêmê*. He does not continue here by asking Critias to suppose that *sôphrosunê* is this *epistêmê* of ignorance, and then ask about its "whatness." Critias makes no protest to this by the time Socrates says "Let's consider it another way."[22] Critias does not say, "Wait, Socrates! We haven't talked about the *epistêmê* of the lack of *epistêmê*, whether it knows what it does not know, or only that it does not know." Again, Critias is still ignorant of his ignorance, which prevents him from attaining real understanding.[23]

C. Argument Two (170e–171c)

Having concluded that this *sophron* individual knows only that he knows and not what he knows, Socrates now makes a new argument, which moves to an even stronger conclusion: that this *sophron* individual will be unable to tell those who know from those who pretend to know.[24] The conclusion Socrates is trying to reach is not simply the specific application of the prior argument to the case of the real and pretend doctor.[25] Rather he is arguing toward a conclusion that will cut away the ground that was left at the conclusion of the first argument: now that he has shown that this "knowledge that" will carry no "knowledge what," he will show that such a state of affairs is impossible—there is no such "knowledge that" without "knowledge what," and so Critias's restrictive view of knowledge is exceptionally incoherent. On the other hand, Socrates suggests that these difficulties are not insuperable, and this is because Socrates throughout the argument moves from the Critian picture of *sôphrosunê* to the Socratic, which somehow escapes the perplexing incoherence that should plague Critias, whether he admits it or not.[26]

Socrates begins the second argument with a hypothetical conversation between this *sophron* individual and the man who is either a "true or false" doctor. But the mere possibility of this conversation is itself undercut by the problem that immediately emerges: according to Critias's view of knowledge, the *sophron* individual and the doctor are confined to their own discrete spheres of expertise—they have *acquired nonoverlapping knowledge territory,* and therefore cannot talk to each other at all. The very conversation in which one is supposed to distinguish the false doctor from the true one is incoherent. Such incoherence prevents the *sophron* individual from distinguishing the true doctor from the false one.

Socrates makes this argument by first claiming that the *sophron* individual will not talk to the doctor about medicine, for medicine is an *epistêmê:* while the *sophron* knows *epistêmê,* the doctor qua doctor knows only health and disease, but not *epistêmê* (and amazingly, the doctor is thus ignorant of medicine!).[27] The *sophron* individual will thus know that the doctor has an *epistêmê,* but to know whether this *epistêmê* is medicine, he must have discussed with him the subject matter of medicine, health and disease.[28] If he is to determine that the doctor knows these subjects, then he must determine whether the doctor "speaks truly and acts rightly" concerning them, but apparently only someone possessing knowledge of medicine could do this.[29] The *sophron* individual insofar as he is *sophron* is thus unable to distinguish the true doctor from the false one, nor any other pretender to knowledge from one who really knows. For he could only do this by having, in addition to his *sôphrosunê,* the same knowledge they have. Having *sôphrosunê,* he will be like the other craftsmen, only able to identify another *sophron* individual, whom Socrates here calls *homotechnon.*[30]

The result of this argument is thus stronger than the prior one. Earlier Socrates argued that the *sophron* individual would know only *that* he knows and not *what* he knows.[31] He then suggested that, given this state of affairs, the *sophron* individual would thus seem to be incapable of distinguishing the false doctor from the real one. Expanding upon this thought ("considering it another way"), he has now shown, if his argument is sound,[32] why this state of affairs not only seems to be the case but must be the case. And the stronger consequence for Critias is that his *sophron* individual cannot even have the bare "knowledge that" without having "knowledge what." For on this model, the Critian *sophron* cannot distinguish the pretend knower from the real knower, but is somehow still able to say that this "knower" does have *epistêmê*. That is, when he is confronted by the man who claims to be a doctor, he would somehow be in the position of being able to say, "Yes! This person has *epistêmê!*" (this is supposedly the "knowledge that" of this *sophron*), without being able to say whether his *epistêmê* is pretend or real (this is the elusive "knowledge what"). But clearly this state of affairs is absurd: for how could this individual ever say that the person *really* has *epistêmê*, when he does not have the resources to further say that it is real rather than pretend? What Socrates has now shown is that "knowledge what" cannot be so separated from "knowledge that" and the upshot for the Critian *sophron* is utter incoherence. He must take back his prior claim that he even knows *that* he knows. This *sophron* is only ignorant of his ignorance.[33]

From this argument come two very interesting results. First, contrary to Critias's hope, it seems that introspection is not enough. Critias responded to Socrates's repeated encouragement to "look within" by saying that this self-knowledge was the *sôphrosunê* that they were seeking. But now we see that "looking within" is not enough, if what one finds there is not in accord with the truth. As Santas says, this search for the definition of *sôphrosunê* reveals that truth and evidence are not worn on the sleeve.[34] But even more than this, it shows that the investigation requires the *right* sort of "looking within," which Socrates has shown will be subject to the critical examination from others.[35] When Critias looks within he sees that his original view, which aimed to be comprehensive in its all-knowing scope, now turns out to be empty and abstract. If this latter view is the reality beneath Critias's doctrine, then it turns out that Critias does not know himself, despite his attempt to "look within."[36] To look within and see the truth requires one to look without as well. [37]

The second interesting result from the argument follows right on the heels of this. The implication from the argument is that if one could ever find a definition of knowledge, and thus perhaps have knowledge of knowledge, it would not be the great boon we might hope it to be. On this model, it might be necessary to have this knowledge, but because it is so limited in its scope, much more needs to be "added" to it, if it is to do us any good. This model of epistemology, or even of self-consciousness, has an impact that is much more limited than we might have thought.[38]

We now can make sense of the strangest statement of this argument: that the doctor is ignorant of medicine.[39] For this is indeed a puzzling moment, since the very idea of the doctor who understands health and disease but has no understanding of medicine seems absurd. How could he have an understanding of health and medicine without the *epistêmê* of medicine, and how could he "have" this *epistêmê* and be ignorant of it? I believe this is a perfectly fair question, and on the interpretation I have here presented, it reveals the problem with Critias's conception of *sôphrosunê*. Critias's view of self-knowledge aims at an architectonic knowledge that is both hierarchical and self-reflexive and thus would have comprehensive knowledge of everything and itself. It turns out, however, that when it is construed in this manner, it does not reach beyond its narrow confines to be able to know any meaningful content. There is no room in Critias's account of "knowledge of knowledge" for "knowledge of objects," and thus it turns out to be an empty knowledge of nothing in particular, incoherent because it cannot even determine whether it *itself* is pretend or real, false or true. But this is not due to an error on the part of Socrates or Plato. It stems directly from Critias's views. That is, it is the empty and narrow Critian reflexivity that leads them to make such a counterintuitive and *illuminating* statement about the knowledge of doctors, which is a misrepresentation of knowledge due to Critias's ignorance.[40]

Socrates has not hereby called into question the Socratic conception of *sôphrosunê* as knowledge of ignorance, nor has he attacked the possibility of his own way of life. The conception being questioned so far is the Critian conception of *sôphrosunê*. It is Critias's self-related conception of knowledge of knowledge that has been on the table for the whole of Socrates's second challenge, while Socrates's small addition of "knowledge of ignorance" has hovered in the background, only alluded to and hinted at indirectly, as we discussed. The results of this argument regarding the limitations of introspection and epistemology thus apply to Critias's model of knowledge, and not Socrates's.[41]

Finally, the use of medicine as an example should remind us that Socrates himself "pretends" to know medicine at the beginning of his discussion with Charmides. He then talks at length about the proper understanding of the nature of medicine itself. Is Socrates's knowledge of medicine pretend or real, and how could we tell?[42] Socrates again brings up the doctor's knowledge of "disease"[43] in addition to the healthful, reminding us of Critias's earlier omission of "disease" and its analogue "knowledge of ignorance." Does not Socrates have some understanding of what *real disease* is? Socrates claims that this *sophron* individual, in his examinations, must be able to judge whether someone speaks truly and acts rightly. Self-knowledge is thus again connected to the way we live our lives, to our flourishing as whole human beings. Is this not what Socrates examines? Well, in the argument it is only a physician who can begin to do this. Yet Socrates has told Charmides that he is a physician.[44] It is not surprising then that Socrates says the knowledge of the doctor needs to be added to *sôphrosunê*: perhaps this tells us that the knowledge of the *true* doctor—the Socratic physician—and the knowledge of the true *sophron* individual (the one with Socratic self-knowledge) are one and the same knowledge. Critias is neither a Socratic physician nor does he possess Socratic self-knowledge. The question raised by this argument, then, concerns the possibility of Socratic self-knowledge. If Socrates has shown that Critias's conception of *sôphrosunê* is incoherent, how might the Socratic alternative, knowledge of ignorance, be explained to meet these objections, and be accounted for so that Socrates's own life activity is thereby not only understood but is itself saved from this Critian incoherence?[45] Critias will still not see this as the path to be followed, but perhaps Charmides is beginning to see that the self-knowledge of his guardian is no real self-knowledge. The young boy should look beyond "his own things" if he wants to have real and not pretend wisdom.

The argument now flows naturally into the benefit of *sôphrosunê*. For by now it is becoming evident that according to Critias's view *sôphrosunê* can do us no good. Recall that at the beginning of this venture, Socrates proposed to investigate the possibility and benefit of Critias's definition of *sôphrosunê*. Socrates's first challenge was mounted directly against the possibility of knowledge of knowledge, asserting the utter strangeness of the phenomenon of self-relation. Unable to solve the problem of establishing possibility, Socrates and Critias granted it and moved on. As we saw, the second challenge is an overt attack on the limit of this conception, and thus begins to suggest that it is of no benefit. But this overt attack on *benefit* again implies that Critias's conception is not *possible*, for its narrow reflexivity and lack of content renders it incoherent. This prompts Socrates to wonder aloud about the good of *sôphrosunê*.

At this point in the dialogue, the observer who is not consumed by *thumos* but instead gripped by wonder will pause longer over the question, How is Socratic self-knowledge related to knowledge of the good?[46] This much, we can say at this point, is Plato's response to wondering about the foundation of the moral and intellectual stance of Socrates. Plato has therefore raised a question about the Socratic conception of *sôphrosunê* and how it might survive the challenges presented to the Critian conception.[47]

Finally, it should be observed that Socrates's challenge here is addressed not only to the Critian conception of *sôphrosunê* but also primarily to one part of it: knowledge of knowledge. No mention is made here of knowledge of all the other knowledges.[48] Socrates's forthcoming challenge—what is the benefit of *sôphrosunê?*—makes clear that he is actually still aware of this aspect of Critias's view, and accordingly he presents an intricate argument, based on the ethical and political dimension of *sôphrosunê*, to deal with it. The argument takes direct aim, ultimately, at the root of Critias's vision of *sophrosune*—his *thumos*. Socrates has demonstrated to Critias that his view of *sôphrosunê*—as knowledge of knowledge—commits him to the view that the *sophron* individual will be in an absurd position: he will have the ability to examine another person's claim to possess an *epistêmê*, while being completely powerless to say *which epistêmê* it is. If my argument is correct, this results from Critias's flawed understanding of knowledge, leading to an unnatural division between "knowing that" and "knowing what." To further understand that this flawed conception of self-knowledge is rooted in the *thumos* of Critias, we must consider what comes next in the conversation.

D. The Greater and Smaller Benefit
of *Sôphrosunê* (171D–173A)

At this point Socrates asks the question that he earlier suggested as the second part of their examination: "Then what benefit (*ôphelia*) would there be to us from *sôphrosunê*, being this sort of thing?"[49] Socrates explains why this question will be particularly difficult for Critias by presenting two possible benefits of *sôphrosunê*. The first and "greatest" benefit of *sôphrosunê* is that of an error-free life. The second and "smaller" benefit is that it aids one in learning. These two benefits are not mutually compatible. In fact, Socrates gives us reason to reject the first view both when he presents it and in the next part of the conversation when he presents his dream of a city ruled by *sôphrosunê*.[50] But Socrates never raises doubts about the second, smaller benefit of *sôphrosunê*, which we will return to in part 3A. Critias responds to the description of the first benefit with an emphatic endorsement, but he is hesitant to agree that the second smaller one captures the real good of *sôphrosunê*. In what follows, I will show how Socrates uses both images to expose the *thumotic* condition of his interlocutor that underlies his endorsement of the first benefit, his hesitation to accept the second, and ultimately his failure to understand how *sôphrosunê* can be good at all.

What then does it mean to say that the greatest benefit of *sôphrosunê* would be an error-free life? Socrates reminds us that the *sophron* individual "knows what he knows and does not know, and that he knows the former, and does not know the latter." Socrates thus reintroduces the notion of knowledge of ignorance that had dropped out of the previous exchange. He also assumes that such an individual is able to examine another individual with regard to this condition, and claims that *sôphrosunê* would be the "greatest benefit" to us. This is because *sôphrosunê* would allow those having *sôphrosunê* as well as those who were "governed (*erchonto*) by us," to lead lives without error (*anamartêtoi . . . ton bion diezômen*).[51] Regarding any matter over which *sôphrosunê* presides, "we would not attempt to do what we did not know, but finding those who know we would put it in their hands (*paredidomen*), nor would we allow others whom we governed (*erchomen*) to do anything but what they were likely (*emellon*) to do correctly . . . having knowledge (*epistêmê*) of it."[52]

The governing of the household and the polis alike would be governed beautifully (*kalôs*),[53] and the result is happiness (*eudaimonia*) for all: "For with error abolished (*exêirêmenês*), and being lead (*hêgoumenês*) by rightness, in every action (*praxei*) men would thus necessarily (*anankaion*) be disposed to do beautifully and well (*kalôs kai eu prattein . . . diakeimenous*), and doing well (*eu prattontas*), they would be happy (*eudaimonas*)."[54] The city Socrates here describes is one that achieves true happiness (*eudaimonia*) for its individuals by expunging error from its midst, which creates the condition for all human beings to do well and beautifully. Critias emphatically agrees that *this* is why he said it would be good (*agathon*) to know that one does and does not know.[55] Critias sees in this city a community that is ruled by his hierarchical, comprehensive view of *sôphrosunê* as "knowledge of all the other knowledges."

This error-free society is in fact the *second* city that has been conceived in the dialogue so far. Socrates suggested another image in response to Charmides's suggestion that *sôphrosunê* might be defined as "doing one's own things," a definition that he stole from Critias in order to show up his guardian and divert the refutation away from himself. The first city, called the "egocratic city" by Schmid, is based on an "every man–every job" principle, which is Socrates's intentionally perverse rendering of the mysterious phrase "doing one's own things."[56] It was at this point that Critias could restrain himself no longer, as he watched his ward mangle his own beautiful words. The discussion now has led Socrates to discuss an ideal city with Critias, and it is significantly different from the city earlier described for Charmides. Consider Schmid's description:

> The first, purely private city is an anti-erotic dystopia of isolated, selfish individuals who apparently devote all of their efforts to cover and care for their naked bodies, so much so that they never even touch one another, much less engage in conversation oriented to truth and happiness. . . . It is a city without love or beauty or moral wisdom. But the second city includes many elements that look forward to the *Republic*: the presumption of mutual goodwill (at least among the rulers); the division not merely in terms of *technai*, but in terms of rulers and ruled, with the authority of the leaders apparently resting on their excellence; the notion that happiness is a function of "doing well" (*eu prattein*) and the identification of well-doing with action in accordance with knowledge; the quality of beauty as well as goodness; the assignment of work by merit.[57]

The city Socrates here describes with Critias is thus a much more human one, in that it is built upon the need for others and strives to actualize the parts of the human soul concerned with beauty, goodness, truth, and love. While the error-free society is meant to bring about happiness (*eudaimonia*), even if this, as I will argue, cannot be accounted for on Critias's model of *sôphrosunê*, the earlier "egocratic" city was built with no such end in mind. The earlier city served a purpose in Socrates's discussion with Charmides: it provoked his guardian Critias to join the discussion and submit himself to Socrates's dialectic. The new *sophron* city is thus a more serious image, carrying more significance than mere argumentative utility.

As Schmid suggests, the city built here not only points back to the previously constructed one but also bears strong similarities to the city Socrates conceives later in the *Republic*. Kahn even suggests that the picture here is foreshadowing the "one man–one job" principle that becomes the staple of the *kallipolis* in the *Republic*.[58] But while both the possibility and the benefit of this city are doubted here, since Critias cannot close the gap between "knowing that" and "knowing what," in the *Republic* the task is more positive: Socrates argues for both the possibility and the benefit of the city there.[59] It is obvious that some changes must take place in order to move from the present discussion in the *Charmides* to the elaborate discussion between Socrates and Glaucon and Adeimantus. For the time being, we should note, as Schmid does, that while the error-free city in the *Charmides* is built, in some way, upon the recognition of ignorance, in the *Republic* the emphasis is placed on the rulers' knowledge of the highest and other sciences.[60] This may make it seem that Critias's view is vindicated after all, but it will become clear in the remainder of the dialogue that this could not be the case. The problem with this error-free city, as Socrates points out,[61] is that they have just discovered that no such error-removing *epistêmê* has been found. Critias's flawed version of *sôphrosunê*, which could not move from "knowing that" to "knowing what," is utterly unable to do the greatly beneficial job assigned to it in this city. In other words, this picture shows that *sôphrosunê* will be a benefit only if it can do what the Critian conception cannot do.[62]

This is underscored by the ambiguous use of "*eu*" at 172a, which Tuckey observes.[63] For Socrates suggests that all the citizens in this polis would "do well" (*eu prattein*), on account of doing only what they know. But while it is clear that one would do "well" in the sense that one would achieve success in one's *craft* without error, it is less clear how *this* doing well would lead to the doing well that is happiness (*eudaimonia*). That is, this city seems to achieve "technical perfection" through its "lack of scientific error," but Socrates now suggests that this by itself does not seem to ensure human happiness.[64] No *epistêmê* has been found to move us from technical perfection in each knowledge to happiness itself, or from craft precision in each skill to moral excellence. Critias has shown, contrary to his hopes, that his earlier move from what is well *made* to what is well *done*, cannot in fact be grounded in the view of the good—as equivalent to what is "one's own"—which he had earlier espoused. He is still hampered in that he takes no view of the whole. He sees only a part.

In sum, the city Socrates has constructed here is meant to show that the Critian conception of a ruling knowledge, a seemingly comprehensive *technê*, is not actually able to bring about one's good. Although Critias is attracted to the "great" benefit of *sôphrosunê* as a self-certain *epistêmê* that produces an error-free life, he is compelled to agree that such a benefit rests only on the possibility of a knowledge earlier found to be impossible. Finally, Critias says, "I see."[65]

The error-free city is therefore suspicious. But Socrates has not *yet* rejected it. He has shown Critias only that its possibility rests upon establishing the possibility of a meaningful "knowledge of knowledge." If a "great man" were able to establish the possibility of this knowledge of knowledge, then we have no reason *yet* to assert that that there is anything fundamentally incoherent about the claim that the error-free life is the grand benefit of *sôphrosunê*. Socrates will raise precisely this objection as the conversation moves forward. But he does so only after first asking Critias to consider a "smaller" benefit of *sôphrosunê*, his second image.

Socrates describes the second image in this way:

> Well then, I said, is this the good (*to agathon*) of knowing (*epistasthai*) *epistêmê* and the lack of *epistêmê*—which we are now finding (*heuriskomen*) to be *sôphrosunê*—namely, that the man having this, will learn (*mathêsetai*) whatever he learns more easily and all things will appear to him more clearly (*enargestera*), since in addition to each thing which he learns, he beholds (*proskathorônti*) the *epistêmê*; and concerning the things which he has learned himself, he will examine (*exetasei*) others more beautifully (*kallion*), while the ones examining (*exetazontes*) *without* this [*epistêmê*] will do this in a more feeble (*asthenesteron*) and paltry (*phauloteron*) way? Are these the sorts of benefits we will have (*apolausometha*) from *sôphrosunê*? And are we looking for (*blepomen*) something greater and are we seeking (*zêtoumen*) it to be something greater than it really is?[66]

Socrates puts forth an image that aims for a "smaller" benefit of *sôphrosunê* than was previously called for in the image of the error-free society. Now he claims two boons for us if we actually have this virtue. First, the *sophron* individual will learn more easily: because he "beholds" the *epistêmê* itself, he will understand things "more clearly." Second, having learned these things, he will then be able to examine others more beautifully[67] than the person who lacks *sôphrosunê*. These, Socrates suggests, may indeed be the truest benefits of *sôphrosunê*, while their earlier notion had mistaken it for something "greater than it is." Critias responds only: "Perhaps" (*tacha*).[68] It is significant that Critias is hesitant to accept this suggestion. It does not fulfill his grand aspiration for a comprehensive knowledge that entitles the one who possesses it to rule over a utopian society.

Socrates now continues the conversation by saying that the joint inquiry of Critias and Socrates has been useless (*hêmeis ouden chrêston ezêtêsamen*).[69] He says this is so because he observes (*kataphainetai*) some strange things (*atop' atta*) about *sôphrosunê*, if it is indeed the way they have been describing it. Socrates now says that, if we assume that an *epistêmê epistêmês* is possible, and that *sôphrosunê* is the knowledge of knowledge and ignorance (*to eidenai ha te oide kai ha mê oide*), then we must still inquire whether *sôphrosunê* will be of any profit (*onêsis*) to us. For he now suggests that he and Critias did not "beautifully agree (*ou . . . kalôs hômologêkenai*)" in their calling *sôphrosunê* a great good (*agathon*).[70] The "greater" benefit of *sôphrosunê*, which seemed so *attractive*, led to a step in the dialogue between Critias and Socrates that was *not beautiful*. What seduces Critias is not what is really beautiful, even if it appears to be on first glance. Recall that Critias and Socrates made this agreement because it seemed good to them in the management of the household and the city that each should do what he knows and hand over everything else to others who know: *sôphrosunê* seemed good, for it created a knowledge-based society free from error. So Critias now asks, "Did we not beautifully agree (*kalôs hômologêsamen*) [in saying these things]?" Socrates replies that he does not think so, and Critias echoes his ·earlier statement: "In truth, Socrates, you speak strange things (*atopa*)."[71] And Socrates agrees with Critias, for it is this very "strangeness" which he says prompted him to fear (*phoboimên*) that they had not been inquiring rightly (*orthôs*). For to him it now seems that *sôphrosunê* accomplishes nothing good for us whatsoever.[72] If Socrates is persuasive about this point, then it is the ultimate reductio ad absurdum for their argument. Not only has Socrates already shown, if subtly, that Charmides and Critias by their own admissions cannot possibly possess *sôphrosunê*, but now it seems that Critias, by his own admissions, would not be benefitted at all even if did possess it. Once again, it would seem that Critias does not know his own good.

Naturally, Critias responds "How so?" (*pôs de*)," as it becomes clear that the foundation on which Critias is standing seems in danger of crumbling. Socrates responds that he thinks he himself is talking nonsense (*lêrein me*) but says "it is necessary to examine what appears and not rashly disregard it, if one cares for oneself even a little."[73] He thus concludes a rather lengthy introduction to an argument that will attempt to show how unstable Critias's position really is. Before turning to the argument itself, we should pause to make some observations about this introduction.

The suggestion that *sôphrosunê* may be no good to us is surrounded on both sides by the mention of the strangeness (*atopos*) of this idea. Socrates prefaces his remarks in this way, and Critias responds to his remarks in the same way. *Atopos* does refer to strangeness, but its literal meaning is "out of place" or even "unlocated" or "disoriented." The very idea that Socrates is introducing—that *sôphrosunê*, by this argument, may indeed not be good for us—is one that has no place in our conceptual framework, if you will. The idea itself seems to have no place, for our understanding of ourselves has *no place for it*. If it is true that *sôphrosunê*, understood as some kind of self-knowledge, is not good for us, then it seems that we neither understand what is our own good, nor have we really understood ourselves. The idea is *atopos*, for if it is true, it renders us *atopos*. *We* have become dislocated, if this argument is correct. We do not know where, or even who, we are.[74]

But we should ask, in examining the argument, whether this "dislocation" or "lack of orientation" applies to the Socratic conception of the benefit of *sôphrosunê* or to that of Critias. Critias has not yet even seen the "strangeness" that Socrates is on the verge of describing. His understanding is only partial: he does not see the whole. The agreement between Socrates and Critias, which Socrates is now claiming not to be "beautiful" (*kalos*) may be rooted in this lack of understanding, and lack of self-knowledge, on Critias's part. We will now see that there is a "nonbeautiful agreement" not only in the agreement between Critias and Socrates in the conversation but between Critias and Socrates *themselves*. To ally Critias with Socrates is to do something ugly. Their visions, ultimately, of self-knowledge and the good cannot be put together in a way that is anything other than monstrous. If one "cares for oneself even a little,"[75] one must wonder about the perplexing reality that renders one *atopos*. For if we truly care about ourselves, and our account of the world seems to leave us truly "dislocated," should we not seek to reunderstand what we thought we knew about ourselves? This is the question raised for the philosophically minded observer of the conversation—whether it be Charmides, or Socrates's unnamed addressee to whom this story is narrated, or Plato's reader. We have begun to see reasons that taking the question seriously, as a question, is connected to the very achievement of Socratic *sôphrosunê*. We must hold on to this thought as Socrates explains how the Critian ideal is in fact incompatible with it.

Chapter Seven

Socrates's Beautiful Dream? (173a–174b)

Critias says Socrates's words about self-care and examination are in fact beautifully (*kalôs*) spoken, and so Socrates reports to him his dream, in which he again describes a city that is in most parts similar to the previously constructed one:[1]

> Hear then, I said, my dream (*onar*), whether it has come through horn or ivory. For if *sôphrosunê* really ruled over (*archoi*) us and were as we are now defining it, then everything would be done according to knowledge (*epistêmas*), and neither would someone who says he is a pilot—but isn't—deceive us, nor would a doctor or general or anyone else who pretended to know (*eidenai*) what he does not know escape our notice. These things being so, would they not result in our having better bodily health than we do now, and safety in the dangers of the sea and war, and wouldn't we have dishes and all our clothes and shoes and things skillfully (*technikôs*) made for as, and many other things, because we are using (*chrêsthai*) true craftsmen? And if you like, let us concede (*sunchôrêsômen*) that prophecy (*mantikên*) is the knowledge (*epistêmên*) of what is to be (*tou mellontos esesthai*), and that *sôphrosunê*, knowing it (*epistatousan*), will keep away impostors, and set up the true seers (*manteis*) as prophets (*prophêtas*) of the future. Thus equipped, I grant (*hepomai*) that humankind (*to anthropinon genos*) would indeed act and live (*zôiê*) according to knowledge (*epistêmonôs*)—for *sôphrosunê*, guarding over it, would not allow

ignorance (*anepistêmosunên*) to creep in and be our accomplice. But that acting according to knowledge (*epistêmonôs*), we would thus do well and be happy (*eu prattoimen kai eudaimanoimen*), this we are not yet able to understand, dear Critias.[2]

In the guise of a dream, Socrates presents his biggest challenge to Critias, and to those listening to the conversation: if *sôphrosunê* is the supreme ruling knowledge, that grasps even what will come to be, it is still not clear how the life lived with this knowledge will be happy and good. It is truly an amazing moment: here we have Socrates asking his interlocutor, "Why is the life according to knowledge really worth living?" The preceding conversation raised doubt about the answer to this question, and it might seem shocking to hear such doubt from the mouth of Socrates. But as he says, if we care for ourselves even a little, we must examine what appears to us and not rashly disregard it, even if it appears to contradict what one holds to be good as one's own. How then are we to understand this latest conclusion of Socrates's?

Socrates's remark that the present insight comes from a dream immediately calls into question its epistemic status.[3] Socrates begins by making clear that he does not know whether the dream comes through horn or ivory. The reference is to the *Odyssey*, where Penelope reports her dream to a disguised, returning Odysseus.[4] Penelope claims that dreams that come through the ivory gate are deceitful, while those that come through the gate of horn come true. To decide whether this dream is true or deceitful, it is necessary to discern what it is really *about*. I will argue that this dream of Socrates seems to be, in fact, the fantasy of Critias: for the ideal human life for him is one that hopes to attain ignorance of nothing and thereby ground its own self-interested conception of what is good. Hyland is thus right to say that Socrates's evocation of a dream is an attempt to remove responsibility for it,[5] for indeed the one "responsible" for this fantasy is not Socrates but Critias. To go a step further, Socrates's evocation of a dream here exposes Critias's unconscious fantasy to those who are closely watching. As he so often does with his interlocutors, in bringing them to see what they are deeply committed to, Socrates is attempting to wake Critias up. The parts of Critias that were earlier glimpsed in bits and pieces will now be visible for everyone to see.

What then will it mean to call this exposed set of unconscious beliefs true or false, and decide whether the dream comes through horn or ivory? It could mean that we can call a dream false that purports something about the world that cannot be.[6] This will turn out to be the case for Socrates's dream here. But Socrates's use of the dream image is also evocative of Critias's lack of self-knowledge. In the midst of a dream, we are supremely dislocated, unoriented (*atopos*). It is not simply that we think we are awake: it is that the distinction between dreaming and waking has somehow left our conceptual toolbox. What we experience seems somehow "real," but it is not clear what this word means in the context of the dream. Socrates in the *Republic* suggests that in dreaming we mistake what is a similar thing for the thing to which it is similar.[7] Indeed, in dreaming there is a breakdown of our distinction between the thing itself and its image, between the apparent and the real.

Therefore, we should notice that it is in this "disoriented" state that Socrates presents what will turn out to be the deepest insight into Critias's view of *sôphrosunê*. For it is here, in this "dislocated" realm, where we will see Critias expose the most problematic aspect of his view of self-knowledge and the good. Socrates's dream will leave us with one of two options: the self-knowledge of Critias is either false or disoriented. In either case, a different vision of *sôphrosunê* is required if we are to reorient ourselves or say something true about ourselves and what is good for us.

Let us turn then to what the dream is about. In the first sentence, we can see the Critian notion of *sôphrosunê*. Socrates describes *sôphrosunê* as "ruling over" us and all the other *epistêmai*, and again drops reference to the knowledge of knowledge and of knowledge of ignorance. At the outset, the narrative therefore shifts the emphasis from knowledge of ignorance to the mastery held by one possessing the hierarchical, architectonic notion of self-knowledge endorsed by Critias. Critias does not comment that the model of agency Socrates has presented seems starkly different from his own.[8] For while Critias may hope that the rulers—among whom he perhaps ranks himself—are free and self-governing, here Socrates clearly describes them as being ruled by *sôphrosunê*. Ultimately, Critias appears committed to the notion that *sôphrosunê* is connected to a human being's self-mastery and mastery of everything around him, but according to Socrates the key seems to lie elsewhere: one must allow *sôphrosunê* to be master. Critias does not notice this. But if *sôphrosunê* were understood as Socratic knowledge of ignorance, then we would need to figure out what it means for such a knowledge *to rule us*.

This thread is not followed. For as Socrates goes on to describe the kind of life that results from possessing this error-free knowledge, it becomes clear that the Socratic vision of *sôphrosunê* has been lost, nor is it even necessary in such a dream society. The city Socrates describes is one that renders philosophical questions and philosophical wonder otiose. Mastery of ignorance replaces inquiry. *Sôphrosunê* is supposed to achieve its mastery over ignorance with the introduction of a kind of wisdom not yet mentioned as a definition of *sôphrosunê*—the wisdom of what is to come (*mantikê*).[9] It may seem odd that Socrates introduces this notion. But Socrates had already said to Critias that knowledge of knowledge could only yield for the knower a "knowledge that" such a person knew anything, and this turned out to be incoherent when Socrates demonstrated that a "knowledge that" without a "knowledge what" was inconceivable. This prophetic knowledge, then, is introduced because it is supposed to be the kind of "knowledge what" that Socrates and Critias were earlier unable to find. But Socrates is skeptical of the vision that he sees in his dream. He points out to Critias that he and Critias have not yet been able to explain how any knowledge is able to make human beings do well and be happy.

Critias responds to Socrates's doubt at the end of the dream by saying, "But you will not easily discover some other end (*telos*) of doing well (*eu prattein*), if you reject [acting] knowledgeably (*epistêmonôs*)."[10] This response by Critias aligns with the somewhat shocking words we have just heard Socrates utter. If indeed he has asked, "Is the life according to knowledge really worth living?," then Critias's response is quite reasonable: "Show me another life worth living, Socrates!" On the surface it seems that Critias is giving one of his most philosophical responses. He is suggesting that the only true *telos* of doing well is acting according to knowledge, and this does seem to echo things Socrates says: Tuckey, for example, suggests that Critias is directly referring here to Socrates's "axiom" that virtue is knowledge.[11] But why does Critias praise knowledge so highly, and what does he mean by it? The previous conversation has shown us that whatever Critias means by "living according to knowledge," it is not the knowledge of ignorance that Socrates has emphasized. How then does Critias himself understand this claim, and in what sense is it like and unlike the view of Socrates?

Socrates responds to Critias by saying, "Then explain one other small thing to me."[12] The "small thing" Socrates asks for is: *of what* (*tinos*)? If a person living according to knowledge does well and is happy, then what is this person's knowledge of? We should notice that Socrates does not endorse nor deny Critias's comment but asks him what the object is of this knowledge that is the *telos* of doing well. It becomes clear that Critias does not believe that acting according to knowledge makes one lead a happy life, but only according to knowledge of *certain things*.[13] Socrates thus reembarks on a rational criticism of the irrational Critian fantasy of *sôphrosunê*. Critias does not realize that this is the beginning of the same objection that has repeatedly plagued his conception of knowledge: just as his earlier notion—"knowledge of knowledge"—was so depersonalized and reflexive that it was empty of content, so too this new notion will be shown to be incapable of grounding the kind of benefit that he believes should result from possessing *sôphrosunê*.

In again asking Critias what this knowledge is *of*, Socrates also presses him again about certain crafts: does the knowledge of shoemaking or brassworking or woodworking bring about happiness (*eudaimonia*)? Critias's first response is definitive, "By Zeus, No!"[14] As Schmid points out, these crafts seem particularly focused on the shaping of physical matter, and such shaping is not the kind "doing well" that Critias has in mind.[15] One is also reminded here of Critias's earlier condescending words about the craftsmen who are as worthy of honor as prostitutes. The candidate Critias endorses is the one whom Socrates has just introduced in the dream city, the seer (*ho mantis*). Critias also has Socrates add that it is the man who not only knows all things to the come but also everything that has been and is, for no man knows more than he does.[16] Clearly knowledge of ignorance has vanished, finally, from the conversation.

The introduction of prophecy in the conversation could be a memento mori for some listeners, whether they be Charmides himself, the anonymous addressee, or Plato's readers. It is a reminder to us, potentially, of the intractable nature of human temporality and ephemerality. But Critias is attracted to this prophetic knowledge because it transcends these bounds. He endorses a knowledge not available to human beings, at the very least, from a phenomenological standpoint. To ascribe this capacity to a virtue is to claim for human beings a godlike power that clearly ascends past the limits of human wisdom. Why then is Critias so willing to accept this power as constitutive of *sôphrosunê*? Such a knowledge must fulfill his aspiration (*his dream*) for an architectonic knowledge that is a higher and thus more beautiful art than the base crafts he earlier rejected.[17] This shows that he is again, at the very least, rejecting any traditional notions of *sôphrosunê* associated with human epistemic limits. But perhaps more importantly, the acceptance of this power as a definition, or at least a pseudodefinition, of *sôphrosunê* carries with it a radical rejection of the Socratic viewpoint. This rejection is deeply rooted in the *thumos* of Critias. For in seeking to grasp within the scope of knowledge all that is to come, all that is, and all that has been, Critias is essentially positing that the truly *sophron* individual will be ignorant of nothing.[18] Although Critias has previously been unable to put together his vision of the good and self-knowledge, he refuses to admit his own ignorance in anything but a superficial way. In his assent to Socrates's dream, and his praise of the seer, we see Critias attempt to bridge the gap between self-knowledge and the good by changing the purview of self-knowledge from knowledge of ignorance to knowledge of everything. *Sôphrosunê* now emerges as the attempted eradication of ignorance and the dominant mastery of an architectonic knowledge that fulfills the *thumotic* drive of Critias. As Levine points out, "We have before us the formulation that more adequately captures Critian [*sôphrosunê*] in its most comprehensive sense, reflective of his unbounded ambition."[19] No move could be more diametrically opposed to the Socratic approach.

Critias thus praises the seer for his omniscience. Having knowledge of all things past, present, and future, he will do well and be happy. Such praise is indeed suspicious, for it seems to aspire to an ideal that is beyond the ken of the wisdom of humans, who are temporally bound. But this suspicion by itself would not be a criticism of his view. For even if Critias is attempting to transcend human limits, it could be claimed that such a transcendence brings one to the domain of the good. Perhaps, the objection goes, it is the case that the transhuman knowledge that Critias and Socrates here imagine would lead to the best life for human beings, if it were within reach.

But Socrates does indeed reject it. We can see this in his question to Critias: supposing such a human being exists, which knowledge (*epistêmê*) makes him happy?[20] Critias's position is problematic: even if we grant that the *sophron* individual will have knowledge of all things to come, "we do not yet understand" how this will lead to happiness.[21] This is because Critias has not yet been able to tie a notion of the good to any other knowledge, including prophecy. In the *Laches*, Socrates makes an argument that casts light on the problem Critias here faces: "The soothsayer ought to know only the signs of things that are about to come to pass, whether it be death or disease or loss of property or victory or defeat in war or in any sort of contest. But whether the suffering or nonsuffering of these things will be *best* for a man is a question which is no more for a soothsayer to decide than for anyone else."[22] There is a division here between events and their goodness, which for Critias appears as an unbridgeable gap. Critias keeps trying to get at the good by incorporating more architectonic knowledge. What he does not see is that greater mastery of self and others will not by itself be enough to lead us to understanding of the good, if it is not already guided by such an understanding. Critias has not been able to show how technical excellence leads to moral excellence, how "knowledge that" leads to "knowledge what," how one's own things are good.

Chapter Eight

Sôphrosunê as Knowledge
of Good and Bad (174b–175a)

Critias thus finds himself in a difficult position. He has claimed that the seer, who has knowledge of all things past, present, and future, will do well and be happy on account of this knowledge. But Socrates presses him about one thing "in addition":[1] which knowledge makes this seer happy? Will it be all of them alike? Critias says that it is not all of them alike that do so, and Socrates again introduces the problem of the *object* of knowledge—what among the events past, present, and future does this seer know?[2] Socrates produces examples. The first two are entirely rejected: neither the knowledge of draughts nor the knowledge of mathematics will be the *epistêmê* that makes the seer happy. Socrates then suggests the knowledge of health, and Critias responds, "More so (*mallon*)." Apparently, they are getting closer.[3] Critias must move from the technical realm to the moral realm: Socrates begins with examples of the crafts, narrowly confined to the shaping of physical matter, then widens the scope to activities that engage the mind—draughts and mathematics. He is trying to move Critias from the narrowly confined arts, with their partial perspectives, to a "holistic art of living," to a view of "human life as a whole."[4] In so doing, he makes clear that Critias's candidate of knowledge of all things past, present, and future is an incorrect understanding of the whole. It too turns out to be only partial.

Socrates then says a strange thing: "And that which I say (*lego*) most (*malista*) . . . is what?" It is natural to read Socrates's response here as saying: "Well and good. Which knowledge makes him most happy?" But it should be noted that Socrates speaks in the first-person singular—"I say (*lego*)"—before Critias answers. In giving his answer, Critias may be trying to say what he thinks Socrates always says makes human beings happy.[5]

It is only now that Critias says that it is the knowledge of good and of bad that makes the seer happy, thus submitting his final definition of *sôphrosunê*.[6] Notice that this is the first time in this current conversation that the knowledge of a negative has surfaced. Socrates has jolted something in Critias's memory, but again it has come forth without understanding, as Socrates's ensuing questions will evince. But Socrates now responds to Critias with the same word he earlier labeled Charmides: *miare*.[7] Just as Socrates had earlier called Charmides a "bloodstained one" for reporting the words of his guardian Critias without thinking them through and thus disengaging from self-investigation, now Socrates throws this appellation at Critias himself for perhaps reporting the words of *Socrates* without thinking them through. Socrates now claims that Critias has been leading him around and around in a circle and concealing his real opinion from him.[8] Even if Critias was not intending to conceal his opinion about *sôphrosunê*, he has not been honest with Socrates about his deepest thoughts about *sôphrosunê*. For all along, Critias had held that it was the knowledge of good and bad *alone*, not some other knowledge of all other knowledges, that produces happiness in one's life.[9]

Socrates is right to say that this claim has led them in a complete circle, for we have arrived once again at the notion of the good without properly understanding self-knowledge. The two notions have not been coherently put together by Critias, and again he makes a last effort to hold on to both. All along he has been unable to show how one leads to the other. He cannot justify the good of his desire for his own things by appealing to a notion of self-knowledge, nor can he justify that a knowledge of all things (ignorance of nothing) leads to true self-knowledge or to the notion that his own things are good.[10] The edifice he has constructed around himself will soon crumble.

It is important to note that Socrates never endorses the "the knowledge of good and bad" as a definition of *sôphrosunê*. Some commentators have still supposed that Critias has offered here, at last, what Socrates has been trying to lead him to all along.[11] Socrates thus begins his final reply to Critias, which closes the door on Critias's conception of the knowledge of good and evil. For Socrates now makes clear that Critias's conception of knowledge is still built on the model of a technical mastery of a particular subject matter, narrowly confined, discrete from all other masteries.[12] Socrates suggests that if one were to take away this knowledge of good and evil, medicine would still give us health, shoemaking would give us shoes, weaving would still provide clothes, and similarly the pilot's craft would prevent loss of life at sea, and the general's in war. Critias agrees, and here Socrates proposes the difficulty: though these crafts will produce their proper subject matter, "the chance of having each of these things well and beneficially done (*eu kai ôphelimôs*) will be out of our reach if this [*epistêmê* of good and evil] is lacking." Critias agrees.[13]

This argument that persuades Critias works by subtraction. If one takes this sole *epistêmê* away from all the others, then they shall still be effective somehow, but not beneficial. But how can this be? Is it really possible for these crafts to be effective without some knowledge of benefit? For example, a shoemaker can know when he has produced a bad shoe and may know this by some other evil obtained from the wearer of the shoe: blisters, perhaps. But then the shoemaker needs to know how shoes effect the *health* of the foot, if he is to make good shoes, or any shoes at all. Likewise, the doctor who treats the poor man who wears the shoes also must have a sense of the effect the foot sickness has on the whole person: does the ailment not seem to be worse if it prevents a marathon runner from walking than if it is just a mere discoloration of the toenails? And it does not seem that health is definable apart from some knowledge of benefit, more generally. In fact, Socrates's question here provokes us to wonder if it is even possible to have knowledge of anything's essence without also understanding in what way it is good. Might the knowledge of good be the source of knowledge about other things?[14] This connects directly to Socrates's speech in the prologue about Zalmoxian medicine, and it is telling that Critias still does not understand its import. For he sees no absurdity in this notion of craft knowledge without knowledge of benefit, just as he saw no absurdity in the situation of "knowing that" without "knowing what." Finally, it is impossible for knowledges to be utterly discrete. But the impossibility of the discreteness of these knowledges passes over Critias, revealing that Critias's understanding again mistakes his partial grasp for the whole.[15]

Therefore, Socrates now concludes that Critias's conception of the knowledge of knowledges and lack of knowledge (*epistêmôn . . . kai anepistêmosunôn he epistêmê*) is not, after all, *sôphrosunê*. Since *sôphrosunê* is something beneficial, and that which is beneficial belongs to another knowledge—the knowledge of good and bad—and belongs to this alone, then the knowledge of knowledges will once again be bereft of benefit.[16] Critias attempts to save his conception, by repeating that the knowledge of all others[17] will in fact be beneficial to us for it "rules over (*epistatei*)" the other *epistêmai* and would thus "govern (*archousa*) the *epistemê* of the good."[18] What does this mean?

Critias has attempted to subordinate the knowledge of good and bad to the overarching knowledge of knowledges. This attempt will fail. The very attempt reveals something important about Critias's character—he reveals an unrestrained, blind *thumos* in contrast to Socrates's self-aware moderation. But first we should consider why it does not work. Critias sees *benefit* itself as an added part, not included in the whole, and thus itself requiring a special knowledge. According to Critias, the good is yet another commodity on a par with all others, to be combined or not combined with other commodities but not in any way that would imply that the good is the source of the benefit of these activities. Socrates goes on to ask Critias—again—what the product will be of this knowledge that "rules over" the others, including the knowledge of the good.[19] Clearly it cannot be health, for that is the object of medicine, and *sôphrosunê* is not medicine but "only the knowledge of knowledge and lack of knowledge, and nothing else (*epistêmês monon . . . kai anepistêmosunês epistêmê, allou de oudenos*)."[20] Socrates then immediately moves from health to benefit (*ôphelia*). This too was given to another "craft (*technê*)" just now:[21] the *epistêmê* of good and evil. Critias has no way out of this argument, and there is no way out of the argument *for him*. To appeal to Critias's notion of knowledge "ruling over" another is no help, if Critias also maintains—however inconsistently—a conception of knowledge that isolates its subject matter so much that benefit is cut off from all other knowledges. This is the end of the argument with Critias, and the nature of *sôphrosunê* is discussed no further. The key questions again are: Does Charmides see that Critias's knowledge is of no benefit? And has Socrates himself really been refuted here?

Several commentators suggest that if Socrates's argument is sound here, then the proper conclusion to make at this point is that "knowledge of good and bad" is itself the proper definition of *sôphrosunê* that Socrates is looking for.[22] But even if this were true, it remains a task (and not an easy one) for the reader to show how knowledge of good and bad is related to self-knowledge.[23] The most important result for those watching the conversation, like Charmides, is that the self-standing Critian view of *sôphrosunê*, as *knowledge of knowledge*, is shown to differ from the knowledge of good and bad, and the link between them is mysterious. We should remain suspicious about Critias's vision of knowledge of good and bad. For in praising the knowledge of the seer, Critias claims that this knowledge of all things past, present, and future alone will make us happy. If he insists that this is true, then the knowledge of good and bad is actually otiose. It should also be kept in mind that such a knowledge transgresses the epistemic limits of human beings, and thus neglects the knowledge of ignorance entirely. Socrates would surely not suggest that human happiness resides in this prophetic knowledge more than in knowledge of ignorance. It has been clear throughout that Critias is ignorant of his ignorance, fails to know himself, and does not know what is truly good. How then can he claim, in Socratic fashion, that the knowledge of what is good and bad is what makes one happy?[24]

The challenge for Charmides, or the unnamed addressee, or the reader of the dialogue, is finally to show how self-knowledge and knowledge of the good cohere not only with each other but also with knowledge of ignorance. What Socrates has shown to Critias, repeatedly, is that he has kept sacrificing one notion for another. Commentators who have turned to "knowledge of good and evil" as a definition of *sophrosune* have been unable to avoid a similar difficulty, and thus in their very interpretation of the dialogue have fallen prey to the Critian circle themselves. I will show later that the only way out of this Critian Circle, and the consequent aporia at the end of the dialogue, is through coming to grips with Socrates's knowledge of *ta erotika*.[25]

Now we may ascertain why Socrates himself doesn't say that *sôphrosunê* is, indeed, this knowledge of good and evil.[26] For indeed, not only does he refrain from explicitly endorsing this conclusion, he specifically claims ignorance about the ultimate "answer" more than once.[27] Kraut suggests that this definition actually fails, though it is failing a different sort of test than the previous definitions have failed. Though Socrates had earlier refuted Critias by appealing to benefit, knowledge of good and evil could clearly not be so refuted. Rather, Kraut argues, it is because this definition cannot pick out those acts that are virtuous from those that are not, that the "knowledge of good and evil" fails as a definition of *sôphrosunê*. Though it "relabels" *sôphrosunê*, it "doesn't tell us what it really is."[28] What would such a criterion be? As we have seen, Critias has led Socrates in a circle, and the Critian circle is problematic: it reveals that Critias is unable to successfully bridge the gap between self-knowledge and knowledge of the good. It is this very failure that underlies the problem that Kraut notices: the definition that Critias suggests supplies no standard for right behavior because self-knowledge and knowledge of the good have still not shown to be tied together, or how they could be so put together.

Critias seeks moral expertise—certain knowledge of everything that will "rule over" the world around him. This moral expertise, built on the foundation of the technical model of knowledge, self-destructs as it incoherently transcends the epistemic limits of human beings. In aiming to be comprehensive and reflexive, yet narrowly confined and discrete, it amounts to nothing but absurdity: "knowledge that" without "knowledge what" and effective crafts without benefit.[29] In its transcendence of human epistemic limits, this moral expertise is clearly incompatible with the Socratic concern for knowledge of ignorance. The Critian notion of *sôphrosunê* remains problematic at the end of the dialogue. Critias's *thumotic* dream of an architectonic master-knowledge that subordinates all other knowledges, even the knowledge of the good itself, reveals that he is committed to a different vision of wisdom than is his interlocutor, Socrates. Critias finally reveals that he holds "his own things" above all other things.[30] The Socratic model of self-knowledge—a knowledge of ignorance that emerges when one is caught by perplexity in need of a community of interlocutors—begins to appear as the very opposite of Critias's *thumotic* vision. It is the further investigation of *this* self-knowledge and the activity that strives to achieve it that is prompted by the argument of the dialogue. What makes Socratic self-knowledge possible? And why is it good for us? These are questions provoked for the ones listening to the conversation. But Charmides and Critias will refuse to acknowledge such a provocation as the conversation now approaches its ominous end. We will return to this ominous ending of the dialogue after we first discuss the psychogenesis of the tyrannical soul in books 8–9 of the *Republic*. This analysis will shed light on Critias's character and definitions of *sôphrosunê* and also prepare us to fully absorb the ending Plato intends the reader to see.

Thumos and Tyranny in *Republic* VIII–IX

Chapter One

The Psychogenesis of *Thumos* and the Decay into the Tyrannical Regime (*Republic* VIII)

Like the mythic psychogenesis of *erôs* provided by Aristophanes, books 8 and 9 of the *Republic* offer another psychogenesis of the kind of *thumos* driving the tyrant, and, if I am right, Critias and Charmides. This psychogenetic account is nested within a larger story about constitutional decay: Socrates discusses with Glaucon and Adeimantus how the aristocracy (rule of the best) they have built in speech will eventually and inevitably be transformed into a regime whose chief characteristic is love of honor or love of victory, thus calling it a timocracy or timarchy. From there, this "Laconian" regime eventually transforms into an oligarchy, then a democracy, and finally a tyranny. Alongside the account of transformation of regimes in the city is an investigation into the corresponding soul type that is supposed to mirror the political constitution.[1] The entire project of the *Republic*, we should keep in mind, is an attempt to answer the question about the putative benefit of justice at the level of the individual soul. The story of constitutional decay (political and psychological) is therefore an investigation into the nature of the soul's desires and how the fulfillment of these desires to excess[2] ultimately leads to regimes that are *pathological*, through a corrupting transformation of the desires themselves. While the timocratic regime replaces the regime that loves wisdom with a regime that loves honor, the oligarchic regime replaces the regime that loves honor with a regime that loves money. Subsequently, the democratic regime replaces the regime that loves money with a regime that loves freedom. Finally, tyranny comes to replace the regime that loves freedom. Tyranny stands as the ultimate pathological constitution, in which the lawless desire that defines the regime brings about its own destruction.

The whole account therefore yields an inverse image of Diotima's crucial depiction of the ascent of *erôs*: here we receive not an ascent, but a journey downward, reminding us of the very first word—*katabên*—Plato uses to begin the *Republic*, and of the *katabasis* of the philosopher into the cave in book 7. But unlike these prior descents, this is a descent of *erôs* driven by *thumos* from *sôphrosunê* to madness.[3] In the current chapter, I will show how *thumos* plays a major causal and motivational role in Adeimantus's and Socrates's discussion of regime decay up to tyranny in the city at the end of book 8. Throughout the decay of regimes, Socrates indicates to us that *thumos* is the real heart of the polis, in all its forms. Educating, restraining, or channeling it is *the* political problem. In the following chapter, I will turn to the unhappy ending of this account: Socrates's and Glaucon's story of the destructiveness of *thumos* for the tyrannical individual in book 9.

Socrates himself signals to us at the beginning of the account that the story of constitutional transformation is rooted in a failure on behalf of the rulers to understand something about *erôs*, in their failure to properly understand and achieve the right breeding relations of the citizens.[4] The details Socrates provides here are intentionally confusing and unclear, and it serves to shroud the beginning of the story in some mystery, perhaps appropriately. As a result of this failure to have the right kind of erotic knowledge, the rulers of the aristocracy mistakenly mix the classes of the regime in a way that leads to war, hatred, and faction (*stasis*).[5] It is when such *stasis* has arisen that a compromise between warring citizens emerges in the form of a constitutional transformation: in this case, while the iron and bronze classes pull the regime toward moneymaking and the possession of property, the gold and silver classes pull the regime toward virtue. A "middle" way is found by the rulers, however: the ownership of land is to be distributed and held in private, while the workers who were previously supported by the guardians as "free friends" are now enslaved by them. As a result, the rulers now occupy themselves fully with war and guarding the ones they have now enslaved. On the political level, we can say that warriors (rather than philosophers) are now in charge of the city. The society has changed from one that is organized around the love of wisdom to one that is organized around the love of honor and victory.

At the psychological level, Socrates tells a story of the birth of the timocratic youth out of the disagreement between the youth's parents regarding the best life. His father, who eschews honors and ruling offices, aims to seek the pleasures of the rational part of his soul. Meanwhile, his seemingly more *thumotic* mother objects to her husband's passive willingness to be outdone by less philosophical souls. In this domestic conflict other educators encourage the young boy to gratify his appetitive and spirited part.[6] He thus comes to a "middle" way and turns himself over to his *thumos*, the part that "loves victory" and becomes a "man who loves honor."[7] So the birth of the timocratic regime in the city brings forth warriors as rulers (replacing philosophers), and the birth of the timocratic regime in the soul brings forth *thumos* as ruling (replacing reason).

At each successive stage of constitutional decay, it becomes clearer from the perspective of both the city and the individual that *thumos* lies at the core of this psychogenetic account, even in the post-timocratic regimes that are not explicitly ruled by *thumos*. On the political level, every regime change is brought about by excessive desire (*aplêstia*) for the good that defines it. But the role of *thumos* is crucial in this *aplêstia*.[8] A timocracy transforms into an oligarchy when the rulers, who now have private houses to amass wealth and material goods like never before, eventually change the laws in their favor, by instituting a property qualification for those who rule.[9] On this account, poverty thus does not arise naturally but is a consequence of the rulers' *pleonectic* desire to transcend the limits of their previous regime. It is essential to this account that "wealth is in tension with virtue," as Socrates says, and that the more *honorable* they find money, the less *honorable* they find virtue.[10] Socrates does not argue for the necessity of this, but Adeimantus agrees wholeheartedly. If they are right, then it is clear that rulers who are caught up weighing the relative honor of virtue and money will "finally become lovers of moneymaking and money; and they praise and admire the wealthy man . . . while they dishonor the poor man."[11] It is the rulers' *thumos* that calls upon them to expand and propagate their power, now in the form of money. It is also *thumos* that motivates them to seek the reward of honor for being rich and the punishment of dishonor for being poor. It is clear that Socrates sees this as a change for the worse. The city is now composed of rich and poor, and so is no longer properly one city, but two.[12] If, according to Aristophanes's speech, *thumotic erôs* longs for a lost whole, then this city will fail to achieve this dream for its citizens. Instead, this regime is the first to create what Socrates calls "the greatest of evils": "Allowing one man to sell everything that belongs to him and another to get hold of it; and when he has sold it, allowing him to live in the city while belonging to none of its parts, called neither a moneymaker, nor a craftsman, nor a knight, nor a hoplite, but a poor man without means."[13] Such citizens are no longer properly citizens at all. The greatest evil of the oligarchy is that it allows its citizens to fall below what we might call a poverty line. There is no safety net for such people in an oligarchy, and they lose their status as participatory members in the society, becoming nothing but spenders. The oligarchy thus creates an entirely new class of people in the city, whom Socrates calls drones.[14] The drones are created by yet another of the rulers' actions that we can see is *thumotically* motivated and justified. For it is the desire for wealth *without bounds* that encourages and perhaps even necessitates the creation of the drone class. Some of these disenfranchised and discontented inhabitants (such as beggars) are barely noticeable by most of the city, but many drones have stingers—they are the thieves and temple robbers who perpetrate crimes against the city out of desperation. And the response to these drones is purely *thumotic*: it holds down these stinging drones by force.[15] But Socrates suggests that these stinging drones are a symptom of the deeper disease that now plagues this city: a per-petual civil war (*stasis*) between rich and poor. Socrates claims that these stinging drones behave the way they do from lack of education and bad upbringing, and are a sign of a badly ordered regime.[16]

On the psychological or individual level, Socrates again turns to personal family dynamics to give an account of the emergence of the oli-garchic individual. Such an individual is the son of a timocratic man and initially admires and imitates his father. But if he comes to see his father dishonored in some way so as to lose his property, then his admiration for his father has to compete with his own hatred of his own new poverty and his fear of falling victim to a similar fate. Such an individual "thrusts love of honor and spiritedness out of the throne of his soul . . . and turns greedily to moneymaking."[17] We might say that the oligarchic individual pushes *thumos* out of his soul to make room for appetite. But we should resist the temptation to say that *thumos* has been supplanted by appetite in this story of psychological constitutional transformation. Bear in mind the young man's motivations: he possesses both fear of living out his father's fate and an aspiration for a life that is better than his father's fate. Both his fear and this aspiration are driven by *thumos*. Without *thumos*, the son of the timocrat would not feel entitled or deserving enough to reject the role model of his father and embrace a new one. Such an ambition bespeaks a kind of courage to make such a move, even if it is motivated, to be sure, by a deep-seated fear. And for the young man, even if he comes to live according to his necessary appetites only, it is crucial that his *thumos* is oriented toward the *honor* money gives him: he loves "the enjoyment of no other honor than that resulting from the possession of money."[18] While the oligarchic man is thus defined by a certain kind of appetite, that appetite is only able to pursue its object without the power of *thumos*. Like the oligarchic regime in the city, he lives with a perpetual civil war between the appetites in his soul, so that he too has to use *force* to control the appetites he fears.[19] Socrates goes on to say that such an individual remains afraid of the appetites within himself, with whom he continues to "make war" because these appetites themselves have a "love of victory."[20] The oligarchic man, who is miserly and yearns to become as rich as possible, should not at all be confused with the *thumotic* timocrat. It is appetite that rules him. But Socrates's use of such violent imagery in the soul of the oligarchic man brings out the *thumotic* valence in his whole psyche. Even in a soul defined by necessary appetites, the story suggests, *thumos* has significant causal power. As the decay continues, the role of this causal power only expands. Even though the democratic and tyrannical regimes and souls are ruled by a kind of appetite, the political and psychological significance of *thumos* increases.

In turning to a democratic regime, we can see the causal power and psychological and political consequences of *thumotic erôs* in its very inception:

> [Socrates:] Doesn't the transformation from an oligarchy to a democracy take place in something like the following way, as a result of the excessive desire (*aplêstian*) for the good that oligarchy sets down for itself—needing to become as rich as possible?

> [Adeimantus:] How?

> [Socrates:] I suppose that because the rulers rule in it thanks to possessing much, they are unwilling to control those among the youth who become undisciplined (*akolastoi*) by a law forbidding them to spend and waste what belongs to them, in order that by buying and making loans on the property of such men they can become richer and more honored (*entimoteroi*).

> [Adeimantus:] They do that most of all.

> [Socrates:] Isn't it by now clear that it's not possible to honor *(timan)* wealth in a city and at the same time to possess *(ktasthai)* moderation *(sôphrosunên)*, but one or the other is necessarily neglected *(amelein)*?
>
> [Adeimantus:] That's quite clear.
>
> [Socrates:] Then, by their neglect *(paramelountes)* and allowance of indiscipline *(akolastainein)* in oligarchies, they have sometimes forced *(ênangkasan)* well-born human beings to become poor.
>
> [Adeimantus:] Quite so.
>
> [Socrates:] Then I suppose these men sit idly in the city, equipped with stings and fully armed, some owing debts, some dishonored *(atimoi)*, and some both. Eager for revolution *(neôterismou)*, they hate and plot against the ones who now possess *(ktêsamenois)* what is theirs, and against others too.[21]

Thumos still serves important functions in this regime. Although the regime is now organized around the appetite for money, *thumos* is importantly weaponized in this pursuit. The oligarchy ensures that "honor" has a place but channels such honor only to the possession of property and wealth.

Because Socrates continues to insist that the honor of wealth is in tension with the honor of virtue, *sôphrosunê* itself comes to be dishonored by the rebels who are poor, and there is now properly no ethical restraint upon the behavior of the ruling oligarchs. But because this regime now praises money instead of virtue, there is also no ethical justification for the rich to be rich. Rulers are no longer philosophers or warriors and can point to no wisdom or courage that is their special trait to distinguish them from the ruled. The difference between the rich and the poor is a difference not in ability or power but only in artificial status. Recall that the drones with stings appeared because the rulers in the oligarchy would not limit buying or selling to create a safety net for its citizens. Because of this excessive desire for limitless wealth, some who had property become poor and disenfranchised. The class of drones is created by the transgressive desires of the rich. Meanwhile, the newly disenfranchised poor citizens now look at their rulers, and because they see no natural difference in power or ability between them and themselves,[22] they do not think their disenfranchisement is *deserved*. They themselves still believe they are entitled to the life the rich have, which is the *thumotic* motivation and cause for their thoughts about revolution. They are shamed; they don't have what they feel belongs to them; they rebel. When the poor are in private with each other, they converse about the lie the rich have perpetrated upon them to take their property, and they incite each other to revolt "for they [viz., the men in power] are nothing."[23] Democracy in a city finally comes into being through violence, motivated by a claim of entitlement to power. It is bloodshed, not debate or compromise, that transforms the oligarchy into a democracy. Only after a forcible taking of power from the rich by the poor, or after the rich surrender to the poor because they are afraid, does the new good of democracy—freedom rooted in equal rule—come to light.[24] Socrates, with pronounced irony, says that many people, such as "boys and women," would judge this regime to be "the most beautiful of all" for it is similar to a "many-colored cloak decorated in all hues . . . all dispositions."[25] In this regime, the love of freedom manifests in the diversity of characters appropriate to a city that allows all citizens to live as they please. The regime does not compel any to rule[26] nor does it compel any citizen to refrain from ruling. The democracy exhibits an unparalleled tolerance (*suggnômê*) for all types of self-expression, which its inhabitants find perhaps most pleasant about it. But Socrates is careful to point out that democratic tolerance and freedom have been achieved at a price:

> A disdain (*kataphronêsis*) of what we were exalting (*semnunontes*) when we were founding the city—that unless a man has a transcendent (*huperbeblêmenên*) nature (*phusin*) he would never become good if from earliest childhood his play isn't among what is beautiful (*kalois*) and all his practices aren't such—how magnificently it tramples all this underfoot and doesn't care at all from what kind of practices a man goes to political action, but honors (*tima*) him if only he says he's well disposed toward the majority.[27]

The regime without rulers, where citizens are all equal with one another in ruling and being ruled, is one that secures this freedom only after it "tramples underfoot" the notion that the young must be brought up in a beautiful way, where they are encouraged to pursue what is beautiful and become good before they take their turn ruling the city. Put another way, the democracy has no other value but tolerance, and therefore leaves individual citizens as arbiters of their own good.[28] In the first two regimes the good was that of the philosopher or the warrior, and we could thus say that an education toward wisdom or an education toward courage was beautiful and needed for the education of the potential ruler. The oligarchy eradicated the ethical restraint of virtue, and once a democratic revolution takes place, no virtue is required for those who rule. The only desirable trait of one who rules is that he will not interfere with the citizens' freedom and self-expression. A ruler who is interested in talking about what is good or beautiful apart from this is not to be trusted. The democratic regime has no respect for the notion of an exceptionally good individual who pursues what is exceptionally good. Such a notion is treated with extreme *disdain* (*kataphronêsis*)—it is beneath democratic esteem. We can see already that the love of freedom has not obviated Socrates's need to use *thumos* to explain the transformation of this regime. Indeed, its origin in violence, its dedication to the distribution of power, its elevation of the individual as the sole arbiter of what is good—all this betrays a *thumotic* desire for self-propagation as fundamental to the origin and nature of democracy. One might suggest that such a regime is the apotheosis of this *thumotic* urge, if it were not the case that tyranny emerges from it. But before we finally turn to the emergence of tyranny, we should consider Socrates's account of the democratic man.

At the individual or psychological level, the democratic man comes from a stingy, oligarchic father who insists that his son focus on satisfying his necessary desires only, while restraining his unnecessary desires that do not aim at moneymaking. In order not to "argue in the dark,"[29] Socrates and Adeimantus define the necessary and unnecessary desires in the following way:

> [Socrates:] Wouldn't those we aren't able to turn aside (*apotrepsai*) justly (*dikaiôs*) be called necessary, as well as all those whose satisfaction benefits (*ôphelousin*) us? We are by nature necessitated (*anangkê*) to desire (*ephiesthai*) both of these, aren't we?
>
> . . .
>
> [Socrates:] And what about this? If we were to affirm that all those are unnecessary of which a man could rid himself if he were to train (*meletoi*) from youth on and whose presence, moreover, does no good—and sometimes the opposite of good—wouldn't we speak beautifully (*kalôs*)?[30]

Socrates appears to distinguish between the necessary and unnecessary desires based on their dispensability and their benefit. It is not clear whether a desire must meet both or only one of these criteria to count as necessary. That is, if a desire is not dispensable but does us harm, should it count as necessary? Socrates introduces as an example the desire to eat, which he says is necessary according to both criteria, and Adeimantus agrees. Indeed, Socrates points out that the satisfaction of this desire is necessary for the preservation of life. Such a case is relatively clear. Socrates also suggests the necessity of the desire for a food that is beneficial to "good health" (*euexia*).[31] If we follow Socrates's reasoning, then any desire that goes "beyond" (*pera*) and seeks foods aside from this, which people could curb or eliminate through training and education, should be classified as unnecessary—such unnecessary desires, Socrates goes on to say, are harmful not only to the body but to the soul as well, "in respect of being practically wise and moderate (*pros te phronêsin kai to sôphronein*)" and its *sôphrosunê*.[32] Socrates does not explain in detail here how such desires interfere with the capacities of the soul for *phronesis* and *sôphrosunê*, but it is important to this account that *sôphrosunê* is in tension with the desires that exceed the natural limits of the necessary desires, which he now calls "useful for our works (*chrêsimous pros ta erga*)."[33]

The oligarchic father, we can now say, is focused on satisfying his necessary desires as now explained. He wants nothing more for his son than that he too will live a pleasant life satisfying such necessary desires. However, such a young man is bound to come across other people in the city who indulge their unnecessary desires. Socrates reminds Adeimantus that the oligarchy created a class filled with such people—the drones—who are ruled by their unnecessary desires and pleasures. When the young boy interacts with these drones, eventually, he will "taste their honey" and "begin his change from an oligarchic regime within himself to a democratic one."[34] The young man, like his father before him when he was young, now becomes the site of a civil war (*stasis*) within his own soul, as he internalizes the voice of his father and the voice of the drones, and when he thus "battles with himself" the voice of the father is at first strong enough to prevail, but soon the voice of the drones—which have multiplied in number and grown in strength—prevails, for the youth, who has no training or education in how to fight these appetites, has but a weak rational part with which to defend himself.[35] Because his reason is weak, the young boy's soul is won over by force—the drones are able to trick the youth with a transvaluation of values like the very one that took place during the plague that stands in the background of Socrates's conversation with Charmides and Critias.[36] The *thumotic* language of this maneuver is striking:

> And if some help from his own kin (*oikeiôn*) should come to the stingy element in his soul, those boasting speeches close the gates of the *kingly wall* (*basilikou teichous*) within him; they neither admit the auxiliary (*summachian*) force itself nor do they receive an embassy of speeches of older private men, but *doing battle* they hold sway themselves (*kratousi machomenoi*); and naming shame simplicity, they push it out with *dishonor*, a fugitive; calling moderation (*sôphrosunê*) *cowardliness* and slinging mud at it, they banish it; persuading that measure and orderly expenditure are rustic and illiberal, they join with many useless desires in *driving them over the frontier*.[37]

It is no accident that Socrates describes what takes place inside the young boy with the language of a battle in which the garrison of the young man yields to the invasion of the foreign force and then prevents the reinforcements from getting inside the castle walls to offer assistance. The battle inside his soul is one of strength in contention with strength. Moreover, the voices of the drones do not speak to the oligarchic youth about the delightful pleasures of the appetite in order to lure him away from the life of his father. Rather, their transformation of the son's language redefines the values his father has attempted to instill, values that he hoped would undergird his son's pursuit of necessary desires and pleasures. These values are now defined as "dishonorable" and are covered with mud. What the father called necessary, because he saw it as healthy, the voices of the drones now label as not only vice but impure and filthy. The voices of the drones are speaking to the oligarchic youth to arouse his *thumos* to fight with them. They seek to supplant the attachment to his own things, so that the son's *oikeiôn* will no longer "hold sway" over him. The son's path to becoming a democratic soul is not possible without the appeal to the *thumotic* element within him. Only such an appeal will prepare the way for the youth to reject the teachings of his father and claim that he is entitled to transgress such limits and define new ones, which is precisely what he does in assenting to the drones' transvaluation of values. Because neither the reason nor the spiritedness of the young boy has been thoroughly exercised through proper training and education, he is left without recourse to respond to the drones' appeal to his *thumos*. If someone says to him that some pleasures are *better* than other pleasures, "he shakes his head at all this and says that all are alike and must be honored on an equal basis."[38] We could say then that the law of equality governs the democratic man.[39] But the young boy's espousal of the law of equality comes about, somewhat paradoxically, from the *thumotic* rejection and disdaining of *thumos'* own natural alliance with reason. This allows him to transgress the limits that have been set up around his desires. And Socrates says he lives just like this, gratifying whichever desire happens to arise in him, moment by moment, calling this life "sweet, free, and blessed."[40]

But Socrates points out that there is a dark side to this sweet and free regime. The story of constitutional decay has been a journey downward: the democratic regime now sits only one step removed from tyranny, which Socrates sarcastically calls the "most beautiful."[41] We will see that the democratic regime as Socrates understands is, at best, a fragile state waiting for a possible tyranny to burst forth and violently overtake it. At worst, the democratic regime may actually plant the seed for its true and necessary tyrannical nature to sprout forth. In my view, if we pay attention to the story being told about *thumos*, we can see that Socrates gives us reason that the worst case is actually more likely. To begin, the tyranny emerges in a similar way to its predecessor constitutions (with the exception of the best). The corruption of the soul here arises from the excessive desire of *its* predecessor:

Socrates: Does the excessive desire (*aplêstia*) for [freedom (*eleutherian*)] and the neglect of other things transform (*methistêsin*) this regime and prepare the need for tyranny?

Adeimantus: How?

Socrates: I suppose that when a democratic city, once it's thirsted (*dipsêsasa*) for freedom, gets bad (*kakôn*) wine-bearers as its leaders and gets more drunk (*methusthêi*) than it should on this unmixed draught, then unless the rulers are very gentle and provide a great deal of freedom, it punishes them, charging them with being polluted (*miarous*) and oligarchs.

Adeimantus: Yes, that is what they do.

> Socrates: And it slings mud (*propêlakizei*) at those who are obedient, alleging that they are willing slaves of the rulers and also nonentities (*ouden ontas*), while praising and honoring, both in private and public—the rulers who are like the ruled and the ruled who are like the rulers. Isn't it necessary for freedom to go everywhere (*epi pan ienai*) in a city like this?[42]

The same *thumotic* disease that dissolved the oligarchy comes to plague democracy well—the *thumotic pleonexia* that leads to an excessive desire, this time, of what democracy defines as good: freedom. *Thumos*, as the engine of desire, is the cause for the democratic citizens to take themselves as the sole authorities to decide what desires to satisfy and how far to go in pursuing satisfaction. Put another way, the democratic realization of freedom culminates in the individual subject arrogating the right for himself to determine the limits of his own desires. In this passage, Socrates compares the arrogation to a wine upon which the democratic individuals become drunk. This drunkenness serves as a symbol of an unnecessary desire transgressing the limits of the good functioning of the soul. Notice that in their drunkenness, the democrats accuse of *miasma* any rulers who do not grant enough freedom. Like the voice of the drones before, they bring forth the language of filth and impurity to speak to the *thumos* of their fellow democrats. This is only confirmed when Socrates uses the same word to describe the mudslinging (*propêlakizei*) that the democrats inherited from the voices of the drones in the oligarchy, and describes the insult the democrats will launch at the oligarchic rulers: they should not *honor* them because they are nonentities (*ouden ontas*). They do not count for anything. It is *thumos* that most wants to count for something.[43] Do not follow such leaders, the democrats appear to be saying, because then you too will count for nothing. Such is *thumotic* motivation.

Socrates then expands upon what he means by saying that the love of freedom will "go everywhere" in a democratic society. In a purely democratic regime, the law of equality governs all. Children have no shame before or fear of their parents; teachers are frightened of students and fawn upon them, while students think little of their teachers; the old imitate the behavior of the young; the slaves are no less free than the ones who bought them; men and women are equal; animals, too, are walking freely in roads, bumping into whomever they like.[44] It is difficult not to laugh at Socrates's final suggestion about animals walking where humans walk. But in this humorous comment is a serious insight about the nature of the democratic regime. Socrates emphasizes this when he sums them all up and asks Adeimantus: "Do you notice how soft (*hapalên*) they make the citizens' soul, so that if someone proposes anything that smacks in any way of slavery (*douleias*), they grow violently irritated (*aganaktein*) and can't stand it? And they end up, as you well know, not at all attending to (*phrontizousin*) the laws, written or unwritten, in order that they may avoid having any master (*despotês*) at all."[45] Socrates brings to light here the real fantasy[46] of the democrats: the avoidance of anything that resembles a master over them. Such an avoidance comes from an almost paradoxical "softness" (*hapalên*). For it is through this softness that the democratic individual feels a violent irritation at anything that sounds like mastery. The softness of the democrat is therefore no ordinary gentleness but more like an extreme sensitivity[47] that becomes quite agitated at even the hint of its hated object. The *thumos* of the democratic individual is thus still engaged, but it has taken on a new form: *thumos* ruled by the hatred of mastery over it looks like "softness." When *thumos* in the regime has reached this developmental stage, the regime becomes the "beautiful and mighty origin from which tyranny grows (*hê archê houtôsi kale kai neanikê hothen turannis phuetai*)."[48] *Thumos* grows naturally toward tyranny, because it hates vulnerability and longs to throw off any master. But in achieving its longing it is appropriate that it looks, paradoxically, like something alien to its very nature—softness. *Thumos*, as we have seen, is bidirectional: though it naturally wants to free itself from any master and propagate itself for the sake of itself, it also is naturally obedient and needs reason as its master. The democratic fantasy, rather than gratifying a deep longing of *thumos*, brings about an identity crisis by satisfying *one* of its bipolar longings. In this identity crisis, the democratic soul becomes susceptible to being subdued and the same disease that destroyed oligarchy, comes to transform democracy. The regime, like any natural thing—season, plant, body—is transformed by this excess in the opposite direction:[49] "the greatest and most savage (*agriôtatê*) slavery out of the extreme (*akrotatês*) of freedom."[50] The *thumotic* fantasy of limitless self-assertion thus dissolves into a limitless self-subjugation.

At this point, we are compelled to wonder whether such a dissolution is necessary or merely possible. In my reading, Plato gives us reason to think that the resulting dissolution is not necessary but at least likely in the event that human beings do not take proper precautions to prevent it. The most important precaution involves philosophical inquiry, which can offer a therapeutic treatment to the disease that plagues both oligarchy and democracy. Recall that the very same disease that arose in oligarchy comes about in a democracy in the form of the drones, both the ones with stings and the ones without, which are like phlegm and bile in the political body and need a good "doctor and lawgiver" to cut them out as quickly as possible.[51] In an oligarchy, the drone class is not *honored* and is pushed out of the ruling offices, but in a democracy the drones are the leading class, and the ones among them who are "fiercest" (*drimutaton*) speak and act on their behalf while the rest "sit around the dais buzzing, not putting up with another speaker," so that the drones rule everything (with few exceptions) in a democracy.[52] In order to see where tyranny comes from, Socrates points out that there are two other classes in a democracy apart from the drones who rule: the rich (*plousioi*), whom Socrates calls the drones' *pasture*, and also the people (*dêmos*), who do not possess very much and work their own farms. When this third class assembles, they are the most numerous and most powerful class. But Adeimantus points out they are willing to assemble only to get a "share of the honey," and the ruling drones make sure they do get a share by taking it from the rich and distributing it among the people, while keeping the greatest part for themselves.[53] All three of these classes are thus motivated by the *oikeion* principle, for each claims to be entitled to what belongs to the other class. But when the drones take the wealth from the rich, the rich then defend themselves and lay themselves open to the drones' charge that they are working against the people and are oligarchs. The rich have no choice but to fulfill the prophecy of the drones: "they at last end up, whether they want to or not, by becoming truly oligarchs; they do not do so willingly, but the drone who stings them implants this evil too."[54] At this point there come impeachments and lawsuits on both sides. The two classes—the rich and the people—are locked in a contest about the most *thumotic* of all subjects: the entitlement to power and property. As long as these two classes exist, then, *thumos* remains the political problem of any society in which there are rich and poor.

Socrates claims that the people are accustomed (*eiôthen*) to "set up some one person as their own champion and to foster him and make him grow great."[55] Tyranny thus begins with the transformation of this single individual. Socrates calls the transformation of this leader into a tyrant, the transformation of a human being into wolf:

> The man who tastes of the single morsel of human innards chopped up among all the pieces of the other sacrificial offerings must necessarily become a wolf.[56]

Isn't it also the same for the leader of a people who, taking over a particularly obedient mob (*ochlon*), does not hold back from shedding the blood of his tribe (*emphuliou*), but unjustly brings charges against a man—which is exactly what they usually do—and, bringing him before the court, murders him, and doing away with a man's life tastes of kindred (*suggenous*) blood with unholy (*anosiôi*) tongue and mouth, and banishes, and kills, and hints at cancellations of debts and redistributions of land; isn't it also necessarily fated, I say that after this such a man either be slain by his enemies or be tyrant and turn from a human being into a wolf?[57]

The story of constitutional decay has so far been a *thumotically* driven descent. At each successive stage, the excessive desire for the good defined by the regime leads to the dissolution of the regime through the *thumotic* drive to transgress the limits defined by the predecessor's regime. But the creation of the tyrannical regime culminates in the very denaturing of the human soul itself: the leader of the regime, in turning cannibal,[58] becoming a wolf, and shedding the blood of his own tribe, has finally transgressed limits of his own nature, and Socrates remarks now that the transgression has reached the level of *unholiness*. The *thumotic* desire for more in the tyrant seeks for godlike power and status but instead creates a monster where formerly there was a human being.[59] In a desperate bid to continue to hold on to his power, this monster now incites the people to bring violence and war against the rich. Deeply motivated by fear of his own vulnerability, the tyrant comes to make what Socrates calls the "notorious tyrannical request":[60] he asks the people for bodyguards. But the fear will not subside for the tyrant. The possibility of revolt will persist, and therefore he is always stirring up war, so that he can either ensure that his citizens continue to believe they need him, or maintain a pretext to kill those who do not support him. Yet all this makes his citizens hate him more.[61] Any of his supporters who speak the truth to him come to be charged with betraying him, and so are exiled or killed. He purges the city in the opposite manner of a doctor who longs to excise the worst part of the body: he instead cuts off the best parts of the political body and surrounds himself with the worst. He thus comes to have no friends, and the only ones who will guard him are the drones who do it for the money or the slaves that he has freed.[62] The tyrant will use up all the city's resources, and when these run out, he will have no choice but to rely on his own father's property for support. At this point, there may very well be enough discontent among the citizens so that they claim "that it is not just for a son in his prime to be supported by his father" and that "they didn't beget and set him up so that when he had grown great they should be slaves to their own slaves and support him . . . and they now bid him and his comrades to go away from the city—like a father driving a son along with his troublesome drinking fellows out of the house."[63] Finally, Socrates says, the people will know what kind of a monster they have created, when he disarms his own father and kills him. The tyranny is complete when the wolf has become a parricide.[64] The deepest *thumotic* fantasy of the tyrant has now been realized. The drive to self-propagate in the face of all vulnerability comes to fruition in the very act of slaying his own parent, asserting himself as self-created and the creator of his own law. Deference to one's father is finally repulsive for the tyrannically *thumotic* man. In killing his own father, he openly declares that he himself determines what his limits are, and he himself may enforce limits on others while being beyond them himself. The monstrous beast aspires to stand outside the city thinking he is a god.[65]

Chapter Two

The Psychogenesis of *Thumos* Part 2: The Decay of the Tyrant (*Republic* IX)

The story of *thumotic erôs* in the growth of the tyrannical regime shows that *thumotic* transgression of limits is clearly essential to its logic. This is made even more manifest in Socrates's discussion of the growth of the tyrant at the psychological or individual level. In order to describe the tyrannical individual and how he comes to be from the democratic man, Socrates returns to the distinction he made between necessary and unnecessary desires.[1] He now suggests that the unnecessary desires admit of a further distinction within them: "Of the unnecessary pleasures and desires, there are, in my opinion, some that are hostile to law (*paranomoi*) and that probably come to be in everyone; but, when disciplined (*kolazemenai*) by the laws and the better desires, with the help of argument (*meta logou*), in some human beings they are entirely gotten rid of or only a few weak ones are left, while in others stronger and more numerous ones remain."[2] Among the unnecessary desires and pleasures, then, are some that Socrates calls "paranomic"—they run counter to *nomos*, and so we should call them "hostile to law" or "lawless."[3] Desire, if unchecked, is most explicitly said here to lead to a breaking of law. What kind of desire is it that leads to such transgression? Here Socrates suggests that we look at the desires that "wake up in dreams"[4] when the rest of the soul sleeps. Sleep gives rise to dreams in which certain desires are not only expressed but also fulfilled when the rest of the soul has let down its guard against such paranomic wishes. "Surely some terrible, savage, and lawless form of desires is in every man, even in some who seem to be ever so measured. And surely this becomes plain in dreams."[5] Socrates is very clear that the "rest of the soul" that lets down its guard against the paranomic desires of dreams refers only to the rational part of the soul and not to the *thumotic* part. He says that the rest of the soul is rational and tame and ruling (*logistikon kai hêmeron kai archon*) while this part is both full of beasts and savage (*theriôdes te kai agrion*).[6] This savage part, as though it has been released from shame and prudence, now "dares to do everything," even attempting intercourse with parent, beast, or god. No act of shamelessness (*anaischuntias*) is beyond its daring when it awakens.[7]

Socrates contrasts the wild, lawless dreams of this man with the dreams of someone who has a "healthy (*ugieinôs*) and moderate (*sôphronôs*) disposition."[8] The person with *sôphrosunê* will prepare his own soul for the potential lawlessness of sleep by directly addressing the three parts within him. First, he "awakens his rational part" and "entertains it with beautiful speeches and speculations," which brings about a condition of *sunnoia autos hautoi*.[9] Socrates does not expand upon what this phrase means, and translators have offered various interpretations such as "understanding with himself,"[10] "harmony with himself,"[11] and "accord with himself."[12] The suggestion does seem to be that the rational part must be nourished with beautiful speeches and speculations in order for the soul not to be at war with itself in sleep. If the rational part is not so nourished, it is too weak to guard against the rebellion of the *thumos* and appetitive part, which seek their own mastery of the self and bring about civil war in sleep. This is confirmed by Socrates's suggestion that the appetitive part needs to be offered neither a lack nor an excess. One should not go to sleep too hungry or too full, so that the appetitive part will not "disturb the best part by its joy or pain, but rather leave that best part alone pure (*katharon*) and by itself, to consider (*skopein*) and to long (*oregesthai*) for the perception of something that it doesn't know."[13] The appetites, if satisfied prior to sleep, will not disrupt the soul with their pains or pleasures, and instead leave the rational part to be philosophical. Notice that desire does not fall silent during sleep even in the person with *sôphrosunê*. Rather, *sôphrosunê* prepares the human being, even in dreams, to experience philosophical desire, rather than paranomic desire. In dreams, philosophical desire manifests as wonder at what is beyond comprehension. Reason is not merely instrumental calculation but that which puts us in touch with the good for our whole soul. But this cannot happen if the third part—*thumos*—is not also nourished properly prior to the onset of sleep. "He tames (*praunas*) the spirited part (*to thumoiedes*) in the same way (*hôsautôs*) and does not fall asleep with his spirit (*toi thumôi*) aroused because there are some he got angry at."[14] Socrates says that the *thumos* is tamed in the same way that the appetites are tamed, which suggests that it too must not disrupt reason with its pain or pleasure caused by a lack or an excess. Socrates specifically mentions the excess that would cause *thumos* to disrupt one's sleep if one goes to sleep with *thumos* aroused in anger. Socrates is silent, however, about the problem caused by the analogue of hunger in *thumos*, leaving us to speculate how a lack of *thumos* is detrimental to one's *sunnoia*, and may also lead to paranomic desires. One possibility is that the individual with too little *thumos* does not care enough about his own worth to search for wisdom.[15]

Socrates is clear, however, that the paranomic desires that show up in dreams are a result of both *thumos* and appetite. For the person with *sôphrosunê*, whose dreams produce paranomic desires least, will "quiet" (*hesuchasas*) both the spirited and appetitive parts.[16] This is the sole mention of *thumos* in Socrates's account of the tyrannical individual. Although Socrates is silent about *thumos* for a majority of this discussion, his remark here emphasizes that lawlessness applies not only to appetites but also to *thumos*.[17] We are thus given a new context to reconsider Charmides's definition of *sôphrosunê* as "quietness." Socrates here suggests that *internal* quietness—the calming of one's own spirit and appetite—is indeed a feature of the person with *sôphrosunê*. It is a deeper account of quietness than the one offered by Charmides, who could not see past external behavior in talking about the quietness of someone possessing *sôphrosunê*.[18] But Socrates's account here also makes an important amendment to the first definition, one that neither Critias nor Charmides suggest to Socrates. The internal quietness here comes along with the awakening of the rational part—where *phronesis* resides—that is "most likely to grasp the truth."[19] *Sôphrosunê*, then, is somewhat *incomplete* if philosophical wonder at the beautiful is not seen as the proper outcome of the quietness associated with it. Recall that the rational part achieves a kind of *sunnoia* prior to sleep. But such a harmonious oneness stands opposed to the paranomic dreams of the tyrant. While the man with *sôphrosunê* achieves *sunnoia* with a kind of mastery over his unconscious *thumotic* desires, the tyrant turns out himself to be mastered by them.

On the psychological level, then, the tyrant comes to be when a democratic father raises his son with his perspective and values—a love of freedom and equality that is grounded in the satisfaction of all desires, except for those that are paranomic. His son, however, just as his father did in his youth, comes to encounter other individuals in his city who show him what lies beyond the limits placed by his father. The tyrant's emergence is thus a return of the repressed paranomic desires.[20] The ones who introduce him to the satisfaction of paranomic desires call such satisfaction "complete freedom" (*eleutherian hapasan*)[21] and nurture in him an *erôs* resembling a great winged drone, so that when the drone buzzes around him, the "sting of longing" is planted within him and he is "stung to frenzy" until all shame and moderation is expunged from his soul.[22] Socrates suggests this as the explanation for why we call the man who is erotic, drunken, and mad a tyrant.[23] Such an individual attempts to rule not only over human beings but also over gods.[24] The tyrant thus exposes an unconscious and dangerous aspiration (suggested by Aristophanes's myth to be universal) to assert power over the cosmos.

Commentators are right to point out that we need some explanation for Socrates's apparent unwillingness to cite *thumos* as a major contributing factor in discussing tyranny. Indeed, *thumos* seems essential to the account of the timocracy, a regime that is defined by the dual features of love of victory and love of honor,[25] but as we have seen there is only one mention of *thumos* in the discussion of the tyrant.[26] The villain in the story of tyranny seems instead to be *erôs* itself, who Socrates claims has been called a tyrant since antiquity.[27] Socrates goes on to say that the soul of the tyrant is in turn piloted in all its parts by *erôs the tyrant*.[28] Paul Ludwig points out that "Plato could have more explicitly made *thumos* the chief characteristic of the tyrant and reserved *erôs* for the chief characteristic of the philosopher" but instead the tyrannical individual is described as "*erôs* incarnate."[29] Why then does the account of tyranny here associate it with *erôs* rather than *thumos*?[30] I suggest that it is precisely because the nature of *erôs* in this story is *thumotic* through and through, as exemplified in the account given by Aristophanes's speech in the *Symposium*, that *erôs* so understood is indeed the villain of this tale. Put another way, books 8–9 of the *Republic* do not speak of *erôs* except as attachment to one's own things, and Socrates is silent about any kind of philosophical *erôs* or any *erôs* that is not governed by what we earlier called the *oikeion* principle, a principle that dominates the polis if my account so far has been right.[31] But this silence makes sense given the new context of Socrates's argument about *thumos* and *erôs:* the earlier account of *thumos*, presented in book 4 with the story of Leontius, presented it as obedient to reason, even reason's natural ally, so long as it is not uncorrupted by bad upbringing. But this notion of *thumos* gives way to one that is not held in check by reason or education and is thus much more dangerous and subversive, because reason is too weak to guard against it.[32] As a result, *erôs* without any rational restraint comes in the story of the tyrant to dominate the soul in expressing itself in the most dangerously *thumotic* way: the story of regime decay reveals souls whose desires want, at all costs, exclusive possession of the object of desire. The excessive longing of such souls "can no longer maintain the separation of *erôs* from *thumos*."[33] Rather, the story of constitutional decay into tyranny is a story of a soul whose *erôs* is corrupted from within by the power of a *thumos* gone wild. There is thus a single disease that weakens the soul in each successive stage of constitutional decay, culminating in what Socrates sarcastically labels the "most beautiful" regime.[34] Tyranny eventually comes about for the soul in which *thumos* is the engine of desire.

The life of the tyrant bears this out. Socrates emphasizes that the *erôs* within the tyrant brings forth "many awful (*deinai*) desires (*epithumiai*), needing many things"[35] that in turn cause the tyrant to plunder any resources or income at his disposal. When these are used up, his desires will *of necessity* cry out like starved hatchlings (*enneneotteumenas*) in the nest of his soul.[36] It is then *necessary* for the tyrant to face great anguish and distress if he does not find a way to secure more resources or income.[37] The repeated reference to necessity here underscores how little choice the tyrant has in satisfying these paranomic desires. He lives at the mercy of his need for lawless pleasures and does not rule over them. We can now see how appropriately named this regime is: while the names of prior regimes refer to their ruling power (aristo*cracy* or olig*archy*), the name tyranny makes no such allusion in its name. There is no such thing as a tyrannocracy: the tyrant does not rule but is enslaved to his desires.

In answering to the beck and call of his paranomic desires, the tyrant comes to act just like the desires within him. Just as his younger, new, lawless desires come to usurp the place of the older, lawful ones, so too he comes to usurp the place of his mother and father, taking their property and seizing it by force if they are not willing to give it up.[38] No boundaries apply to the tyrant in his relationship to his parents. He feels no sense of shame before their authority but instead sees their authority as worth nothing. Deference to parents is ultimately repulsive to the tyrant. He is willing to strike his mother or father, or even enslave them, for the sake of his infatuation with a recently found mistress or boyfriend.[39] It is not long before he defeats the opinions his parents attempted to instill in him in his childhood, replacing them with newly released lawless opinions that serve to defend his lawless desires. Both his lawless desires and his lawless opinions are those Socrates earlier discussed as only emerging in dreams when the rational part of the soul let down its guard.[40] But now he is tyrannized by *erôs*, and what he only sometimes was in dreams he becomes permanently when awake.[41] The tyrant, then, lives a life in which his paranomic desires, formerly unconscious and repressed, have now become conscious only to take over his soul and rule. In such a condition, no deed is off-limits to him. The tyrant's *erôs* is transgressive of all *nomos*.[42] What other individuals find thinkable in the realm of fantasy or dreams, whether it be parricide, cannibalism, or incest, the tyrant dares to do. His life is the result of letting loose repressed desires that come to dominate his actions.[43]

Those who attempt to resist the tyrant will face enslavement, exile, or death. His language is that of violence and force, mastery and slavery, and everything is either a means for him to satisfy his desire, or an obstacle that must be eradicated. Socrates points out that the tyrant therefore comes to live a life without any meaningful connection to another human beings. Because there are no limits to his lawlessness, all other human beings end up as only potential slaves who give in to his wishes or as potential masters who attempt to restrain his will. The complete and final result of letting loose his *thumos* produces a man who "never has a taste of freedom or true friendship."[44] In summing up the tyrant, the worst man in this story of constitutional decay, Socrates once again reminds Adeimantus that he is "awake, presumably, what we described a dreaming man to be."[45] Because he has no true friends or allies, and because he must treat citizens in his regimes as slaves or potential threats, he is in constant fear for his life, and perpetually seeking validation of his reputation. His attempt at shamelessness is an unfulfillable fantasy, and he cannot escape from the demands of his own *thumos*. Rather, he lives his life enslaved to the eyes of others. The tyrant's life is unfree, dissatisfied, poor, afraid, and grieved, just like the political regime that bears his name.[46] The tyrant thus lives in state that is a mixture of savagery and fear. He is finally *thumos* at war with himself. His vulnerability to death is ever on his mind, and his violence is rooted in his permanent and ever-expanding denial of his own mortality, a denial that enslaves him to erotic, drunken, madness. Ultimately, the tyrant ceases to function as a unitary agent: in his attempt to perpetually pursue the satisfaction of paranomic desires in his mad denial of vulnerability, his soul becomes a place of internal chaos without any coherence—tyranny is properly the lack of a constitution rather than a distinct kind.[47]

Let us therefore take stock of the nature of the tyrant's soul and the role *thumos* plays in transforming him into a wolf, madman, and waking nightmare. When the tyrant's repressed paranomic desires are let loose, their release brings about anarchy in his soul. The tyrant's *erôs* takes the form it does because his *thumos* has no rational restraint: he thus provides the exemplar of *thumotic erôs* taken to the extreme. It is important that the tyrant's *erôs* has no object other than to express itself. As Laurence Cooper points out, the tyrant's desire is not at all directed upward or sublimated, as Diotima's account of *erôs* in the *Symposium* suggests.[48] Rather, the tyrant's *erôs* seems to be in love with nothing other than the power of *erôs* itself. It has no object that transcends its own self-expression as itself.[49] The tyrant as the extreme of the *thumotic* man thus aims at the extreme of victory, invulnerability, and self-sufficiency,[50] and will transgress all boundaries that pose limits on his self-propagation. This *pleonectic* urge is the apotheosis of an unrestrained *thumos*, which needs the restraint of reason or law not to run amok. But in such a condition the tyrant will achieve none of what he aims for. Not only does he end up enslaved to those he attempts to master, but because his desire is now boundless, it is truly insatiable.[51]

This insatiability is best accounted for by considering the role his *thumos* plays, rather than the appetites of the tyrant. We must thus say something about the standard reading of the structure of the soul of the tyrant. According to this view, the soul of the tyrant, like that of the democrat and oligarch, is primarily governed by appetite, directed in each case at a different pleasurable object (money, freedom, lawlessness), and that the pleasurable object becomes more corrupt the further one descends.[52] And while it is correct to see the oligarchic, democratic, and tyrannical souls as ruled in this way, the standard view has not paid significant enough attention to the explanatory power of *thumos*, especially in the tyrannical soul. In the tyrant's soul, it is his *thumos* that most craves for, yet fails to achieve, satisfaction and thus explains his violence and madness.[53] *Thumos*, whose natural ally is reason, is most aroused by the vulnerability exposed when appetites take control of the soul. We saw this in the case of Leontius, but Socrates also introduces another image to demonstrate this, in which a multiheaded beast, a lion, and a human being are molded together as one inside a human being:

> Then let's say to the one who says that it is profitable for this human being to do injustice, and that it's not profitable to do just things, that he is claiming only that it is profitable for

> him to strengthen the manifold beast, the lion, and what's
> connected with the lion by feeding them well, while starving
> and weakening the human being so that he can be pulled
> wherever either of the other leads. And he doesn't accustom
> them to one another or make them friends, but allows them
> to bite and fight and devour each other.[54]

Arruzza points out that this passage shows that *thumos* "cannot be corrupted into becoming a *willing* ally of the appetites against reason. In
this worst-case scenario, it will be enslaved."[55] and moreover, the rule of
the appetites is incompatible with the desire of *thumos*, for if *thumos* is a
desire for control prompted especially by the threat of vulnerability and
loss of agency, then boundless appetites will fail to fulfill this yearning.[56] If
the appetites rule, then the desire for autonomous expansion of self—the
natural goal of *thumos*—is ultimately thwarted by the forced subjugation
of *thumos* by appetite. Leontius presents such a case of enslavement when,
unable to successfully defeat the appetite to look at the corpses and align
his appetites with his reason, he then angrily reproaches his own eyes that
have robbed him of his agency and expose him to self-dissolution. The
tyrant is best understood when we see the enslavement of his *thumos* and
his *thumotic* reaction to this slavery: his shamelessness, his violence, and
his aggression. As we have seen, when *thumos* no longer has the restraint
of reason it is no longer able to repress the desires that are lawless (paranomic). Indeed, we should say that not only can it no longer repress them
but it *contributes* to their nature and drive for satisfaction. These appetites
are not only made more powerful by the ancillary causal role that *thumos*
plays. They are in fact *thumotic* appetites, because they are steeped in the
hatred of vulnerability and the desire for control and power and manifest
themselves in a greed (*pleonexia*) to propagate oneself beyond all limits.
When such desire is thus unrestrained by reason and enslaved by appetites,
it takes the form of beastly, savage, mad *erôs*.[57]

Indeed, Socrates's use of animal metaphors confirms the role that
the enslaved *thumos* plays in the psychic structure of the tyrant. We have
already seen Socrates compare *thumos* to a dog in book 2, an image introduced to highlight the importance of the *oikeion* principle: the dog's ability
to be gentle to friends and harmful to enemies highlights that *thumos* is
fundamentally concerned with the attachment to one's own things (and
a hostility to the threat of the other).[58] But in book 8 *thumos* is cut loose
from reason, enslaved by appetites, and, as we have seen, Socrates claims

that the tyrant himself is transformed into a wolf.[59] With this image, Socrates completes his tale of psychic decay. The transformation into a wolf is the final step of the soul's degeneration from rational agency directed toward what is good, into savagery and self-dissolution. As Arruzza points out, "The use of the image of the wolf, as well as the insistence on the two aspects of attachment to power and excessive violence, is a plausible basis for arguing that spirit is involved in the tyrant's behavior."[60] But in my view, Plato is making even a stronger claim: it is *thumos* that is the most important driving force of the tyrant's dissolution. The wolf, unlike the dog, no longer makes a distinction between friend and enemy but is entirely predatory toward all it confronts. There are finally no limits to its desire for domination, consumption, and possession of its world.[61] The dog has been let loose from the restraint of reason and all *nomos*: the wolf is thus the exemplar of paranomic *thumos*. It is *thumos* in its most debased state. Unlike the *thumos* of a well-bred dog, which is domesticated and restrained by the rule of reason, or even that of the lion and the snake, which is at least bidirectional and potentially tamed, the wolf's *thumos* is corrupted and degenerated to the extreme of violence and aggression.

Chapter Three

Critias the Tyrant

It is indeed the very bidirectionality of *thumos* that makes tyranny possible—its ability to be restrained by reason and its susceptibility to the enslavement of appetite. When the latter occurs, *thumos* moves the soul with a lawless greed (paranomic *pleonexia*) that drives it to a boundless and brutal predatory self-propagation that seeks domination of all around it. The image here is worse than the other image Socrates introduces in book 9, in which we can infer that a *thumos* enslaved to the appetites, dominating one's reason, would look very much like a lion and a multi-headed beast carrying around a weak and powerless human being.[1] But in the same way as the life of the circle-people in Aristophanes's myth, the image demonstrates a "longing for wholeness"[2] that disguises a dream of control, victory, and self-sufficiency fueled by a more dominant fear of vulnerability. Both seek not to understand and respond to a world that provides a horizon to their desires but to define the limits of the world by their desires. The *thumos* of the tyrant motivates him to do "anything necessary to preserve his power in order to satisfy his *pleonexia* and insatiable *erôs* and appetites."[3] Moreover, the tyrant rebels against all law to pursue his dream. But such a pursuit must end in failure. The tyrant's paranomic *pleonexia* will not stop short of attaining complete invulnerability to that which is beyond the circumscribed vision of the world defined by his own will. The *Republic*'s story of the genesis of the tyrant thus dramatizes the views of self-knowledge adumbrated by Critias and Charmides. In particular, the contentless reflexivity of Critias's notion of "knowledge of knowledge," circumscribed by no good beyond itself, is the metaphysics of one with a paranomic ambition to shape the world according to his

185

own will, unrestrained by any limit set from outside his gaze.[4] The account of the *Republic* shows that this paranomic *pleonexia* renders the tyrant a villain to his fellow human beings and to himself. As we have seen, both the tyrannical city and the tyrannical soul are poor, wretched, and full of suffering. Moreover, the soul does not truly escape law or convention by rebelling against it.[5] Indeed, the tyrant's desire does not even transcend his *thumotic* yearning for recognition by those whom he dominates. He remains enamored of their adoration and calls for their death or worship, just as Zeus demonstrates to the circle-people. The tyrant's attempt to own his subjects can bring about such worship only through force and thus he achieves no real satisfaction for this longing. He is greeted with fear rather than respect; he must perpetually fear those whose worship he seeks. Unrestrained by any proper limit, his pursuit culminates in his own self-dissolution as he becomes enslaved to the beast within. The tyrant, finally, in his dream to be invulnerable and self-sufficient, becomes instead a man who is incapable of governing himself. Enslaved rather than free, he does least what he wants, a beast rather than a human being.

Critias, in taking over the conversation from Charmides, rebukes the young boy in anger when he sees "his own things" disrespected and then goes on to offer a monologue (the longest uninterrupted speech in the dialogue) positing as a definition of *sôphrosunê* his own un-Socratic interpretation of the Delphic Oracle.[6] The view behind this speech becomes most manifest in Critias's attempt to expand it into the "knowledge of itself and other knowledges," which Socrates shows to be metaphysically, epistemologically, and ethically problematic.[7] Ultimately, Socrates reveals that Critias's vision of self-knowledge is incoherent because it has no standard beyond itself: its very reflexivity makes it bereft of content and meaning. Critias fails to demonstrate that this view of self-knowledge is either possible or beneficial because he cannot explain how it can be entirely reflexive, unrestrained by any good outside of it, and still be a genuine knowledge of anything. This problematic feature is the ultimate confirmation and refutation of the *thumotic erôs* of Critias, for the tyrant's *thumotic erôs* aspires to a condition of self-sufficiency and self-determination that is the very psychological underpinning of the epistemic claim Critias here affirms. We could say that Critias here describes the metaphysics of the tyrant's desires pushed to the extreme. It is evident that, just as Charmides cannot escape the dialectic of ruling and being ruled, Critias never frees himself from his own vision of self-determination. It underlies his conspiracy with Charmides at the end of the dialogue to threaten Socrates with force. The world is finally a representation of nothing but his own will. The two tyrants, at the end of the dialogue, have not changed from the beginning, in which we saw Critias pimp Charmides out to Socrates, boasting about his beautiful possession that holds the gaze of all present. His possession of Charmides is his power, and at the end of the dialogue, Critias will have him taught by Socrates not because he believes that philosophical wonder will turn the young boy's soul to the good but only to demonstrate that he still holds power over the young boy and over Socrates. To put it bluntly, neither Critias nor Charmides desires to know. Even at the end of the dialogue, when Charmides admits that he does not know what *sôphrosunê* is, he acts more as a cheeky commentator on the rivalry he sees between the authorities of Socrates and Critias. How is he supposed to know what this virtue is, if these two reputed wise men do not? Charmides effectively places himself in a winning situation, if the game has all along been a *thumotic* contest for control. He has vindicated his own ignorance by reminding those listening that both his "teachers" are unable to elucidate the nature of this virtue. But such ignorance does not inspire in him a genuine curiosity to know what *sôphrosunê* might actually be. He, like Critias, does not pick up on the possibility that this admission of ignorance could very well be connected to the nature, possibility, and benefit of *sôphrosunê*. Both Critias and Charmides are blind to a Socratic alternative to the vision of self-knowledge that has been refuted in the dialogue.

We readers are meant to catch sight of the Socratic alternative: a genuine wonder that inspires and is inspired by philosophical dialogue. It is a potential antidote to the *thumotic* tragedy that awaits those who follow Critias and Charmides. In the *Charmides*, Socrates alludes to this alternative by discussing *sôphrosunê* as knowledge of ignorance combined with a collaborative inquiry into the unknown. But this alternative is never seriously pursued in the *Charmides*, because Charmides and Critias do not see its value. We can now say that the *Republic* offers us an account of *thumotic erôs* that explains why Charmides and Critias are particularly unsuited to carry out an investigation of Socrates's alternative. In order to undertake this investigation, the *thumotic erôs* of Critias and Charmides must be transformed. I believe that in the *Symposium*, Plato proposes a method of transformation, a therapeutic treatment, of this *thumotic erôs* in the form of philosophical wonder: tyrannical *thumos* must be restrained by philosophical *thauma*. It is now time to make good on this claim. We will first return to the ominous ending of the dialogue.

The Ending of the Dialogue and Socratic *Sôphrosunê*

Chapter One

Back to War—Ugly Critias and Charmides (175a–176d)

Having finally brought Critias to the conclusion that *sôphrosunê* can be of no benefit to us, and thus completed the reductio ad absurdum that this inquiry has become, Socrates asks Critias to "see" just one more thing, that he himself must be a worthless investigator:

> Then do you see, Critias, how appropriately (*eikotôs*) I feared a while back and how justly (*dikaiôs*) I reproached myself for inquiring (*skopô*) not at all usefully (*chrêston*) into *sôphrosunê*? For I don't suppose that what is agreed (*homologeitai*) to be the most beautiful thing (*kalliston*) of all things would have appeared to us to be of no benefit (*anôpheles*), if I had been any help (*ophelos*) in searching beautifully (*to kalôs zêtein*). But now we have been defeated (*hettômetha*) in every way and we are unable to discover (*heurein*) which of the beings (*tôn ontôn*) the lawgiver (*nomothetês*) gave this name, *sôphrosunê*.[1]

Socrates blames himself for the inquiry and makes clear as he continues that he is *solely* responsible for the failure of the discussion.[2] The taking of such responsibility is extremely grand and seems to be ironic, yet there is something deeply significant about it as well. Some commentators suggest that Socrates's self-effacing remarks here should be taken at face value, for they reveal a Platonic critique of what has been Socrates's approach in the dialogue.[3] In fact, there is no good evidence that suggests that Socrates should be blamed for the failure to define *sôphrosunê*.[4] It may very well

191

be the case that we need to distinguish the views of Plato from those of Socrates in order to understand what is being said and enacted in the dialogue. But in addition, and in my view this is even more important, the views of Socrates and Critias need to be distinguished, as I have argued above in detail.[5] Nonetheless, it is still the case (as I will show) that Critias (and Charmides) are indeed unable to learn from Socrates. Is Socrates then to be blamed for their failures? And if so, is it the elenctic method that is to blame for yielding such poor results? Or could the Platonic critique be not of Socrates but instead focus, more expansively, on the natures and limits of philosophy and politics themselves, and the nature and limits of the human soul and its proper education?

The words of Socrates at this juncture are aimed not only at Critias but also and particularly at those listening. It is difficult to imagine that one attending to this conversation closely will hear them as a critique of Socrates's character or method by the author as he writes the dialogue. For Socrates's avowal of responsibility for failure casts quite a poor light over his fellow interlocutors. To claim such grand responsibilities implies that Critias himself had little, if anything, to contribute to the investigation of this virtue.[6] Critias may or may not hear the implication of these words. If he does not, it is because he is happy not to be the one blamed for the failure of the inquiry. This would show him up as being doubly self-ignorant and thus *asophron*—first, for his lack of understanding, and second, for his ignorance of this lack of understanding. But if indeed he catches the undertone of Socrates's remarks, he must be, as Schmid says, "burning with frustration,"[7] as he earlier did when Charmides mangled his words like a bad actor. But if so, this would also show him up, yet again, as one who is *asophron*.[8]

Moreover, those watching will have observed, repeatedly, that Critias cannot after all possess *sôphrosunê*, and that he is ignorant of himself and what is truly good. Charmides should again be wondering who his proper "guardian" should be. For Socrates's remarks are once again turning back toward Charmides. Can Charmides stand up and admit his own ignorance, and thus come closer to "knowing his own things" and knowing the good, and thus assert his true self to his guardian Critias? One can see Socrates putting this choice to Charmides in the words he uses in this very passage. For the first time in the dialogue, Socrates calls *sôphrosunê* the "most beautiful of all things."[9] Not only does this reraise the question of the "beauty" of *sôphrosunê*, and how this should be properly understood, it recalls the only other time in the dialogue that the epithet "most beautiful" is used: in connection with Charmides's appearance. Socrates hints again here that it is not the beauty of Charmides's body that he should be concerned about but the beauty of his soul. If Charmides does not actually possess *sôphrosunê*—recall that this is the question that launched the conversation—then perhaps he is not "most beautiful" after all. If not, everyone watching would be wrong about him, especially his guardian Critias.[10] Does Charmides hear this? Or does he hear Socrates's puzzling reference to the "lawgiver,"[11] whom he says has given the "name *sôphrosunê*" to one of "the beings"? This enigmatic statement refers back to the dream city Socrates constructed in which the one who ruled had the prophetic ability of knowing all things past, present, and future. It is this person who Critias identified as happiest, and is in a sense his *ideal*. Yet it is this person who Socrates now suggests we just cannot make any sense of. Failure to understand the most beautiful thing has left Socrates in a place of wonder, as he admits his own ignorance and need of wisdom. Indeed, while Critias has shown an aspiration for a comprehensive knowledge that yields an architectonic mastery over all other knowledges, Socrates reveals himself throughout and here again to be committed to knowing what he does not know.[12] Whereas Critias asserts a master wisdom that is victorious over ignorance, Socrates claims here that they have actually been "defeated" by the inquiry itself,[13] but ironically it was an immoderate hubris on the part of the inquiry that has brought about this defeat. Socrates has enough self-knowledge and *sôphrosunê* to examine, test, and evaluate the inquiry itself,[14] while Critias does not. Socrates is suggesting to us that the very discussion itself has not been "ruled by *sôphrosunê*." Such a conversation would proceed differently from the one he has undertaken with Charmides and Critias.

Therefore, Socrates explains that the discussion has not in fact reached a suitable ending point. For he now asserts that he and Critias made three concessions that were not warranted by the argument.[15] They first conceded that an *epistêmê epistêmês* existed, even though their examination of other *dunameis* suggested the strangeness, if not impossibility, of such a notion.[16] Secondly they conceded that this *epistêmê* could indeed know all the others, even though Socrates had shown that it would only reach "knowledge that," never "knowledge what."[17] Finally, Socrates introduces a third concession that has not yet been explicitly mentioned, made for the purpose of guaranteeing that the *sophron* individual knows what he knows and does not know: "And we made this concession in a most magnificent manner (*pantapasi megaloprepôs*), without considering the impossibility of someone knowing, in some sort of way, what he does not know at all: for our agreement says he knows these things. But I think there could be nothing more irrational (*alogôteron*) than this."[18] As Socrates recapitulates, it should be clear that the very concessions were granted to sustain Critias's formulation. Though the notion of knowledge of ignorance is connected to the formulation Critias presented, it was never explored deeply enough, as Critias twisted and perverted Socratic words to fit his own view. But it is nevertheless quite surprising to hear Socrates at this moment comment that the knowledge of ignorance itself seems to be the most irrational (*alogoteron*) state of affairs there could be.[19] Critias again is silent here, and we should not be surprised. For Critias, knowledge of ignorance is not the important issue, and that is his downfall. But it is the crux of the Socratic picture of *sôphrosunê*, and though he has had the wrong interlocutor to say much that is positive about this cognitive state of affairs, still he has enacted it in his deed. This enactment must be held side by side with the claim that it could be *alogon*, even if the argument "mocked the truth" and was a "fabrication" as a result of these "fictitious" concessions.[20] Nonetheless, Socrates concludes that either *sôphrosunê* is not beautiful, or that he himself had not been investigating beautifully. Socrates refuses to endorse the former, and thus expresses his doubts about the inquiry itself. His continual endorsement of the beauty of *sôphrosunê* itself goes hand in hand with his endorsement of the Zalmoxian teaching about the whole, which he reintroduces in turning the discussion back to Charmides's possession of *sôphrosunê*.

Socrates claims that he is not distressed (*aganaktô*) for himself[21] but rather for the young boy, who has such a *sophron* soul but will "have no profit (*onêsêi*) or benefit (*ôphelêsei*) from having *sôphrosunê* in all your life."[22] Socrates is now directly confronting Charmides with the question that he has hinted at all along. The argument of the dialogue is now over. All that remains is to determine what effect it has had on young Charmides. Thus, having come to an unsatisfactory conclusion to his discussion with Critias, Socrates once again puts Charmides at center stage. Can the youth now look within and determine whether he has *sôphrosunê*? What are the consequences of this conversation, Socrates is asking, for him? Socrates now reminds Charmides of the incantation he learned from the Thracian doctor, and implies that there is a choice: either they must reject the Thracian doctrine of medicine he earlier presented, or reject the current inquiry, and Socrates does the latter.[23] But as he does so, he immediately raises the question to Charmides all over again, and tells him to "see" if he has *sôphrosunê* and has no need of Socrates's Thracian charm, and can thus regard Socrates as a "babbler" and worthless at "inquiry," while he himself would be as happy as he is *sophron*.[24]

The reraising of the question about Charmides's possession of *sôphrosunê* is a crucial test to see if Charmides has gained anything from Socrates. For his answer will in fact tell all, perhaps not about the nature of *sôphrosunê*, but about the young boy's nature. Has Charmides "seen" what has transpired between Critias and Socrates? If so, he should be able to admit his ignorance and say that he is *in need*. The most beautiful Charmides would then show his own potential not to be solely the object of everyone's erotic gaze upon him but in addition he could reveal that he is an erotic seeker of wisdom. This would require that he stand on his own before his guardian and move toward authentic self-knowledge, succeeding where his guardian seemed to falter. The question Socrates poses to Charmides now is: can you choose the truth above all else? Can he prize what is genuinely good and beautiful above his *thumotic* attachment to his own things?

It may look at first as if Charmides's answer displays a victory for Socrates, for he says that he does not know and needs the charm from Socrates:

> Then Charmides said: But, by Zeus, I do not know (*oida*), Socrates, whether I have it or don't have it. For how could I know (*eideiên*) when even you two (*humeis*) are unable to discover (*exeurein*) what sort of thing this is, as you say. But I am not persuaded (*peithomai*) by you, and I believe, Socrates, that I need the charm, and will not prevent (*kôluei*) being taught by you every day of my life, until you say I have had enough (*hikanôs exein*).[25]

If Socrates's intention has been to show Charmides that the "knowledge" he has taken from his culture and his guardian is mere illusion, then Charmides's admission of ignorance might reveal that he has finally succeeded and has had a positive effect on Charmides.[26] But as the dialogue comes to a close, we shall see that Charmides's newly gained self-knowledge is not what it first appears.[27] Most importantly, Charmides suggests that *he* could not know whether he has *sôphrosunê*, for Critias and Socrates themselves have been unable to discover it. This remark is telling in a number of respects.

First, Charmides has not followed one of Socrates's final moves: he has ignored Socrates's claim of responsibility for the failed inquiry. Instead of saying that he could not possibly discover it when Socrates has just failed, he uses the plural (*humeis*) and implies that both Socrates *and Critias* have contributed to the conversation. Charmides is not ready to kick away the influence of his guardian. Secondly, even if Charmides were ready to stand on his own, apart from the influence of his guardian, and assert that it was indeed only Socrates who was responsible for the search for *sôphrosunê*, this itself would be only a superficial insight. For Charmides's claim here is that he cannot discover it in the face of the failures of his wiser elders, Socrates and Critias. This shows nothing more than Charmides's habitual bow to authority, rather than an authentic insight into his own limitations and a readiness to examine himself. His admission of ignorance is still rooted in his dependence and fully based on what he perceives as an inability of others who he sees as authorities.[28] Finally, notice the use of two words in Charmides's final utterance here. He claims he is not "persuaded" (*peithomai*) by Socrates, and that nothing will "prevent" (*kôluei*) him from being taught by him. Charmides here suggests that his recent admission of ignorance is not truly heartfelt: he really believes he does have *sôphrosunê*, and that Socrates has not been entirely persuasive. But doesn't this refusal to accept the necessity of the conclusion without a good counterargument reveal his ignorance and unwillingness to face the truth about himself and his guardian? Consider that "*peithomai*," from the verb "*peithô*," although primarily meaning "to be persuaded," also signifies "obey" in its passive voice. The mere sound of the word implies that Charmides is not "obeying" Socrates and is still ruled by Critias. At the very least, we should notice that Charmides still sees relationships in terms of ruling and being ruled. He then confirms this by using the word "*kôluei*": nothing can *prevent* him from talking with Socrates. Even his talk of future conversations with Socrates shows that he is not at all ready or able to abandon his view of relationships defined by a ruler and a ruled. And as we shall soon see, even his readiness to depart from Critias is short-lived.[29]

For at this point, Critias intervenes once again. Before Socrates can respond to Charmides's suggestion that Socrates give him the charm, Critias addresses Charmides: "Now, Charmides if you do this it will be proof (*tekmêrion*) to me that you possess *sôphrosunê*, if you submit (*parechês*) to being taught by Socrates and do not abandon this in anything big or small (*toutou mête mega mête smikron*)."[30] Although Charmides was speaking to Socrates, Critias here reasserts his authority.[31] It is Critias who now demands "proof" of the youth's *sôphrosunê*, and makes clear that it will only be with his approval that the young boy may consort with Socrates. Notice also how Critias describes the act of learning from Socrates: he exhorts Charmides to "submit" to Socrates's teaching, in much the same way that the boy should submit to his elder guardian. Critias ends by saying that the boy must not abandon this whatever happens, "big or small." One must wonder if Plato is playing a joke here, for it is Socrates, after all, who states in the *Apology* that he knows he is wise with respect to nothing either "big or small" (*oute mega oute smikron*).[32] But while Socrates will admit to knowing nothing either "big or small," Critias uses the phrase in a very different context: the call for Charmides to submit to Socrates and not abandon him come what may is not a call for him to investigate but to be ruled. The forthcoming exchange between Charmides and Critias is perhaps the most revealing of this closing scene:

> I will follow, Charmides said, and not abandon this. For I would do dreadfully *(deina)* if I did not obey you *(peithomên)*, my guardian, and not do what you commanded *(keleueis)*.
> Well now, said Critias, I command it.
> Then I will do it, said Charmides, starting this very day.[33]

Charmides shows that his loyalty to Critias trumps all else. Charmides does not now seek Socrates's incantation because he is truly aware of his self-ignorance but because he is commanded to do so by the very person whose power Socrates sought to diminish. As Schmid says, "[Charmides] has accepted a life of moral heterarchy, in which he will remain forever the slave of his guardian master."[34]

Socrates's response to this exchange further confirms this point. For he does not celebrate a victory in argument (even quietly), nor does he eagerly agree to take on young Charmides as a student. He does not at all praise Charmides's answer but is instead suspicious.[35] He asks, "What are you two plotting *(bouleuesthon)* to do?" Charmides responds, "Nothing. We have already plotted *(bebouleumetha)*."[36] Socrates's suspicion has now been confirmed. What might have appeared to be an authentic admission of ignorance, and thus a real improvement in Charmides's soul, has turned out to be a farce. Discussion with Socrates may continue but only under the shadow of a "plot" between Charmides and Critias, thus undermining any real improvement in the soul that Socrates could possibly hope to achieve. And the story only becomes worse as the "dialogue" continues. For Socrates now asks, "Will you use force (*biasê*) and not even give me a pretrial (*anakrisin*)?" Charmides responds affirmatively, "since [Critias] commands it (*epitattei*)."[37] He now says explicitly that he and his guardian are an unbreakable pair[38] with which Socrates must deal. The "plot" then is clear: as an unbreakable pair, Critias and Charmides will be able to defeat Socrates. Critias does not get consent from Socrates but simply commands it, thus provoking the anonymous addressee and the reader to think of Critias's and Charmides's future.[39] As Levine notes, "Whereas Socrates outmatched Charmides by himself and outmatched Critias by himself . . . this twosome (and what they represent) is a more formidable unity."[40]

Charmides suggests that Socrates "take counsel" (*bouleuou*) about what to do, and Socrates responds that counsel will be useless, for it cannot stand up to their use of force:

> For if once you attempt to do anything and use force (*biazeomenoi*), no human being will be able to oppose you (*enantiousthai*).
>
> Then do not oppose me, said Charmides.
> Then I will not oppose you, I said.[41]

Thus the dialogue ends ominously. Charmides has shown himself to be unaffected by Socrates's inquiry, and now Socrates is forced to confront the more powerful dyad of Critias and Charmides, who have thrown dialectic aside in favor of persuading with force. It is in this way that Socrates's discussion about *sôphrosunê* with the two future members of the Thirty Tyrants comes to a close. Many readers of the dialogue who have paid attention to this ominous ending have wondered how such a turn of events could come about. In fact, the ending of the dialogue is the logical outcome of what has come before, and we have already seen foreshadowing hints of this foreboding turn of events in the arguments that Critias has put forth, most notably in his endorsement of Socrates's "dream" of the best-ruled city. Plato shows that Socrates, not Critias, has the prophetic knowledge that Critias so admired. Plato has historical access to the "future" actions of Critias and Charmides, but he portrays Socrates himself as able to see the future of Charmides and Critias in the lack of *sôphrosunê* displayed before him in the present.[42] When he says that he will not oppose them, he is saying that he will not use force against them and thus be corrupted by them. Socrates is not the one on trial here as the corruptor of the youth, but rather Charmides and Critias (and what they represent). No Socratic error has brought this ending about. At the end of the dialogue, we may say that Socrates's pursuit of wisdom still remains unexamined.[43] And indeed we have reason to claim that Socratic knowledge of ignorance has not at all been refuted, nor has its companion activity of self-examination and testing of others in the pursuit of wisdom. This may very well be the essence of *sôphrosunê* as Socrates embodies it. But it requires further examination, an examination that needs to come to terms with and overcome the ugly *thumos* of Charmides and Critias, in order to approach the genuine beauty of wisdom that Socrates *seeks*.

Chapter Two

A Return to the
Smaller Benefit of *Sôphrosunê*

The ominous ending of the dialogue threatens despair upon the unnamed listener and the reader. The violent *thumos* of tyranny threatens the destruction of the polis and the soul of the philosopher. It is at this point that we should recall what Socrates called the "smaller benefit" of *sôphrosunê*.[1] Recall that the *thumos* of Critias prevents him from fully acknowledging the "smaller benefit" Socrates proposes. Critias instead desires an all-encompassing, architectonic, reflexive wisdom in an error-free life. Such is the vantage point of the tyrant described in *Republic* 8–9, whose self-enclosed world renders him isolated and alienated even from himself. But Socrates claims that he and Critias had sought to be making the benefit of *sôphrosunê* something "greater than it is" and proposes instead that it is the ability to learn more quickly, understand more clearly, and examine more beautifully. He thus describes the very actions he himself undertakes here and elsewhere, as presented by Plato. As Tuckey points out, the appearance of the word "examination" *(exetasis),* used twice in this passage, seems to make a textual connection to Socrates's description of his own activity in the *Apology* and it seems closely bound to Socrates's method of *elenchus*.[2] The examination Socrates here describes as the "lesser benefit" of *sôphrosunê* is perhaps then not as "small" as he is claiming it to be. Socratic self-knowledge is something "in addition" to the learning already taking place in the learner, and so it improves its quality.[3] But Socrates is implying that learning might not merely be improved by *sôphrosunê*, but that the virtue itself may very well be essential to all our learning. For it is this "addition" that helps us test our claims to wisdom to see if and why they are true. Without the ability to examine ourselves and others, we can say that our claims to knowledge are only opinions and beliefs, and we have no reason to say that we *know* we should act on them. In such a condition, we are radically incomplete, limited, and deficient in our knowing, because we do not have the virtue that adequately preserves and guards any wisdom that we may have.[4]

It is no coincidence that Socrates suggests that the examination of *others* will be more *beautiful* if one possesses *sôphrosunê*. Socratic examination, if indeed it is essential to *sôphrosunê*, is embedded in a political community and requires open dialogue with other claimants to wisdom who acknowledge their incompleteness in their attempts to seek what is good. The conversation with Critias and Charmides began with the disruptive power of the beautiful Charmides, whose very power placed him in an odd relationship to his community. He is worshipped as something outside it, and Critias, as his guardian, has a possessive relationship with this beautiful youth who inspires such a reaction by his fellow citizens. But Socrates's "examination" of both Charmides and Critias has so far shown that neither understands beauty to be much more than this power Charmides has over others, even as both of them are unable to explain how their notions of *sôphrosunê* could possibly yield any genuine self-knowledge or any good other than the expression of one's own will. Charmides's views are too dependent on authorities over him who have defined his sense of selfhood, and so he fails to examine himself—indeed he has no self apart from the view of others. Critias's views point to nothing outside his fundamental beliefs that ground them, and so he fails to examine himself and only asserts himself and his self-justified power. Socrates, in contrast, presents the "smaller" benefit of *sôphrosunê* as importantly connected to our dialogical engagement with others in order to seek wisdom. Socratic self-knowledge then is inextricably linked with our *erotic* nature—our fundamental desire to complete ourselves by gaining wisdom. Philosophy conceived as the love of learning is the alternative that Socrates puts forth here as the benefit of *sôphrosunê*. Neither Critias nor Charmides has shown himself, so far, to be good at learning or even motivated to learn. Their engagement in the search for wisdom does not portray a *beautiful* examination aimed at learning but an *ugly* desire for victory. They are deficient not because they lack wisdom but because they lack the wonder at anything beautiful beyond them that would reorient them and inspire them to ask questions of themselves about how to live their lives. Their *thumos* prevents them from attaining this.

It is therefore important to distinguish this "smaller" benefit from the benefit of the error-free society that Critias endorsed as the "greater benefit" of *sôphrosunê*. Indeed, neither the word "*exetasis*" nor its cognates is ever used in describing the "greater" benefit. As appealing as this first image was to Critias, Socrates himself could never be the ruler of this error-free society because the two images are not in fact compatible. And we should not lose sight of the fact that this picture emerges only after the Critian quest for "knowledge of knowledge" is shown to be problematic. That is, on Critias's understanding of "knowledge of knowledge" there is no way to achieve the beneficial "knowledge of refutations" that Socrates seems to be describing in this passage. Because Critias's view cannot move from "knowledge that" to "knowledge what," his chimerical "knowledge of knowledge" will not allow for any beneficial examination whatsoever.[5] Can the dialogical approach of Socrates provide an answer to the question, What is the *good* of *sôphrosunê*? This is not explored in the remainder of the conversation. Just exactly why this picture of *sôphrosunê* is good is left an open question for those present.

Socrates also does not explain why he calls this benefit "smaller" or why the previous benefit is "greater." We should note, however, that this is not the first time in the dialogue that the relation of "greater than" and "lesser than" has made an appearance. Earlier Socrates used the example of something being "greater than itself" to call into question Critias's understanding of self-related faculties.[6] I suggested earlier that this should make us wonder about the suitability of mathematics as a model for self-knowledge. It should come as no surprise then that such a reference is made at this moment in the conversation. Socrates is reminding us that the dialogical examination that seems to exhibit *sôphrosunê* is not the kind of *technê* or mathematical science that Critias earlier saw, and perhaps still sees, as paradigmatic of all knowledge. At the same time, the phrase suggests something about Critias's repeated attempt to transcend our human limits. For in desiring *sôphrosunê* to be something greater than it is, is he not desiring human beings to be something greater than they are?[7] Socrates is again trying to correct Critias's view of the human's relation to the divine, to bring him down from his groundless godlike ascendancy. Critias refuses to acknowledge his place, and this makes him ignorant of his ignorance. And has not Socrates shown this to Charmides in the very image he has chosen? For, if Socrates has suggested that the "lesser benefit" of *sôphrosunê* is an improvement in one's learning, Charmides, being a schoolboy, should see by now that he himself and his guardian Critias are perhaps quite slow at learning, and therefore they are indeed not *sophron* gentlemen. Socrates would seem to be suggesting to the youth, again, that Critias is not the best teacher, and if Charmides wants to indeed *be a better student*, he must change his ways. We now know that the ending of the dialogue suggests that Charmides does not take the warning from Socrates. Can the unnamed listener or the reader heed the warning? And can we explain to ourselves the possibility and benefit of *sôphrosunê* as exemplified in the Socratic search for wisdom? I have suggested that a way to this is available in examining wonder at the beautiful in the *Symposium*. It is now time to make good on this claim.

Part 3B

Thauma and *Sôphrosunê*
in the *Republic* and *Symposium*

Chapter One

The *Theoros* Returns (*Republic* 327a–328b and *Symposium* 172a–174a)

I have argued that Plato presents an analysis of the *thumotic erôs* of Critias and Charmides in the psychogenesis described in Aristophanes's myth in the *Symposium* and in the account of tyranny in books 8–9 of the *Republic*. Underlying this *thumotic erôs* is an acquisitive orientation to the beautiful that is fueled by a hatred of vulnerability, especially to the self-dissolution threatened by one's mortality. Its culmination is the paranomic *pleonexia* of the tyrant: an unbounded ambition to protect, replicate, and propagate oneself and deny the otherness of the other. *Thumotic erôs* denies any real alterity and subordinates the good to what it defines as its own things. It is a perversion of desire in which other-directedness has been thoroughly corrupted into boundless *pleonexia*. Socrates in the *Charmides*, both in speech and deed, reveals a philosophical alternative and therapeutic response to this tyrannical ambition. While Charmides and Critias have on multiple occasions shown their unwillingness to admit ignorance and their desire for victory that culminates in the ominous ending, Socrates has shown an ability to control himself in the face of beautiful Charmides, at the threat of ugly Critias, and at the hands of both of them together. He is willing to admit his ignorance and attend to what is best. Such is the demonstration of his *sôphrosunê* in action, in sharp relief to the *thumos* of Critias and Charmides. In what follows, I will suggest that Socrates's *sôphrosunê* is essential to his philosophizing. We can call it his *zetetic* excellence. It is not *thumotic* but grounded in his own brand of *erôs*, which differs importantly from the *thumotic* desires we have seen in Critias and Charmides. Socratic *erôs* turns out to merge with *sôphrosunê*, if we attend

207

to its connection with wonder (*thauma*). We will begin exploring this alternative by first turning to the dramatic openings of all three dialogues, in which Plato sets the stage for our inquiry by describing Socrates as a *theoros* who has come back to the city as a witness. As Andrea Nightingale suggests, Plato models philosophic *theoria* on civic *theoria*, in which "the *theoros* journeys forth as an official witness to a spectacle, and returns as a messenger or reporter: at the end of the journey, he gives a verbal account of a visual, spectacular event. The journey as a whole, including the final report, is located in a civic context."[1] Moreover, in contrast to the denial of alterity that is constitutive of the *thumotic erôs* of tyranny, "the gaze of the *theoros* . . . is characterized by alterity: the pilgrim brings his foreign presence to the festival, and he interacts with people from other cities and cultures. He thus returns home with a broader perspective, and brings information and ideas from foreign parts into the city."[2] We can see this portrayed in the openings of the *Charmides*, the *Republic*, and the *Symposium*:

> We came (*hekomen*) yesterday evening from the army camp at Potidaea, and because I had arrived (*aphigmenos*) after some time away, I gladly sought my habitual conversations (*sunêtheis diatribas*). And so I went into the wrestling school of Taureas, opposite the temple of Basile, and there I came upon quite a number of people, some of whom were unknown to me, but most of whom I knew. And as soon as they saw me unexpectedly entering, they greeted me from a distance on every side; but Chaerephon, like the madman that he is, jumped up from their midst and ran to me, and grasping me by the hand—
> Socrates, he said, how did you survive the battle?[3]

> I went down yesterday with Glaucon the son of Ariston to the Peiraeus in order to offer my prayers to the goddess and also because I wanted to see *(theasthai)* how they would conduct the festival, since this was the first time they celebrated it. I thought that the procession sent by the Thracians was no less fine. After we had offered our prayers and seen the spectacle *(theôrêsantes),* we began to head back to town.[4]

> In fact, your question does not find me unprepared. Just the other day, as it happens, I was walking to the city from my home in Phaleron, when a man I know, who was making his

way behind me, saw me and called from a distance. . . . "Apollodorus, I've been looking for you!" he said. "You know there once was a gathering at Agathon's when Socrates, Alcibiades, and their friends had dinner together; I wanted to ask you about the speeches they made on love. What were they?" [5]

All three dialogues are narrated in the first person. The speaker in the *Charmides* and the *Republic* is Socrates, narrating to an unnamed listener (and for the reader's benefit) an event that has already taken place after Socrates had made a journey and witnessed a spectacle about which he brings news to those who have stayed behind and not seen it for themselves. I have already discussed[6] the connection between this narrative device and the theme of self-knowledge in the *Charmides*. I suggest that in the *Republic* and the *Symposium* as well, the narrative device is connected to the explorations in these dialogues of the pursuit of self-knowledge and its political implications. And as Nightingale suggests, the "*theoria* at the very opening of the *Republic* . . . anticipates the discussion of metaphysical *theoria* set forth in books V–VII."[7] In the current part, we will see how the *Symposium* sets up a similar narrative dynamic, one in which the *theoria* described at its very opening comes to anticipate the metaphysical *theoria* in its central moment, the account of the ascent of *erôs* in Diotima's speech.

But we should note a complexity regarding the narrator of the *Symposium*. Though this dialogue is indeed narrated in the first person to an unnamed listener, it is not Socrates but his devotee, Apollodorus,[8] who for the second time in two days recites a story that he himself had heard from Aristodemus, another devotee of Socrates. So we are further removed from the event than we are when we open the pages of the *Charmides* and the *Republic*. Indeed, Apollodorus is no witness but relays what he witnessed from another, which turns out to be a tale about Socrates's journey to Agathon's house, where something strange happens to him on the way,[9] and he ultimately relays what he has witnessed from Diotima. I will return to the purpose of this, and I will argue that this complexity is tied to the therapeutic role that wonder plays as a response to tyrannical ambition. For now, I would suggest that all three narratives emphasize what Nightingale has outlined as the journey of the *theoros*, even within the more complex framework of the story of the *Symposium*.[10]

As Blondell points out, it is particularly important that Socrates himself is on a journey to Agathon's house when something strange happens to him:

> For a brief period no one knows where Socrates is—a slave must be sent to find him (174e–175a). Only then do we find out that he has been standing in a neighbor's doorway, resisting any invitation to come in (175a7–9), with his mind (*nous*) only on himself. He has stopped moving, standing still on the road as he sometimes does, according to Aristodemus (175b). The situation is *atopos*, "strange," or more literally "out of place," at least in the view of Agathon, who wants to stop it by sending someone (presumably a slave) to fetch him.[11]

This event, which takes on even greater significance when we hear the speech of Diotima, causes Socrates himself to be a source of wonder. His strangeness (*atopia*) is met with resistance by the poet Agathon, and furthermore, not a single person at the party ventures to ask Socrates about his experience. Even Aristodemus, the adoring disciple of Socrates who shows up without him and urges Agathon to allow Socrates to come in on his own time, seems to *presume to know* what this experience and others like them are about. When Socrates does arrive, Agathon suggests that Socrates clearly has obtained some wisdom while standing on his neighbor's porch and will impart it to him perhaps through touch, while lying down on the couch next to him.[12] Agathon does not inquire about Socrates's wisdom or his "strange" experience, and this prompts Socrates's ironically bemoaning rejoinder that wisdom is not like water that flows from a full cup to an empty one, for if it were, it would be Socrates who would receive the bountiful wisdom Agathon could poor into him, wisdom so bountiful that more than thirty thousand Greeks could be called as witnesses.[13] In contrast, Socrates claims that his own wisdom is paltry (*phaulê*) and as disputable (*amphisbêtêsimos*) as a dream.[14] Socrates ironically calls attention to the difference between his own claim to know nothing of much importance, which we saw to be of such significance in his discussion of self-knowledge with Critias, and Agathon's more resplendent knowledge. Agathon is clever enough to see that Socrates is mocking him and claims that Dionysus will be the judge between them. In just what way Dionysus will serve as judge between these two can be seen only when Socrates gives his own speech about love. But when Socrates questions Agathon about his speech in praise of *erôs*, it becomes clear that Agathon's own knowledge betrays an ignorance of the fundamental nature of *erôs* itself, continuing the theme that has been announced even before a word has been said about love, that of *erotic failure*.[15]

From the response to Socrates's experience by all at the party to Agathon's speech about love to Alcibiades's account of his relationship with Socrates (and others), Plato stages a series of erotic failures that remind the reader of the political backdrop of the conversation. As Mateo Duque points out, following Debra Nails and Walter Ellis, the reader and unnamed listener would be aware that Agathon's party "is on the eve of several characters being accused of sacrilege, and later being exiled or dead. Alcibiades was accused of the destruction of the Herms and the profanation of the Eleusinian mysteries. Also, the relative peace that Athens had enjoyed (Nicias's Peace) was about to end with Athens embarking on an unprecedented imperial expedition to Sicily."[16] Alcibiades was critical in stoking what Thucydides called the *erôs* that the Athenians had for this expedition, an *erôs* that manifested in the elders as a desire for conquest, and in the youth as a longing to gaze upon what is absent.[17] It is a *thumotic erôs* for a diseased notion of *theoria*[18] that fuels this expedition, much like the crowd's reaction to the entrance of Charmides to the Palaestra in the *Charmides*.[19] Furthermore, in his own speech in the *Symposium*, Alcibiades is portrayed as admitting that his own *thumotic* love of fame and power drives him away from following Socrates. Not only is he complicit in a great erotic failure of the Athenians, he himself perhaps turns out to be a particularly important erotic failure, similar to Charmides and Critias, in his inability to turn from the destructiveness of his own *thumos* to follow the transformative wonder that Socrates arouses in him in their conversations.[20] The *thumotic erôs* that drives one to a diseased *theoria* must be contrasted with the *erôs* of the philosopher that culminates in philosophic *theoria*. Like the *Charmides* and the *Republic*, the *Symposium* provides for the reader the spectacle of the Socratic conversation itself, provoking us (along with the unnamed listener) to wonder about its limitations and possibilities, and how to follow Socrates in a way that is neither destructive of Socrates nor of ourselves.[21] Alcibiades, Critias, and Charmides in their relationships with him reveal ways of "following" Socrates that betray a deep, tyrannical *thumos* in their *erôs* for him, or for what he represents to them. And although I will not have the space to demonstrate this in the present account, I would suggest that Alcibiades in the *Symposium* could be a stand-in for both Charmides (in his youthful devotion and political charm) and Critias (in his prideful ambition for mastery). The *Symposium* shares with the *Charmides* and the *Republic* a very possible and plausible tragic outlook that awaits the reader who does not learn from Socrates's conversations, whether this (erotic) failure comes from the illusions of a Charmides or Critias or of an Alcibiades. Socrates's account of *erôs* in the *Symposium* thus serves a very political function—it is the expression of a vision that can potentially be a salve for the wound described by Aristophanes that manifests itself most tragically as the paranomic *pleonexia* of the tyrant, which is the motivation for Socrates to act as a *theoros*.

It is philosophic wonder that is the crucial distinguishing feature of the philosophic *theoros*. Wonder is not only the beginning of the journey of the philosopher but also the journey's culmination, and is thus an essential feature of the entire activity.[22] Indeed, as Nightingale nicely puts it, "wandering is translated into wondering"[23] and therefore it is not only the case that the *theoros* returns from a foreign spectacle with new information and ideas to impart to those waiting at home. The philosophic *theoros* himself is also significantly transformed[24] in this contemplative activity, and thus "returns to the city as a stranger to his own kind. This *atopos* individual becomes a sort of agent of alterity, and must confront the problem of bringing alien ideas into the city."[25] As we have seen in the openings of the three dialogues, Socrates is portrayed as returning from such a mysterious spectacle—the war, the festival, the higher mysteries of love taught by Diotima—in order to bring new ideas to the city. But in what way should we account for Socrates's own self-transformation in witnessing these spectacles? How might Socrates's own search for self-knowledge be understood in light of his wandering and wondering? Socrates's activity is one that is significantly hindered (if not utterly forestalled) by the *thumotic erôs* of Charmides and Critias, whose attachment to their own things blinds them to see what is beyond their own horizons. And in the figure of Alcibiades and the Sicilian expedition in the *Symposium*, we have an instantiation of an erotic failure—a *thumotic erôs* that longs for a diseased *theoria*. The philosophic *theorôs* who wanders into the realm of the other does so out of a recognition that he lacks what the tyrant claims to possess. He does so out of a recognition of his incompleteness and thus continues to strive to find fulfillment in an intimate relationship with alterity, rather than in a struggle to dominate it. It is crucial that wonder, as I have suggested, is not only the beginning of this journey but also its culmination. The philosopher's *erôs* will be distinguished from that of the tyrant in that he not only seeks and investigates the alterity of the good and the beautiful but actively surrenders to this alterity without being destroyed by it. Thus, the wonder attained from wandering is transformative of the soul of the philosopher in a way that escapes the tyrant. To demonstrate this more fully, we should turn our attention to Socrates's own account of *erôs* in the *Symposium*, which begins with his questioning of Agathon.

Chapter Two

Erôs Is a Lack

Socrates Questioning Agathon (*Symposium* 199c–201e)

As we discussed above in part 1B, Aristophanes's speech in the *Symposium* gives an account of an *erôs* that is *thumotic* at its core. The desire for wholeness that he describes is a desire for one's lost self; the completion at the center of Aristophanes's speech is an apotheosis of the ego. Such an erotic love has no genuine interest in alterity but rather sees the beloved as a reflection and extension of one's own identity. When pushed to the extreme, such a *thumotic erôs* is dangerous. Indeed, Aristophanes's speech ends with a call for his listeners to curb their ambitions and not again compete with the gods for power. If my argument in part 2B is right, such a story of unrestrained tragic ambition is spelled out in books 8–9 of the *Republic*, in which we see that the human with unbridled *thumos* aims at extending the self beyond limit and remaking the world in his image. This is the story of the tyrant's paranomic *pleonexia*.

In the *Symposium*, Socrates does not directly address Aristophanes's account, though it is clear to anyone listening that he means for us to think of him.[1] He begins, in fact, by critiquing Agathon regarding an agreement that Socrates himself shares with Aristophanes. That is, Socrates begins his discussion of *erôs* by emphasizing an important element of Aristophanes's account that Agathon overlooked in his own encomium. That feature is that *erôs* is a lack, and is fundamentally connected to our human incompleteness, and our need to remedy this condition.

Socrates gets Agathon to admit that all *erôs* is of something, just as a father or mother are essentially a father or mother *of* a child, and a brother or sister are both *of* a sibling.[2] Socrates is suggesting that it is important to keep in mind that *erôs* is essentially relational or intentional, regardless of what the object may be to which it is related. To conceive of a love that has itself as its object and nothing outside it would be absurd. This is perhaps why narcissists are seen to be incapable of loving. Love is essentially other-directed.

Kosman has called this feature objective intentionality[3] and has suggested that, according to both Plato and Aristotle: "Cognition . . . reaches out toward a world other than itself, which it posits as its object. But at the same time it involves a mode of self-awareness that is, as it were, nonobjective, a consciousness of the *subject as aware* in which the *subject as aware* is *present to itself* but not *before itself* in the mode in which the posited object of consciousness is before its consciousness." This admission calls to mind for us Socrates's own disagreement with Critias about the "*tinos*" (of what?) or the intentionality of self-knowledge.[4] While Critias insisted upon the stringent reflexivity of self-knowledge (to the point of incoherence), Socrates continued to suggest that even self-knowledge, like all other *epistemai*, must be related to an object distinct from itself. *Erôs* is no exception to this. The objective intentionality of *erôs* addresses the empty, narrow, restrictive notion that Critias is saddled with in his conversation with Socrates. In virtue of its other-directedness, *erôs* is not narrowly confined to an inert subject matter that fails, from the outset, to provide any ethical guidance or knowledge or potential understanding of the self. While Critias's depiction of self-knowledge is demonstrably ineffective to yield an adequate account of self-knowledge (and quite likely incoherent as well), it is not clear out of hand that the objective intentionality of *erôs* is either incoherent or unable to explain self-knowledge. In fact, I would like to suggest in what follows that the intentionality of *erôs* helps us understand the alternative that philosophic self-knowledge presents to the enclosed, *thumotic* self-deception of the tyrant. To see this, consider what Socrates brings Agathon to see next:

Socrates: Keep this in your memory, this something of which *[erôs]* is. But tell me this much: does *erôs* desire that of which it is the *erôs*, or not?

Agathon: Certainly.

Socrates: And is it when he has, or does not have, that which he desires and loves, that he desires and loves it?

Agathon: It is at least likely that he does not have it.

. . .

Socrates: To me it seems to be [not only likely, but] wondrously *(thaumastôs)* necessary. How about you?

Agathon: It seems so to me also.[5]

Socrates suggests to Agathon that the intentionality of *erôs* demonstrates its needy and incomplete nature. *Erôs* is deeply connected to the desire of that which is not possessed. At first, Agathon affirms that this is likely the case, but after Socrates asks him to examine *(skopei)*, he comes to agree with Socrates that it is not only likely but necessary—a *wondrous* *(thaumastôs)* necessity has been revealed about *erôs*. It is essentially a lack, revealing the incompleteness of human striving. *Erôs* is never consummated once and for all. It is appropriate that Socrates calls this revelation *wondrous*. For it brings to light an insight about human striving that will help us behold the particular beauty and truth of human action. Throughout the *Symposium*, Socrates never goes back on this claim about *erôs*, even as the discussion brings additions and modifications. Indeed, as Socrates specifies, it might very well appear that one could have an *erôs* for what one already possesses, like a strong athlete who continues to exercise his muscles. But a reflection on our temporality and ephemerality suffices to show that this desire too is a lack: the athlete's *erôs is* aimed not at the strength he now has but at keeping his strength in the future.[6] *Erôs* is thus rooted in our time-boundedness, and its content is defined by its futurity. It is a yet-to-be good that *erôs* desires, whose possession is not present.

Agathon is thus forced to conclude, in contrast to his earlier claim, that *erôs is* neither beautiful nor good, for by his very nature he desires and thus lacks both.[7] This sets Agathon's mind spinning,[8] and he asserts that he is no longer able to refute Socrates. But Socrates now, as he also does with Critias and Charmides, insists that it is the truth that is on trial here, rather than Socrates or Agathon,[9] and at this point he lets Agathon go. In an unusual move, perhaps unparalleled in the dialogues, he abandons the method of asking Agathon questions and instead tells a story of his own conversation with a priestess of Mantinea, whose name was Diotima. It was thus a foreign prophetic woman who taught Socrates everything he knows about love. It is doubtful that Diotima existed,[10] but it is nonetheless more important to reflect on Socrates's claim that his philosophical education is in her hands. First, *erôs is* now associated with a divine mystery that requires a special kind of preparation to approach. The nature of love is thus perhaps not graspable by mere human rationality, unaided.[11] In addition, just as Socrates has questioned Agathon, he now presents himself as having been in Agathon's position: as a student of Diotima who answers her dialectical questioning. Socrates, therefore, in contrast to Agathon, shows himself as aware of his own incompleteness (his ignorance of love) and in need of a teacher to learn. Indeed, he says that he formerly held a view of love similar to Agathon's—that he was a "handsome god, attracted to beautiful things"[12] that Diotima persuaded him to reject. This is a rare moment in the Platonic dialogues. Only in the *Parmenides* do we witness a younger Socrates learning from a teacher about the difficulties of positions he once held.[13]

It is also remarkable that Socrates chose a woman to stand in as his teacher about *erôs*. It becomes clear from what Diotima says about *erôs* that her gender is no accident. This is most notable in her connection between *erôs and* pregnancy (of all human beings) and her subsequent emphasis on the creative side of *erôs*, which supplements its acquisitiveness.[14] As Halperin notes, "Diotima's conceptualization of *erôs* derives from a specifically feminine perspective"[15] and her point of view establishes a "distance between [her] outlook . . . and the customary approach . . . of the Athenian Demimonde."[16]

It is finally significant that Diotima is not a prophetess in name only. Socrates points out that she even "put off the plague for ten years by telling the Athenians what sacrifices to make."[17] Clearly Diotima's erotic wisdom displays great power, if she was capable of such a feat. But we should reflect further upon what Socrates intends to say by pointing out this detail. What are the consequences of the delay of this plague? Recall that this is the very same plague that serves as the recent backdrop for the discussion that takes place in the *Charmides*, which brought about a transvaluation of values that gives urgency to Socrates's opening question upon returning from battle about the status of philosophy and the young at home.[18] Consider what Laurence Cooper, following Benardete, claims:

> Had Diotima not delayed it by ten years, the plague would
> have struck Athens far less severely, since, as it happened,
> its deadliness was multiplied by the ongoing urbanization of
> Athens and by the wartime decision to bring Athenian villag-
> ers and farmers inside the city walls. (Both the urbanization

and the withdrawal into the city were Pericles's doing, in the service of the erotic imperialist project.) Even more important, Athens in all likelihood would have won the Peloponnesian War; and Alcibiades would likely have been saved from exile, and Socrates from death. So Diotima's "erotic wisdom"—or Athens's use of it—proved disastrous.[19]

Cooper goes on to speculate that it is the mastery of nature that Socrates here critiques, and ties it to the erotic delusion that the present will go on forever; the "intoxicated lover does not really imagine that his beloved will ever grow old, and erotic statesmanship cannot quite believe the splendor of the city could ever dim."[20] I would suggest, if Cooper is right, that such an intoxication is caused by *thumos* and is thus a diseased *erôs*, just as Nicias claims about the ambitious desire that provokes the Athenians to launch the Sicilian expedition. I believe we shall see that Diotima herself is committed to a vision of *erôs* that in at least some ways is diseased by a *thumotic* striving. As we explore Diotima's discussion with Socrates, we should thus be extremely concerned to see exactly what Socrates learns from her.

Before turning to her discussion with Socrates, let us thus take stock of what Socrates has established in a few Stephanus pages. To sum up: *erôs* is a lack, rooted in our essential time-bounded incompleteness, aimed at the possession of a future good. Socrates does not go back on this claim, even as it is supplemented with Diotima's forthcoming notions about pregnancy and creation. In what follows, I will discuss how Socrates's discussion with Diotima reveals important insights not only about *erôs* but also the human soul (*psychê*) itself. This is not only because *erôs* is part of the soul but also because the soul is essentially erotic. However, I believe that we must disentangle what Diotima takes to understand as the erotic soul and what Socrates comes to understand by it. To begin to see this, let us now attend to the discussion itself.

Chapter Three

Erôs Is Between—Diotima Questioning Socrates (*Symposium* 201e–203a)

Socrates reports that he asked Diotima if she meant to say that love, in being neither beautiful nor good, was instead ugly and bad. This question inspires an interesting rebuke from Diotima. She tells Socrates to *be quiet*, using a word that has religious connotations (*ouk euphêmêseis*).[1] Socrates's notion is in some way impious in Diotima's eyes. It does not respect the limitations of human knowledge about the divine. Diotima then offers as a counterexample the role that correct opinion plays "between" knowledge and ignorance.[2] People with correct opinion rise above the level of mere ignorance by hitting upon a true answer but fall short of being knowledgeable because they are unable to explain their opinion or justify it with an argument. Socrates agrees, and Diotima suggests that the divine being Eros is similarly in a *metaxic* or in-between state: "Then do not compel (*anankaze*) what is not beautiful to be ugly, or what is not good, to be bad. Also, since you yourself agree that Eros is not good or beautiful, do not in any way consider (*oiou*) that he must (*dein*) be ugly and bad, but something between (*metaxu*) these two."[3] Socrates saw Diotima's words as a denial of a divine feature of Eros, a denial that borders on blasphemy. He reports that he still thought that everyone—both those who know and don't know—agreed Eros to be a great god (*megas theos*),[4], and when Diotima asked, "Will you dare (*tolmêsais*) to deny that any god is beautiful and happy?," he himself swore by Zeus that he would not say this.[5] But Diotima reminded Socrates of their earlier agreement—that Eros fundamentally lacks the beautiful and good things that he desires, and Socrates maintains that he still endorsed this claim. He therefore asked

221

Diotima, "How could Eros be a god, yet not possess anything good or beautiful?"[6] The conclusion is inescapable. Eros, who is neither beautiful nor good, is not a god. Diotima emphasized that Socrates *himself*, by his own admission, did not believe Eros to be a god. Socrates agreed, but he was puzzled, asking if Diotima was suggesting that Eros was therefore mortal. Finally, Diotima suggested that just as he is in between the beautiful and the ugly and the good and the bad, so also does he reside in between the mortal and the immortal. Eros is not a great god but a great *daimon*, "for everything *daimonic* is between the divine and the mortal"[7] and has a unique and essential power (*dunamis*):

> Interpreting and ferrying to gods things from human beings and to human beings things from god: the requests and sacrifices from human beings; from gods the orders and gifts in return for sacrifices; for it is in the middle (*mesoi*) of both and completes (*sumplêroi*) them, so that the whole itself has been bound together (*sundedesthai*) by it. . . . A god does not communicate (*meignutai*) with a human being; but through this occurs every communion (*homilias*) and conversation (*dialektos*) between gods and human beings, whether awake or asleep. And the one who is wise about these sorts of things is a *daimonic* man.[8]

Using three different words (*meignutai, homilias, dialektos*), Diotima emphasizes that there is no community between gods and human beings without the *daimon* exercising its power to unite them. It is the role of the *daimon* to bind the whole cosmos together, enabling human beings and the divine to connect. Human beings and gods too, in themselves, are thus incomplete. As Strauss points out, "Neither gods nor men are self-sufficient; the self-sufficiency is created by the [*daimons*],"[9] who serve as a mediating power between them.[10] Without the *daimons*, there would be little hope of any relationship between human beings and gods, who thus rely on the power of the *daimons* for completion and connection. We should note here, that Diotima's introduction of the *daimon* is a fundamentally important corrective response to the tragic vision outlined in the speech of Aristophanes. In his story, the human relationship with the divine begins in conflict, a competition for power that results in abject servitude and a humbling abnegation of the original human *thumotic* drive to assert their own power. The conclusion of Aristophanes's speech calls for human beings to remember that an ascent to the gods will only bring further unspeakable punishment, and that we should confine our *erôs* to our human halves, for our own self-protection. But Diotima's introduction of the *daimon*, as a very bridge between the mortal and the immortal, suggests a different vision of the cosmos, in which an ascent to the divine is neither impossible nor hubristic but instead a natural feature that binds all into a rational whole. Ironically, Diotima's speech is much more akin to a divine comedy in response to the tragic outlook presented by Aristophanes.

Chapter Four

Diotima's Psychogenesis of *Erôs* (*Symposium* 203a–204d)

When Socrates heard about the power (*dunamis*) of Eros, he asked her about his mother and father.[1] Just as Aristophanes offered a psychogenetic account of Eros, describing his nature and origin, so too does Diotima tell a story of the origin of love. Diotima's story agrees in part with Aristophanes's account but also moves beyond it, allowing for the possibility and the benefit of an ascent to the divine. This is tied directly to Eros's parentage and birth. Eros was conceived on the same day as Aphrodite's birth, when the mortal woman Penia (whose name means "poverty") sought to transcend her impoverished state by getting the best of the drunken Poros (whose name means "resource"). Poros was son of the god Metis, and Penia hoped to become pregnant with his child.[2] Penia's action—a rape—casts a dark shadow on the birth of this lover of Aphrodite and beauty. Eros is thus tied to an important ambiguity even in the act of his conception. To further complicate this ambiguity, Diotima's account appears to suggest that the cunning and intelligence of Eros comes from his resourceful father, but the action of Penia seems to show more cunning than the passive victim Poros, who seems to exert no agency at all in the birth of his son. The myth seems to invent two, where there is more accurately a two-in-one. We need to keep these complications in mind as we examine Diotima's account of Eros's inheritance from his parents:

So because Eros is the son of Poros and Penia, his lot in life is set to be like this. First, he is always poor, and he's far from gentle (*hapalos*) and beautiful (*kalos*) as many believe, but is tough, shriveled, shoeless, and homeless . . . having his mother's nature, he is always living with need (*endeiai sunoikos*). But according to his father, he plots against (*epiboulos*) the beautiful and the good, and is courageous, reckless, and impetuous, a marvelous hunter (*thêreutês deinos*), always contriving some devices (*plekôn mêchanas*), resourceful and desirous of practical wisdom (*phronêseôs epithumêtês*), philosophizing through all his life, a marvelous (*deinos*) wizard, druggist, and sophist (*goês kai pharmakeus kai sophistês*). He is by nature neither immortal nor mortal. But sometimes on the same day he blooms and lives when he has plenty of resources (*euporêsêi*), then he dies but comes back to life through the nature of his father. And his resources are always gradually passing away, so that Eros is never either without resources or rich, and is in between (*en mesôi*) wisdom and ignorance as well.[3]

Diotima's account of Eros's inherited nature emphasizes his "in-between" nature. Eros is impoverished and needy like his mother, and not gentle and beautiful as someone like Agathon would have us believe. Eros's need for what he lacks remains a fundamental feature of both the *daimon* and the desire. On his father's side, Eros has inherited a courage that sometimes looks like recklessness combined with an awe-inspiring or even wonder-inducing (*deinos*) ability to contrive devices, cast spells, make charming medicines, and give seductive speeches all in the attempt to plot against the beautiful and the good. It is an odd description. Not only is it the case, as we have seen, that Penia seems to be the more cunning and resourceful one of the couple, it is a strange story to tell about the nature of *erôs*, if the desire is meant to be like the god. The needy Eros is one who plots devices and seeks to use magic and sophistry to satisfy his need for the beautiful and the good. There is something shameless about Eros when he is in pursuit of the beautiful and the good. And indeed, Socrates himself tells Charmides, citing Homer, that shame is not good for a man in need when Charmides offers shame (*aidôs*) as a definition of *sôphrosunê*.[4] Indeed, although there may be some differences, there seem to be several intriguing similarities between the account Diotima has offered here of the figure of Eros and the presentation Plato gives us of Socrates.[5] Socrates, like Eros, is often barefoot and puts on shoes for special occasions such as attending a celebration at Agathon's house. He himself, it is reported by many, is not a beautiful man, though he is very much a seeker of it in many forms, as we witness in the dramatic opening of the *Charmides*.[6] Critias suggests to Socrates to offer Charmides a charming medicine for Charmides's headache (not the only time Socrates has contrived a device (*mechanê*): consider the fictional device he puts to use in Diotima), and indeed Socrates may indeed have such a therapy, which I believe comes to be manifest in what I would suggest is the most salient feature of the clearly invited comparison between Eros and Socrates—the *metaxic* (in-between) state they share. As a messenger between gods and humans, and as a mixture himself between god and human, the nature and birth of Eros is thus a psychogenetic myth that portrays an important part of Socratic philosophy: his knowledge of ignorance. Indeed, earlier in the *Symposium*, Socrates claims that the "erotic things" are the only things he know about.[7]

We now have a myth that can render some sense to this claim. This myth about Eros makes it fundamental that he is *daimonic*, and identifies Socrates with the *daimonic* in a way that is not emphasized in any other dialogue, including the *Republic* and the *Phaedrus*.[8] Here, as we have seen, *erôs* is first of all aimed at what it lacks. Its object is other than is itself; it is other-directed. Therefore, to understand one's own erotic nature is to understand oneself as *in need*. In recognizing how one can and cannot satisfy this need, one understands one's own possibilities and limits. To have an understanding of one's own lack therefore is to have a knowledge of what one does and does not know. Socratic self-knowledge is thus importantly tied to this *metaxic* feature of *erôs*. It is most apt that Diotima reports that Eros, much like Socrates, philosophizes his whole life and apparently it is a task that is never quite finished. Philosophizing turns out to be constitutive of the human condition, situated between a divine knowledge and a brute ignorance:

> None of the gods philosophizes and desires to become wise—for he is so—nor if there is anyone else who is wise, does he philosophize. Nor, in turn, do those who lack understanding (*amatheis*) philosophize and desire to become wise; for it is precisely this that makes lack of understanding dangerous (*chalepon*), that if someone is not beautiful and good, nor wise (*phronimon*), it seems to him, he thinks himself sufficient (*hikanon*). . . . For wisdom (*sophia*) is one of the most beautiful things, and Eros is love (*erôs*) of the beautiful; and so by necessity Eros is a philosopher, and as a philosopher he is between (*metaxu*) wisdom and lack of understanding (*amathous*).[9]

The gods and the ignorant share a self-sufficiency, even if it is justified in the case of the god (who indeed possesses wisdom), while it is illusory for those who lack understanding and only think they know what they don't know. It is no accident that Diotima calls this latter condition a dangerous (*chalepon*) one. Critias, for one, reveals a dangerous willful ignorance of his own incompleteness. The philosopher, however, is aware of his incompleteness, even if it threatens to be insuperable. Unlike Critias, who claims to be in possession of wisdom, Socrates constantly chases after it, and when he runs out of resources and is unable to complete his search for wisdom, with a new inquiry he blooms and comes to life again. Socratic self-knowledge is thus importantly tied to *erôs* in this way. As McNeill puts it, "Like Eros, Socrates is characterized by a seemingly limitless capacity for generating discourses while in conversation with others, a peculiar resourcefulness which seems to be connected with his ability to 'divine' what kinds of education are appropriate for what kinds of human souls."[10]

Furthermore, I would suggest that Diotima's account also invites us to think about how and why Socrates in his *metaxic*, erotic state could be said to bind the whole together and make communication possible between the human and the divine. As we have seen, the role of the *theoros* described by Nightingale fits here precisely: "The philosophic [*theoros*] . . . acts at the interface between time and eternity, the personal and the transcendental. The dialogues dealing with *theoria* offer a literary and philosophical exploration of this dynamic tension."[11] "As a human being, he must journey again and again to the metaphysical region. . . . And he must 'return' each time to the terrestrial and human world, since he is an incarnate human being. In short, he must shuttle back and forth between two worlds."[12]

The *theoros* who leaves the city and returns after having gazed on the distant wisdom in the eternal realm is himself *daimonic* in Diotima's sense. Indeed, this further demonstrates what Diotima calls the "homelessness" of Eros and illuminates its connection to Socratic philosophy.[13] The *theoros* is a wanderer, and in traveling abroad to bring wisdom back that transcends the knowledge at home, such a wanderer is thus never quite at home in his city. It is in this sense that he is *atopos*. If such a wanderer can be identified as *daimonic*, then he is also, as Diotima says, at home with his need (*endeiai sunoikos*). Let us remind ourselves, that such a journey seems to be perpetual: the *daimonic* philosopher, like Eros, seems to forever renew himself and die, falling short of complete wisdom,[14] but whose *very incompleteness* keeps him in pursuit. It is this incompleteness, finally, that is constitutive of his philosophic activity, and so Socratic philosophy and *erôs* come to have the "same purpose."[15] What this purpose is, and how it might complete the *daimonic* inquirer, comes to the forefront with Socrates's next question for Diotima.

Chapter Five

The Good of *Erôs* (*Symposium* 204c–206b)

Having learned from Diotima of the nature and origin of Eros, Socrates then asked Diotima "What use (*chreian*) is he for human beings?"[1] This is to be Socrates's next lesson. Socrates's use of the word "use" recalls for us the form of his conversation regarding the possibility and benefit of *sôphrosunê*. There, too, Socrates first sought for the nature (the sort of thing) *sôphrosunê* could be, and afterward inquired into the benefit it might bring to human beings. The second question, as we saw, was prompted by a strong intuition held by both Critias and Socrates that *sôphrosunê* is indeed beneficial for us. Here, too, Socrates had the same hunch in talking to Diotima. Indeed, the speech Socrates is giving at Agathon's party is part of a party conversation to praise Eros. Of the speakers, only Aristophanes and Socrates describe his origin story, and thus the other speakers miss important elements of the nature of love. They fail to adequately account for the benefit he brings to human beings and subsequently the reason he should be praised at all.

Diotima's own account of the nature and origin of Eros fundamentally revises the prior speeches, especially those of Agathon and Aristophanes. We have seen how she rebukes Agathon's account by emphasizing the needy, incomplete, in-between nature of the *daimonic* Eros, who lacks beauty and is thus not a beautiful god. But now we will see that Diotima's account introduces another element in dealing with the benefit of *erôs*, that fundamentally revises Aristophanes's account of *erôs* as a desire for one's other half.

Diotima began by saying,[2] "The one loving (*ho erôn*) beautiful things loves (*herai*): what does he love (*ti herai*)?" To which Socrates responded,

"That they become his (*gesthai hautôi*)." But this prompted Diotima to press Socrates: "What will he have when the beautiful things have become his own?" Socrates, apparently having run out of resources, had difficulty answering this, and so Diotima changed the question from the beautiful to the good: "What will [the one loving the good things] have when they become his own?" Socrates now felt better equipped (*euporôteron*) to answer the question this time, "he will be happy (*eudaimôn*)."

Diotima thus began by insisting to Socrates, just as Socrates insisted to Critias, that they get at the "of-what" of *erôs*. It is important that Diotima does not disagree with Socrates's claim that the lover, whether of beautiful or good things, wants these things to become his own. As Bloom points out, "The possessiveness of love is underlined here. Love is not just contemplation of a beautiful object, but requires the active pursuit of it so as to possess it."[3] So far then, Diotima has not challenged this feature of Aristophanes's own account of the acquisitive nature of *erôs*. But a new conversation is launched in this exchange that emphasizes what we earlier called the intentionality or object-relatedness of *erôs*. This culminates in Diotima's explicit rebuke of Aristophanes's speech:[4] the love of one's other half is wrongheaded. Diotima's reformulation of love as aimed at the good seeks to move beyond the speeches of Agathon and Aristophanes, which are both *thumotic*. Agathon's account renders love as complete and self-sufficient, while Aristophanes's incompleteness still seeks a fulfillment in the extension and propagation of self. Diotima's account will thus respond with a notion of the good that transcends the loving self. As Strauss puts it, Diotima denies that the object of love is one's own things.[5] But Socrates has difficulty answering Diotima's question about the "of-what" regarding the possession of beautiful things. Why does Socrates have a difficult time answering Diotima's question when it is framed in terms of beauty? Why does it become easier to answer the question when Diotima suggests they replace the beautiful with the good?

The substitution of the good for the beautiful cuts two ways. On the one hand, Diotima's move and Socrates's easy acceptance of it implies that the interchangeability of the two suggests a near identification of the terms. On the other hand, the very change of terms and the ease with which Socrates is able to determine what one has when one acquires good things (in contrast to his difficulty saying what one has in possessing beautiful things) suggests instead an important difference between the beautiful and the good.[6] Barney has suggested that the two notions play different roles in our psychic economy: "What is good is so by virtue of its effects on some subject: 'good' is thus a causal concept, closely tied to the 'beneficial' . . . *Kalon* has no operationalized counterpart analogous to 'beneficial': what is fine is not fine by *doing* anything to or for anyone."[7] Consequently, the beautiful, according to Barney, turns out to more like an object of *admiration*, than an object of desire. Admiration differs from desire, in not being acquisitive:

> If the primitive sign of wanting is trying to get, what then is the primitive sign of admiring? . . . Admiration seems to seek *intensified* contact; but that contact might consist in emulation and a seeking of kinship . . . or simply a contemplative prolongation of the admiring gaze itself. It may well lead to no detectable action at all . . . admiration, even at lower levels of intensity, involves a forgetfulness of self. It borders on surprise and wonder (*thaumazein*): the admired object absorbs our full attention.[8]

The beautiful is thus an object of a passion that seems to be different in kind from *erôs*, if indeed *erôs* is necessarily an acquisitive desire. Such a picture complicates the psychological account of the *Republic*, in which anything in our "psychic economy" must conform to a vision of *erôs* as acquisitive. I have attempted to argue[9] that such an account of *erôs* is thoroughly *thumotic*,[10] and it is important that Diotima is here alluding to its limitations. As Barney points out, the passion of admiration—culminating in wonder—appears to suggest a seeking in our soul that is neither aimed at possession nor satisfied by it. Admiration seeks an "intensified contact" but not an acquisition of an object. There is also, importantly, a forgetting of the self that is in tension with what Bloom calls the "utilitarian" pursuit of good things that Socrates seems quick to endorse and ready to describe when Diotima brings it up. I would suggest that this is an important part of Socrates's philosophic education at the foot of Diotima. As we will see, at the height of Diotima's ascent of *erôs* there will be a contemplation (*theoria*) without acquisitiveness.

Shortly after substituting the good for the beautiful, Diotima introduced (seemingly out of the blue) the notion that *erôs* aims at an eternal possession of the good: "This wanting (*boulêsin*) and this *erôs*, do you suppose they are common to all human beings, and all want the good things to be theirs always (*hautois einai aei*), or how do you mean it?"[11] Socrates explicitly agreed that it was common to all human beings, though it appears he only tacitly consented at this point to the new feature of permanence. Socrates explicitly agreed to it when Diotima summed up their view of *erôs* as "of the good being one's own always."[12] We should note that Diotima's definition of love, then, does not entirely reject Aristophanes's "love of one's own" for it is important at this point, that the good (unlike the beautiful) is acquired. But Diotima's explicit addition of "always"—a turn to an immortal permanence—will lead to an important modification of Aristophanes's account.[13] According to Diotima, human beings and animals seek this immortality through reproduction:

> For *erôs* is not . . . of the beautiful as you believe. . . . It is of engendering (*gennêseôs*) and bringing to birth (*tou tokou*) in the beautiful. . . . Because engendering is born forever (*aeigenes*) and is immortal as far as that can happen to a mortal being.[14]

> . . . Mortal nature seeks as far as possible to be forever and immortal. Mortal nature is capable of immortality only in this way, the way of generation, because it is always leaving behind another that is young to replace the old. . . . By this device (*mêchanêi*), Socrates, the mortal shares in immortality . . . but the immortal has a different way.[15]

As Gabriele Lear points out, "Beauty is the goddess of erotic generation, the mortal form of immortality."[16] Diotima's new emphasis on generation modifies the earlier account of *erôs* as purely acquisitive. Indeed, the notion that all human beings are pregnant implies that our deepest longing is to "give rather than take,"[17] and that *erôs* is therefore not an appetite like hunger.

But *thumos* still hides behind this generative *erôs*. It is important that beauty in this account so far is tied up with our vulnerability to the threat of death, directly linking it to a *thumotic* longing. This *thumotic* longing to outlast our ephemerality and replace ourselves with something akin, is displayed (albeit more or less unconsciously) in the acts of animal and human childbirth, bodily growth, psychic and moral development of oneself and others, studying, seeking fame, self-sacrifice for love of another, and education of others.[18] Diotima suggested to Socrates that even he could be initiated into the these mysteries (*muêtheiês*) of the erotic things (*ta erotika*), but she doubted his ability to understand the highest mysteries (*ta de teleia kai epoptika*).[19] In the next chapter, we will discuss these highest mysteries and what Socrates learned from them. For now, we should wonder why Diotima is more confident in Socrates's ability to understand or be initiated into these lower mysteries. I would like to suggest that it is because the lower mysteries reveal a *thumotic erôs* that we and Socrates are more likely to understand their nature. This is because Diotima has not yet revealed a love to us that is truly a denial of our own things, and shows how fundamental our *thumotic* attachment to our own things is.[20] In presenting to us as *erotic* human longings these desires to replace ourselves with something that is akin, whether it be through offspring, fame, students or the like, she is actually eroticizing *thumos* itself, and this allows us as mortal beings to understand what *erôs* is like. It is in fact Aristophanes's description of love in disguise, which very description resonates with our quite legitimate intuition that human love speaks to a lack, requires a reciprocity, and is importantly relational between humans. The lower mysteries, too, speak of longings rooted in a lack (our hatred of our own ephemerality), and our yearning to defeat this vulnerability and assert ourselves. They too speak to a human relationship or community, which gives meaning and context to the love itself. The immortality one attains in these lower mysteries is one that always involves another human being speaking about us, remembering us, or carrying on work that we accomplished until death brought it to its close. But the beautiful itself, when we hear of the highest mysteries, requires an ascent that will take us beyond this *thumotic erôs* to an *erôs* that is "without copulation or reciprocity."[21] The admiration that culminates in wonder will play a critical role here, and it is this wonder that transforms the *erôs* of the *thumotic* longing for immortality into a philosophic life. The nature of such a philosophic life will renew for us the question of our relationship with our human community.

Chapter Six

Diotima's Ascent (*Symposium* 210a–212a)

In spite of her warning to Socrates that he might not be capable of being initiated into the highest mysteries of *erôs*, Diotima still made the attempt to teach him. She began playfully, punning on the word "*erôs*" by saying that she would speak (*erô*), and then possibly alluded to her own *thumos* in saying she would not stint (*apoleipsô*) in her effort or zeal (*prothumias*).[1] She thus suggested to Socrates (and the reader) that he and others must follow the *thumotic* Diotima in order to be initiated into the highest mysteries. At the top of the ascent, we should ask what, if anything, remains of this *prothumias*. We must also inquire about Socrates's ability to follow Diotima, and ask whether it is this or something else that provokes applause from those listening to Socrates's speech. What would it mean to follow Diotima, and what evidence can we give that Socrates does this?

Diotima suggested that he who is to move correctly (*orthôs ionta*)[2] will begin, when young, to go to beautiful bodies, and first he "must love one body and there generate beautiful speeches (*gennan logous kalous*)."[3] The first step in what turns out to be an ascent of *erôs*[4] begins with a physical encounter with an individual beloved, but we should note that it is not primarily sexual, for the act generates beautiful speeches. Instead, I would suggest that the love of the individual body's work appears in the beautiful conversations between the lover and the beloved. Diotima here thus appears to be referring to the pregnancy that played a crucial role in her account of the lower mysteries of love. We should notice that even at this first step of the ascent, we are on a higher level. Whereas, according to the lower mysteries, offspring in the form of children are the first main example of a mortal being's pursuit of immortality, no children are mentioned as resulting from this encounter. One might suggest that the pursuit of fame could be encapsulated by the engendering of *logous kalous*, but it is not all clear that the individual production of these beautiful speeches serves such a purpose. And as Diotima continues her speech, the pregnancy seen in the lower mysteries will be a less and less dominant image. We will see that by the time the procreative or generative element of the erotic ascent reemerges at the end of the story, it is vague, seemingly inconsistent with her account, and appears to play an insignificant role overall.

Diotima continued by pointing out that the lover of the one individual body must[5] "realize (*katanoêsai*) that the beauty that is in any body whatsoever is related to (*adelphon*) that in another body"[6] and "if he must pursue beauty of form (*eidei*, punning on *ei dei*), it is great foolishness (*anoia*) not to think (*hegeisthai*) the beauty in all bodies is one and the same."[7] It is this realization that necessitates that he be a lover of all beautiful bodies and leads him to look down with disdain (*kataphrônesanta*) on the obsession with an individual body as an insignificant thing (*smikron*). What causes the *necessity* of this first step up on the ascent of *erôs*? Why *must* the lover come to look down on the individual body as insignificant? It seems that a new insight has drawn his attention away from the previous beloved, which he previously took to be fulfilling his deepest longings. In this way, the move upward appears to be an intellectual ascent, marked by an education in the truth about beauty, that apparently rises from the particular to the universal, the individual to the general. But it is not clear at all that the beauty of all bodies, in comparison with the beauty of the individual, is indeed more beautiful. In what sense is this erotic experience *higher* than the one that has preceded it? For Diotima, there seems to be no doubt that the rise to this step is almost effortless, with one who leads rightly. But at this point, we are left without a reason to endorse such a smooth necessity. We will be given a reason only when we come to the apex of the ascent. But as we ascend, I believe the explanation for the necessity becomes more obscure, not less. To see this, consider Diotima's turn to the next step: the soul.

Diotima said, "After this he must think that the beauty in souls is more honorable (*timiôteron*) than the beauty of their bodies."[8] We should notice that Diotima uses a possibly *thumotically* charged word (*timiôteron*) to rank this new beloved object (beauty in souls) above the previous one (beauty in bodies). It is a word that played a dominant role in her account of the lower mysteries when she pointed to the desire for immortality in the pursuit of fame. But at the same time as she uses this language, she downplays the essential feature of *thumos* (its desire for self-propagation, a personal assertion of one's own things) by omitting what we might, with good reason, expect to be the step above all bodies: an *individual soul.* Diotima makes no room in her account for the individual soul, I would say intentionally, because the move from the particular and individual to the general and universal is an abstraction that depersonalizes the self, and this depersonalization is only augmented the more we ascend. This is especially odd when we consider that the work of the *erôs* of one body was to produce beautiful speeches. Should this not be even more paradigmatic of the loving activity of one individual soul? Indeed, Diotima says at this point that now the lover will "engender (*tiktein*) and seek (*zêtein*) such speeches as will make the young men better (*beltious tous neous*)."[9] The plural (*tous neous*) indicates that the conversation with one individual disappeared after the first step. Moreover, they are no longer called beautiful speeches: the good in the form of what is better (*beltious*) has again replaced the *kalon.* There is no implication that they are shared, reciprocal, philosophical conversations, yet there does seem to be an educational effect on the beloved. But Diotima does not explain why this feature, at this stage of the ascent, should necessitate ranking it higher than the love of all bodies. But as her speech transitions to the next step, Diotima introduces language that begins to suggest the meaning in the order of these steps of the ascent.

Diotima now suggests that the previous step at least, but perhaps even all three previous steps, takes place "in order that (*hina*) [the lover] may be compelled (*anankasthê*) to behold (*theasthai*) the beautiful in practices (*epitêdeumata*) and laws (*nomois*) and to see (*idein*) that all this is akin to itself (*hautoi suggenes*) so that (*hina*) he will come to think (*hêgêsêtai*) the beauty of bodies is something insignificant (*smikron*)."[10] This is the first time that Diotima talks of beholding (*theoria*), and thus explicitly introduces into the ascent the passion culminating in wonder. The lover may gaze on his beloved in the earlier stages, but Diotima does not mention it. Conversely, at this stage Diotima shifts the language away from desire. The practices and laws are objects for our contemplation. Though in the first three steps (body, bodies, souls) the lover is explicitly said to love the objects, in this step Diotima omits any reference to any loving desire toward the practices and laws.[11] In addition, Diotima implies that there is a stronger necessity here in using the verb *anankasthô*, and we are thus compelled to wonder at the compulsion at work here. This step of the ascent is the most mysterious so far. For the step from the beauty of souls to the beauty of practices and laws is a step away from the human. And this is so even given the human-made nature of laws and practices. The first three steps are conceivably, at least, reconcilable with our intuition that love involves an intimate reciprocity, perhaps exemplified in Aristophanes's speech. Though we were suspicious of the *thumotic* (and perhaps even tyrannical) roots of Aristophanes's speech, still we were able to recognize his account of human relationships as erotic. In this step of Diotima's ascent, however, there is no possibility for reciprocity, as the lover comes to gaze upon that which is soulless and neither gazes back nor desires the lover in return. *Erôs* is thus becoming less recognizable to us as *erôs*, as it abstracts more from a relationship between human beings.[12] Thus it is revealing that Diotima here introduces that *erôs* involves a kind of kinship (*suggenes*), but the kinship is not between the beautiful and the viewer but between the beautiful and itself. Unlike the gods and human beings, who in their lack of self-sufficiency require a *daimon* to bind them together and make communication possible, the beautiful here stands complete whether or not the viewer beholds it. The viewer's relationship to the beautiful is one of gazing from a distance rather than being with it. It is mysterious how such an erotic experience captures the intimacy we saw in Aristophanes's account of lovers finding each other's halves. To be sure, Aristophanes agrees with Diotima's implication that this intimacy is not only about sex, but Aristophanes would be right to question whether the love that is now being described adequately resembles love in our human experience of it.

The turn away from human intimacy continues as Diotima now suggests that after practices and laws, the lover must come to see (again, not desire) "the beauty of knowledges (*epistêmôn kallos*),"[13] a vision that Diotima says will transform him, for "in looking (*blepôn*) at such great (*polu*) beauty, [he will see it] no longer in one thing, like a servant (*oiketês*) who is fond (*agapôn*) of a boy or some human being or a single practice . . . but having been turned (*tetrammenos*) to the great sea of beauty, he beholds (*theôrôn*) it and gives birth to many beautiful and magnificent speeches and thoughts (*kalous logous kai melgaloprepeis . . . kai dianoêmata*) in boundless (*aphthonôi*) love of wisdom."[14] The vision of the great sea of beauty inspires a turning of the lover's soul. Former loves of individual bodies, souls, or even practices now appear narrow-minded and unbefitting the magnificent multitude of beauties he now beholds. Diotima says that the love of such beauties for someone who has made this turn will now appear servile and unambitious. Such language should appeal to the *thumos* of one who sees his own station as above the menial household laborers that Diotima disdains. Rather, the one who makes this erotic ascent is strong and courageous enough[15] to turn away from the insignificant realm of the individual and particular and contemplate the magnificent multitude of beauty writ large. In doing so, we should notice that Diotima reintroduces the generation of beautiful speeches, which had disappeared after the first step. Now the beautiful speeches are also magnificent, mirroring the great sea of beauty, and are paired with thoughts. But why then does Diotima describe this as not only an intellectual conversion but as a *thumotic* one?

We should remark first that although Diotima reintroduces generation of speeches and thoughts at this point, it is no longer clear at this point that such speeches and thoughts are embedded in discourse with an other. They seem to come rather from a solitary ecstatic vision of the great sea of beauty with no explicit mention of a return to conversation with other human beings. Her description of the ascent of *erôs* continues to denude it of the erotic as we understand it, even as she continues to use *thumotic* language. This strange tension is exhibited in her use of the term "*pholosophia aphthonôi*," which I have, following Avi Sharon, translated as "boundless love of wisdom." Prompted by the seemingly boundless beauty of knowledges, the lover himself is moved by a boundless love of wisdom. This apparently attractive notion looks less so if we call to mind how incoherent and dangerous is Critias's contentless self-knowledge that is restrained by no standard outside itself. There is a danger that the love of wisdom itself, if indeed restrained by nothing, could itself be turned toward a tyrannical pursuit of mastery. Indeed, Diotima emphasizes that when this boundless desire is strengthened and increased (*sôstheis kai auxetheis*), that it now comes to one knowledge of this sort that sees the beautiful itself. Diotima's optimism for this should raise our suspicions, both regarding her use of *thumotic* language and her continued abstraction from the human erotic encounter. But Diotima claims that at the apex of the ascent, the beautiful yields a reason, a justification, for all prior erotic efforts. At the apex, the beautiful itself by itself is described:

> Try to pay attention as best as you can. You see, the man who has been educated to this point in the erotic things, beholding (*theômenos*) the beautiful things in the right order and correctly, in now going to the completion (*telos*) of loving, will

> all of a sudden catch sight of (*exaphnês katapseitai*) something wondrously (*thaumaston*) beautiful in its nature, that thing, Socrates, for whose sake (*heneken*) were all his prior labors. First, it always is and neither comes to be nor perishes, neither increasing nor passing away. Second, it is not beautiful this way and ugly that way, nor beautiful at one time and ugly at another, nor beautiful in relation to one thing and ugly in relation to another; nor is it beautiful here but ugly there, as it would be if it were beautiful for some people and ugly for others. Nor will the beautiful become visible (*phantasthêsetai*) to him in a kind of face or hands or anything else that belongs to the body, nor in any speech or any knowledge. It is not anywhere in another thing . . . but itself by itself with itself, it is always one in form; and all the other beautiful things share in that. (210e–211b)

Upon coming to the summit of this ascent of love, *erôs* arrives at the goal of its efforts. What is portrayed is the eternal beauty itself, not composite but one, not coming to be or passing away, nor subject to change at all. Neither spatial, nor temporal, nor inhering in space or time, it is radically transcendent of our sensible world. It is not relative to context, or individual views or perceptions, and does not appear in any bodily form, or wisdom. Yet this utterly transcendent good is what most satisfies the deepest longing of our souls. What does it mean to say that such a transcendent beauty is the satisfaction of our longings, and is indeed the completion (*telos*) of all prior erotic pursuits, which are now justified by the glimpse of this wonder? According to Diotima, it seems that it is its very eternal permanence that is constitutive of the beautiful itself. It exists beyond all relations and displays what Gabriele Lear calls "self-sufficiency and lack of change," and it is "impervious to the passage of time."[16] Lear rightly goes on to point out how different this is from Diotima's earlier account of mortal striving for immortality, especially in the lower mysteries: "We mortal human beings are always trying to become beautiful and good . . . but can never be permanently so . . . we are so far from being self-sufficient that our selves persist in time only in the being of our literal and metaphorical children."[17] But unlike us, the beautiful itself manifests what Lear calls "transcendent being," and that it is "godlike in its relationship to time and change. In fact, its manifestation of its atemporal imperviousness to change is exactly what strikes lover as being so wonderful about beauty."[18] Diotima's view of beauty thus presents it as a supremely immortal being, and it is this immortality that Diotima claims is the ultimate goal of all our erotic striving. Now we can see the justification for the necessity Diotima describes in the ascent and the order of the steps. As one ascends the ladder, one's *erôs* is directed at more and more *being*. The ascent to the beautiful itself is a continual move away from the realm of becoming, toward a being that is so transcendent it appears to have no contact with that which changes anymore. The glimpse of it, which Diotima says occurs "all of a sudden" (*exaiphnês*), is so powerful that this vision would shake a human being to his core. If the lover were to catch sight of it, it would be not only transformative but fundamentally disruptive of the lover's understanding and experience of his own erotic pursuits. Indeed, it is not clear how *erôs* can reach its goal without ceasing to be *daimonic*. For in ascending to that which has more being, we also come more and more to look with disdain—*thumotic* contempt—on the erotic pursuits of the lower steps, mired as they are in their vulnerability to change and decay. The ascent to the self-sufficient beautiful itself would thus engender a new seeing that thus compels us to regard these lower forms of *erôs* as insignificant and unworthy of our devotion. Diotima's account calls forth a very reevaluation of our values, in light of the ultimate transcendent being of the beautiful. This is why Diotima suggests to Socrates that it is there, in looking at the beautiful, that life is worth living (*biôton*) for a human being[19] and goes on to ask him:

> Do you think that a worthless life (*phaulon bion*) would come to be for a human being looking there (*bekeise blepontos*) and beholding (*theômenou*) it by that which he must, and being together (*sunontos*) with it? Or do you not conclude (*enthumê*) that only here, in seeing in the way the beautiful is seeable (*horônti hôi horaton to kalon*), will he come to give birth (*tiktein*) not to images (*eidola*) of virtue—because he does not lay hold of (*ephaptomenôi*) an image—but true, because he lays hold of the true; and that once he has given birth to and nourished (*threpsamenôi*) true virtue, he begins to become loved by the gods (*theophilei*) and, if (*eiper*) it is possible for any human being, to become immortal as well?[20]

In these final two questions are Diotima's only plausible allusions to a post-ecstatic descent to the world of human relationships. For Diotima's questions reintroduce the generative power of love, as she implies that the one beholding the beautiful gives birth to true virtue, which one might suppose to be constitutive of human actions in community. She also introduces the language of "touching" (*ephaptomenôi*) and "being with" (*sunontos*) it, but she implies that this language is subordinated to the "seeing" of the beautiful, in the way that it is seeable. It seems that an intellectual apprehension has completely replaced a reciprocal loving encounter. We are not seen by the beautiful, nor recognized by it as seeing. The "being with" the beautiful does not overcome the irreducible distance and difference between the viewer and the spectacle. Diotima suspects, rightly, that Socrates may object that such a life, if indeed it is most worthy to be lived by a human being, is not a human life at all. And it is for this reason that she claims, again with *thumotic* language, that those who have not yet reached this summit and glimpsed it (and are consequently "laying hold of" images in the realm of change and decay), live a life that is less worthy, too paltry to be befitting one who has beheld the magnificent sea of beauty. But Diotima leaves unexplained what exactly is engendered when one gives birth to "true virtue," and whether or how it is an ethical virtue that has some relation to other human actors. Up to this point, her account of the vision of the beautiful itself implies that if anything is engendered, it is a self-transformation that is so arresting and disruptive, that it seems to remove the human being from his attachments to others, rather than reestablish connection with them. Human community seems to be among the things that are *disdained* by the one who ascends to the apex. True virtue, following this line of reasoning, appears to have more to do with the intellectual excellence involved not in human praxis but in contemplation of that which is impervious to change. It is here that a human being could become immortal. But we must emphasize that Diotima's claim for the immortality of human beings rests on an explicit "if" (*eiper*), and just as she gives no explanation of the nature of true virtue, neither does she give any explanation or justification for this possibility. In fact, she leaves Socrates and the reader with unanswered questions.

Indeed, it is important that Socrates himself reports no answer he gave to Diotima's questions about the life of the human being beholding the beautiful. We then are left to wonder, given the self-sufficient, transcendent being of the beautiful itself, and the nature, conversely, of the incomplete, mortal, ephemeral human beings who seek to commune with it, how should we understand the possibility and benefit of human interaction with the beautiful itself? When the human soul reaches the apex of the ascent, it is no longer clear how the human soul gazing upon the beautiful remains a *human* soul belonging to a human community. At the same time, the replacement of acquisitive language with the language of vision and beholding (*theoria*) emphasizes an irreducible distance that the beautiful maintains between itself and the viewer. As "partners" in an erotic relationship, the communication between the lover and the beautiful itself is without *erôs* as we understand it. *Erôs* as Diotima describes it comes, when one reaches the beautiful itself, to look not like the *erôs* of a human being but like that of a divine being in no need of others.

If this is true, we could suggest that Diotima presents an ascent that abstracts from human intimacy and replaces it with a vision of a spectacle that culminates in a self-forgetting self-dissolution. And here we should wonder how it relates to the tragic self-dissolution that is the great danger of a tyrannical expression of *thumos*.[21] We have thus reached a point that takes us back to the conflict between Socrates and Critias and the nature of *sôphrosunê*. For I wish to argue that their visions of self-knowledge lead in two very different and incompatible interpretations of the significance of Diotima's teaching about *erôs*. I will argue that to see the beautiful itself as the culmination of our desire for immortality actually gratifies a *thumotic* longing that leads only to a tragic self-dissolution. I believe that Socrates offers us a better way for comprehending our relationship with the beautiful, and it is revealed in our response of admiration or wonder,[22] which exhibits a *possible* kinship between the beautiful and the mortal viewer, and a *benefit* in the engendering of *sôphrosunê* understood neither as an intellectual or ethical virtue but a *zetetic* one, an excellence of soul that is necessary for excellence in inquiry. This kind of Socratic self-forgetting, if it is not dangerous, comes from a wonder that puts us in touch with, though at a remove from, being as such. Socratic philosophy, and the wonder that is its origin and culmination, remains thoroughly *daimonic*, a feature that Diotima introduced but most significantly fails to emphasize in her account of the beautiful itself. For Socrates, self-knowledge entails no oblivion of self. I will show that if Diotima's account is to be of help to us, it is of the utmost importance that we neither forget the fundamental lesson about *erôs* as in-between (*metaxu*), nor should we, *if* this is possible, *thumotize* the ascent of *erôs*. In developing these claims, we will see more clearly the connection between Diotima's apotheosis of the beautiful and our human longings for wisdom and connection to one another.

Chapter Seven

Beautiful Socrates and the Connection between *Sôphrosunê* and Wonder

There is a dangerous possibility of a *thumotic* (even tyrannical) reading of Diotima's speech. I would suggest that Critias, in his promotion of a self-certain and enclosed vision of the good, detached permanently from the yearnings of others, promotes such a view. Critian self-knowledge purports to be a self-reflexive wisdom restrained by no normative guidance outside itself. It is the self-knowledge of a tyrant, whose hatred of alterity is rooted in an illusion of self-sufficiency. A Critian view of Diotima's ascent would find in its *telos* (the beautiful itself) an attractive, if paradoxical, all-encompassing knowledge of the whole detached from the lower longings not befitting to him. Moreover, one who is dominated by *thumos* will be tempted by the immortality promised at the end of Diotima's speech, which would be read as gratifying the ultimate longing of one whose dominant passion is his fear of his vulnerability to death. This individual sees in Diotima's speech a victory over his own nature in a defeat of time and mortality. If indeed possible, such a *thumotic* soul is released from any restraint upon his desire to expand and propagate his self. This is most clear in the case of our Critian's *thumotic* aspiration. Such an individual would not be fully satisfied by the way mortals achieve immortality according to the "lower" mysteries—the replacement of oneself with someone that is younger is not self-sufficient enough (being dependent upon future generations of other human beings who will perpetuate one's self). It will also disappoint the craving that what remains of oneself is truly *one's own*. As we saw in Critias's rebuke of Charmides when the young boy (according to Critias) mangled his teaching, one can only be replicated up to a point by the words of others. The way mortal beings, according to the lower mysteries, attain mortality is limited in remaining embedded in the *logoi* of other human beings. *Thumos* demands more and sees a potential glimpse of it at the end of Diotima's speech. But such a transcendence is fool's gold for the Critian. For as we have seen, the transcendence Diotima speaks of leaves in doubt the very existence of the self *qua* self when it comes to behold the beautiful itself. Inasmuch as the transcendence described by Diotima is a transcendence, it is not a self-transcendence or one in which the *self endures* throughout the ascent. If the *thumos* of the Critian longs for a victory over death then the existence of the beautiful itself does promise such a victory, but this victory, if it belongs to anyone, belongs to the beautiful itself. The one who beholds it is granted such a victory only at the cost of it no longer being *his* victory over death. At the very moment that *thumos* gains its beloved prize, then, *thumos* is utterly annihilated. Just as a tragic self-dissolution threatened the tyrannical outgrowth of *thumos* in the city,[1] so too a *thumotic* ascent to the beautiful tragically leads not to self-propagation and expansion but self-abnegation. Aristophanes was right to warn lovers not to make another assault on the gods, lest we be cut in half again. This is the price of unrestrained *thumos*.

In what follows, I will argue that this tragedy is averted by the lesson (as I understand it) that Socrates appears to glean from the speech of Diotima. It is by no means clear that Socrates endorses everything that Diotima said to him and based on his comments upon her speech and his behavior in the *Symposium*, I hope to show that the primary notions that Socrates takes from Diotima revolve around her notion that *erôs* is *daimonic* and that wonder is critical to the pursuit of wisdom. I believe Socrates disagrees with Diotima about the nature of wonder and the role it plays in philosophy, and related to this disagreement is another about the role that the beautiful itself plays in our lives. As we will see, the main departure Socrates appears to make from Diotima is in his insistence that self-knowledge is fundamentally an outgrowth of philosophical conversations. One's true self is both known in and constituted by the dialogue of philosophical inquiry, and it is here finally that we will see a therapy for tyrannical self-dissolution. To begin, let us turn to Socrates's comments upon Diotima's speech.

Rather than say what he responded to Diotima's closing question, Socrates tells those at the party that he has been persuaded (*pepeismai*), and having thus been persuaded he says, "I try to persuade (*pithein*) others that for this possession (*ktêmatos*) one could not easily get a better co-worker (*sunergon*) for human nature (*têi anthrôpeiai phusei*) than *erôs*."[2] The appeal to human nature is striking. If I am right, then human nature as Socrates understands it has not been described by Diotima's account. Rather, she has described a "possession" that is a "co-worker" with it. *Erôs*, which Diotima described as acquisitive before turning to the highest mysteries, now itself seems to be called an acquisition, one that supplements human nature in some way. What should we say human nature is like, such that one can find no better co-worker for it than *erôs*? I suggest that the primary part of human nature that Socrates is discussing is its *thumos*, to which Socrates has already appealed in using the language of *possession* (when *erôs* is made to be "one's own"). The same question emerges at this moment that Diotima asked Socrates before giving her speech about the highest mysteries: what will come to be for human nature with the possession of *erôs*?[3] The answer now comes in the next sentence. "Accordingly, I say that every man (*andra*) must (*chrê*) honor (*timan*) Eros, and I myself honor the erotic things (*ta erôtika*) and practice them especially (*diapherontôs askô*); and I recommend them to others, and now and always I praise (*egkomiazô*) the power and courage (*dunamin kai andreian*) of Eros as far as I am able."[4] Socrates has remarkably very little to say about Diotima's speech. Much too little. Eros, finally, should be praised because of its "power and courage" (*dunamin kai andreian*). After Diotima's stunning and disruptive initiation into the mysteries of the transcendent being of the beautiful itself, Socrates makes no mention *at all* of the realm of being and instead uses two words that seem to play little to no role in her speech. In response to a stunning speech, it is a stunningly odd endorsement, if indeed it is one. What power and courage—words that have thoroughly *thumotic* associations—might Socrates be thinking about? The closest Diotima comes to remarks that relate to these two words occurs when she describes the turn away from the soul[5] to the great sea of beauty, a turn that elevates one from being a slavish, small-minded, unambitious lover to one who has much higher aspirations. It is the most *thumotic* moment of her speech, and indeed it appears to be this *thumotic* engine of the ascent that Socrates signals as worthy of honor in his final words about the speech. Indeed, Diotima's account of the erotic neediness of the lover thus speaks more to the *thumotic* hostility to this neediness, with a literal *encouragement* to achieve victory over such incompleteness.[6] Moreover, Diotima even suggests that such *thumotic* hostility is an essential component of the erotic ascent. Her account implies that without *thumos*, the lover who gazes upward will not be motivated to make the ascent.[7] The ascent of *erôs* thus can only be accomplished, Diotima suggests, through a *thumotic* striving—philosophical *erôs* cannot be divorced from *thumos*.[8]

What then should we say about what Socrates learned from Diotima, if these *thumotic* words are the ones he chooses to emphasize? I would like to suggest that Socrates and Diotima see themselves as very differently oriented to the ascent of *erôs*. While Diotima suggested that she herself had seen the highest mysteries, she expressed some doubt about Socrates's ability to achieve such a vision. The question is thereby raised for readers: where should Socrates be placed on Diotima's ascent?

There are moments in the *Symposium* that suggest that Socrates has himself reached the summit of Diotima's ascent. His apparent trances, witnessed both by those at Agathon's party and by Alcibiades on the battlefield,[9] seem to display an inward contemplation without need of other human beings. Socrates appears to be as self-sufficient as the beautiful itself. Many commentators take this to be Plato's suggestion that Socrates has on multiple occasions reached the summit of the ascent of *erôs*.[10] However, Blondell and others also point out that Socrates also resembles the "personified Eros who is a seeker after wisdom but never attains it."[11] Plato thus dramatically displays a fundamental ambiguity in the character of Socrates—he is described as both capable of the self-sufficiency and completion that accompanies the possession of wisdom, and also as irrevocably incomplete in his seeking of such wisdom. I believe that Blondell is right to emphasize both of these sides of Socrates in Plato's text, and gives a persuasive account of the evidence in the dialogue for placing Socrates at every step of the erotic ascent.[12] Following Steve Lowenstam, she suggests that Plato's depiction of Socrates implies that Socrates is through and through *daimonic* in his "shimmying up and down the ladder . . . between mortal and divine realms in a dynamic process of interpretation, communication, intercourse and conversation."[13] The upshot then is that Socrates has no genuine place on the ascent of love. He is, like the *theoros* we previously discussed, "everywhere, and therefore nowhere. . . . He is *atopos*, 'placeless.' . . . This mysteriousness is central to Socrates's allure as an object of desire, as Alcibiades, in his extravagant effort to solve that mystery so clearly demonstrates."[14] Plato's account of Socrates suggests a human possibility that exists outside the ascent that she describes but at the same time turns Socrates himself into an object of wonder for us. It is important that we notice how Plato thus frustrates a desire we may have to locate Socrates more securely on the ascent of love. Plato's intention to frustrate such a desire suggests that the desire itself is wrongheaded, and may in fact be a hindrance to understanding Socrates and *erôs* itself. If we resist the urge to nail down Socrates's *topos*, we find that Socrates himself—of whose activity we may be unable to give a proper account—now himself becomes mysterious to us. He becomes mysterious in his very ability to exhibit the very wonder of *erôs* itself, and the *atopia* that accompanies the *daimonic* nature of *erôs*. The true source of wonder for those of us reading the dialogue may not after all be the beauty at the summit of the ascent, as wondrous as this might be, but the erotic activity of Socrates himself, who shuttles back and forth between the divine and the human. The *Symposium* presents Socrates to us as worthy of contemplation, both at the beginning of philosophy and at its culmination.

For Diotima is surely right that *erôs*, if it leads to the wonder at the beautiful itself, brings about a transformative self-forgetting that, as Bloom points out, rightly gives due to our legitimate desire and ability to be more than just our bodies. But in doing so, she appears to arrive at a conclusion that suggests that the so-called lower forms of *erôs*, including those which bind together individual human beings, "are denied their fulfillment."[15] I do not think we are meant to endorse such a denigration of these lower forms of *erôs*. Instead, it is a sign that Diotima's psychology—her account of the human soul—is incomplete. As Critias does in his account of *sôphrosunê*, so does Diotima fail in her account of *erôs* to make central its irreducibly relational character, and though she introduces to Socrates the notion that Eros is *daimonic*, rather than a god, her final speech about the ascent omits any reference to the *daimonic*, and seems to suppress any claim that human incompleteness is fundamental. The *daimonic* nature of *erôs* is vividly displayed instead in the character of Socrates, who is thus philosophically erotic—he is in-between, rooted in his rootlessness, and *atopos* and thus the dialogue presents him as either nowhere or everywhere on the steps of Diotima's ascent, as we have seen.

Therefore, I suggest that Socrates's praise of the "power and courage" of Eros is connected to the very *daimonic*, in-between nature of love. It is because *erôs* gives a power to transcend one's own partial, limited perspective and wonder at the beautiful, that we can thus call it courageous.[16] It is a bravery to use one's ability to be bigger than one's own limited attachments to our "own things," attachments that can blind us to the source of what is true and valuable always. Put another way, the wonder at the beautiful motivates us to move beyond our *thumotic* attachment to our opinions about the beautiful and the good that are rooted in a preference for those closest to us and most like us. Such an attachment, we have seen, can be perverted and twisted into a tyranny that results in tragic self-dissolution. Moreover, it can feed a desire for one's own immortality that is also a perversion of *erôs* that cannot be satisfied. But Socrates makes no claim to achieve immortality. Rather, both in his speech and his deeds, he endorses Diotima's picture of an *erôs* of a philosophical *theoros* that shuttles back and forth between the divine and human. Such *erôs*, situated between the divine and the human, between the mortal and the immortal, may be constitutive of human beings as such, who are of course vulnerable to death but also have the ability to inquire about this very feature of themselves. And perhaps there is no better co-worker for such philosophical inquiry than the courage to transcend.

But the *thumos* for one's own things cannot be entirely transcended by human beings, and it is important that we not forget this. The boundless philosophizing of Diotima, admired for its courage to transcend, must be mixed with a *sôphrosunê* that comes from wonder at the ever elusive, just-beyond-reach, seen but nonpossessed beauty. That is, wonder and *sôphrosunê* come together in the Socratic recognition of ignorance—the acknowledgment of the epistemic limitations of human beings. While it is courage that moves one to venture beyond the familiar and comfortable attachment to one's partial views, it is *sôphrosunê* as Socratic self-knowledge that is responsive to the limitations of such venturing.[17] Such self-knowledge is a therapy, then, for the Critian perversion of Diotima's teaching, a claim for an apotheosis of self that isolates us from the other. It is no accident that Alcibiades enters at this moment, a moment in which Aristophanes was seeking to be heard over the applause for Socrates's speech.[18] Aristophanes, the one whose speech we *most* recognize as truly erotic in its account of a shared, reciprocal human intimacy, is not heard because of another *thumotic* disruption—it is the noise of a drunken crowd that forestalls a conversation between Socrates and Aristophanes. It is that very conversation that needs to take place.[19] While Aristophanes exalts our human connections to each other above our dangerous, hubristic ascent to the divine, Diotima overcorrects by glorifying the ascent to the divine at the cost of human connection. The beauty of Aristophanes's speech is marred by the ugliness of the gap between the human and the divine. The beauty of Diotima's speech is marred by the ugliness of the divine effacing of the human. Socrates, if he is *daimonic* and in-between, serves as a reminder not only of the existence of the utterly transcendent whole that inspires our erotic longings but also of its permanent elusiveness.[20] Socratic philosophy, and the wonder in which it culminates, binds together—as *erôs* binds together the divine and the human—the views of Diotima and Aristophanes. And in doing so, it corrects the illusory self-sufficiency portrayed in both.

We can see this reminder in Alcibiades's story of his relationship with Socrates, where we hear of Socrates's rejection of him.[21] It is important that we hear of Socrates's rejection only through the mouth of Alcibiades, who emerges in the drama to represent the individual who is, similarly to Critias, unable to successfully bind together the divine and human elements of Socrates. I believe that Alcibiades misunderstands Socrates as either belonging to the realm of the transcendent beautiful or merely to the realm of the interpersonal human. He fails to appreciate that the mystery of Socrates requires us to put these two sides together.[22] But this misunderstanding is rooted in an active rejection of Socrates as existing in an in-between place, a place that would challenge Alcibiades's categories. As Sanday describes:

> Alcibiades actively refuses to pursue the path that Socrates awakens within him. . . . The first strategy of active refusal is to reduce the presences of the beautiful to something human, i.e., to Socrates, and to something like Socrates that can be manipulated. The second strategy is to exalt Socrates, the presence of the beautiful, as something divine, as something beyond the human, and as a paradigm to which Alcibiades and the rest of us mere mortals need not answer . . . philosophy is either a presence, equal to ourselves, that is available to be seduced, or is so alien to us that we could never be blamed for failing to live up to its demands.[23]

Alcibiades attempts at first to woo Socrates by luring him with his own physical beauty, and thus he expects that this man can be manipulated and seduced. When Socrates does not succumb to the seduction of Alcibiades, he then attempts to explain away Socrates's rejection of him as an action of a being that is nothing like the rest of human beings, a class to which he only appears to belong. Alcibiades's claim is that Socrates's rejection is thus an erotic failure, explicable when we realize that Socrates is not properly erotic, for he is not properly human. But though there is a failure here, it is neither Socrates's nor is it precisely an erotic one. The failure belongs to Alcibiades, and it is a failure of courage. Properly speaking, Alcibiades's erotic failure is a *thumotic* one. In elevating Socrates to a godlike status, eschewing his own accountability to live up to Socrates's exhortation, Alcibiades "serves as a negative reminder of the courage required for facing up to the demands of philosophy."[24]

But rather than accept Socrates's rejection as an exhortation to reevaluate his own longings for victory and honor and perhaps open himself to a good that transcends these, Alcibiades's explanation gratifies a need to remain in control and undefeated in love. Thus, in his relationship to Socrates and wisdom, Alcibiades, like Critias, cannot move beyond his subservience to his own *thumos*. He does not transcend his own partial perspective of the nature of the good. He thus lacks the courage that Socrates calls for in his assessment of Diotima's speech. Nor does he have the moderation to accept the wonder that would come from acknowledging his own ignorance. Such wonder would motivate one who was genuinely moved by a love of Socrates to continue to investigate together with him. Indeed, Alcibiades reveals to those listening that the ultimate good Socrates recommended to him, contrary to the proposal of Critias (or even Diotima), is not a wisdom of transcendent beauty but the opportunity to continue their philosophical dialogue.[25] Socrates's invitation to Alcibiades, which he does not accept, is an invitation that the two of them inquire together. Alcibiades, like Critias, sees this activity as too paltry to be of any real benefit. Both of them side with the rewards of honor and victory over the small benefit of philosophy: a wonder at the beautiful that comes with a knowledge of our incompleteness. For Socrates, there is finally a deep connection between Socratic self-knowledge (as knowledge of ignorance), *sôphrosunê*, and the in-between (*metaxic*) state of the *daimonic*. Both Critias and Alcibiades exemplify the failure to acknowledge this incompleteness. But it is the acknowledgment of this incompleteness that generates the Socratic therapeutic response to our *thumotic* drive for power that threatens to tyrannize both ourselves and others. The taming of this self-destructive ambition is thus the ultimate benefit of Socratic conversations and Socratic self-knowledge. This finally makes Socrates himself beautiful and the conversations he inspires most beautiful of all and worthy of our wonder.

Concluding Remarks

Plato's *Charmides* deserves more attention. Its conversation about *sôphrosunê* is significant not only for readers of Plato but for all who are concerned with the possibility and benefit of the radical self-examination to which Socrates devoted his life. It is no coincidence that these questions emerge in a search for the nature of *sôphrosunê*, for the virtue is inextricably linked to Socratic philosophizing. It is part of his *zetetic* excellence; it is the virtue that makes for good inquiry. This is because *sôphrosunê*, in its Socratic sense, is related not only to self-knowledge but also to a philosophical wonder at the beautiful that transcends one's own incompleteness. It is also no mere rhetorical flourish that Socrates conducts the inquiry with two members of the Thirty Tyrants, dramatically framing the inquiry with the opposing forces of war and beauty, violence and love. The erotic context demands that we must actually bring together the seemingly disparate and potentially conflicting notions of *sôphrosunê* and *erôs*.

Erôs presents a danger to us, psychologically and politically, if dominated by a boundless *thumos*. This is first seen in Charmides's entrance to the dialogue, when Critias parades Charmides before a crowd of hapless witnesses, who risk being consumed by the youth's beauty. But Charmides's own *thumos* is driven by the authority of his guardian, Critias. He thus never comes to see himself as free of Critias's rule over him and cannot see past the gaze of others in the attempt to examine himself. His first two definitions of *sôphrosunê* potentially reveal important elements in the moral dimension of the virtue, but Charmides understands them only through his own understanding of beauty. His notions of quietness and shame are rooted in an external validation: he has received his view of what is best in himself from what others see on his surface. It is only Socrates who is concerned with examining his soul. Charmides, unfortunately, fails to see this beauty of the soul as relevant and compelling and has no room in his account for the beautiful that entices the loving seeker of wisdom. When he offers his third definition, "doing one's own things," we quickly learn that the boy is no longer willing to engage in genuine philosophical inquiry. Rather than submit himself to more painful embarrassment, he proposes an idea he has heard from Critias and relishes Socrates's suggestion that the author of this riddle may not have known what he is talking about. Charmides's courage for philosophy is shallow and short-lived. He is dominated by a *thumos* explored in the stories of Leontius and Aristophanes, a *thumos* ultimately dangerous because it places higher value on one's own things than the good. It is his *thumos* that prevents him from taking up the role of seeker, encouraging him instead to turn the tables on his guardian, Critias. The move does not, however, express genuine desire for independence and search for wisdom, as the ominous ending of the dialogue illustrates. At the end of the dialogue, Charmides remains the slave of Critias and will do his bidding to bend Socrates to Critias's will.

Critias's angry intervention confirms the initial impression he gives at the opening of the dialogue, when he pimps Charmides out to Socrates. His fury is incited by the betrayal of Charmides, and he fears being exposed as not knowing his own things. Charmides is the prized possession of Critias, whom he shows off to display his own status and power. The young boy's betrayal is a threat to the *thumos* of Critias. The move paves the way for Critias to defend his notion of "one's own things" and comes to a culmination in his view that *sôphrosunê* is self-knowledge. Critias thus moves the discussion of *sôphrosunê* away from its moral dimension to a more intellectual one. This intellectual and more abstract conversation becomes utterly divorced from the moral aspect of *sôphrosunê*. Socrates's examination of Critias brings the reader to see that Critian *sôphrosunê* turns out to be at best a strange notion, whose possibility and benefit remain in doubt at the end of the dialogue. Its psychological and political consequences, seen in the imagined societies Critias endorses, lead either to incoherence or nightmares. The contentless reflexivity Critias ascribes to *sôphrosunê* renders it devoid of content, bereft of value for the individual possessing it. Critias's vision of *sôphrosunê*, exemplified in what he takes to be its great benefit, is that of an all-encompassing and reflexive architectonic omniscience. It is finally the metaphysical position of the tyrant, who sees nothing external to himself to be authoritative or worthy of wonder. Critias's *thumos*, unlike that of his ward Charmides, has no guardian. His *thumos* is thus more threatening because it is boundless, and like his view of knowledge, it is restrained by nothing outside of itself and aspires to an absolute invulnerability. We see in his future tyranny the bloody wolf in the city described in the *Republic*. Like Charmides, Critias is unable to successfully import a good of the soul into his account of self-knowledge. His ambition for self-sufficiency leads to a tragic self-dissolution. The tyrant's *sôphrosunê* portrays a human life that is self-enclosed, isolated, and alienated.

There is a Socratic alternative to the *thumotic* failures of Charmides and Critias. Socrates in his inquiry demonstrates both a courage and moderation that makes him a beautiful seeker of wisdom. Socrates's search for *sôphrosunê* begins and ends and begins again with his awareness of his incompleteness. While the *thumos* of Charmides and Critias prevents them from acknowledging their ignorance, the wonder of Socrates motivates him to inquire courageously. His courage drives him to transcend his limited perspective, for fear that he may ultimately miss what is best for him. But this transcendence seems perennially moderated by his awareness of his incompleteness, and this moderation restrains the *thumos* that might otherwise derail his search for wisdom. Both Socrates's courage and moderation are tied up with his *daimonic* status, shuttling back and forth between the immanent and the transcendent. We see this first when he is threatened with dissolution on seeing inside Charmides's cloak. He is able to attend to the more transcendent beauty of the soul by engaging in the act of conversation itself. It is finally the Socratic conversation that demonstrates in action the possibility of self-knowledge and brings about its benefit. The benefit comes not from the content of the conversations but from the virtues of inquiry, the *zetetic* excellences of Socratic courage and *sôphrosunê*. Socratic courage inspires one to reject one's own things as absolute, to transcend one's own *thumotic* attachment to one's own things. Socratic *sôphrosunê* is coupled with a wonder at the elusiveness of the beautiful itself and thus restrains the dangerous *thumotic erôs* that leads to self-dissolution in an ambitiously foolish attempt to conquer nature, time, and death. The danger of tyranny might be enough for us to suggest, then, that philosophical wonder is not just a *zetetic* excellence but a human excellence. In being *daimonic*, Socratic self-knowledge serves as the bridge not only between the immanent and the transcendent but also between the moral and metaphysical elements of *sôphrosunê*. The tyrant lives in a realm where this bridge is impassable. The perspectives of both Critias and Charmides are limited, and Socrates's erotic account addresses this. Wonder at the beautiful emphasizes both the epistemic, intellectual dimension and the moral dimension of *sôphrosunê*.

Let us close by recalling Socrates's opening question in the *Charmides*. Upon returning from war, he longed to know about the youth of Athens and the state of philosophy. If am right, the dialogue and the drama of the *Charmides* answer Socrates's question with a disconcerting thought. The beautiful young Charmides is ugly in his soul, portending his violent tyranny with Critias that will take over Athens. Plato's psychogenetic account of tyranny gives us even more reason for concern. The *thumotic* origin of tyranny seems built into the nature of the human soul, leading it to a perhaps inevitable tyrannical self-dissolution. *Thumos* is the political problem. It must be tamed, channeled, or educated if it is not to destroy the city. The *Symposium* gives us hope that philosophical wonder, a nonacquisitive *erôs* that both ascends to and is limited by the beautiful itself, may rescue us from our tragic *thumotic* fate. This wonder is both the starting point and the culmination of philosophical dialogue, as Socrates seems to understand it, and yields a *daimonic* self-knowledge that escapes the oblivion of self that awaits the tyrannical soul. The benefit of such wonder is thus clear. But a question remains about its possibility. Can the *erôs* for the beautiful overcome the inner, *thumotic* drive for power in human beings? Here we feel the importance of Socrates's opening question in our own *thumotic* times, beset by the challenges of tribalism, partisanship, polarization, and war. In our account, we have seen three cases of erotic (*thumotic*) failures: Alcibiades, Critias, and Charmides. If we include Socrates's death at the hands of the city, perhaps it is naive to hope that philosophical wonder can address the political problem of *thumos*. At this point, we should recall that Plato himself is another student of Socrates, whose very response to this problem has raised these questions for us. The possibility of a therapeutic self-knowledge must be enacted in the reading and discussing of the texts themselves. In writing the *Dialogues*, Plato calls upon the readers themselves to engage in philosophical dialogue and philosophical wonder about the political problem as a problem. Plato invokes us, as Socrates urged Alcibiades, to continue the dialogue with courage and moderation. How we respond to this invocation will demonstrate the possibility and benefit of Socratic self-knowledge. We may decline to answer, and instead succumb to the inner wellspring of *thumos*. But I urge us to answer the call to wonder. Our souls, and cities, depend on it.

Notes

Introduction

1. Two recent works have paid significantly more attention to this erotic setting, Woolf (2023) and Cohen-Taber (2022), and I have profited from their approaches to the text. My own treatment of the *Charmides* goes further in explicitly linking our final understanding of *sôphrosunê* with the *eros* that drives Socratic philosophy. I also argue that the erotic context compels readers to distinguish Socratic *erôs* from the failed *erôs* of Critias and Charmides, which is poisoned by their *thumos*.

Part 1A

Chapter One

1. Translations of the dialogue are my own, though I have consulted frequently the translations mentioned below. In the English translations of the *Charmides* currently in print, *sôphrosunê* has been rendered various ways: "sound-mindedness" (West and West 1986), "moderation" (Watt in Saunders 1987), "self-control" (Waterfield 2005), "temperance" (Jowett in Hamilton and Cairns 1961; Sprague in J. Cooper 1997; Lamb 1927), and "discipline" (Moore and Raymond 2019). All these translations have their advantages and disadvantages. The proposal of West and West, "sound-mindedness," is a straightforward etymological translation of *sôphrosunê*, for example, but to a modern ear it connotes the minimum condition one has in order to prepare one's last will and testament, and it seems utterly mysterious that such a condition would be a virtue for which one should strive. The alternatives offered by Watt and Jowett, "moderation" and "temperance," do not include enough of the cognitive and psychic element of the word, while the translations of Moore and Raymond as well as Waterfield cannot

avoid assimilating *sôphrosunê* to *enkrateia*, from which it must be distinguished. In short, all translations do not, and I would suggest cannot, quite capture the full range of qualities and activities—cognitive, emotional, and behavioral—that this virtue is capable of connoting. It is untranslatable for us, and I will leave it untranslated throughout.

2. 153a.

3. Thucydides, *Peloponnesian War*, 1.67–86.

4. The closest dialogue to the group of seven above is the *Euthydemus*, but in this dialogue the audience of Socrates's narration is known more clearly: it is Crito. The speaker of the *Symposium* is Apollodorus, and Cephalus narrates the *Parmenides*. The *Phaedo* is narrated by its title character, while Euclides tells of the conversation in the *Theaetetus*. I will return in part 3 to compare the narration of the *Symposium* and the *Republic* to the narration of the *Charmides*.

5. 154b. Also see 155c.

6. 155d.

7. Hyland (1981) 25–26; Schmid (1998).

8. Benardete argues that this should lead us to believe that Socrates is narrating the story to Theodorus, or someone like him. See Benardete (1986) 231–232. I don't believe the text gives us enough evidence for his reading, however.

9. 154e, 155a.

10. See Schmid (1998, 3): "With remarkable brevity, the initial scene projects the reader forward to the entire tragic story of the Peloponnesian War, beyond that to the tyranny of the Thirty, and beyond that to Socrates's own trial and execution." This is a very good encapsulation. Missing from it, interestingly for my current treatment, is only the erotic element.

11. Kahn (1996) 187.

12. Schmid (1998); Notomi (2000) 11.

13. Schmid (1998); Notomi (2000) 11.

14. Xenophon, *Memorabilia*, 1.2.12. Some scholars claim that (1) this is a biased and uncorroborated overstatement by Xenophon, and that indeed there was evidence of support for Critias and his regime, and that (2) Plato himself was no critic of Critias and presents him in a positive light in his dialogues. See Notomi (2000) 240–248; Tuozzo (2011) 52–89. Even if Notomi's (and Tuozzo's) claim about bias in appellation is true, Notomi himself admits that the failure of the oligarchy under Critias's rule exhibited an ignorance and lack of *sôphrosunê*, which Socrates (and Plato) address in this dialogue. Therefore, the exploration of *sôphrosunê* with men who were called tyrants on account of their lack of *sôphrosunê*, in fact, seems intentional on Plato's part. Tuozzo's attack on Xenophon by relying on countervalent opinions does not demonstrate the falsity of his character (or at least his reputation) as a tyrant. Tuozzo's attempt to build up Critias relies on passages taken out of context and it is not clear that the Critias he alludes to in the *Timaeus* and Aristotle's *Rhetoric* is the same Critias as that

presented in Plato's *Charmides*. Regarding the *Charmides*, it is most telling that Tuozzo makes light of the ominous ending of the dialogue. His claim that Plato saw Critias or his regime in a positive light is not borne out by the *Charmides* or Plato's other works, as I will show.

15. See Notomi (2000) 242–243; Schmid (1998); Levine (2016) 1–3.

16. See 156a. Xenophon also suggests that the two had other meetings, which led to conflict between the two. See *Memorabilia*, 1.2.30. Cf. Hyland (1981).

17. According to Tuozzo's argument, of course, this very question and the ones that follow should not even come up.

18. I owe this comparison to Stewart Umphrey.

19. See the discussion of *thumos* and *thauma* in the introduction.

20. See 154b, 158b, and 173a. Cf. Brouwer and Polansky (2004) 233–245; Lampert (2010) ch. 2; Burger (2013); Joosse (2018); Raymond (2018).

21. Moore and Raymond (2019) 41.

22. 153a. Thucydides discusses this as the battle that was one of the "spoken causes" of the Peloponnesian War. It took place in 432 BCE.

23. Thucydides 2.53.4 translated by Woodruff (1993).

24. This discussion of the body's relation to the soul, and its political backdrop, will become thematic when Socrates begins his diagnosis and treatment of Charmides.

25. The *Lysis* and *Theaetetus* also take place at gymnasia.

26. 153c.

27. 154a.

28. See Dover (1978).

29. If I am right about the psychopolitical difficulties presented by Charmides and Critias in the *Charmides*, and their subsequent analysis and treatment in the *Republic* and *Symposium*, then my argument suggests a rough reading order for these dialogues—*Charmides, Republic, Symposium*—if we are concerned with pedagogical and therapeutic effectiveness. For such effectiveness, nothing depends on a claim about a dramatic or compositional order of the dialogues. To see a contrasting view of the order of these three dialogues, with a very different set of assumptions, consider Altman (2010).

30. The return from war reminds us of Socrates's extraordinary courage on the battlefield, described eloquently by Alcibiades in the *Symposium*.

31. Levine (2016) 23–26.

32. 153b.

33. Regarding the appearance of Chaerephon, Hyland (1981, 21–23) points out that the presence of this democratic individual is coupled with the tyrannical interlocutors. Not every "Socratic" is a tyrant then. For an alternate view, see Moore 2013.

34. Cf. 170a and *Gorgias* 509a. Benardete (1986, 233) suggests that this implies that Socrates's *sôphrosunê* shows an "indifference to simply human

concerns." But to put it another way, Socrates does not fear what most humans fear, and indeed, the way that Socrates's *sôphrosunê* goes wherever he goes will be tied to his erotic nature according to both Diotima's speech and Alcibiades's depiction of him. I shall return to this in Part 3.

35. 153d.

36. There was at this point already discontent with the fighting that would only escalate. The siege of Potidaea was an enormous expense for the citizens, costing the city two thousand talents, which amounts to around two years of income. See Thucydides 2.70.2 with Roberts (2017) 88.

37. *Symposium* 219e–220e.

38. See Monoson (2014).

39. Cf. Hyland (1981), 273; Schmid (1998) 3–6; Murphy (2000) 287–288.

40. Levine (2016), 27.

Chapter Two

1. 154a.

2. 154a.

3. See Levine (2016) 28.

4. Because of this narrative voice, we are thus able to watch Socrates watch himself and also watch himself as he watches others (who are unaware of him as a watcher, of course). This would not at all be possible if the dialogue were not narrated by Socrates.

5. 154b–c.

6. See Cohen-Taber (2022) 119–121. Woolf (2023) 62. As mentioned in the introduction, while I agree with Cohen-Taber's emphasis on *erôs* and beauty in the dialogue and also support Woolf's insight that *sôphrosunê* is linked in the character of Socrates to "attention," I do not finally endorse their conclusions about the nature of *sôphrosunê* and argue instead that Socratic *erôs* plays a more essential role in the definition of *sôphrosunê* itself.

7. See for example, Plato, *Euthydemus* 303b; *Apology* 20e, 30c; *Protagoras* 319c.

8. 154a.

9. See *Republic* 565e.

10. See Moore & Raymond (2019), 42. As they point out, Socrates warns about the dazzling effect of the tyrant's outward appearance in the *Republic*. See 576d, 577a, 591d, and 619a.

11. Socrates seems to experience what looks like this in the *Symposium*. It is noteworthy that it is not provoked by the beauty of human form. I will discuss this in part 3.

12. 154d.

13. 155b.

14. See Hyland (1981) 35. As he points out, it ends with one as well.

15. 154e. Cf. Levine (2016) 55–58. Notice that Socrates responds to Critias by saying "Let him come." He thus from the outset questions Critias's ability to relinquish his hold on Charmides.

16. 155b–c.

17. Cf. Levine (2016), 30–31; Schmid (1998), 6, 91; Rosen (1973) 637–639.

18. 155c–d.

19. Cf. Hyland (1981) 37; Schmid (1998) 91; Levine (2016) 34.

20. Benardete (1986) 236.

21. See Levine (2016) 60–62 and Tuozzo (2011) 108–110.

22. See Tuozzo (2011) 110. Touzzo is right to point out the connection between this passage and the other Platonic passages about gazing upon the beautiful. But I disagree with his conclusion that *sôphrosunê* emerges at this moment in the gazing on such beauty. What is seen here is a beauty that threatens to destroy the one who gazes upon it, as Socrates indicates in his interpretation of the wisdom of Cydias. This indicates a different lesson about the nature of *sôphrosunê* and the beautiful as it relates to Charmides's possession of it, and the effect it has on other people, as I explain in the rest of the paragraph. I agree with Woolf (2023, 72), who points out that this moment "indicates Socratic self-recognition of a failure to occupy what he evidently takes to be his proprietary stance."

23. It may thus be no accident that Charmides's first definition of *sôphrosunê* is *hesuchia* (quietness). I will discuss this part 1A.4.

Chapter Three

1. 155e.

2. 154a.

3. 154e.

4. 158c.

5. 156a.

6. See Benardete (1986) 233: "The question of *sôphrosunê* is a question about the transmissibility of philosophy as self-knowledge." Cf. Kosman (1983) 204–205; Bruell (1977) 144–145.

7. It should not be surprising therefore that Critias's attempt to put forth a "science of the self" is bound to fail, for Critias, as I will argue, is unable to capture any real notion of reflexivity in his formalistic approach. Charmides also attempts an examination of himself, but it too will fail. Socrates's attempt will not, however, and Plato's dialogue is precisely the philosophical medium to show this process of self-examination.

8. 160d.

9. Cf. Vlastos (1985) 9; Burger (2013) 10; Schmid (1998) 28.

10. See the similar opening of the *Republic*, in which Polemarchus threatens Socrates with force in order to prevent him from leaving for Athens. Socrates offers persuasion as an alternative to force. See 327c.

11. See Hyland (1981), 35–36, 40; Levine (2016) 55–62; Tuozzo (2011) 110–111. Tuozzo argues that Critias's question is actually his own attempt to test Socrates. As will be seen below, it backfires on Critias badly, as the youth reveals that his guardian was too quick to praise his qualities. Critias never takes back any claim that Socrates should treat Charmides, thus vindicating Socrates even if at the same time he is unwilling to fully admit his own self-ignorance and his ignorance of Charmides.

12. But perhaps it could be said that Socrates too is resorting to a kind of force, in conspiring with Critias to deceive Charmides to strip his soul. In response to this, we should note that once Charmides has laid himself bare, if indeed he is able to do it, it will turn out that Socrates's deception contains at least a partial truth. His examination of Charmides will actually bring the boy closer to admitting his ignorance, and thus closer to a more real *sôphrosunê*, and in some way cure his "headache." See Coolidge (1993) 24–28 and below.

13. Cf. Woolf (2023) 79–80.

14. 156b–c.

15. 156d–157a.

16. 156e.

17. 156e–157a.

18. Levine (2016), 67–68; Schmid (1998) 17. Contrast Tuozzo (2011) 118–123.

19. See Coolidge (1993) 29n9.

20. As our earlier discussion indicated, Socrates seems deeply concerned with the disease of the city—the kinds of lives the citizens in Athens are living.

21. "Source" thus may be a misleading word. On my reading, Socrates is not making a claim that the Stoics or Kant might put forward about the will—that it alone could be the real origin of all things good and evil. Perhaps Socrates is saying this, but there does not seem to be evidence for it in the text. See Moore and Raymond (2019) 49–50. Rather, the soul appears to be responsive to the good that comes from without. Indeed the soul's relation to the good seems to be properly erotic: the soul desires that the good become its own always. Problems for us arise, however, when we attach ourselves to goods that are only partial instead of the whole good itself, as Charmides and Critias do. Socrates's speech about Zalmoxian medicine will thus come back in Diotima's account of the ladder of love, and help us think through the puzzles that emerge immediately following.

22. See Coolidge (1993) 26.

23. Cf. *Republic* 445a–b; *Gorgias* 277a–279c, 503e–505b. Thus it becomes incumbent to turn to the discussion of *erôs*, *thumos*, and wonder in the *Republic* and *Symposium*.

24. Socrates implies at 158b–c that he does not know whether the charms will work on Charmides at all.

25. Recall that Socrates's opening question concerned how philosophy and the youths had fared while he was away from home.

26. See Nightingale (2004).

27. 156d–157a.

28. Tuckey (1951) 18, 103.

29. Schmid (1998) 15, 50–51.

30. For the standard form of the *elenchus*, see Vlastos (1983).

31. Recall that Socrates's description of the physician of the soul used the word *therapeia* to describe this treatment.

32. Cf. Schmid (1998) 68: "The Socratic dialectic challenges him not only to acquire the correct moral opinions, but to question himself and think for himself and develop his own moral rationality."

33. 157b.

34. Cf. Coolidge (1993) 35; Schmid (1998) 70; Levine (2016) 72.

35. We should notice how problematic this is. The ideal city in the *Republic* is built around the one man-one job principle. As Rosen (1973) 626 says, "The diversity of the sciences raises a doubt as to the possibility of a philosophical science competent to rule the entire city." This is a problem for the beginning of Aristotle's *Nicomachean Ethics* as well, which points to political science as the architectonic knowledge of the highest end or ends.

36. Schmid (1998) 83.

37. 158b–c.

38. A blush is a physical manifestation of a troubled soul. On display, then, is the "whole" soul interacting in its bodily parts. A blush is essentially connected, as I will discuss below, to one's perception of others' views. One would not blush by oneself. Thrasymachus blushes in the *Republic* at 350d. Dionysodorus blushes in the *Euthydemus* at 297a. Socrates never blushes in Plato's portrayals of him.

39. 158d. The word is *atopon*, literally "out of place." The traditional definition of *sôphrosunê* included knowing one's place, knowing one's role in the social hierarchy. See North (1966).

40. 158c.

41. See Schmid (1998), 25–26, 99; Blondell (2002), 75–80.

42. Recall Socrates's opening question—he asks about the state of philosophy and the youths. The two turn out to be connected.

43. 159a.

44. The assumption seems especially well designed to move Charmides along in his therapy. Although Charmides does not notice, readers will surely wonder that this assumption raises numerous questions: Are we right to think that *sôphrosunê* is comparable to Charmides's headache and that he must have some internal perception about if indeed he has it? Even if he has some internal

perception, does that warrant an opinion (let alone a correct one) about it? What kind of self-examination is needed in order to distinguish a good opinion from a bad one about one's internal state, and has Charmides himself undertaken any such proper self-examination? The results of the ensuing enquiry, and Charmides's failure to answer Socrates, will provide answers—at least in dramatic form—to these questions.

Chapter Four

1. 159b.

2. Santas (1973) 107. Cf. Bruell (1977) 152.

3. Schmid (1998) 23. Cf. North (1966) 5–9; Santas (1973) 107; Hyland (1981) 56.

4. 159b.

5. 153d.

6. Lear (2006). Lear argues that the problem is that the young have heard "childhood stories" before they have the adult, rational capacities to recognize them as stories. By the time they do recognize them, the stories have already done their psychological work, and are like seeds for an explosion that will take place later in life. In Cephalus's case, in the *Republic*, his unconscious anxiety about death surfaces to plague his old age. I suggest that, in the cases of Critias and Charmides, the seeds explode into their "tyrannical" future. The efficacy of the *elenchus* may be deficient as a cure to this problem, and Lear argues persuasively that the Myth of the Cave is meant as "mythic therapy" to help us, the readers, who are not so different from Charmides on first reading the *Republic*.

7. See *Republic* 389d–e; 430e, 431c; *Symposium* 196c; *Gorgias* 491d, 506d–507c; *Laws* 696b–e; *Timaeus* 44a–d, 80b–87d.

8. *Statesman* 307a–b; *Gorgias* 508a; *Republic* 560d.

9. Santas (1973, 108–110) asserts that the definition seem to have no rhyme or reason and is thus too strong.

10. Tuckey (1968) 19.

11. Cf. *Lysis* 207d–208e and *Protagoras* 324d–326e. Both passages further indicate why quietness and not "self-mastery" is the definition offered by young Charmides. It would indeed be hubris for an Athenian youth to claim that he is master of himself, when his culture has taught him that his teachers, parents, and other elders are his masters. Perhaps it is no coincidence that the understanding of self-mastery as *sôphrosunê* comes in the *Republic*, where Socrates's interlocutors are not young Athenian boys. This makes some sense of the absence of the discussion of "self-mastery" in the dialogue. Consequently, the dialogue seems to take a different direction as a result of the different emphasis coming from this

absence. It is only after Socrates's examination of Charmides's first definitions that the discussion here emphasizes what could be called the intellectual rather than the moral aspect of *sôphrosunê*. For other passages where Socrates links being *sophron* to self-mastery and control of desire for pleasure, see *Gorgias* 491d; *Phaedo* 68c; *Philebus* 45d–e; and *Laws* 710a. Consistent with my view, in the first three passages Socrates is not talking with a youth; in the *Laws* Socrates is absent, but the Athenian stranger is talking to Clinias, an elderly gentleman from Crete.

12. Cf. Moore and Raymond (2019) 57.

13. 159b.

14. Possible translations of *kalos* are "beautiful," "noble," "admirable," "honorable." This ambiguity has been evident in our discussion of Charmides's relationship to his own beauty and it must be kept in mind as we continue. Therefore, I will leave *kalos* untranslated in the ensuing passages.

15. 160d and 160e.

16. 159d and 160b.

17. 160a.

18. 160b. For a detailed spelling out of the steps of the argument, see Santas (1973) 113–114.

19. *Hesuchia* does connote a sort of slowness, and so Socrates isn't completely talking past Charmides by opposing quickness to quietness. See North (1966) 102–104.

20. 160b–d; my emphasis.

21. Santas (1973) 116–117.

22. 159b.

23. Socrates himself associates order with *sôphrosunê* at *Gorgias* 504d and *Republic* 431e.

24. See Bruell (1977) 154.

25. The same question arises for the arguments regarding the soul. For, as Bruell notes (1977, 154), Socrates leaves out discussion of desires, hopes, and fears. Is quickness rather than quietness really more worthy of praise with respect to these? Surely not.

26. Kosman (1983) 216; my emphasis. Part of Kosman's aim in resurrecting *sôphrosunê*-as-quietness is to show the relation of the beginning definitions to the understanding that emerges from the dialogue as a whole.

27. See Tuckey (1968) 19; North (1966) 156; Santas (1973) 110–111; Moore and Raymond (2019) 57–60.

28. 159c. It should accordingly not be surprising that "good and bad" become thematic later in the dialogue, and that Socrates will appeal to "the good" as soon as Charmides offers another definition.

29. See Levine (2016) 109–110; Hyland (1981) 61–62; Kosman (1983) 204. This also makes some sense of the stipulations that Socrates makes at 159a

(regarding having an opinion about something within and being able to speak Greek), for both highlight Charmides's problem: he is unable to look within, he belongs to another.

30. See 160b.

31. See 154e and 158a.

32. See 155c–156d. Whether Critias could be so moved to genuinely seek wisdom is a question I will pursue in parts 2A and 2B.

33. See Schmid (1998) 25: "Neither quiet behavior nor its opposite can be judged virtuous, but the account of virtue must be sought at another level."

Chapter Five

1. 160d–e.

2. Inserting the idea of courage at this point raises the question about the relation between these two virtues. See Hyland (1981) 68–69; Kosman (1983) 215; Annas (1985) 123–125.

3. See Tuckey (1968) 19; North (1966) 155–156; Santas (1973) 110–111; Schmid (1998) 25.

4. 160e.

5. 160e.

6. 154e.

7. See Levine (2016) 115–116.

8. The problematic relation between the beautiful and the good is evident in the *Republic*, I will argue, and is directly addressed in Diotima's speech in the *Symposium*.

9. 161a–b.

10. See Raymond (2018).

11. *Odyssey* 17:347.

12. In *Protagoras* 313c–d, for example, Socrates describes the scene upon entering the house of Callias with imagery from Odysseus's descent into the underworld (*Odyssey* 11:601). Then Critias makes an entrance soon after (316a).

13. See 377b ff.

14. Moore and Raymond (2019) 64.

15. "I have one wonderfully good trait, which saves me: I'm not ashamed to learn." So says Socrates, *Lesser Hippias* 372c.

16. Schmid (1998) 28.

17. Schmid (1998) 29. Along these lines, Kahn (1996, 189) points out that what is missing from the conception *sôphrosunê*-as-*aidôs* is knowledge. But what kind of knowledge would supplement it? In my view, it would involve a proper understanding of the good and *to kalon*. Cf. Annas (1985) 116n21.

18. Perhaps correcting this mistake will thus supply grounds for the claim that *sôphrosunê* is good, which is premise (2) above. Hyland (1981, 70–71) attempts to reject this premise.

Chapter Six

1. 161b.

2. A version of Meno's skeptical question is thus raised here. Must we already have self-knowledge in order to begin looking for it?

3. Charmides cannot accept another kind of beauty than the one he has, one that is deceiving to all, concealing an ugly soul.

4. 161b–c. As Levine (2016) 121 says, *miare* or "blood-stained one," connotes something "different from the popular estimate of the youth's benign beauty." The bloodiness, he goes on to say, refers to both the tyrannical future and war in the background. Cf. Bruell (1977) 156; Hyland (1981) 76; Schmid (1998) 30–31.

5. 161c. Charmides says that the person who uttered this doctrine "seemed to be wise" (162b; my emphasis).

6. 162c–d. Critias's motives for denying authorship of the saying are unclear. There is also debate among scholars about whether or not the phrase is original to Critias or if he himself may be parroting Socrates. See Moore and Raymond (2019, 66–67) and the literature mentioned there. The status of this debate and its resolution does not bear on my argument.

7. Bruell (1977, 158), for example, sees a "liberated" boy in the moment that Charmides looks mockingly at Critias (162b). But in fact, this liberation is only superficial, and Charmides is just as controlled by Critias even in saying this, as the dialogue shows in its ending. For starters, Charmides does not understand this definition, and though he laughs at Critias, it is still the case that Charmides's "own" is to be, at least for the moment, the dependent of Critias. Cf. Schmid (1998) 31.

8. 161c.

9. Bruell (1977) 157; Hyland (1981) 70.

10. 161d–e.

11. 161e–162a.

12. He does so twice: 162a and 162b.

13. 162b–c.

14. See Levine (2016) 34, 60. Contrast this with Blondell (2002) 127; Beversluis (2000) 158–159. Cf. Hyland (1981) 56–57.

15. See *A Greek-English Lexicon* (Liddell and Scott, rev. Jones, 9th ed., Oxford 1940). Cf. Levine (2016) 120; Schmid (1998) 31.

16. See *Euthyphro* 4c.

17. 174b.

18. The reader thus sees them stained with blood they haven't shed yet.

19. Socrates uses the word *"miare"* only two other times in Plato's dialogues. He calls Theages *"miare"* in the dialogue bearing his name at 124e, and labels Phaedrus one at 236e. In the respective passages, Theages has just claimed that he wishes to be a tyrant, and Phaedrus has just shown himself to be a lover of rhetoric, holding power over Socrates by refusing to say Lysias's speech. Regarding the futures of Charmides and Critias, it seems that they are dramatically connected with Charmides's hearing the quote from Critias and the possibility (though disputed) that Critias heard it from Socrates. (This is compatible with Theages's and Phaedrus's fondness for the speeches of others.)

20. 161c.

21. This is in fact what happens in the *Republic*, where doing one's own things denotes a one man–one job principle rather than an every man-every job principle. The question is raised: What should "one's own things" really mean? Does it apply to one's soul? And if so, what kind of theory of the soul do we need to explain this? How is it related to the good? The beautiful? The truth? See Annas (1985) 117–118.

22. "One's own" remains with us in the following chapter, and I will discuss more implications of this part of the dialogue in parts 2 and 3 as well.

Part 1B

Chapter One

1. See 443d.

2. *Cratylus* 419e.

3. Hobbs (2000) 3. Cf. Arruzza (2018) 186-187. One could also add resentment, spite, envy, and, as I mentioned above, tribalism and partisanship.

4. See Hobbs (2000, 4) for a good summary of skeptical views in the secondary literature.

5. Cf. Hobbs (2000) 30; Arruzza (2018) 191; Brennan (2012) 109–110; J. Cooper (1984) 14–15; Wilburn (2021) 52–54; Singpurwalla (2013) 56; J. Lear (2006) 118.

6. Cf. Hobbs (2000) 44, 67–78; Umphrey (1982) 378–379; Wilburn (2021) 71–73.

7. Although *thumos* is not explicitly mentioned in the earlier argument of the text, the *drama* prior to this moment has already introduced us to it, notably in the discussion of persuasion and force in the opening frame (327a–c), Thrasymachus's beastly anger at Socrates (337b), and Socrates's praise of Glaucon's

courage in inquiry (357a). Similarly, Glaucon's disgust at Socrates's city of pigs appears to be motivated by *thumos*—there is no *thumos* in the city, and perhaps Glaucon's need for "relishes" is itself *thumotic* (372a–d). Cf. Wilburn (2021) 72; Craig (1994) 43, 117.

8. 374b.

9. Craig (1994, 19–20) makes the argument that war and philosophy are conjoined from the beginning to the end of the discussion in the *Republic*. In what follows, I agree with Craig's emphasis on the desire for victory as the defining feature of *thumos*, but I will argue instead that philosophy as Socrates presents it in the *Symposium* is a therapeutic response to the *thumotic* desire for victory.

10. 373e.

11. Smith (2016) 34. See also 40–45.

12. 359b–c.

13. Arruzza (2018) 149.

14. 366d.

15. Cf. Wilburn (2021) 30–31, 60.

16. Although it is not central to my argument here, we can see that much of book 3 of the *Republic* could be seen as a political and educational program aimed at the body (gymnastic) and soul (music) to respond to the dangerous side of *thumos*, especially in the potentially *pleonectic* aspirations of the citizens, and use it instead for the sake of justice in the city as a whole. The "one person–one job" principle, for example, is an attempt to restrain a *thumos* that seeks a boundless mastery of everything. No *thumotic* modes of music are allowed. And although there is *wonder* at the imitative poet who can imitate all forms of narrative (such as Plato?), he is to be banished from the city as dangerous (398a). Indeed, the living situation of the guardians—especially the banning of private property—is directly aimed at *thumotic* attachment to one's own things (416d–417a; cf. 422a–424b). The guardians must never put anything before the city, and thus their *thumos* for themselves is channeled (not ever transcended or annihilated) into defense of the city (412e). Indeed, both parts of the "noble lie" are aimed at counteracting the citizens' *thumotic* urge to put either themselves or their kin above that of the city (414d–415c). This is immediately followed by a fear that the guardians may descend into savagery, turning from dogs to wolves (416a), an image that will return in book 9. Finally, the eventual definition of justice as "doing one's own things" (433b) is a reorientation of the very nature of *thumos*, which, if untrained, is misguided by a dangerous notion of what counts as "one's own things." Cf. 443d.

17. Cf. Brennan (2012) 105; Hobbs (2000) 9; Weinstein (2018) 166. As Wilburn (2021, 58) points out, "The two faces of *thumos* [i.e., savageness and gentleness] can be reconciled because the opposite motivations in question are experienced with respect to different and opposite objects or individuals."

18. Tarnopolsky (2007) 304.

19. 374c–d. The word for "well-bred" is "*gennaios*," often translated as "noble." As Rosen points out, it is important to keep in mind that such dogs are not like all other animals because they are trained. We may wonder at this point, however, how trainable are our natures—even if they are philosophical. See Rosen (2005) 83. This makes them different from the three other animals that come to illustrate the nature of *thumos*: the serpent, the lion, and the wolf. Cf. Arruzza (2018) 203–204, 209. I will discuss this more fully in part 3B, chapter 4.

20. 376a. I will argue in part 3B that it is wonder that can accomplish the therapeutic harmony of the tension in *thumos*.

21. Wilburn (2021) 40–41.

22. 376c.

23. 376c.

24. 375c.

25. To call the dogs philosophic is a strange claim, and we will come to doubt its seriousness by the end of our discussion of *thumos* in part 2B. Several commentators have pointed out that the most important attribute of these dogs—that their knowledge is rooted in a distinction between what is familiar and what is foreign—is in tension with genuine philosophical inquiry. See Weinstein (2018) 172–173; McNeill (2010) 256–257; Saxonhouse (1988) 34–37; and Nichols (1988) 50–51. Brennan (2012, 116) argues that this even indicates that *thumos* can't by itself grasp the good. Rosen (2005, 84) points out that Socrates himself gives no actual human example of a philosophical dog. Cf. Wilburn (2021, 44–46). In the next two chapters, it will become clearer why this example is so very suspicious. Both the account of love in Aristophanes's speech in the *Symposium* and the investigation into tyranny in books 8 and 9 of the *Republic* suggest that the ability to faithfully follow the *oikeion* principle poses deep problems for one who is erotic.

26. "*Oikeion* appears on the scene almost as soon as spirit does." Brennan (2012) 115. Also Wilburn (2021, 61): "For *thumos* the world is divided up into the *allotrion* and the *oikeion*, and the desires and emotions for which it is responsible are dictated by an agent's sense of their position and role in the world of human or animal interaction." Brennan goes on to argue that *thumos* is totally social and connected more to honor than it is to anger, competition, or aspiration. Compare the definition of Arruzza (2018) 191: *thumos* is a self-assertion of one's superiority over others. Similarly, Wilburn also argues for the social rootedness of *thumos* (2021, 71–73). But Wilburn seems to concede that the most basic and primitive part of *thumos* is tied to aggression, savagery, and violence and that the aggressiveness of *thumos* is at least temporally (I would say by nature) prior to its gentle side (2021, 60, 71). Brennan also admits that a human being isolated on an island could still be *thumotic* (see 119). In the light of these points, I will argue that the social aspect of *thumos*, rooted in the love of honor (*philotimia*), is

a secondary manifestation of the deeper roots of *thumos,* connected to an aversion to vulnerability to death. Cf. Weinstein (2018), who argues that *philotimia* is a kind of *philonikia* (love of victory), and Craig (1994) 75–79, 101–102.

27. Cf. Rosen (2005) 84–85.

28. I will discuss this threat in more detail at the beginning of part 3A.

29. Leontius's own name is yet another reference to animality in the story of *thumos.* His very treatment of himself, once could suppose, is lionlike. See Craig (1994) 18.

30. The principle of noncontradiction is introduced at 436c. Socrates never makes an argument for the necessity that the soul be subject to this principle. For further discussion, see Weinstein (2018).

31. It is not unreasonable to associate *thumos* with appetite. When desire is introduced, it is actually described as *thumotic*—it wants the object to become *its own* (437c).

32. For helpful commentary on the "psychic parthood" and logic of tripartition discussed here, see Wilburn (2021, 4–25) and Weinstein (2018). While my own discussion of *thumos* is rooted in Socrates's argument for the tripartite structure of city and soul, it does not depend on that argument being sound. Indeed, the very division of the soul into three parts could come from a *thumotic* imposition of order on an object that may be resistant to such cognitive control. But even if there are more or fewer parts of the soul, the psychological investigation into *thumos* still reveals important insights into the souls of tyrants such as Critias and Charmides, and their lack of philosophical wonder.

33. 439e–440a.

34. 440a. Such a claim is quite consistent with our earlier discussion of the savagery of *thumos,* even if now Socrates talks of *thumos* while considering it as an auxiliary to reason. Cf. Wilburn (2021) 34.

35. See references in Saldaña (2021) 3n6.

36. Bloom (1968) 376. Cf. Craig (1994) 101.

37. Allen (2000) 139.

38. For the following, I am heavily indebted to the distinction between purity and danger that Mary Douglas outlines in her work of the same name. See Douglas (1966).

39. See Saldaña (2021)15; Parker (1983) 39; Douglas (1966) 67.

40. Hobbs (2000) 17; Ferrari (2007) 181; Bieda (2012) 147–148; Wilburn (2021) 36.

41. Tarnopolsky (2015) 12.

42. See Carroll (1990) 47. Cf. Douglas (1966) 3, 67: "Holiness means keeping distinct the categories of creation. It therefore involves correct definition, discrimination and order." Also see Kristeva (1982, 3–4): "If dung signifies the other side of the border, the place where I am not and which permits me to be, the corpse, the most sickening of wastes, is a border that has encroached

upon everything . . . [the corpse] disturbs identity, system, order." One can also compare Freud (1961) 46–47 on beauty, order, and cleanliness as distinguishing features of civilization.

43. Socrates and Adeimantus earlier banned both the tale of Achilles's profession of love to the corpse of Patroclus and the tale of dragging Hector around Patroclus's tomb (391b).

44. See *Republic* 581b and *Timaeus* 70a.

45. *Republic* 442c.

46. See Mansfield (2006) 219–221.

47. Cf. Wilburn (2021) 182, 184, 189–192.

48. Courage in the city is defined at 428c and it is specifically called "political" courage at 429c. It is primarily connected to *doxa* and the notion of what is lawful, so courage in the soul turns out to be obedience to the ruling wisdom of the soul about what ought to be feared. In this context, *sôphrosunê* (430e) is considered to be a kind of "self-mastery" in the city and later revised on the level of soul to be a "friendship of parts" of the soul (442c–d). The definition of *sôphrosunê* ends up looking very much like the definition of justice as each part "doing one's own things." I would suggest that the *sôphrosunê* revealed in this discussion is still a kind of *thumotic* moderation, one that undergoes important revision in Diotima's speech in the *Symposium*. It will perhaps turn out to be closer to what Socrates eventually calls wisdom, which involves knowledge of the soul and what is good for it (442c). We should keep in mind that the turn from the city to the human being in book 4 (435b–d), as Socrates is about to begin examining whether the soul has the same three parts (*eide*) as the city, actually rejects the "longer way" Socrates claims is necessary to conduct a full inquiry into these matters. Indeed, Glaucon expresses *thumos* once again and urges Socrates not to grow weary but to examine (435d). The "longer way" is thus left as a task for the reader to pursue. Perhaps, if my account is right, the account of wonder in the *Symposium* is part of it.

49. 441a–c.

50. For the following, I am grateful to Weinstein (2018) 89–90.

51. The story of Odysseus thus connects *thumos* not only to endurance but also the doglike behavior that lives according to the *oikeion* principle. It is an illustration of self-*mastery*. Cf. Wilburn (2021) 59. A difficulty may emerge in the *thumotic* person's apparent readiness, occasionally, to sacrifice his life. But if we are more precise about what such an individual takes his self (or his own things) to be, the difficulty is resolved. The dishonor that a base or cowardly act would bring to such a person may be a death of self greater than what is meant by "self" in "self-preservation." As we have already seen, the *thumotic* person—like Leontius—may see his own body as lowly and alien from his "higher" self.

52. 441a.

53. See Umphrey (1982) 378–379.

Chapter Two

1. Translations from the *Symposium* are from Nehamas and Woodruff (1989), though at times with my own revisions. I have also consulted Benardete (2001).

2. Obdrzalek (2017) 71.

3. Bloom in Benardete (2001) 108.

4. Although *thumos* is not explicitly mentioned in Aristophanes's speech or the rest of the *Symposium*, I will argue here and in part 3 that is still being addressed in the particular desires that are discussed. I agree with Cooper that "Aristophanes' whole account of *erôs* speaks to the relation between *erôs* and [*thumos*], but in its effective subordination of the former to the latter . . . it rejects rather than elaborates Plato's teaching." L. Cooper (2008) 60n10.

5. 189e–190a.

6. 190b. Benardete (2001) translates the phrase *phronêmata megala* as "proud thoughts."

7. Lacan (2015) 89: "In Plato's work, and well before him, this shape, *Sphairos* . . . is a being who is 'self-identical on all sides, without limits . . . reigns in its royal solitude, full of its own contentment, and of its self-sufficency.'"

8. 190b. The word Aristophanes uses is "*epicheireô*."

9. 190c.

10. 190c. "Honors" translates "*timai*" while "sacrifices" translates "*hiera*."

11. 190c–d.

12. This word will return in Diotima's account of *erôs* and have a new connation.

13. 191d.

14. "Man is an experiment of the gods." Benardete (2001) 186.

15. Cf. Bloom in Benardete (2001) 107.

16. In 190e–191a, Aristophanes points out that the human navel is a physical reminder of the wound of human nature. The artificiality of this separation is emphasized in the description of the tool Apollo uses to smooth out the wrinkles made by this separation.

17. 191d, 192e.

18. 192c. Aristophanes's speech emphasizes that *erôs* is not a desire for sexual pleasure but union with the missing half in the physical embrace. This comes to light more fully in the offer of Hephaestus. See below.

19. 191b–d.

20. 192c–d. See Bloom in Benardete (2001) 108.

21. 193b.

22. 192d–e.

23. 196d. Cf. *Odyssey* 8, 266–366. This tale is banned by Socrates and Adeimantus in their attempt to tame the too *thumotic erôs* in the stories of Homer. See *Republic* 390c.

24. Obdrazalek (2017) 78.

Part 2A

Chapter One

1. 162c–d.

2. 162c.

3. 162d.

4. The weaponizing of shame, which has been refuted as a definition of *sôphrosunê*, is thus patently lacking *sôphrosunê*.

5. Schmid (1998) 33.

6. 162d–e.

7. Notice the use of *epimeleia*, of which the strongest connotation is "attention." See *A Greek-English Lexicon* (rev. Jones, 9th edition, Oxford 1940). The word also suggests "treatment" or "care" and was used during Socrates's introduction of the Thracian physicians of the soul, who treat the part only by attending to the whole. How to understand the soul and the part–whole relation are questions looming over this discussion, but, as we shall see, Critias does not make them the focus.

8. Whereas Charmides fled from Socrates by throwing Critias's words at him, Critias will not flee, because there is no other he can flee to. There is disagreement among scholars about the originality of Critias's definition here. Some commentators suggest that Critias has heard the doctrine from Socrates. See Santas (1973) 118; Schmid (1998) 178n22; Lampert (2010), ch. 2; Burger (2013) 225–227. Others claim there are good reasons to suppose that Critias was the first to define *sôphrosunê* as "doing one's own things." See Moore and Raymond (2019) 66n94 and the references there. My argument at this point does not depend on the resolution of this issue, but I do find it more likely that Critias is imitating Socrates here, and that there is an irony for readers to catch: Critias himself is a bad actor reciting Socrates's poem. While Critias responds with anger at Charmides, however, Socrates calmly and temperately examines and refutes the hubristic Critias. As the dialogue nears its close, we will have more reason to suggest this.

9. 162e.

10. *Works and Days*, 311. The rest of the line reads "but idleness is a disgrace."

11. 163b–c.

12. Cf. Levine (2016) 164.

13. Cf. Hyland (1981) 64.

14. *Memorabilia* I.ii.56–58.

15. See Levine (2016) 191n14.

16. Hesiod placed value on the common labor that was a service to the community. Critias's contortion thus betrays him as "the kind of arrogant aristocrat Hesiod criticizes, as a man who lacks political moderation." Schmid (1998) 34. Cf. Tuckey (1968) 21 and Brennan (2012) 240n12.

17. Cf. Levine, 164–172.

18. 163c.

19. Cf. Tuozzo (2011) 176–178.

20. Hyland (1981) 83. Cf. Schmid (1998, 34): "Critias's underlying thought is clear: the true meaning of *sôphrosunê* does not consist in making or even doing what is beautiful; it rather focuses on the idea of procuring benefit for oneself and avoiding all harm as 'alien.' . . . Critias identifies the good with what benefits himself, in the sense of a calculating, narrow egoism."

21. Critias, the potential tyrant, also manifests this teaching in his deeds throughout the dialogue.

22. Thus, Kahn (1996, 190) is right to point out the similarities between the passage here and the passages in the *Lysis* and the *Symposium*, where the good and one's own are linked. But he does not note the tyrannical perversion of the doctrine that is at play in the Charmides.

23. 163d.

24. Ibid.

25. 197d.

26. 194c–e.

27. Cf. Hyland (1981) 81–83; Schmid (1998) 178n22. Perhaps Critias has taken a step forward in actually placing the notion of the good at the forefront, thus supplanting the beautiful. For the good takes us past the appearances, toward the real. Cf. *Republic* 382b, 505d–e; *Lysis* 219c–e; *Gorgias* 466a–468c; *Symposium* 205a. But Critias's understanding of the good as self-benefit ultimately mars this step forward. So the transition from the beautiful to the good, and from dialogue with Charmides to discussion with Critias, will turn out to be a move not from the conventional notion to a more philosophic understanding but from a conventional notion to a radical, sophistic, tyrannical perversion of a potentially philosophic understanding. See Levine (2016) 170–172.

28. 163d.

29. The other is at 167a.

Chapter Two

1. 164a.

2. Also wondrous was the effect of Charmides's beauty on those who gazed upon it. See part 1A, chapter 1.

3. Schmid (1998) 36.

4. Cf. Hyland (1981) 84. I am not intending to say that self-knowledge in a kind of *modern* sense (knowledge of one's own particular personality or soul) is required for virtue. I am suggesting that what is required is knowledge of self qua human being, and I believe that this knowledge may turn out to be inseparable from knowledge of the good. I think this is what Socrates is revealing in this section of the text. Critias, however, misses this or, more ominously, refuses to see.

5. Santas (1973, 118) claims that Critias does not emend his definition around the notion of the good (with something like "knowing good things and doing good things") because he fears "the Lachean objection that it is a definition of the whole virtue, not [*sôphrosunê*]." This is possible, but I think an even bigger problem exists for Critias: knowledge of the good and self-knowledge are not coextensive according to his doctrine of self-benefit, and he will be unable to smuggle self-knowledge into his view. Perhaps a Socratic understanding of "knowing the good and doing it" has self-knowledge built in, but the Critian understanding does not.

6. 164a.

7. 164b.

8. See Levine (2016) 174; Tuozzo (2011) 299.

9. Cf. Tuckey (1968) 24.

10. 164d–165a.

11. Perhaps the biggest mistakes in interpreting this speech have been to attribute its content to Plato and/or claim that Critias's interpretation of the Delphic Oracle yields a philosophically important insight into *sôphrosunê* that Socrates should endorse. Hyland (1981, 88–93) commits both errors. And as Schmid (1998, 179 n32) points out, Friedlander, Guthrie, and North also come close to the one or both of the errors in their readings of the passage. More recently, see Tuozzo (2011, 186–188) and Moore (2015, 69–70). In what follows I hope to make clear that the view Critias is putting forward, consistent with what he has heretofore presented, cannot be Socrates's (or Plato's) opinion, nor does it highlight a praiseworthy feature of *sôphrosunê* properly understood. Instead, it presents a distorted vision of *sôphrosunê* that undercuts its significance. Cf. Levine (2016) 177–179.

12. See Tuckey (1968) 9–10, 24; Kahn (1996) 191; Moore (2015) 14–22.

13. Cf. Levine (2016) 177: "The self-knowledge that Critias has in mind here is not a new definition but is continuous with the foregoing. It is the specific mode of self-understanding implicit in Critias's earlier opinion."

14. When Charmides put forth an opinion that really turned out to be Critias's own view, Socrates first called it an *"ainigma"* before he began picking it apart, much to Charmides's delight. Socrates's image of the *ainigma* thus pulled Critias into the conversation, a goal that emerged upon seeing Charmides abandoning the inquiry. It is thus illuminating that Critias here uses the word again to refer to the Oracle. Critias presents this riddle to defend his earlier riddle, which turned out to be incoherent.

15. 165a.

16. Ibid.

17. 165a.

18. Levine (2016) 178.

19. In contrast, Tuozzo (2011, 186) claims that a greeting "[expresses] some conception of a good end and [expresses] a wish that the addressee will attain it." In the same vein, Moore (2015, 70) argues that the "salutation could also encourage acknowledging oneself as a potential object for transformative conversation." Both these readings, though admirable, fail to show any textual evidence to support them. Moreover, they stretch too far the notion of a "greeting" (which Critias has already quite adamantly denied to be advice) in saying that a greeting is a form of encouragement or an expression of some good. If I wish to express to someone that we share a good and I wish to encourage her, then the words I use after I greet the person will serve better to express this. For in many circumstances, the greeting itself will be the same whether or not I have a wish that the person should attain some good or acknowledge herself as deficient. Those beliefs and desires are simply not embedded in my practice of greeting and are revealed only by the other kinds of communication that put the greeting in context. In addition, the content of a greeting seems to be a matter of pure convention. Whether one says "Hail!" or "Cheers!" or "Ciao!" is a phenomenon that seems to carry no significant content, philosophically speaking, and is dependent on the customs in one's community, customs that are human, all too human.

20. This has been hinted at since the beginning of Critias's speech, with his emphasis on the "dedicator" who "put up" the inscriptions. The human source of the inscription is highlighted, while the intention of the god is only mentioned secondarily. Schmid (1998, 179n35) points out that Critias says the inscription was put up "as if" it were from the god, and (180n36) that he repeatedly calls his account his opinion (*dokei moi*). This not only emphasizes the human element of the speech but also stresses Critias's vision of himself as a knower. Cf. 165a, where Critias pairs the dedicator with himself. Of course, as Schmid points out, calling it an opinion signals its "low epistemic status" even if Critias is thereby trying to shield himself from refutation.

21. Schmid (1998) 38. Cf. Levine (2016, 178–179), where he discusses the practical Thrasymachean consequences of this view: "Looking to no other standard

than itself . . . and wholly self-directed, the injunction Know Thyself amounts to a divine exhortation to self-insistence . . . [it is] the lion's way: do as you please, as you are inclined; indulge your passions, desires, appetites, ambitions, aggressions without regard to any externally imposed standard of good and bad."

22. Hyland (1981, 90) claims in contrast to this that Critias's characterization of "know yourself" as a greeting is "a well-chosen image for the kind of responsive openness to things which . . . [is] the interrogative stance of philosophy." But Critias does not in fact embody any kind of openness, as I will show.

23. Tuozzo (2011) 299–300.

24. Tuozzo (2011) 302

25. See Tuozzo (2011) 297.

26. 165a–b.

27. 165b. Critias even says he would not be "ashamed" to retract what he has said at 164d, further recalling Socrates's earlier refutation of Charmides.

Chapter Three

1. For *gnosis* as acknowledgment, see Moore (2015) 9–11.

2. 165c. This is the first mention of *epistêmê* in the argument. Translating it is difficult. I have opted to leave it simply as "knowledge," though the plural "knowledges" does sound unnatural to us. But other translations that sounds more natural ("sciences" or "kinds of knowledge") import connotations to the words that are simply not there. Socrates's examples of *epistêmai* do include what we might call "sciences" but are not limited to them. Translating "*epistêmai*" as "kinds of knowledge" implies regrettably that there are kinds that need to be distinguished, which is not at all entailed by the use of the word.

3. Cf. Roochnik (1986) 298–300; Tuozzo (2011) 193–194. For examples in Plato's dialogues, consider *Parmenides* 134a–b; *Republic* 477a–78a; and *Protagoras* 352c.

4. Tuckey (1968) 38.

5. Tuckey (1968) 38–44. Others who take a similar view include Hyland (1981) 95–96; Schmid (1998) 43; and Schofield (2006) 149.

6. Levine (2016, 199n58) rightly suggests that the question raised at this moment could be phrased: "Is *epistêmê* as Critias understands it exhaustive of human cognition?"

7. 165c.

8. See Rosen (1973) 632; Hyland (1981) 98; Levine (2016) 182.

9. 165c–d. The reintroduction of "medicine" harks back to the Thracian physicians of the whole. The relation of their knowledge to the *epistêmê* being discussed is a background question here.

10. 165c.

11. 165d. Socrates seems to be equating *technê* and *epistêmê* here.

12. 165e. Indeed, Socrates has hinted to us here that the "beautiful work" of self-knowledge could itself be "beautiful work." That is, as I will explain in more detail in parts 3A and 3B, the activity of knowing oneself in Socratic terms may turn out to be inseparable from, if not identical to, a cognitive activity that is itself beautiful through beholding what is beautiful. This activity is philosophical wonder.

13. Cf. Republic 438a.

14. See Sprague (1976) 29–42; Levine (2016) 182–183; Tuozzo (2011) 198–199.

15. 165c.

16. Annas (1985, 35–36) claims that this does not happen in the Charmides because there is a confusion between self-knowledge and knowledge of knowledge. But the root of the confusion here is essentially connected to Critias's (dis) orientation to the beautiful and the good.

17. 165e–166a.

18. Notice that Critias does not follow suit and mention medicine here. Medicine is a tricky *epistêmê*, given the pretense under which Socrates agreed to go to work, and the discussion of Thracian healing of the whole.

19. This should not be taken to mean that Socrates necessarily disagrees with Critias here. Rather, Socrates is comparing self-knowledge to the crafts in order to reveal what, if anything, is distinctive about the knowledge Critias is describing. Cf. Tuozzo (2011) 194.

20. 166a.

21. 166a–c. It is not clear why Socrates does not mention geometry in responding to Critias. Geometry is crucial to the educations of the guardians in the *Republic*.

22. 166c.

23. See the review of the scholarship in Tuckey (1968) 33–37; Schmid (1998) 181n14; and Tuozzo (2011) 198–199.

24. Schmid (1998) 47, 182n16.

25. Tuckey (1968, 39) asserts that it rests on nothing but Critias's "sophistic love of antithesis."

26. For this and the following, see Tuozzo (2011) 199–200, 305.

27. See especially *Statesman* 259e–260c; *Euthydemus* 288e–291a.

28. Cf. Levine (2016) 186.

29. Stalley (2000, 271) claims an *epistêmê* of knowledge in general is needed because it just is general (Cf. *Ion* 531a–533c) and because of the phenomenon of examining others. Tuozzo (2011, 305) argues that *sôphrosunê* knows itself and the other knowledge because if we want to know if the other knowledges are beneficial, we need the one that is the standard for benefit. Both these claims may be right, but neither explains why it is the Critian conception of a ruling science and not the Socratic conception of knowledge of ignorance which addresses

these problems. That is, *sôphrosunê* will turn out to be vitally connected with the knowledge of limits in a way that Critias's definition, but not Socrates, fails to be. It is this vital Socratic connection that is the answer that Tuozzo and Stalley call for, or so I will argue.

30. I will further justify this language in part 3B.

31. Cf. Moore (2015) 6; Levine (2016) 188–189.

Chapter Four

1. 166c–d.

2. 166e.

3. 165b–c.

4. See Bruell (1977) 166.

5. Cf. *Apology* 22e–23a.

6. Schmid (1998) 45.

7. By using the phrase "philosophical detachment," I am referring to nothing more than Socrates's exhortations to transcend our *thumotic* desire for glory and fear of looking inferior, in favor of the philosophical pursuit of the true good itself. Socrates has explicitly said that Critias should not worry who among them is being refuted, but he has subtly forced the onlookers, including Charmides and the reader, to wonder about Critias's false claims to know. Cf. Levine (2016) 206.

8. 166e.

9. 21d. Consistent with Socrates's other uses in the *Charmides*, the passage in the *Apology* mentions not *epistêmê* but *eidenai*. Accordingly, at 167a Socrates replaces "*anepistêmosunê*" with "*ha me oiden*."

10. Cf. Tuozzo (2011) 190.

11. One of the puzzles of the dialogue is that this seemingly Socratic teaching is apparently refuted. I will be arguing that this is not the case.

12. 164a.

13. I will return in 3art 3B to the connection between this and the account of *erôs* in the *Symposium*.

14. Cf. Levine (2016) 206–211; Schmid (1998) 56–57.

15. 167a.

16. Levine (2016) 215.

17. 20c. While Moore (2015) attempts to situate the Delphic speech in the *Charmides* amid other Delphic references in the dialogues, he does not address the *Apology*.

18. As I say below, it is not only the oracle but Chaerephon whom Socrates cites to explain himself to the city.

19. 20d–20e.

20. 21a.

21. 21b. Critias also said the Oracle was a "riddle." But the meanings of the two riddles are not identical.

22. 21c.

23. 21d–e.

24. See Moore (2015) 42. Cf. Levine (2016) 222–223.

25. Recall Charmides's failure to exercise this freedom in his discussion with Socrates.

26. *Charmides* 172c.

27. See Levine (2016) 218–219.

28. Levine (2016) 219.

29. Nor does he think it even desirable.

30. 173a ff.

Chapter Five

1. 167a–b. This second beginning and third libation thus divides the conversation accordingly. Critias first offered "doing one's own things" as a definition of *sôphrosunê* and subsequently revealed that he subsumed the good under "his own," and so the first new beginning was called for: the shift from *sôphrosunê* as doing one's own things to doing good things. See 163e.

2. 166e.

3. Cf. Levine (2016) 238. Clearly, if awareness of ignorance is essential to *sôphrosunê*, then we must first have some understanding of what "knowledge" is, since ignorance is defined as the lack of knowledge. The discussion in the *Charmides* does not reveal to us what Socrates's understanding of knowledge is. Cf. Tuozzo (2011) 209–235. But it does make suggestions about how not to think about it, as I will try to show in the current chapter. I will defend in more detail a positive account of self-knowledge connected to wonder about the beautiful in parts 3A and 3B.

4. Hyland (1981, 108–109) has an interesting discussion of the connection between the definitions and the different libations: why "one's own things" would be an appropriate libation to the gods, and "know yourself" to the heroes, as well as Critias's final definition to Zeus. The first seems to bring with it the conventional view of piety that would be the correct response to the gods. The second calls attention to the mortality of heroes, and the final one to Zeus aims for complete divine wisdom. This is suggestive, but it is not clear that these definitions are understood by Critias or Socrates in the way that Hyland specifies, nor is it clear what the content of the "second libation" really is. Hyland wants to equate it with "know yourself," but strictly speaking it seems to be the "doing of good things," and it is unclear how to relate this to the libation to the heroes on Hyland's interpretation.

5. As will become clear, it is a mistake to suppose that Socrates's remarks shows that his own conception of *sôphrosunê* is problematic. It is Critias's doctrine that is attacked in what follows, and Socrates's refutation will reveal that he, in fact, knows what he knows and does not know. The question of the possibility and benefit of this is thus left open, not closed, by the dialogue. Cf. Levine (2016) 236; Schmid (1998) 87.

6. Along these lines, Schmid (1998, 85) claims that 167a (the mention of knowledge of ignorance) marks the high point of the dialogue. We now descend again, but not without gaining insights into what *sôphrosunê* is not. The remainder of the dialogue shows it is neither "theoretical-objective [nor] technical-productive knowledge" but perhaps another kind of knowledge is possible.

7. 167b.

8. Those who follow the first interpretation above may lose sight of the "what" of the knowledge of knowledge and ignorance. Socrates's second challenge to Critias is that though he might have knowledge "that," he does not have knowledge "what." This will become clearer in what follows.

9. 167b.

10. 167c. The word for "see" is *ide*, recalling *eidenai* once again. Socrates again seems to be showing that he knows what he does not know. The question is: can Critias have this kind of "sight"? When Socrates first introduced the "possibility and benefit" question, he talked of knowledge as *eidenai;* now that he is "at a loss," he introduces knowledge as *epistêmê*.

11. 168e.

12. 167c–d. The use of *ennoei* again is significant. Socrates is telling Critias to turn to himself once again. What he says about the soul will thus be directly tied up to the state of his soul. Socrates's question makes those watching wonder whether Critias's own thinking is the kind of self-related act that would at least demonstrate in deed the possibility of the kind of self-knowledge that he and Socrates are trying to establish in speech.

13. Tuozzo (2011, 212–213) calls this the "exclusionary proviso" and points out that "Socrates puts first, and thus emphasizes, this feature of the analogues he adduces: they do not have as an object what all other cases of the relevant psychological phenomena have as their object." He argues that the exclusionary proviso is true only if we also make the assumption that "all first-order seeings see colors [and] all colors are seen by first-order *seeings*." Critias is not required to make this assumption, but he makes no objection to Socrates.

14. Socrates does this for the example of both seeing and hearing, but excludes the analogue to ignorance in the remainder of the examples of mental faculties. See below. Cf. Levine (2016) 239.

15. 167c–168a.

16. Hyland (1981) 114–117; Bruell (1977) 73–76; Schmid (1998) 90.

17. 167d.

18. Cf. Levine (2011) 238–239; Hyland (1981, 115) sees this as well and suggests that Socrates is showing that *epistêmê* cannot grasp the "lack." I would suggest that the issue is not with the use of *epistêmê* but with Critias's and Charmides's mistaken conceptions of knowledge and the good.

19. This is the very topic of Aristotle's *De Anima* 3.2. Cf. Tuckey (1968) 45; Bruell (1977) 173–76; Kahn (1996) 195n21; Schmid (1998) 90; Tuozzo (2011) 226–233.

20. See Tuozzo (2011, 213): "[T]here is nothing odd about a fear of fears, a love of love, and opinion about opinions. . . . But there is something odd about a fear that does not take the terrible as is intentional object, or a seeing that sees no color, or a love that is not directed to its object as something beautiful." The example of *erôs* and beauty is most interesting and I will return to it in parts 3A and 3B. Cf. Tuckey (1968) appendix 4; Santas (1973) 123; Hyland (1981) 115–117; Schmid (1998) 90; Tsouna (in Carone (1998, 274–275) argues that this reflexivity problem is solved by distinguishing first and second order knowledge. This may go some extent to dealing with the *epistêmê* of other *epistêmai*, but clearly won't handle the purely self-directed *epistêmê*, especially when we add the "exclusionary proviso." It should also be kept in mind that what is at issue is a Critian conception of knowledge that is deeply flawed. The dialogue is showing why a certain understanding of self-knowledge and the good is illusory, and there is another understanding that Socrates implicitly offers for our consideration. Cf. Tsouna (2022) 206–209.

21. Although Socrates specifies what the objects of seeing and hearing are (color and sound), he does not specify in his questions to Critias what the objects of opinion or knowledge are.

22. Cf. Moore (2015) 94–95.

23. Tuckey (1968, 41–42) claims that if we knew the nature of the object of knowledge, then we would know how knowledge could be reflexive. He believes Plato has not solved this problem in the *Charmides* and takes it up later, with the theory of ideas. Tuozzo (2011, 304–333) similarly points to a solution in the discussion of knowledge of the Idea of Good presented in the *Republic*. I will argue in part 3B that this solution fails unless we provide an account of the erotic faculty, which can have the attribute of its distinct, intentional object and thus become beautiful itself as it is aimed at beauty. See Tsouna (2022) 212–213.

24. As mentioned, Socrates encourages Critias to "see" if he "knows." Cf. Moore (2015) 93. All along we are right to wonder about the relationship between seeing and knowing, especially since there is a linguistic connection: knowing (*oida*) is the perfect tense of seeing (*horao*). It is also relevant that perhaps no relation is more significant than between *doxa* and *epistêmê*, emphasized repeatedly by Socrates saying "*dokei moi*" and "*dokei soi*."

25. For the following, I am indebted to the interpretation of Tuozzo (2011) 219–224.

26. 168b.

27. 168b–c.

28. 168c–d.

29. Again, in these examples Socrates does not mention the analogue for the "lack" of *epistêmê*. Its omission suggests that the Socratic alternative to Critias's viewpoint is not at issue here.

30. Socrates seems to be suggesting this. See below.

31. 168d.

32. Schmid (1998, 94) says that Socrates is rejecting here a metaphysics of self-relation that is "modeled on quantitative relations." Cf. Tuckey, appendix 4; Levine (2016) 245–247; Santas (1973) 123; Moore (2015) 93.

33. Cf. Tuozzo (2011) 223. Socrates does not reintroduce the desires and cognitions or emotions. Hyland (1981, 119) claims that the result of an *epistêmê* having the being in relation to its faculty is "empty science." Hyland perhaps goes astray in identifying *epistêmê* with the modern, positivist notion of science he seeks to reject. But his suggestion that we look to *erôs* in trying to understand the self-relating activity of the soul seems right to me.

34. 167c–d.

35. 168d.

36. 168e.

37. Cf. Levine (2016) 247; Schmid (1998) 95; Moore (2015) 93.

38. 168e–169a.

39. 169a. Tuckey (1968) 46–48 suggests that such an *epistêmê* of *epistêmê* is what we would consider "epistemology," and that Socrates is really getting at the question "How can I know that I know?," a question that Plato does not here have the tools to answer. But along these lines, Bruell (1977, 182) points out that the *diarêsis* or "division" Socrates calls for would turn out to be an *epistêmê* of *epistêmê*, and so the possibility of self-relation would be shown even in the act of discovering self-relation. Tuozzo (2011, 225–233) argues that the call for a great man here is a Platonic invitation to members of his academy to take up this diaresis and suggests that Aristotle does so. Tuozzo admits, however, that Aristotle does not ultimately give us a an account of the "relatum of knowledge" (what I earlier called its distinct, intentional object), and that without this, we still don't know which cases of knowing are capable of self-relation. An adequate account of self-relation here would need to go beyond Aristotle's account of relatives.

40. 169a–b.

41. Levine (2016) 248; Tuozzo (2011) 236–238.

42. 169b.

43. Levine (2016) 249–250. If we recall Socrates's earlier account of Zalmoxian medicine, we can note that Critias's self-relation and even that of Charmides are deficient in their failure to take into account what is their proper "whole." Both of their self-relations are inevitably partial in their dependence on others' views of them.

44. See below.

45. 169c–d.

46. Cf. Bruell (1977) 184; Santas (1973) 107; Levine (2016) 255; Hyland (1981) 142–143; Schmid (1998) 101–102. More recent commentators have missed the alarming significance of this "yawn perplexity," and that it undermines attempts to see Critias as genuinely philosophical.

47. Levine (2016) 256.

48. See Schmid (1998) 101–103, 113; Levine (2016) 257–258; Hyland (1981) 122–123. Notice that Socrates once again calls Critias a "wretch" (*miare*) in the closing moments (when Critias once again tries to resurrect "knowledge of the good") and accuses him of moving in a circle. The bloodstained image thus highlights the connection between tyranny and the inability to understand oneself and the good. Cf. Schmid (1998) 151.

49. Cf. Schmid (1998) 35, 140–141, 148; Bruell (1977) 158.

50. 135a. Kahn (1996, 196n22) points out this parallel and claims that the phrase in both passages are just "figures of speech," and that Plato is not talking about himself.

51. See *Phaedrus* 245c–e and *Laws* 894e–896a.

52. I will provide my own response in part 3B. I believe that the erotic orientation to the beautiful that culminates in philosophical wonder is meant to both (1) combat the *thumos* that blinds one to a self-relation that is self-knowing, and (2) instill a wonder that is both self-knowing and generative, and thus an antidote to Critias's tyrannical blindness.

53. Not only does Critias not see "self-motion," but, as Bruell (1977, 180) points out, he also doesn't consider that the examples of quantitative relations and hearing and seeing are tied to the body. Might *epistêmê* not be? This seems to be the case in the divided line, at least. See Bruell (1977) 180. Halper (2000, 313–314) suggests that Critias fails to "recognize a noetic faculty distinct from sense, emotion, and opinion . . . a realm beyond the sensible where self-relation is possible." This fits in well with Critias's attempt to bring the Delphic inscription to the human level.

Chapter Six

1. 169d. He says that he and Critias will examine it again some other time. If there is such a discussion "some other time," Plato never shows it to us. The meaning of *epistêmê epistêmês* still remains unclear.

2. The procedure is similar to that employed in the *Meno* to discover whether or not virtue is teachable. In this dialogue we may see the transition from the method of *elenchus* to that of hypothesis. Cf. Vlastos (1983); Kahn (1996) 196, 309–313. Earlier we wondered about the very notion itself of demonstrating possibility. It seems that actions, though incapable of explaining possibility, seem

to be able to show it, and we have already seen some glimpses of Socrates showing *sôphrosunê*, and thereby the possibility of the Socratic conception of self-knowledge, in his questioning of Critias. Thus the trouble to account for possibility that is spoken here seems to refer specifically to the Critian conception of self-knowledge: the moment suggests that while Socrates's view of self-knowledge may already appear, through his actions, to be possible, Critias's view here is only hypothetical.

3. 169d.

4. Cf. Hyland (1981) 123. As Bruell (1977, 186n52) points out, Socrates's raising of this question shows that we can in no way say that the definition of self-knowledge or *sôphrosunê* that Critias is proposing can readily be expanded into the Socratic knowing of what one does and does not know.

5. See Schmid (1998) 106, 119. Santas (1973, 124) calls the two arguments (170a–e and 10e–171d) the "best and most significant" in the dialogue.

6. 169d–e.

7. Cf. Bruell (1977) 185; Tuozzo (2011) 239–242. Tuckey (1968, 55–57) suggests that there is great confusion around *gignoskein* and *epistasthai* in this passage, a confusion that he attributes to Socrates. Even if one grants that there is confusion here, it is not clear that the confusion is Socrates's and not merely that of Critias, who is the one who reintroduces *gnôsis* after all.

8. 169e.

9. Dyson (1974, 106) claims that Socrates puts aside Critias's suggestion as irrelevant. This is true, but misleading, if Dyson is thereby accusing Socrates of foul play. It is Critias who has failed to see the significance of the problem that Socrates will now explain, which perhaps Dyson has not seen as well, in making this remark. Socrates does appear to subtly reinterpret Critias's suggestion here, by saying that having "that which knows itself (*to hauto gignoskon*)" will bring about self-knowledge. He does not repeat Critias and say that an *epistêmê epistêmês* is the same thing as *to hauto gignoskon*.

10. 170a. Cf. Levine (2016) 274. This would further seem to suggest that this *epistêmê epistêmês* is not the Socratic knowledge of ignorance that many commentators take it to be. They of course would respond that Critias doesn't really have *epistêmê epistêmês*. But as Socrates goes on to show, this is really no rejoinder, for the conception of *epistêmê epistêmês* will be deeply problematic.

11. 170a. Bruell (1977, 187) points out that the odd phrasing "*ou gar manthanô hôs esti to auto ha oiden eidenai kai ha tis mê oiden eidenai*" seems to suggest that Socrates cannot understand how knowing what one knows is the same as knowing what one does not know. The point is that knowing what one does not know is a unique kind of knowledge, not really comparable to knowing what one knows.

12. 170a.

13. See Tuozzo (2011) 243–244.

14. 170a.

15. Again, Socrates's choice of examples is interesting. The nature of the "arts" of politics and medicine has been a question hovering in the background throughout the previous discussion. The rest of the discussion will accordingly make us wonder about the relation between *epistêmê epistêmês* and the "arts" of medicine and politics, and raise the question how to understand these latter properly, perhaps in a way that will evade the problems that the discussion presents (Especially given Socrates's claim to treat Charmides's headache, his subsequent speech on Thracian medicine, and Critias's first picture of a well-functioning city). For Critias, at least, it seems that politics and medicine are the same kind of thing. Critias also overlooks Socrates's omission of the knowledge of the "sick" and "unjust" from his definitions of medicine and politics. This highlights again Critias's inability to see ignorance, no matter how much lip service he pays to it. Also, Critias has not only missed Socrates's omission of the "lack of health or justice," he has not seen that Socrates has moved the lack to the *epistêmê* itself: Socrates asks about the *epistêmê* or lack of *epistêmê* of health or justice. Were Critias's own understanding consistent with Socrates's he would see that the lack is in the wrong place. For the "lack of *epistêmê* of health" is by no means medicine: it is just plain ignorance of health.

16. 170b. As Kahn (1996, 197n23) says, the arts are "individuated" here, similarly to discussions in the *Gorgias* and *Ion*.

17. 170b–c.

18. Cf. Tuozzo (2011) 247–248; Levine (2016) 273; Moore (2015) 96–100. The inability of this *epistêmê epistêmês* to rise from "knowledge that" to "knowledge what" has been foreshadowed already in the dialogue: A related problem was seen when Critias was earlier driven to the conclusion that a doctor could treat his own patient, and thus be *sophron*, without knowing that what he was doing was good. This prompted Critias to introduce self-knowledge as *sôphrosunê* (164d). Critias's response is an insistence that the *sophron* individual has the "knowledge that" he is *sophron*, but he later responds with an *epistêmê* of itself and all the others, which seems like it should be a "knowledge what." But this too appeared to be problematic as soon as Socrates mentioned the self-relating capacities: this *epistêmê* is not "of" what the other vision and hearings are "of" (167c), and so where does its "whatness" lie? The present argument now shows how difficult it is for Critias to hold "knowledge that" and "knowledge what" together.

19. Schmid (1998) 113. Of course, one could say that in reality Critias only "thinks he knows." But I think Schmid is right in pointing out that Critias is an embodiment of the problematic view he is trying to defend. It is not clear how Socrates is using the words "*gignoskein*" and "*epistasthai*" throughout this interchange. Both Hyland and Tuckey interpret the latter part of the dialogue as an attack on the suitability of *epistêmê* as a candidate for self-knowledge, and urge that "*gnôsis*" replace it. Perhaps in this spirit, it would appear that Socrates uses the words indiscriminately without paying attention to fine distinctions that

should be made, especially at 170b–c, where the *epistêmê* is supposed to help the *sophron* individual "know what he recognizes." This view seems to be right in the following sense: it is quite unclear how to neatly draw the distinctions between these words in this passage, and it is further unclear how Socrates would do so. But this makes it even more unclear that the issue Socrates is bringing Critias to see revolves around the unsuitability of *epistêmê*, when compared to *gnôsis*. We should observe that Critias goes along readily with Socrates use of the terms, and perhaps if there is confusion about them, it is a confusion that reveals something about his flawed understanding of knowledge and the good. This might be revealed by an examination of the word use here, but I believe it is revealed by the point of the argument itself, which shows that the Critian conception is empty of content.

20. 170c.

21. Recall that the entire conversation with Charmides rests on Socrates "pretending" to know the cure for Charmides's headache. Cf. Levine (2016) 274. Woolf (2023, 192–194) argues that Plato is here calling the reader to a kind of "scrutiny" that involves deep philosophical engagement with the text, rather than a passive acceptance of some doctrine. I agree and suggest that it is of the utmost importance that Critias (and perhaps the unnamed listener of the *Charmides*, who never asks the narrator a question) fails to do just this.

22. 170e.

23. A similar point can be made about the charge Tuckey (1968, 55–62) makes to Socrates's opening question of the argument. Socrates's beginning point was that the *epistêmê epistêmês* is not the same thing as the *epistêmê* of justice or of health, and Tuckey asserts that this assumes an analogy between the self-related *epistêmê* and the others, which is not in fact tenable. I think this is right, but it shows once again Critias's (not Socrates's or Plato's) lack of understanding: recall that Socrates and Critias earlier agreed that self-knowledge was unique and dissimilar to a productive *technê* like medicine (165c–166a) or a theoretical science like calculation (166a–c). As Schmid (1998, 111–112) points out, Critias does not object to lumping these two *epistêmai* together, and he does not at all stress either dissimilarity to self-knowledge. Schmid even suggests that Socrates is here testing Critias to see if he has learned, and the gentleman has failed.

24. 170e–171c. Recall that Socrates on beginning a conversation with Critias, agrees to "pretend" to be a doctor. The "true or false" doctor is the very example that Socrates examines in the ensuing argument, compelling us to wonder about the status of Socrates's own pretending, and raising the possibility that Critias himself may be the "real pretender," in that he doesn't know his own ignorance.

25. 170e. Schofield (2006, 122–123) suggests the text should even be emended to alleviate some of this confusion, and claims that while the first argument shows how *epistêmê epistêmês* cannot lead to "knowledge what," the second argument reveals a specific instantiation of this general truth, with regard to the real and pretend doctor. Santas (1973, 126) also makes an interpretation along these lines.

But as Schmid (1998, 114) points out, this explanation does not do justice to the end of the argument that suggests a combination of *epistêmê epistêmês* with "knowledge what" at 172b–c, which would be precluded by the general/specific arguments here. My own interpretation of the conclusion and argument here is closer to that of Tuozzo (2011, 248–254), who claims that this second argument establishes that "there is no single kind of knowledge that enables one to know that kinds of knowledge a person does and does not possess" (251).

26. Cf. Schmid (1998) 115.

27. 170e–171a.

28. 171a–b.

29. 171b

30. 171c.

31. 170e.

32. Tuozzo (2011, 251–254) argues for the soundness, which I endorse. If knowledge is construed on model such that each branch is narrowly confined to its own subject matter, then knowledge of knowledge will yield only "knowledge that," not "knowledge what," which is an absurd state of affairs because these two conceptions cannot be divorced.

33. Cf. Levine (2016) 276; Morris (1989) 57; Schmid (1998) 115–118. Bruell (1977, 192–193) sees the error here slightly differently: while the artisan has a kind of *epistêmê epistêmês* in knowing the limits of his art, his failure to apply this across the board leads him to think he knows what he does not know. I think this is a correct description of the artists whom Socrates describes interrogating in the *Apology*, but it doesn't quite capture Critias's failure here, which is more deeply rooted in the narrow reflexivity of his conception, which empties it of content. It thus might be misleading to compare, as McKim (1985, 69–70) does (this *sophron* individual to the *peirastic* inquirer in Aristotle's *Sophistical Refutations* (172a–b), who has knowledge of the common principles (*ta koina*) but knowledge of nothing in particular. Even this peirastic inquirer has more knowledge than the Critian *sophron* individual, for he sees what is in common to all knowledges, whereas knowledges for the Critian *sophron* individual are discrete and confined to their own subject matter. The Critian *sophron* is incoherent in a way that the peirastic is not.

34. Santas (1973) 128.

35. Thus Socrates, in showing himself able to examine others, seems to dramatically display that real *sôphrosunê* is not Critian in nature.

36. Cf. Levine (2016) 282.

37. See Moore (2015) 98–100.

38. Santas (1973, 128–129) points out that it is not the "almighty" science one might hope for. Hyland (1981, 126) also suggests that Socrates is calling into question philosophy as epistemology or study of consciousness, because these appear to be cut off from the good.

39. 170e.

40. Tuckey (1951, 61–62) sees the perplexity caused by this argument in the divorce of "knowledge of knowledge" from "knowledge of the object," but then attributes this divorce to a confusion on Socrates's (or Plato's) part between two kinds of disanalogous knowledge. This may be an accurate description of the confusion is there, but the confusion belongs to Critias, not Socrates. See Tsouna (2022) 237.

41. McKim asserts that the Socratic conception and the Critian conception are one and the same. This is quite remarkable given McKim's criticism of others who have interpreted the current passage out of context, neglecting dramatic details. These dramatic details, as we have begun to see, suggest that the Critian conception and the Socratic conception are far from identical. McKim also suggests that Plato should be distinguished from his protagonist Socrates. One should wonder, of course, why not also distinguish Socrates from his interlocutor Critias? McKim refuses to do so and says instead that it is a mistake to believe that Plato presents Socrates as an ideal embodiment of *sôphrosunê*. This interpretation goes astray, for in lumping Socrates together with Critias, it misses Socrates and the key issue of the dialogue: how is self-knowledge, as knowledge of ignorance (and not just knowledge of knowledge) connected to knowledge of the good? See McKim (1985) 60–65. Cf. Tuckey (1951) 49; Hyland (1981) 127–128; Levine (2016) 276—280; Tuozzo (2011) 264–266. Commentators remark how strange it is that Socrates might be questioning the possibility of the Socratic way of life he discusses in the *Apology*. It would be strange, if that were indeed the case. For how can Socrates examine others if he only has "knowledge that"? Kahn's response to this conundrum is that Plato is showing that Socrates needs not special expertise but must have knowledge of good and evil, and thus must go beyond the *elenchus*, which has only a negative effect, to a more "technical" and positive foundation for the moral and intellectual stance of Socrates. See Kahn (1996) 198–222. But it is quite strange that Kahn appeals to *technê* as Plato's answer to the problems here, since Socrates had implied in the previous part of the dialogue that *technê* was a highly suspect model, at best, for understanding the nature of self-knowledge.

42. Woolf's response to this is to expand "knowledge of knowledge" to the knowledge of the logical relations of propositions. See Woolf (2023) 195–206. I do not see evidence for this proposal in the dialogue.

43. 170e.

44. Cf. Schmid (1998) 118; Levine (2016) 274.

45. See Tuozzo (2011) 251–252 and the authors cited there. My full account of the Socratic alternative that does not fall victim to Critian incoherence will come in part 3B, in which I argue that philosophical wonder provides an antidote to the empty reflexivity here envisaged.

46. Cf. Moore (2015) 99.

47. Recall that the meaning of "knowledge of knowledge" is not specifically made clear at 167a, and so the results that have manifested regarding epistemology, psychology, self-consciousness, may or may not apply to Socratic knowledge of ignorance, properly understood. See Schmid (1998) 191n2.

48. It is surprising that this is overlooked by the commentators who object so strongly to the move from knowledge of knowledge to knowledge of knowledges at 169e–170a.

49. 171d. Cf. 169b–c. Recall that at 167a, Socrates was not confident about the possibility of knowledge of knowledge but seemed quite confident that *sôphrosunê* is good.

50. 173a–174b. I will discuss this in the next chapter.

51. 170d–e. Socrates consistently uses the first-person plural in talking about both the benefit and in the ruling.

52. 171e.

53. 171e. The word *kalôs* is used twice in the passage and appears four more times before Socrates introduces his dream, in which the word is absent.

54. 172a.

55. 172a.

56. 161d. ff. See Schmid (1998) 127.

57. Schmid (1998) 127–128.

58. See Kahn (1996) 204; Levine (2016) 277. But see Reeve (1988) for an argument that Plato is not committed to this view.

59. See Kahn (1996) 204–205.

60. See Schmid (1998) 128.

61. 172a.

62. See Kahn (1996) 204–205.

63. See Tuckey (1951) 74.

64. See Tuckey (1951) 73–75 and Schmid (1998) 135. Tuckey points out that Socrates quickly moves from "*eu prattein*" to "*eudaimonia*," a move he thinks is a sophism. It may be, but it is meant to show the weakness in Critias's understanding of the connection between knowledge and the good.

65. 172a. The reference to sight once again recalls the discussion of the possibility of *sôphrosunê*. Socrates earlier made repeated reference to Critias's sight, after they discussed the strangeness of a "seeing of seeing" and other self-related faculties. At first glance, it would thus seem that Critias has made some progress here with Socrates, for he now sees what he could not see before. But as the dialogue proceeds, it shows that this "insight" is not as real as it appears. And on further reflection on the present passage, we can see that Critias's seeing of the impossibility of this image does not amount to much. For the image constructed here is built on a complete recognition of ignorance. It is this that Critias has failed time and again to achieve or admit. And we have already seen glimpses of

Critias's alternative picture of *sôphrosunê* as a hierarchical, comprehensive, ruling science, which seems to preclude the very notion of knowledge of ignorance that the rulers seem to have in this city.

66. 172b–c.

67. The reappearance of "*kalos*" recalls its role in earlier arguments, where it wasn't clear how to relate it to the good and self-knowledge. Socrates seems to suggest that it has some role: a more beautiful examination is connected to true *sôphrosunê*, defined as Socratic self-knowledge. But the nature of this connection is not specified, and we must return to it.

68. 172c.

69. 172c.

70. 172d.

71. 172e.

72. 172e–173a.

73. 173a.

74. Consider Glaucon's reaction to Socrates's description of the cave's prisoners in the *Republic* (515a). There too "*atopos*" seems to imply that we do not know how to locate the image, or if it is true, then we do not know how to relocate us. We have to reunderstand our place. The remainder of the dialogue can be seen as an attempt to accomplish this.

75. 173a.

Chapter Seven

1. 171d–e. The slight modifications Socrates makes to it, which I discuss below, expose more clearly the incoherence of the Critian view of *sôphrosunê*.

2. 173a–d.

3. See Levine (2016) 282; Moore & Raymond (2019) 101. At the very least, a dream needs to be interpreted in order to ascertain its meaning. It is therefore fundamentally ambiguous.

4. Odyssey 19: 562–567. For commentary on the significance of the Odyssey passage, see Lampert (2010) 216–218; Tuozzo (2011) 266–267; Burger (2013); Moore & Raymond (2019) 100n81.

5. Hyland (1981) 132.

6. I should emphasize that we are discussing an imagined dream, rather an experienced dream, in talking about the best-ruled city.

7. Republic 476c.

8. The following is indebted to Schmid (1998) 135–136.

9. At 169b Socrates did claim that he had a hunch (*manteomai*) that *sôphrosunê* is beneficial and good, foreshadowing the appearance of *mantikê* here. I will show that the prophetic knowledge in the dream is no better than a hunch

about the most important things. We must thus wonder whether Socrates's own "hunch" is subject to the criticism he levels at the prophetic "knowledge" in his dream. If so, we must investigate what is required to transform this "hunch" into a knowledge that will not be subject to this criticism.

10. 173d.

11. See Tuckey (1951)76. Cf. Santas (1973) 130; Schmid (1998) 137.

12. 173d. At the beginning of the conversation (154d), Socrates said that Charmides would be irresistible (*amachon*) if he had "one small thing in addition" to his beautiful body. This small thing turns out to be *sôphrosunê*. Small things are often big things, according to Socrates. Cf. Tuozzo (2011) 273; Levine (2016) 283.

13. 173e.

14. 173e.

15. Schmid (1998)137.

16. 173e–174a.

17. See 163c, 173e. Cf. Tuozzo (2011) 269.

18. 174a.

19. Levine (2016) 284.

20. 174a.

21. 173d.

22. *Laches* 195e–196a; my emphasis.

Chapter Eight

1. 174a.

2. 174b.

3. Recall that Socrates himself is "pretending" to be a doctor able to treat Charmides.

4. See Schmid (1998) 137. Not only is the idea of health more closely connected to the good than the previous knowledges Socrates has mentioned, especially since it is the kind of practical benefit that Critias has shown himself to admire, but it also recalls the discussion of health in the prologue, where Socrates explained the Zalmoxian understanding of medicine. In one sense, Socrates might say that happiness comes from the true health of the soul, but it is still not clear that Critias catches this much.

5. Levine suggests that this is final confirmation that Critias's ideas are not original to him but rather are distorted perversions of teachings that he has imbibed from Socrates. See Levine (2016) 288–289. I do not see a better explanation for the very odd use of the first-person verb here.

6. 174b.

7. 174b, 161b. We should react to the use of this word with surprise, if not shock, at its harshness. Cf. Levine (2016) 285. Tuozzo downplays the use of

the word, translating it as "dirty dog" and claiming that it is a "jocular vocative." See Tuozzo (2011) 277–278. But Tuozzo does not acknowledge the severity of Socrates's criticism of Critias here. My own reaction to its appearance is more similar to that of Levine.

8. 174b–c.

9. 174c. As Tuozzo (2011, 279) puts it, "No science can produce any benefit in the absence of knowledge of good and bad."

10. The Critian circle shown here demonstrates again the "yawn reflexivity" that Critias displays. His own self-relatedness yields no self-understanding or knowledge of the good.

11. I will return to this suggestion below.

12. Several commentators claim that this was the very problem that lead Critias to the conclusion that his *epistêmê epistêmês* could yield only "knowledge that," not "knowledge what," for it was narrowly confined to itself. See Tuckey (1951) 84–86; Schirlitz (1897) 519; Martens (1973) 82; Hazebroucq (1997) 319n2; von Kutschera in Heitsch and von Kutschera (2000) 46. But as Tuozzo (2011, 282) points out, Socrates has already granted at this point in the conversation that the prophetic knowledge is a candidate for the "knowledge what" of *sôphrosunê*. He argues persuasively that the claim here refers back to 167b, in which Socrates reintroduced the "exclusionary proviso," which shows that "knowledge of knowledge" is only of itself and so is divorced from a knowledge of objects.

13. 174c–d.

14. See Levine (2016) 289.

15. Cf. Tuozzo (2011) 280–281.

16. 174d.

17. Notice that "ignorance" is once again dropped in Critias's formulation

18. 174d–e. Notice also that "evil" has dropped from Critias's formulation. Again Critias's conception of the "ruling" knowledge reveals his self-interested view of the good, as opposed to the Socratic alternative—knowledge of ignorance.

19. Schmid rightly suggests that at the end of this argument Critias should be taken back to his earlier "insight" about self-knowledge without a product, a doctrine Critias clearly did not believe but offered just to escape Socrates's objections. See Schmid (1998) 141.

20. 174e. Again the exclusionary proviso appears. See Tuozzo (2011) 284.

21. Notice that Critias does not object to the reintroduction of a "craft (*technê*)" of good and evil, even though he and Socrates earlier saw tremendous difficulties in using *technai* as analogies for self-knowledge and *sôphrosunê* (165e–166a). Critias just shows himself to be at best confused, and at worst, unwilling to learn from Socrates. Cf. Schmid (1998) 140.

22. See Tuckey (1951) 81; Hyland (1981) 136; McKim (1985) 59.

23. Cf. Tuozzo (2011) 280 and 285–286; Levine (2016) 289–293; Until one takes up this task, as Levine points out, all knowledge is profoundly and dan-

gerously "ambiguous." Knowledges themselves do not dictate whether they are beneficial or harmful, and so without the boundary of knowledge of the good we can easily become tyrannical by assuming our own partial perspective applies, without restriction, to all.

24. Hyland (1981, 133–136) suggests here that if *sôphrosunê* does not bring happiness, then either virtue is not knowledge, or the virtuous are not necessarily happy, or *sôphrosunê* is not really a virtue, which are all conclusions that greatly trouble Socrates. Hyland proposes that we may avoid these conclusions by abandoning the notion of *epistêmê* itself, and embrace a different kind of knowledge of our finitude. Setting aside the question about the value of *"epistêmê,"* I think this statement is correct if Hyland means that the Critian conception of a knowledge that transcends our epistemic limits is impossible and not beneficial, while the Socratic alternative of knowledge of our limits is the opposite. But Hyland seems to lump the Critian view in with Socrates, and in spelling out the alternative the picture becomes more confused, for Hyland relies on the Critian knowledge of all things past, present, and future to explain the Socratic version. He suggests that Critias's seer has knowledge of the "structure of time," meaning a knowledge that we are temporal beings, mortal, and erotically yearning for what is beyond our incomplete selves. This knowledge of the "structure of time," he suggests, and knowledge of good and evil are inseparable. Instead of seeing Socrates as exploding Critias's hubristic doctrine from within, Hyland goes astray by reinterpreting it to make it look Socratic, which it cannot in fact be. In similar fashion, it should now be clear why the suggestion that knowledge of good and evil that Critias makes here cannot be readily identified with a Socratic insight that has been the goal of the discussion. What seems to have been shown so far is that the Critian conception of self-knowledge is quite problematically connected with the good, if at all, and the resulting picture of *sôphrosunê* teeters at the edge of incoherence.

25. I will turn to this task in part 3B.

26. Tuckey unsatisfactorily answers that the Charmides is an undogmatic Socratic dialogue and that this task is left to the reader. See Tuckey (1951) 81, 88. McKim's answer is that Plato is presenting the failure of Socratic self-knowledge, since the elenchus cannot attain the knowledge that is virtue. See McKim (1985) 60.

27. See 165b–c, 166c–d, 175c–176b. Cf. Kraut (1984) 254.

28. See Kraut (1984) 255–256, 258.

29. Carone responds to this problem by suggesting that "mere acquaintance" and knowledge of knowledge are enough to survive the challenges Socrates makes to Critias. I have by now shown that this cannot be the case, but even if she is right, Carone collapses the Critian and the Socratic views here. She may be right to claim that the *Charmides* shows that we are not moral experts and that we must "introspect" to seek virtue, a task continued by the *Republic*. But not all introspections are equal, and Socrates's discussion with Charmides and Critias shows that introspection by itself is not enough. Carone seems to think

the problem is one of correct definition, but in fact it runs much deeper in the soul. See Carone (1998) 280–283.

30. See Levine (2016) 291–292. It is Critias who refuses "to be ruled" by *sôphrosunê*, perhaps indeed because his desires are in the way, and Socrates moves beyond the rational—to the realm of dreams—in order to illustrate this to Critias, Charmides, and others listening. The dialogue between Critias and Socrates suggests that Critias's view of knowledge, built on the narrow *technê*-based model of specialized expertise, is fraught with difficulty when applied to the conceptions of self-knowledge and knowledge of the good. This is why, ultimately, one cannot claim that the "knowledge of good and evil" presented at the end of the dialogue is a proper definition of *sôphrosunê*. For it misses the point that Critias missed as well, that self-knowledge has a different structure than craft-knowledge, and this craft-knowledge can in no way be a "component" of this self-knowledge. The failure to nail down *sôphrosunê* in the *Charmides* stems from flawed conceptions of human self-knowledge and the human good, and Critias's inability to put forward a connection between them. Knowledge of ignorance, especially if this is understood on a model unlike the *technê* model Critias has embraced, has not been touched by the very specific arguments Socrates has made to Critias. The argument does not reject Socratic wisdom, but it forces us to question it: how does the Socratic knowledge of ignorance relate to knowledge of the good and self-knowledge?

Part 2B

Chapter One

1. See J. Lear (1998, 219–239) for a compelling account of Plato's project in presenting both a psychological and political account of constitutional decay. Lear argues that Plato's treatment analyzes the political regime as an externalization of the psyche, while the psychic regime is an internalization of the political culture, and that the best regime is the only one that harmonizes political externalization with psychic internalization. All other regimes are pathological. The question then arises about the pathology, of both psyche and polis, that eventually gives rise to tyranny. In what follows, I will argue that the pathology is rooted in an unrestrained and uneducated *thumos*.

2. 563e. Cf. Bloom (1968) 418. Craig argues that the story of the decay bespeaks a "natural disposition" in the regimes to be torn asunder. See Craig (1994) 28. He also argues (273) that all regimes pursue a particular pleasure, and the story is therefore about a decay of appetite. I will argue that the role of *thumos* should be given more weight here. All parts of the soul, this story reveals, turn out to be *thumotic*. See McNeill (2010) 261.

3. See Craig (1994) 327.

4. 546a–d. This is often called the "nuptial number."

5. 547b.

6. 550a.

7. 550b.

8. "Spirited affection for, and desire to protect, friends and *oikeioi* remain salient features of human psychology and behavior even in unjust cities . . . it is just that they are directed toward those private subsets of the city—family members, friends, or political confederates—that each person considers allies in his own pursuit of pleonectic good." Wilburn (2021) 83.

9. 551b.

10. 550e.

11. 551a.

12. 550d.

13. 552a.

14. 552a–c.

15. 552e.

16. 552e.

17. 553c.

18. 553d.

19. 554c–e. Cf. J. Lear (1998) 235.

20. 555a.

21. 555b–d.

22. 556d.

23. 556d.

24. 557a–b.

25. 557c. Cf. 558c.

26. 557e–558a.

27. 558b–c.

28. J. Lear (1998, 237) argues that "for Plato, this is not a serious psychological possibility: humans need a socially grounded culture to internalize." It could be that the democratic regime here described is a type for which there are no perfect specimens.

29. 558d.

30. 558d–559a.

31. 559b. This is reasonable as far as it goes, and Adeimantus goes along with Socrates. In another context, Socrates might force his interlocutor (as he does with Charmides and Critias) to further examine the nature of good health and what makes it good. Perhaps Socrates does not do so here because the conversation with Adeimantus takes place after the middle books of the *Republic* that serve as this missing discussion.

32. 559b.

33. 559c. Griffith's translation suggests that the necessary desires "contribute to some function."

34. 559d–e.

35. 560a–c.

36. See part 1A, chapter 1.

37. 560c–d; my emphasis.

38. 561c.

39. 561e.

40. 561d. He is the first individual, after the transformation from the best regime, who is said to spend time doing philosophy. It may thus appear that Socrates may have reason to call this the best regime to live in.

41. 562a. Cf. 563e.

42. 562c–e.

43. Hobbs (2000) 3. The *thumotic* Thrasymachus levels this insult at Socrates at 341c.

44. 562e–563d.

45. 563d–e.

46. Adeimantus himself says that Socrates is telling him his "own dream" at 563d. Adeimantus's tone and attitude seems to convey that it is more of a nightmare.

47. Griffith, whom I follow, offers the translation of "sensitive" for *hapalos*.

48. 563e.

49. 563e.

50. 564a.

51. 564b–c. Recall Socrates's description to Charmides of his own role as a doctor of the soul.

52. 564d–e.

53. 565a.

54. 565c.

55. 565c.

56. 565d–e.

57. 565e–566a.

58. The act of cannibalism displays a vicious exertion of power and expression of dominance over one's own kin. It is *thumos* at its frightening extreme. For a disturbing account of this in chimpanzees, see De Waal (2019) 186–187.

59. I will return to this in the next chapter.

60. 565b.

61. 566e–567b.

62. 567d–e.

63. 568e–569a.

64. 569b–c.

65. Cf. Aristotle, *Politics* 1253a29.

Chapter Two

1. This distinction was made at 558d–559d.

2. 571b.

3. Socrates does not actually give a name to the "lawful" class of desires, and indicates their existence only negatively. They are presumably the class of unnecessary desires that are notparanomic.

4. 571c.

5. 572b.

6. 571c.

7. 571c–d.

8. 571d.

9. 571d–e.

10. Bloom 1968.

11. Griffith 2000.

12. Sachs 2007.

13. 571e–572a.

14. 572a.

15. I will substantiate this claim when I return in part 3 to a fuller discussion of the role *thumos* plays in philosophical inquiry.

16. 572a.

17. It is a common view that the paranomic desires are confined to the appetitive part of the soul, but this passage clearly indicates that *thumos* can become paranomic as well. See Arruzza (2018) 214. And as the account develops, it is *thumos* that drives the soul into the most extreme form of "paranomia."

18. See part 1A, chapter 4.

19. 572a. Again, reason is not merely instrumental but grasping the good of the whole.

20. Cf. J. Lear (1998) 235; Arruzza (2018) 171–172, 214–216. While the democratic man gives free reign to his unnecessary appetites, the implication now seems to be that the lawless ones are kept at bay in the realm of dreams. The tyrant releases what the democrat kept concealed.

21. 572e.

22. 573a–b.

23. In book 1, Cephalus calls *erôs* a mad master from which he is happy to have escaped. Cephalus, however, has only escaped from *erôs* to be tyrannized by his fear of death. See Pichanick (2018).

24. 573c.

25. 545a.

26. Arruzza argues that in spite of this oddity, *thumos* still plays an important role as causally ancillary. See Arruzza (2018) 185–186, 215–216. I would suggest that it plays even a stronger role.

27. 573b.

28. 573d.

29. Ludwig (2007) 203. Weiss (2012, 15n11) points out that "only the tyrant is referred to as erotic as frequently as the philosopher is (572e, 573e, 574d–a, 578a, 579b, 587b)." Craig (1994, 49) suggests that the harsh description of the intractable *erôs* of the tyrant would seem to call for an exorcist.

30. Several Straussian readings respond to this puzzle by emphasizing the tension between love and politics, especially as it comes to light in the discussion of sexual communism. See Ludwig (2007) 204n2. I would argue that the sexual communism Socrates proposes is actually a response to a *thumotic* problem rather than an erotic one—the desire to care for *one's own* child.

31. See Ludwig (2007) 208–209: "What offends justice is not the erotic desire itself but rather the possessiveness that tends to accompany or follow erotic desire." As Ludwig rightly concludes, such possessiveness is *thumotic*. If there is such a thing as *erôs* without such possessiveness or attachment, it is not to be found in books 8–9 of the *Republic*. I will return to such a non-*thumotic erôs* in the discussion of wonder in the *Symposium*. Weiss even argues that there is no intellectual *erôs* in the description of the philosopher of book 7. See Weiss (2012) 69–70.

32. Singpurwalla (2013) 45.

33. Ludwig (2007) 224. Cf. L. Cooper (2008) 79; Nichols in Zuckert (1988) 58–59. McNeill (2010) 197; Arruzza (2018) 164.

34. 562a.

35. 573d.

36. 573e.

37. 574a.

38. 574a–b.

39. 574b–c.

40. 574d–e.

41. 574e.

42. Cf. Ludwig (2007) 229–230; Craig (1994) 108; Arruzza (2018) 172–173; Weinstein (2018) 151.

43. 575a.

44. 576a.

45. 576b.

46. 577c–578b.

47. Cf. Weinstein (2018) 52.

48. L. Cooper (2008) 30.

49. L. Cooper (2008) 112.

50. Nichols (1988) 57.

51. This is shown by a later passage at 586a–b comparing people without the restraint of virtue and reason to cattle: "After the fashion of cattle, always

looking down and with their heads bent to earth and table, they feed, fattening themselves, and copulating; and, for the sake of getting more of these things, they kick and butt with horns and hoofs of iron, killing each other because they are insatiable; for they are not filling the part of themselves that *is*, or can contain anything, with things that *are.*" Cf. Bloom (1968) 423; Arruzza (2018) 174. My own reading differs from Arruzza's, in that she is inclined to see the tyrant's desires as rooted in a sexual *erôs* (178). I do not think sexual *erôs* explains the most salient features of tyrannical desire—neither its paranomic nature nor its excessive attachment to its own things. I would suggest that it is a *thumotic erôs* instead.

52. See Arruzza (2021, 140) for a summary of the literature espousing this view.

53. Singpurwalla (2013) 64; Arruzza (2018) 197–200

54. 588d–e.

55. Arruzza (2018) 198.

56. Arruzza (2018) 198.

57. Arruzza (2018) 217.

58. "The dog is a good animal example of the way spirit can come to consider somebody else as a part of one's own identity, as a watchdog is ready to fight and even to die for those it knows and considers its own." Arruzza (2018) 206.

59. 565d–566a. In book 9, Socrates also compares *thumos* to a lion and a snake (588d & 590b). Both images highlight what we have called the bidirectionality of *thumos*. See Arruzza (2018) 203: "the serpent is a dangerous and aggressive animal, but it can be charmed. . . . The lion embodies a combination of savagery and kingliness, violence and courage."

60. Arruzza (2018) 213.

61. Arruzza (2018) 207: "Plato's own interpretation of the myth of the werewolf aims at emphasizing two main features related to the condition and operation of the tyrant's spirit: ferocity and unrestrained thirst for power."

Chapter Three

1. 588c–589d. See Singpurwalla (2013) 54.

2. Bloom (1968) 424–425.

3. Arruzza (2018) 231.

4. See part 2A above. See Xenophon's characterization of Critias's tyrannical policy in *Hellenica* 2.3.15.

5. Ludwig (2007) 230.

6. See part 2A, chapter 2, above.

7. See part 2A, chapters 3–6, above.

Part 3A

Chapter One

1. 175a–b.

2. Cf. 175e–176a, especially Socrates's repeated use of the first person.

3. See Hyland (1981) 145; McKim (1985) 74–75. Consider also Beversluis (2000, 158–159), who asserts that the examination Socrates has conducted has been worthless all along.

4. See Moore & Raymond (2019) 105–106; Tuozzo (2011) 288; Levine (2016) 295.

5. The picture is even more complicated than this if we remind ourselves that the discussion between Socrates and Critias and Charmides is one that is being narrated by Socrates to an unnamed listener. Again, the reflexivity of the dialogue shows what seems problematic in speech.

6. Cf. Bruell (1977) 200.

7. Schmid (1998) 148.

8. Levine (2106, 294) points out that Socrates has cleverly hidden his blame of Critias in order not to provoke his anger, which emerged upon seeing Charmides mangle his teaching. Socrates is thus still holding out hope for Charmides here.

9. 175a.

10. Levine (2016) 302.

11. Recall that Socrates gave the role of "lawgiver" to Critias at 165d.

12. Moore & Raymond (2019) 105–106; Levine (2016) 295.

13. 175b.

14. This knowledge of inquiry is connected to the "smaller" benefit of *sôphrosunê*.

15. 175b–d.

16. 169d.

17. 173a–d. Tuozzo points out that the first concession is overstated and the second is recharacterized here. See Tuozzo (2011) 291.

18. 175c.

19. It might not be surprising, then, that Hyland uses this passage as evidence that *epistêmê* need be rejected as a model for self-knowledge. See Hyland (1981) 145. Again, I think this conclusion is too quick. Morris, following the work of John Lyons, suggests that this surprising statement can best be understood by distinguishing "understanding from acquaintance." This is grounded in the wide usage of the verb *oide*, which can mean either *epistatai* or *aianôskei*. See Morris (1989) 54. Cf. Santas (1963) 124–125. This also explains the earlier move at 165c from *gnôsis* to *epistêmê* in a straightforward way. Just as recognizing the nature of food requires the *epistêmê* of nutrition, so the understanding of the self requires the *epistêmê* that takes it as its object. On this model, Socrates could be reported to say that one cannot know what one does not know "at all," but this does not

prevent someone from saying they do not know what they are merely acquainted with (and thus know to a lesser degree). The safest response may be made by Tuozzo, who points out the significance of knowing "in some way" in order to avoid a direct contradiction here. See Tuozzo (2011) 293. Tuozzo's point here has the advantage (apart, hopefully, from being correct) of not requiring us to have a theory about the relation between *gnôsis* and *epistêmê* in the *Charmides*.

20. 175c–d.

21. Though Socrates could very well be concerned himself here. See Tuozzo (2011) 295.

22. 175d–e.

23. 175e.

24. 176a.

25. 176b.

26. Cf. Bruell (1977) 202; Carone (1998) 282; Tuozzo (2011) 296–298. On the other side of the spectrum, Beversluis (2000, 158) won't even admit that this could be a victory. To the contrary, he claims that "instead of emerging with his soul improved, he [Charmides] is reduced to incoherent stammering," while Critias looks on like a "helpless parent." As I will explain below, I believe this is a significant misreading of the ending of the dialogue.

27. As Schmid (1998, 147) says, "Each part of the final scene is marked by immoderation."

28. Cf. Levine (2016) 303.

29. Schmid (1998, 150) suggests that Charmides shows very little modesty in this proposal to Socrates, demanding that he give him the charm he desires. However, he also sees his own role as "passive"—being cured by Socrates—which Schmid rightly says "implies the boy has not understood the manner in which one is to submit to Socrates's charms."

30. 176b.

31. Cf. Levine (2016) 304.

32. 21b.

33. 176b–c.

34. Schmid (1998) 151. "Heterarchy" could be translated as "ruled by another."

35. Cf. Levine (2016) 304.

36. 176c.

37. 176c. Tuozzo (2011, 299–300) reads this as playful banter. I believe this is a misreading of the ending.

38. As Levine points out, the only use of the dual in the dialogue appears here. See Levine (2016) 304–305.

39. Cf. Moore & Raymond (2019, 107), especially the discussion of the treatment of Leon of Salamis. See also Tuozzo's discussion of the Thirty's actions in taking away citizenship from those members they saw as potential threats in order to put them to death without a trial. Tuozzo's explanation for this connection to the ending of the dialogue is unsatisfying. See Tuozzo (2011) 301–303.

40. Levine (2016) 305. Cf. Bruell (1977) 202.

41. 176d.

42. See Levine (2016) 306.

43. Cf. Tuozzo (2011) 288.

Chapter Two

1. 172b–c.

2. See Tuckey (1951) 65–71. Tuckey is right to say that Socrates has here presented "a new conception of the benefit of *sôphrosunê*," but this is because for the very first time in the argument of the dialogue, we are getting a speech about what Socratic *sôphrosunê* looks like when it is seen its proper light and not perverted by Critias. Tuckey describes this image as "the ability to think clearly and consistently" and says is the "knowledge of how to acquire knowledge." Also See Santas (1973) 122; McKim (1985) 63; Morris (1989) 49, 50–51, 57–58; Moore (2015) 98–100; Tuozzo (2011) 259–263; Levine (2016) 277–280; Woolf (2023) 206.

3. See Moore (2015) 98

4. Thus, the etymological root of *sôphrosunê*: (*sos* + *phrên*).

5. See Schmid (1998, 120): "Nor would ['knowledge that'] be at all relevant to knowing 'more clearly' what he learns, unless he realizes more clearly what he is coming to know, not merely that he know something. Socrates's conclusion makes no sense, if we regard him as referring to the same conception of the knowledge of knowledge throughout the argument at 169c–172d." But if one sees Socrates as rejecting Critias's model of knowledge in this passage, then this move makes sense. Tuckey (1951, 72) is thus right to suggest that Plato is here envisioning a new "science of dialectic" that will thus not be built on a technical view of "knowledge of knowledge," and thus not prey to the "knowledge that" problem. But this may take us beyond his mere "ability to think clearly," as Schmid suggests: "to the Socratic practice of dialectical questioning, which treats beliefs as opinions to be tested for justification." And if Socrates's preceding arguments about the limits of *technai* are correct, then this dialectical questioning will not fit that model.

6. See 168b–d.

7. Cf. Schmid (1998) 123.

Part 3B

Chapter One

1. Nightingale (2004) 4.

2. Nightingale (2004) 35. Cf. 69: "In sum, the defining feature of *theoria* in its traditional forms is a journey to a region outside the boundaries of one's

own city for the purpose of witnessing some sort of spectacle or learning about the world. *Theoria* involves 'autopsy' or seeing something for oneself: the *theoros* is an eyewitness whose experience differs radically from those who stay home and receive a mere report of the news. On the journey as well as at its destination, the *theoros* encounters something foreign and different. This encounter with the unfamiliar invites the traveler to look at his own city with different eyes."

3. *Charmides* 153a–b.

4. *Republic* 327a.

5. *Symposium* 172a–b.

6. See part 1A, chapter 1, above.

7. Nightingale (2004) 75.

8. The friend who asked him the previous day was a gentleman named Glaucon, who is probably not the same Glaucon in the *Republic*. But a reminder even in name only is nonetheless another connection between these dialogues.

9. See below.

10. Socrates will turn out to be both similar to the *theoros* but also *atopos* himself. I will suggest that this is due to his essentially *in-between* nature. As such, his journey as *theoros* is never complete, and he is at home only in shuttling back and forth. See part 3B, chapter 7.

11. Blondell (2007) 149–150.

12. 176c–d.

13. 175d–e.

14. 175e.

15. Duque (2019) 101.

16. Duque (2019) 101.

17. Thucydides, *The War of the Peloponnesians and the Athenians* 6.24.3: "And a desire to sail fell upon them (*erôs enepese*) all alike: onto the older men who believed that they would conquer those they were sailing against or at least that such a great force could not fail; on the young who longed for the sight and the contemplation of the absent (*tes te apousês pothôi opseôs kai theôrias*) and were confident that they would be safe." Nicias himself is worried about this *erôs*, and calls it sick: "I am fearful seeing those young men sitting here at the bidding of this same man and I urge the older men not to feel ashamed, if they are sitting next to one of them, that they will seem soft if they vote against war, nor to suffer what these men suffer and fall morbidly in love (*duserôs*) with what is absent."

18. We should recall the story in the *Republic* of Leontius's desire to look upon the corpses in the *Republic*, discussed above in part 1B, chapter 1.

19. See part 1A, chapter 2, above.

20. *Symposium* 215e–216b.

21. Admittedly, the spectacle of Socratic conversation the reader receives is limited in that Socrates gives a speech and embeds a conversation with an imagined interlocutor within that speech. But this strengthens the point that the

spectacle in the text can't, nor is it meant to, replace the living conversation it provokes for the readers.

22. Nightingale (2004) 8: "In Plato's conception of *theoria* . . . *erôs* and the affect of wonder play a key role in the activity of contemplation . . . *theoria* is fueled and sustained by erotic desire."

23. Nightingale (2004) 12.

24. Nightingale (2004) 83: "The activity of philosophic *theoria* serves, first and foremost, to transform the individual soul, conferring upon it a state of wisdom, happiness, and blessedness."

25. Nightingale (2004) 36.

Chapter Two

1. See especially 205e, when Socrates through Diotima comments that "a lover does not seek the half or the whole, unless . . . it turns out to be good as well."

2. 199d–e.

3. Kosman (2013) 244.

4. See part 2A, chapter 3.

5. 200a–b.

6. 200d–e.

7. 201a–b.

8. 201c.

9. 201d.

10. J. Cooper (2008, 128) points to the "near-implausibility" of her name and town, which means something like "honored by Zeus from the science of divining" and suggests that Socrates is hinting that she is a fictional device.

11. Cf. *Republic* 505d–e, where the Good is said to be "divined" (*apomanteuesthai*).

12. 201e.

13. I would suggest that it is no coincidence that the *Parmenides* and the *Symposium* are paired in this way. Diotima's account of the nature of *erôs* as in-between can be seen as a response to at least some of the problems regarding the existence of the Ideas that Socrates discusses with Parmenides. Cf. Benardete (2001) 192.

14. Cf. *Republic* 490b. I shall expand upon this below, in chapter 6.

15. Halperin (1990) 117.

16. Halperin (1990) 124.

17. 201d.

18. See above part 1A, chapter 1.

19. L. Cooper (2008) 128.

20. L. Cooper (2008) 129.

Chapter Three

1. 201e.
2. 202a.
3. 202b.
4. 202b.
5. 202c.
6. 202d.
7. 202e. Cf. *Phaedrus* 242b; *Theages* 128d; *Apology* 40a.
8. 202e–203a.
9. Strauss (2001) 190.
10. Strauss (2001, 190), following Krüger, points out that the same role is played by Christ in Christianity.

Chapter Four

1. 203a.
2. 203b–c.
3. 203c–204e.
4. *Charmides* 161a.
5. McNeill (2010) 203: "Clearly this barefoot, daimonic philosopher is meant, at some level, to call to mind Socrates himself; it seems to be an idealized portrait of Socratic philosophy."
6. See part 1A, chapter 1.
7. *Symposium* 177d–e.
8. McNeill (2010) 204.
9. 204a–b.
10. McNeill (2010) 203.
11. Nightingale (2004) 95.
12. Nightingale (2004) 99.
13. Benardete (2001) 193.
14. Nightingale (2004) 100.
15. Chrysakapolou (2013) 101–102.

Chapter Five

1. 204c.
2. The following exchange is 204d–e.
3. Bloom in Benardete (2001) 134.
4. Further evidence that she is Socrates's fictional device.

5. Strauss (2001) 203.

6. See the interesting debate between Kosman (2010) and G. Lear (2010). Cf. G. Lear (2007) 104–105. Strauss (2001, 28) suggests, "The good is not identical with the beautiful, and that is the great theme of the *Symposium*."

7. Barney (2010) 369. Compare Bloom (2001) 134: "We might express the issue here as the conflict between the aesthetic life and the utilitarian one."

8. Barney (2010) 373. Cf. G. Lear 2007 (113–114).

9. See above, parts 1B and 2B.

10. Cf. L. Cooper (2008) 80–81.

11. 205a.

12. 206a.

13. We could say that Diotima, rather than disagreeing with Aristophanes, brings out a latent but implied point in his speech about love, as seen in the offer made by Hephaestus. This offer brought to our attention the tragic element of Aristophanes's *thumotic erôs*.

14. 206e.

15. 207d–208b.

16. G. Lear (2007) 107.

17. Bloom in Benardete (2001) 139.

18. 207d–209e.

19. 209e–210a.

20. See Bloom in Benardete (2001) 138–145; L. Cooper (2008) 60–62.

21. Bloom in Benardete (2001) 147.

Chapter Six

1. 210a.

2. 210a.

3. 210a–b.

4. Although often referred to as a "ladder," Diotima does not use this word. She does, however, refer to ascending steps (*epanabasmos*) at 211c.

5. The *dei* of 210a continues to be operative for the sentence construction through the rest of 210b.

6. 210b.

7. 210b.

8. 210b.

9. 210c.

10. 210c.

11. Cf. Strauss (2001) 232.

12. Cf. Benardete (2001) 196.

13. 210c. Just as the *Charmides* revealed to us, the plural here poses a difficulty for translators. I would suggest here too that "sciences," although not ideal, is preferable to "branches of knowledge" or "kinds of knowledge."

14. 210c–d.

15. Socrates will later emphasize this in his comments about Diotima's account.

16. G. Lear (2007) 97.

17. G. Lear (2007) 116.

18. G. Lear (2007) 117–118.

19. 211d.

20. 211e–212b.

21. See part 2B above.

22. Notice the use of both "*theomenos*" and "*thaumaston*" at 210e.

Chapter Seven

1. See part 2B above.

2. 212b.

3. Cf. 204e. Recall that Socrates was stumped when Diotima asked him what he would obtain by getting the beautiful. Only when Socrates is prompted to think about the good does he say that humans possessing it will be happy.

4. 212b.

5. 210d.

6. Cf. L. Cooper (2008) 41.

7. "Eros cannot ascend to higher objects, to greater and more comprehensive satisfaction, without the help of *thymos*, if only because ascending these peaks requires a prior foundation in thymotically informed discipline or demotic virtue. *Thymos* is born of and for the sake of eros." L. Cooper (2008) 43–44.

8. Cf. Rosen (2005) 229.

9. *Symposium* 175a, 220c–d.

10. See Blondell (2007) note 38 for references.

11. Blondell (2007) 159. As Blondell goes on to suggest (161), the identity of Eros and Socrates is by no means complete or unambiguous.

12. Blondell (2007) 161–174.

13. Blondell (2007) 176; Lowenstam (1985) 94–98.

14. Blondell (2007) 177.

15. Bloom in Benardete (2001) 153.

16. Some readers are dissatisfied with Diotima's account of *erôs* as negative—she tells us what it is not, rather than what it is. Perhaps such a move is appropriate if wonder, rather than wisdom, is the culmination of the ascent.

17. "Men are constantly attracted and deluded by two opposite charms: the charm of competence, which is engendered by mathematics and everything akin to mathematics, and the charm of humble awe, which is engendered by meditation of the human soul and its experiences. Philosophy is characterized by the gentle, if firm, refusal to succumb to either charm. It is the highest form of the mating of courage and moderation." Strauss (1959) 40.

18. 212c.

19. It is related that while Aristophanes's speech appears to be both comic and tragic, Agathon's is neither. At the end of the party, Socrates is talking to each of them about the true poet's ability to write both. See 223d.

20. Cf. Strauss (1959) 39.

21. 215e–216c.

22. Cf. Sanday (2019) 186.

23. Sanday (2019) 199–201.

24. Sanday (2019) 201.

25. 218d–219b. See McCabe (2015) 223, who argues that the self-knowledge of the prisoner in the cave, in contrast to the one who practices philosophical dialectic, is a contrast between a monoperspectival failure that is corrected by a more "stereoscopic" view. In my language, the former is *thumotic*, while the latter wonders at what is beyond.

Bibliography

Allen, Danielle. 2000. "Envisaging the Body of the Condemned: The Power of Platonic Symbols." *Classical Philology* 95 (2): 133–150.

Altman, W. H. F. 2010. "The Reading Order of Plato's Dialogues." *Phoenix* 64 (1): 18–51.

Ambury, James M., and Andy German, eds. 2019. *Knowledge and Ignorance of Self in Platonic Philosophy.* Cambridge: Cambridge University Press.

Annas, Julia. 1985. "Self-Knowledge in Early Plato." In Dominic J. O'Meara, *Platonic Investigations*, 111–138. Catholic University of America Press.

Aristotle. 1926. *Nicomachean Ethics.* Translated by H. Rackham. Cambridge: Harvard University Press.

———. 1932. *Politics.* Translated by H. Rackham. Cambridge: Harvard University Press.

———. 1975. *On the Soul.* Translated by W. S. Hett. Cambridge: Harvard University Press.

Arruzza, Cinzia. 2018. *A Wolf in the City: Tyranny and the Tyrant in Plato's Republic.* Oxford: Oxford University Press.

Austin, Scott. 1987. "The Paradox of Socratic Ignorance (How to Know That You Don't Know)." *Philosophical Topics* 15:23–34.

Barney, Rachel. 2010. "Notes on Plato on the *Kalon* and the Good." *Classical Philology* 105/4:363–377.

Barney, Rachel, Tad Brennan, and Charles Brittain, eds. 2012. *Plato and the Divided Self.* Cambridge: Cambridge University Press.

Ben, N. van der. 1985. *The Charmides of Plato.* Amsterdam: B. R. Gruner.

Benardete, Seth. 1986. "On Interpreting Plato's Charmides." *Graduate Faculty Philosophy Journal* 11:9–36.

———. 2001. *Plato's "Symposium."* Chicago: University of Chicago Press.

Benson, Hugh. 2003. "A Note on Socratic Self-Knowledge in the *Charmides.*" *Ancient Philosophy* 23 (1): 31–47.

Beversluis, John. 2000. *Cross-Examining Socrates: A Defense of the Interlocutors in Plato's Early Dialogues.* Cambridge: Cambridge University Press.

Bieda, Esteban. 2012. "Is Leontius an Incontinent Man? Spirit and Appetite in Plato's Republic." *Diánoia* [online] 57 (69): 127–150.

Blondell, R. 2002. *The Play of Character in Plato's Dialogues*. Cambridge: Cambridge University Press, 2002.

———. 2007. "Where Is Socrates on the 'Ladder of Love' "? In *Plato's "Symposium": Issues in Interpretation and Reception*. Edited by James Lesher, Debra Nails, and Frisbee Sheffield. *Hellenic Studies Series* 22:147–179. Washington, DC.

Bloom, Allan, trans. 1968. *Plato:* The Republic. New York: Basic Books.

———. 2001. "The Ladder of Love." In Benardete 2001:55–178.

Bonitz, H. 1968. "Bemerkungen zu dem Abschnitt des Dialogs *Charmides* 165–172." *Platonische Studien*. Hildesheim: Georg Olms Verlag.

Brennan, Tad. 2012. "The Nature of the Spirited Part of the Soul and its Object." In Barney, Brennan, and Kraut 2012:120–127.

Brickhouse, Thomas C., and Nicholas D. Smith. 1994. *Plato's Socrates*. Oxford: Oxford University Press.

Brouwer and Polansky. 2004. "The Logic of Socratic Inquiry: Illustrated by Plato's Charmides.' " In Karasmanis 2004, 233–245.

Bruell, Christopher. 1977. "Socratic Politics and Self-Knowledge." *Interpretation* 6:141–203.

Burger, Ronna. 1981. "Belief, Knowledge and Socratic Knowledge of Ignorance." *Tulane Studies in Philosophy* 30:1–23.

———. 2013. Socrates' Odyssean Return: On Plato's Charmides. In Denise Schaeffer & Christopher Dustin, *Socratic Philosophy and Its Others*, 217–235. Lanham: Lexington Books.

Carone, Gabriella. 1998. "Socrates's Human Wisdom and *Sôphrosunê* in *Charmides* 164c ff." *Ancient Philosophy* 18:267–286.

Carroll, N. 1990. *The Philosophy of Horror or Paradoxes of the Heart*. New York: Routledge.

Chrysakapolou, Sylvana. 2013. "Wonder and the Beginning of Philosophy in Plato." In *Practices of Wonder*, edited by Sophia Vasalou, 88–120 James Clarke.

Cohen-Taber, Inbal. 2022. *Wisdom and Beauty in Plato's "Charmides."* Portland, ME: Pickwick Press.

Coolidge, F. P. 1993. "The Relation of Philosophy to Swjrosunh: Zalmoxian Medicine in Plato's *Charmides*." *Ancient Philosophy* 13:1–23.

Cooper, John, ed. 1997. *Plato: Complete Works*. Indianapolis. Hackett.

———. 1984. "Plato's Theory of Human Motivation." *History of Philosophy Quarterly* 1 (1): 3–21.

Cooper, Laurence. 2008. *Eros in Plato, Rousseau, and Nietzsche: The Politics of Infinity*. University Park: Pennsylvania State Press.

Craig, Leon. 1994. *The War Lover: A Study of Plato's "Republic."* Toronto: University of Toronto Press.

De Waal, Frans. 2019. *Mama's Last Hug: Animal Emotions and What They Tell Us about Ourselves.* New York: W. W. Norton.

Desjardins, R. 1988. "Why Dialogues? Plato's Serious Play." In *Platonic Writings/ Platonic Readings,* edited by Charles Griswold, 84–92 New York: Routledge, Chapman & Hall.

Douglas, Mary. 1966. *Purity and Danger.* New York: Routledge.

Dover, K. 1978. *Greek Homosexuality.* Cambridge: Harvard University Press.

Duque, Mateo. 2019. "Two Passions in Plato's Symposium: Diotima's to Kalon as a Reorientation of Imperialistic Erōs." In *Looking at Beauty to Kalon in Western Greece: Selected Essays from the 2018 Symposium on the Heritage of Western Greece,* edited by Heather L. Reid and Tony Leyh, 95–110. Sioux City, IA: Parnassos Press—Fonte Aretusa.

Dyson, M. 1974. "Some Problems Concerning Knowledge in Plato's *Charmides.*" *Phronesis* 19:102–111.

Ebert, Thomas. 1974. *Meinung und Wissen in der Philosophie Platons: Untersuchungen zum "Charmides," "Menon," und "Staat."* Berlin: de Gruyter.

Entralgo, P. Lain. 1970. *The Therapy of the Word in Classical Antiquity.* Translated and edited by L. Rather and J. Sharp. New Haven, CT: Yale University Press.

Evans, Joseph C. 1990. "Socratic Ignorance—Socratic Wisdom." *Modern Schoolman* 67:91–110.

Ferrari, G. R. F., ed. 2007. *The Cambridge Companion to Plato's Republic.* New York: Cambridge University Press.

Frankfurt, Harry G. 1971. "Freedom of the Will and the Concept of a Person." *Journal of Philosophy* 68:5–20.

Freud, S. 1961. *Civilization and Its Discontents.* New York: W. W. Norton & Company.

Friedlaender, Paul. 1964. *Plato.* Vols. 1–2. Translated by Hans Meyerhoff. New York: Bollingen Foundation.

Griffith, T. 2000, trans. *Plato: The Republic.* Cambridge: Cambridge University Press.

Griswold, Charles L., Jr., ed. 1988. *Platonic Writings/Platonic Readings.* New York: Routledge, Chapman & Hall.

Grote, George. 1875. *Plato and the Other Companions of Socrates.* Vols. 1–3. 2nd ed. London: J. Murray.

Halper, Edward. 2000. "Is Knowledge of Knowledge Possible? *Charmides* 167a–169d." In *Plato: Euthydemus, Lysis, Charmides: Proceedings of the "Symposium Platonicum" Selected Papers,* edited by Thomas Robinson. Academia: Sankt Augustin.

Halperin, D. 1990. *One Hundred Years of Greek Homosexuality.* New York: Routledge.

Hamilton, E., and H. Cairns, eds. 1961. *Plato: The Collected Dialogues.* Princeton, NJ: Princeton University Press.

Hazebroucq, M-F. 1997. *La Folie humaine et ses remèdes. Platon. Charmide ou de le moderation*. Paris: Vrin.

Heitsch, Ernest & von Kutschera, Franz. 2000. *Zu Platons Charmides*. Wiesbaden: Franz Steiner Verlag.

Hesiod. 1959. *Works and Days*. Translated by Richmond Lattimore. Ann Arbor: University of Michigan Press.

Hobbs, Angela. 2000. *Plato and the Hero*. Cambridge: Cambridge University Press.

Hyland, Drew. 1981. *The Virtue of Philosophy*. Athens: Ohio University Press.

Irwin, Terence. 1977. *Plato's Moral Theory*. Oxford: Clarendon Press.

Joosse, A. 2018. "Sôphrosunê and the Poets." *Mnemosyne* 71:574–592.

Kahn, Charles. 1996. *Plato and the Socratic Dialogue*. Cambridge: Cambridge University Press.

Karasmanis, V., ed. 2004. *Socrates: 2400 Hundred Years since His Death*. European Cultural Center of Delphi.

Klein, Jacob. 1965. *A Commentary on Plato's Meno*. Chapel Hill: University of North Carolina Press.

Kosman, L. A. 1983. "Sôphrosunê as Quietness." In *Essays in Ancient Greek Philosophy*, vol. 2, edited by John P. Anton and Anthony Preus, 203–216. Albany, NY: SUNY Press.

———. 2010. "Beauty and the Good: Situating *The Kalon*." *Classical Philology* 105/4:341–357.

———. 2013. "Self-Knowledge and Self-Control in Plato's 'Charmides.'" In *Virtues of Thought*. Cambridge: Harvard, 227–245

Kraut, Richard. 1984. *Socrates and the State*. Princeton, NJ: Princeton University Press.

Kristeva, J. 1982. *Powers of Horror: An Essay on Abjection*. New York: Columbia University Press.

Lacan, J. 2015. *Transference*. Polity Press.

Lamb, W. R. M. 1927. Rev. 1955. *Plato: Charmides, Alcibiades I and II, Hipparchus, The Lovers, Theages, Minos, Epinomis*. Loeb Classical Library, vol. 12. Cambridge: Harvard University Press.

Lampert, L. 2010. *How Philosophy Became Socratic*. Chicago: University of Chicago Press.

Lear, Gabriele. 2007. "Permanent Beauty and Becoming Happy in Plato's *Symposium*." In Lesher, Nails, and Sheffield 2007, 96–124.

———. 2010. "Response to Kosman" *Classical Philology* 105/4:357–362.

Lear, Jonathan. 1998. "Inside and Outside the *Republic*." In *Open Minded: Working Out the Logic of the Soul*, 219–246. Cambridge: Harvard University Press.

———. 2000. *Happiness, Death, and the Remainder of Life*. Cambridge: Harvard University Press.

———. 2006. "Allegory and Myth in Plato's *Republic*." In *The Blackwell Guide to Plato's* Republic, edited by G. Santas, 25–43. Blackwell.

Lesher, James, Debra Nails, and Frisbee Sheffield, eds. 2007. *Plato's Symposium: Issues in Interpretation and Reception*. Hellenic Studies Series 22. Washington, DC: Center for Hellenic Studies.

Levine, David L. 1984. "The Tyranny of Scholarship." *Ancient Philosophy* 4:65–72.

———. 2016. *Profound Ignorance*. Lanham, MD: Lexington Press.

Liddell, Henry George, and Robert Scott. 1940. *A Greek-English Lexicon*. Revised and augmented throughout by Sir Henry Stuart Jones with the assistance of Roderick McKenzie. Oxford: Clarendon Press.

Lowenstam, S. 1985. "Paradoxes in Plato's *Symposium*." *Ramus* 14:85–104.

Luckhurst, K. 1934. "Note on Plato's *Charmides* 153b." *Classical Review* 48:207–208.

Ludwig, Paul. 2007. "Eros in the *Republic*." In *The Cambridge Companion to Plato's "Republic."* Cambridge: Cambridge University Press.

Mansfield, Harvey. 2006. *Manliness*. New Haven, CT: Yale University Press.

Martens, E. 1973. *Das selbstbezuegliche Wissen in Platons Charmides*. Munich: Carl Hansen Verlag.

McCabe, M. M. 2015. *Platonic Conversations*. Oxford University Press.

McKim, Richard. 1985. "Socratic Self-Knowledge and 'Knowledge of Knowledge' in Plato's *Charmides*." *Transactions of the American Philological Association* 115:59–77.

McNeill, David. 2010. *An Image of the Soul in Speech: Plato and the Problem of Socrates*. University Park: Pennsylvania State University Press.

Miller, M. H. 1999. "Platonic Mimesis." In *Contextualizing Classics: Ideology, Performance, Dialogue: Essays in Honors of John J. Peradotto*, edited by T. M. Falkner, N. Felson, and D. Konstan, 253–266. Lanham: Rowman and Littlefield.

Monoson, S. 2014. "Socrates in Combat: Trauma and Resilience in Plato's Political Theory." In *Combat Trauma and the Ancient Greeks*, edited by Peter Meineck and David Konstan, 131–162. New York: Palgrave McMillan.

Moore, C. 2013. "Chaerephon the Socratic." *Phoenix* 67:284–300.

———. 2015. *Socrates and Self-Knowledge*. Cambridge: Cambridge University Press.

Moore, C., and C. C. Raymond. 2019. *Plato: Charmides*. Indianapolis: Hackett.

Morris, T. F. 1989. "Knowledge of Knowledge and Lack of Knowledge in the *Charmides*." *International Studies in Philosophy* 21:49–61.

Murphy, D. 2000. "Doctors of Zalmoxis and Immortality in the *Charmides*." In *Plato: Euthydemus, Lysis, Charmides: Proceedings of the "Symposium Platonicum" Selected Papers*, edited by T. Robinson and L. Brisson. IPS Series vol. 1. Sankt Augustin: Academia. 287–295.

Nehamas, A., and P. Woodruff, trans. 1989. *Plato's Symposium*. Indianapolis: Hackett.

Nichols, Mary. 1988. "Spiritedness and Philosophy in Plato's *Republic*." In Zuckert 1988, 48–66.

Nightingale, Andrea. 2004. *Spectacles of Truth in Classical Greek Philosophy*. Cambridge: Cambridge University Press.

North, Helen. 1966. *Sôphrosunê: Self-Knowledge and Self-Restraint in Greek Literature*. Ithaca, NY: Cornell University Press.

Notomi, N. 2000. "Critias and the Origin of Plato's Political Philosophy." In *Plato: Euthydemus, Lysis, Charmides: Proceedings of the "Symposium Platonicum" Selected Papers,* edited by T. Robinson and L. Brisson. IPS Series vol. 1. Sankt Augustin: Academia. 237–250.

Obdrzalek, S. 2017. "Aristophanic Tragedy." In *Plato's Symposium: A Critical Guide,* Cambridge Critical Guides, ed. Pierre Destrée and Zina Giannopoulou, 70–87. Cambridge: Cambridge University Press.

Parke, H. W., and D. E. W. Wormell. 1956. *The Delphic Oracle.* Oxford: Oxford University Press.

Parker, Robert. 1983. *Miasma: Pollution and Purification in Early Greek Religion.* Oxford: Oxford University Press.

Pichanick, A. 2018. "Why Might (Or Must?) Philosophy Be for the Young? The Case of Cephalus in Plato's Republic." *Cahiers des études anciennes,* LV | 2018, 145–159.

Plato. 1903. *Opera.* Edited by John Burnet. Oxford: Oxford University Press.

———.1986. *Charmides.* Translated by Thomas G. West and Grace Starry West. Indianapolis: Hackett.

———. 1997. *Collected Dialogues.* Edited by John Cooper. Indianapolis: Hackett.

Raymond, C. C. 2018. "AidwV in Plato's *Charmides.*" *Ancient Philosophy* 38:23–46.

Reeve, C. D. C. 1988. *Philosopher-Kings.* Princeton, NJ: Princeton University Press.

———. 1989. *Socrates in the Apology.* Indianapolis: Hackett.

Roberts, Jennifer T. 2017. *The Plague of War: Athens, Sparta, and the Struggle for Ancient Greece.* Oxford: Oxford University Press.

Roochnik, D. L. 1986. "Socrates' Use of the *Technê* Analogy." *Journal of the History of Philosophy* 24:295–310.

Rosen, Stanley. 1973. "*Sôphrosunê* and *Selbstbewusstsein.*" *Review of Metaphysics* 26:619–642.

———. 1974. "Self-Consciousness and Self-Knowledge in Plato and Hegel." *Hegel-Studien* 9:109–129.

Rosen, S. 1965. "The Role of Eros in Plato's *Republic.*" *Review of Metaphysics* 18/3:452–475.

———. 1973. "*Sôphrosunê* and *Selbstbewusstsein.*" *Review of Metaphysics* 26:619–642.

———. 1974. "Self-Consciousness and Self-Knowledge in Plato and Hegel." *Hegel-Studien* 9:109–129.

———. 2005. *Plato's Republic: A Study.* New Haven: Yale University Press.

Sachs, J., trans. 2007. *Plato Republic.* Indianapolis: Focus Publishing.

Saldaña, Eduardo. 2021. "The Struggle With(in) Leontius' Soul." *Archiv fur Geshicthe de Philosophie* 103 (1): 1–28.

Sanday, Eric. 2019. "Self-Knowledge in Plato's *Symposium.*" In Ambury & German 2019, 186–205.

Santas, Gerasimos. 1973. "Socrates at Work on Virtue and Knowledge in Plato's *Charmides*." In *Exegesis and Argument: Essays in Honor of Gregory Vlastos*, edited by E. N. Lee, A. P. Mourelatos, and R. M. Rorty, 105–132. Assen, Holland: Van Gorcum.

Saunders, Trevor J., ed. 1987. *Plato: Early Socratic Dialogues*. New York: Penguin.

Saxonhouse, Arlene. 1988. "*Thymos*, Justice, and Moderation of Anger in the Story of Achilles." In Zuckert 1988, 30–47.

Schmid, W. Thomas. 1998. *Plato's Charmides and the Socratic Ideal of Rationality*. Albany, NY: SUNY Press.

Schirlitz, C. 1897. "Der Begriff des Wissens vom Wissen in Platons *Charmides*- *und seine Bedeutung* für das Ergebnis des Dialogs." *Jahrbücher für classiche Philologie* 43:513–537.

Schofield, M. 1973. "Socrates on Conversing with Doctors." *Classical Review* 73:121–123.

———. 2006. *Plato: Political Philosophy*. Oxford: Oxford University Press.

Singpurwalla, Rachel. 2013. "Why Spirit Is the Natural Ally of Reason: Spirit, Reason, and the Fine in Plato's *Republic*." *Oxford Studies in Ancient Philosophy* 44:41–65.

Smith, Thomas W. 2016. "Love of the Good as the Cure for Spritedness in Plato's *Republic*." *Review of Metaphysics* 70/1:33–58.

Sprague, R. K., trans. 1973. *Plato*: Laches *and* Charmides. Indianapolis: Bobbs-Merrill. [Republished by Hackett Publishing, 1992. Trans. reproduced in Cooper 1997.]

Strauss, Leo. 1959. *What Is Political Philosophy?* Glencoe, IL: The Free Press.

———. 1964. *The City and Man*. Chicago, IL: Rand McNally.

———. 1963. *On Tyranny*. Glencoe, IL: The Free Press.

———. 2001. *On Plato's "Symposium."* Chicago, IL: University of Chicago Press.

Taran, Leonardo. 1985. "Platonism and Socratic Ignorance." In *Platonic Investigations*, edited by Dominic O' Meara, 85–110. Washington, DC: Catholic University of America Press.

Tarnopolsky, Christina. 2007. "The Bipolar Longings of Thumos: A Feminist Rereading of Plato's *Republic*." *Symposium* 11 (2): 297–314.

———. 2015. "*Thumos* and Rationality in Plato's *Republic*." *Global Discourse* 5 (2): 1–16.

Tarrant, H. 2000. "Naming Socratic Interrogation in the *Charmides*." In *Plato: Euthydemus, Lysis, Charmides: Proceedings of the "Symposium Platonicum" Selected Papers*, edited by Thomas Robinson, 251–258. Academia: Sankt Augustin.

Thucydides. 1998. *The Peloponnesian War*. Translated by Steven Lattimore. Indianapolis: Hackett.

Tsouna, Voula. 2022. *Plato's "Charmides."* Cambridge: Cambridge University Press.

Tuckey, T. G. 1968. *Plato's "Charmides."* Amsterdam: Hakkert.

Tuozzo, T. 2011. *Plato's "Charmides": Positive Elenchus in a "Socratic" Dialogue.* Cambridge: Cambridge University Press.

———. "Two Faces of Self-Knowledge: *Alcibiades I* and *Charmides.*" In Ambury and German 2019, 30–45.

Umphrey, Stewart. 1982. "Eros and Thumos." *Interpretation* 10 (2/3): 353–422.

———. 1990. *Zetetic Skepticism.* Wakefield, NH: Longwood Academic.

———. 2002. *Complexity and Analysis.* Lanham, MD: Lexington Books.

Usher, S. 1979. "This to the Fair Critias." *Eranos* 77:39–42.

Vlastos, Gregory. 1971. *The Philosophy of Socrates.* Garden City, NY: Doubleday.

———. 1981. *Platonic Studies*, 2nd ed. Princeton, NJ: Princeton University Press.

———. 1983. "The Socratic Elenchus." *Oxford Studies in Ancient Philosophy* 1:27–58.

———. 1985. "Socrates' Disavowal of Knowledge." *Philosophical Quarterly* 35 (138): 1–31.

———. 1991. *Socrates, Ironist and Moral Philosopher.* Ithaca, NY: Cornell University Press.

———. 1994. *Socratic Studies.* Cambridge: Cambridge University Press.

Waterfield, Robin, trans. 2005. *Plato: "Meno" and Other Dialogues.* New York: Oxford World's Classics.

Weinstein, J. 2018. *Plato's Threefold City and Soul.* Cambridge: Cambridge University Press.

Weiss, Roslyn. 2012. *Philosophers in the Republic: Plato's Two Paradigms.* New York: Cornell University Press.

Wellman, Robert R. 1964. "The Question Posed at *Charmides* 165a–166c." *Phronesis* 9:107–113.

West, Thomas, and Grace Starry West, trans. 1986. *Plato: "Charmides."* Indianapolis: Hackett.

Wilburn, Josh. 2021. *The Political Soul: Plato on "Thumos," Spirited Motivation, and the City.* Oxford: Oxford University Press.

Wilkins, Eliza Gregory. 1979. *"Know Thyself" in Greek and Latin Literature.* New York: Garland.

Witte, Bernd. 1970. *Die Wissenschaft von Guten und Bosen: Interpretationen zu Platons "Charmides."* Berlin: Walter de Gruyter.

Woolf, Raphael. 2023. *Plato's "Charmides."* Cambridge: Cambridge University Press.

Zuckert, C., ed. 1988. *Understanding the Political Spirit.* New Haven, CT: Yale University Press.

Index